T0060112

ALSO BY MARK PENN

Microtrends: The Small Forces Behind Tomorrow's Big Changes (with E. Kinney Zalesne)

MICROTRENDS SQUARED

THE NEW SMALL FORCES DRIVING TODAY'S BIG DISRUPTIONS

MARK PENN

WITH MEREDITH FINEMAN

Simon & Schuster Paperbacks

NEW YORK · LONDON · TORONTO · SYDNEY · NEW DELHI

Simon & Schuster Paperbacks
An Imprint of Simon & Schuster, Inc.
1230 Avenue of the Americas
New York, NY 10020

First Simon & Schuster trade paperback edition March 2019

SIMON & SCHUSTER PAPERBACKS and colophon are registered trademarks of Simon & Schuster, Inc.

For information about special discounts for bulk purchases, please contact Simon & Schuster Special Sales at 1-866-506-1949 or business@simonandschuster.com.

The Simon & Schuster Speakers Bureau can bring authors to your live event. For more information or to book an event, contact the Simon & Schuster Speakers Bureau at 1-866-248-3049 or visit our website at www.simonspeakers.com.

Interior design by Paul Dippolito

Manufactured in the United States of America

1 3 5 7 9 10 8 6 4 2

The Library of Congress has cataloged the hardcover edition as follows:

Names: Penn, Mark J., author
Title: Microtrends squared : the new small forces driving today's big disruptions / Mark Penn ; with Meredith Fineman.
Description: First Simon & Schuster hardcover edition. | New York, NY : Simon & Schuster, 2018.
Identifiers: LCCN 2018285797 (print) | ISBN 9781501179921 (ebook) | ISBN 9781501179914 (hardcover) | ISBN 9781501179938 (pbk.)
Classification: LCC HM1176 .P45 2018 (print) | DDC 303.4973—dc23
LC record available at https://lccn.loc.gov/2018285797

ISBN 978-1-5011-7991-4
ISBN 978-1-5011-7993-8 (pbk)
ISBN 978-1-5011-7992-1 (ebook)

To Nancy, Jackie, Miles, Margot, and Blair

CONTENTS

Foreword 1

The Building Blocks of Change Today 5

SECTION 1: LOVE AND RELATIONSHIPS

1. Second-Fiddle Husbands 31
2. Never Married 39
3. Open Marriages 46
4. Graying Bachelors 51
5. Third-Time Winners 57
6. Having It Both Ways 62
7. Internet Marrieds Revisited 67
8. Independent Marrieds 73

SECTION 2: HEALTH AND DIET

9. Pro-Proteiners 81
10. Guys Left Behind 88
11. Nonagenarians 96
12. Kids on Meds 102
13. The Speed Eaters 109
14. Wellness Freaks 114
15. Cancer Survivors 120

SECTION 3: TECHNOLOGY

16. The New Addicts 129
17. Digital Tailors 134
18. Technology-Advanced People 140
19. Droning On 145
20. No-PCers 151

21. Unemployed Language Teachers 156
22. Bots with Benefits 161
23. New Luddites Updated 166
24. Private Plane Party Crashers 173
25. Social Millionaires 178

SECTION 4: LIFESTYLE

26. Single with Pet 185
27. Roomies for Life 190
28. Footloose and Fancy-Free 195
29. Nerds with Money 200
30. Uptown Stoners 208
31. Intelligent TV 212
32. Korean Beauty 218
33. Modern Annie Oakleys 224
34. Armchair Preppers 230

SECTION 5: POLITICS

35. Old Economy Voters 237
36. Happy Pessimists 242
37. Closet Conservatives 249
38. Impressionable Elites Revisited 254
39. Militant Dreamers Revisited 260
40. Newest Americans 266
41. Couch Potato Voters 273

SECTION 6: WORK AND BUSINESS

42. Self-Data Lovers 283
43. Bikers to Work 289
44. Virtual Entrepreneurs 295
45. Microcapitalists 301
46. The Fakesters 307

47. Work with Limits 312
48. The New Factory Worker 318
49. Hazel Reborn 324
50. 10XMillionaires 330
Conclusion: Taming Our Microtrends 339

Sources 357
Index 395

MICROTRENDS SQUARED

FOREWORD

We live in strange times in which numbers and facts seem to hold no weight compared to hunch, belief, and opinion. The motivating idea for the original *Microtrends* in 2007 was that just below the surface, right in front of our eyes, there were small changes making a big difference. There was also a method for finding microtrends: identifying unusual new developments, checking the numbers, documenting the shifts and their sources, and then projecting possible implications. Some microtrends would turn out to be boons for business owners: one manufacturer even redid his clothing line to sell to the Sun-Haters, parents who had become fanatical about shielding their kids from the sun. Jim Cramer featured the book for a week on his TV show, explaining the implications for investors. The Tory party in the U.K. established a tax credit for people who were partners but living apart, crediting *Microtrends* as the source. The World Economic Forum held a panel on emerging microtrends. Maureen Dowd wrote in a column "I'm a microtrend"—noting that she'd been identified as one of the Impressionable Elites.

Ten years later the world has entered a new phase of change, and I have written *Microtrends Squared* to make sense of the number of new forces that are emerging and converging now to upend our society in ways that seem inexplicable on the surface. If we dig deeper, we see the contours of clear trends and changes within the chaos, although many of these are working in opposite directions at the same time. As millennials mature, the older generation has reasserted its power. As egghead politics failed, common sense came back in vogue. While our cities were renewed, rural voters roared back into power. As Silicon Valley and the new economy took off, angry old-economy voters spoke up. While technology was providing us with more choices, we have been making fewer choices, burrowing into our comfortable silos. As we sought to eat healthier, protein turned out to be the food of choice. At the same time, globalization and technology continued apace in new directions, some of which may be quite devastating if we fail to understand how to control them and how to make them more transparent.

If you are seeking a simplistic explanation for the disruptions you're living through, you won't find it here. They are the result of a complex set of changes happening all at once. But if you want insight into what is happening, why, and what we need to do to curb some of the dangers of these trends, my aim is to deliver that here. I hope you will also find some new business ideas, some new social trends to consider, and clear explanations of how our lifestyles are adapting to the twenty-first century. I have tried in the opening chapter to place the microtrends you will read about in perspective by reviewing some of the larger forces of change. And in the closing I recommend some specific remedies I believe need to be implemented.

We also revisit a few old microtrends, because they have become even more significant over time. Those who are here without legal documentation have become even more powerful as a political force in the country. Getting married after meeting on the internet has almost become the norm, and this has significant implications on how social class is maintained or mixed up. And the dangers of our educated elites making up their minds not on the basis of evidence but based on talking points they get from the *New York Times* and cable TV is becoming even more acute. It is turning our representative democracy on its head.

On top of all of these developments, I am concerned that obvious facts today are being ignored in favor of popular narratives. One hundred thousand dollars of Facebook ads, mostly run after the election, somehow supposedly affected a race in which the campaigns spent $2.4 billion. Poll after poll shows more people believe in a Russia conspiracy over the election than there are those who have seen any evidence of such a conspiracy. Typically, it should be the other way around: more people believing something is true should have evidence of it than not. It suggests that we are entering a dangerous period in which the public can get worked up over information on hot public topics that later turns out to be false. One of the strong underpinnings of *Microtrends Squared* is that we start with the facts and work our way from there to our opinions, not the other way around.

I want to thank my collaborator, Meredith Fineman, for her tireless devotion to the project, for keeping us on time, and for thoroughly exploring all of the ideas I developed. My researcher Amelia Showalter did a fantastic job with the numbers and background material. I thank them both for their incredible contributions and hard work. I hope you enjoy the new trends and then get out there to find the next emerging microtrends.

THE BUILDING BLOCKS OF CHANGE TODAY

The Power of Microtrends

We live in a microtrends world. It's driven by granular, often opposite patterns of human behavior that seem small but punch above their size. We've identified these powerful patterns as *microtrends*, and the world is full of them. Together, they are the dots of a global impressionist painting that comes to life when you step back and look at it holistically. These forces have only become more impactful in recent years, and they've started to upend society.

Ten years ago, when I first identified these patterns of change in *Microtrends*, I saw a world of boundless opportunities. I was over-the-top optimistic about how microtrends would produce a new world of personalized products on our shelves, and how—in Washington—they would produce an even greater selection of fresh, first-rate political choices. Of course, that's not exactly what happened.

Instead, the Information Age has given way to the Disinformation Age, in which fake information abounds.

The nation founded on free speech is grappling with how to live with free speech in the era of the internet troll.

The optimism around our economy faded with the unexpected crash of 2008, followed by a historically slow recovery over a decade. Only now is it recovering.

Unparalleled consumer choice is leading not to the growth of more start-ups but to the dominance of just a few internet companies, which are amassing more and more power on the basis of data gleaned from willing but unknowing consumers.

And the older generations, who in their own youth led a rebellion, have now dug in their heels against the politics and culture of today's new generations.

What makes the microtrend such a powerful tool in this moment is that it can unpack and explain changes we are seeing that otherwise make no sense. On the surface, for example, the middle class can seem to be shrinking, and this is alarming—but it is only by digging deeper and seeing that education is driving more people into the upper class that we can come to understand these overall statistics at a more molecular level. Often, two diametrically opposed trends are occurring at the same time, which would be invisible in the averages but which leap out when understood as the result of a cauldron of microtrends.

Today in politics, for example, there is no overall ideological shift; instead, one group of moderates became more conservative and another group became more liberal, causing society to become both more liberal and more conservative at the same time, canceling each other out. This increased polarization then produces even more gridlock and confusion. We can see similar tugs and pulls throughout society: while one group seeks more technology, another wants to sit in the Amtrak Quiet Car. Some can't sit through a six-second commercial; others spend hours and hours binge-watching TV. Some live in a world of globalization, while others yearn for a return to greater nationalism. To explain all this, we have borrowed from Newtonian physics: for every trend there is a countertrend. It is human nature in the Information Age: every move or desire in one direction seems to inspire a countermovement by another group in the opposite direction. For every radical group, there is a new conservative group. For every new product in mobile technology, there are those sticking to the flip phone. Only by understanding the complexity of these developments can we make sense of a world that seems senseless, confusing, and even jumbled.

While in 2007 *Microtrends* allowed you begin to navigate the changes of the day, now *Microtrends Squared* lets you better understand the emerging chaos as the seesawing of opposite forces fighting for dominance in the social, political, and cultural worlds. In the last decade technology has sought to exploit and even conquer the world of microtrends with its ability to customize products and our lives based on AI and Big Data. But even as these attempts have transformed our lifestyles, they have also led to some serious unintended consequences that have further clouded society. Microtrends disentangle many of these shifts and lie at the source of many battles for power that have disrupted our world today. As you'll see throughout this book, those ongoing battles will result in some very unlikely winners, losers, and shifts in the overall power map of society.

The Unintended Consequences of Advances in Technology and Shifts in Lifestyle

More Choice Results in Fewer Choices

While the technology behind increased personalization of goods and services has been providing us with more choice in our daily life, we have instead been making fewer choices, burrowing into comfortable silos. We expected that the advances in our ability to customize goods and services would open us all up to a new world of never-ending experimentation. A decade later, exactly the opposite has occurred, and our society has become increasingly polarized, with people finding choices they like and picking them over and over again.

In 2007, *Microtrends* explained how the Starbucks economy had succeeded the Ford economy. In the Ford economy you could have any color you wanted—as long as it was black. The aim of industry was to mass-produce products at the lowest possible cost, and that meant standardization of the goods. But the new economy of the twenty-first century was moving starkly away from that model, instead providing consumers with any color they wanted.

The Starbucks economy was based on creating greater value

through customization, even of simple products like coffee and tea. People everywhere became more individualistic in their tastes and were rebelling from carefully mowed lawns and white picket fences. The marketplace responded to these trends by allowing people to "have it their way," and they did. The theory was that more choice would result in a happier and more satisfied group of consumers. Variety would open consumers up to new experiences, in many ways bringing us closer together, allowing us to mix, match, and try out all sorts of new options.

Something rather surprising happened, however, as consumers got more choice. It turned out they found choices they intensely liked, and they stuck with them. More choice ultimately resulted in people making fewer choices. A society that has become less monogamous in its marriages has become more monogamous with its product choices. Once everyone had the opportunity to choose their perfect drink at Starbucks, most customers now ask for the "regular"—the same grande mocha Frappuccino they get every single day.

Think of America as a restaurant that offers only chicken and fish, two rather boring choices. Then add steak and a selection of sushi to give your menu sizzle. Well, it turns out that chicken and fish eaters were not very attached to their choices. But steak eaters get very impassioned about their steaks. Sushi lovers are an entire community devoted to the best fish from Japan. These metaphorical steak and sushi customers become so satisfied with their new choices that they never again choose anything else. More choices result in a balkanized world in which people, over and over again, revert to their favorite choices.

This is happening in news and politics just as it is in the realm of products and services. Before all the cable channels existed, people watched one of three fairly similar network TV news programs (think of that as the chicken-and-fish era). Once the cable channels came along, a lot of folks found Fox News to their liking and, just like steak eaters, watched nothing else. And after MSNBC moved further to the left, it found its steady constituency (call them the sushi eaters). The world of choice actually produced people experimenting with choice even less often.

Thus, we have the modern paradox we've all witnessed of late: expanded choice did not create a reenergized public always open to trying new things. It produced a groundhog population, digging itself more deeply into its own holes. It encouraged people to stop participating in broadly based activities and instead cocoon into the ones they really liked. But when you spend your time in a smaller and smaller niche, you lose touch with the bigger picture of what is happening in the rest of the society.

The very process intended to make people as happy as possible by expanding choice is ultimately also to blame for the very separations that are disrupting society and tearing us apart. Instead of uniting us, technology is helping to divide us into warring camps, reducing the power of the center. It is a powerful and unexpected result of the world of microtrends that greater personalization created more polarization.

Choices Made for You but Are They for *You*?

There's another interesting development for us to keep an eye on in the world of technology, personalization, and choice. As Big Data and AI evolve, the next level of personalization is increasingly being done for you by hidden algorithms. In theory, they are learning so much about you that they can take you out of the equation and make life even easier—like having your slippers ready when you get home. The executive vice president with AI in his portfolio at Microsoft said to me one day, "The human race, I got that one figured [out] in no time." Yeah, right. He thought he had the process of humans making decisions all figured out.

As we will see in microtrend after microtrend, the drive to customization remains at the core of the new marketplace; in fact, what was originally about getting your coffee right and customizing your car has spread now to just about every aspect of your life, from the real estate you see, to your dating selection, to the news and information you receive. But all of these are now touted as being perfectly suited to *you*, based on thousands or millions of data points. Artificial Intelligence is transforming the world of products you use—and even those you see—as ads are selected and formed in the very instant that you click on an article. Your profile is analyzed, and an ad then appears with the dress you were looking at yesterday on another site. It's all done at the speed of light. You are part of a microtrend with every click.

In the world of microtrends squared, your smartphone is more than a phone; for marketers, it's the ultimate spy, privy to when you get up, when you go to sleep, where you go, and even what you say and buy. In the years ahead, data, not oil or gold, will be the most valuable asset on the planet. With five billion people and counting, on-demand service means getting the right song, movie, ad, car, pet, or helper to the right person at the right time. Data is what makes this entire ecosystem work. The better its resolution, the better the targeting and the fatter the profits for someone in the digital chain.

It starts out innocently enough, but because an AI application is fundamentally a black box process, it may not stay that way—especially when the interests of the companies divert from your interests. For most tech services, you don't pay the tech companies; advertisers pay them and so the advertisers (and *not you*) become the real customers catered to by the service. Even something as simple as a weather app may, as will be explained in a later chapter, be shaded to sell more umbrellas rather than tell you how likely it is to rain. Its purpose gets transformed from keeping you dry to selling products for its advertisers.

Even a decade into this business model, few people realize how much information they are giving out about themselves or how it could be used by political campaigns, issues groups, marketers, and even foreign governments. There are no free apps—only apps that are paid for by you, by advertisers, or by selling your information.

While at Microsoft, I devised the Scroogled campaign, which warned consumers about what was happening. The campaign explicitly told people that Google could and does scan and read your mail, explaining that much of what consumers thought were neutral, free listings for products were in fact hidden paid ads. Consumers responded with surprising enthusiasm for this campaign. About

250,000 people a day would come to the Scroogled website, frantic to find out what was happening with their private information. On a lark, I opened a Scroogled store and in thirty hours 450,000 people came to get merchandise, buying mugs and things with slogans like "Keep calm while we download your data." Of course, Google didn't find it very funny.

The primary use of the data being gathered today is to target you with advertising. But as time goes on, other uses will emerge that may be far more important to your life and possibly far more ominous. Ultimately, what's occurring right now means that the tech companies could be able to create a habits, usage, and preferences profile for every individual from birth to death. Facebook today is probably sitting on the most complete and easy-to-mine dataset ever in existence. As more and more people get DNA tests, genetics will be linked to people's habits and medical data—forwarding research but also scuttling very basic ideas of privacy.

Big Data, aided by the establishment of the cloud as a central repository of information, is now being created based on cases big and small—often in unexpected ways. A leading elevator company, for example, has linked all the elevators they have installed or serviced in the world. They get data about every trip every elevator makes: they know the time, the floor, and number of trips. They use it for maintenance issues, but this data is becoming increasingly valuable and useful as the company gathers information from 50,000 elevators. Facial recognition or encoded fobs tell them where people are going to and can calculate the loads on the elevators—even control them from afar. They are using AI over time to calculate maintenance requirements and even predict accidents. This revolutionizes elevator management though tech, big data, and AI. And if something as simple elevators can be managed this way, how far away are we from collecting data from every watch and Fitbit, and treating people just like elevators? One day soon, doctors who do knee operations will be able to pick out potential candidates even before they know they will need a new knee. They will get a data flag based on their walking and running speeds.

As Big Data gets fed into AI, more and more of what you see and experience is being curated by machines. As you probably know, Amazon recommends products on the basis of what you bought in the past. Netflix does the same in recommending movies or TV shows. Instead of merchandisers carefully designing the display, unseen algorithms are at work, and they gradually take over more and more of what you see and hear. The art of merchandising is being replaced by bots. And this is a great development, right? Everything personalized to fit our needs? Maybe. But it depends upon how the algorithm is set. Think of the Netflix and Amazon home screens as the store windows of those companies. They are free to put anything in those windows based on what they think you will like *and* based on what makes them the most money. So you may like sci-fi films, but they will feature the ones that maximize their profit, not what pleases you the most. And product listings on Google are pay-to-play. Because the service seems free to you, without blaring disclosure, you naturally see this as a service for your benefit. Yet there's the rub: personalization is being gradually warped by bots to create a profit-maximizing world for the companies while you think these services are working on your behalf.

What makes these trends a cause for concern is the growing market concentration in the tech industry. Only one company is selling 50 percent of all online goods. Only one company is a universal social platform. Only one company has a news feed more powerful than the *New York Times*. And only one company has 98 percent of the search engine market worldwide. Start-ups are on the decline. As the tech industry matures, its power in industry after industry is mushrooming. The top five tech companies now dwarf the market cap of the top seven banks.

Another potentially troublesome issue is not just our increasing propensity to let AI take over our decision making but also the use of AI to create companions, or "beings." We are getting closer and closer to having relationships with robots and bots. On the one hand these bots and robots, most commonly seen as Siri and Alexa today, will have a tremendous capacity to make us happy and be at our beck and call. As they improve in their learning of us, they may also be programmed to play on our emotions and bring out our vulnerabilities. In the next ten years they will go from being the annoying digital concierge you get when you call American Airlines to home health aides, sexual companions, and self-driving chauffeurs. These relationships will seem real because they are a dynamic reflection of who you are and how you have responded in the past. But they are not real. They are not sentient in genuine ways: they are nothing more than high-tech Sirens, drawing you into their schemes with their disguised sales pitches. They are the inevitable result of the drive for greater personalization, and they could create further polarization as they siphon humans away with the call of relationships that never disappoint.

Millennials Are Adapting to the Machines

Each day a millennial checks his or her smartphone an average of 237 times. The machines have not adapted to the millennials—the millennials have adapted to the machines, tethered themselves to them, waiting for their commands on what to do, how to dress, and what to eat.

The demands of the Information Age and the new economy are upending how we live: more than two-thirds of high school graduates now enter college, and their average age when their first child is born has been pushed back five years, since 1975, to age 32. No wonder that, with all these additional years of freedom, many millennials have put religion on hold and instead are filling their lives with more technology, more hookups, and more companions—increasingly adding long-term roommates or pets they're treating like children.

At the other end of the age spectrum, we are seeing the fruits of a booming economy and technological revolution: older folk are living with greater prosperity than ever before and increasing numbers of them are making it to their nineties. Whole lifestyles and communities have sprung up around these trends, from the one-year leased apartments springing up around college and universities built for young adults, to the active-lifestyle communities that ban anyone under forty. The same people who complained about young people living in "sin" now live in "sin" themselves in the retirement communities, and the hottest Graying Bachelor is the guy who makes it to age seventy.

Life today is like an accordion, with decades of it being stretched out in new ways now, whether you are young, vigorous, and alone in your twenties or older, wiser, and on the verge of becoming a centenarian. This expansion of the way we spend our formative years and our golden years is perhaps one of the most fertile creators of unexpected change and new microtrends, both in the last decade and in the years to come.

The Winners and Losers in Today's Power Map

We've seen how microtrends have intensified the developments in technology, advertising, and lifestyle, with companies now aiming to personalize their products to a microtrend of one: *you*. As microtrends allow us to make sense of such developments, they also shed light on underlying power shifts at the heart of today's biggest disruptions. These battles are not just about people shifting from liking frozen yogurt back to light ice cream, or buying more dogs. When opposing microtrends go to war against each other, the result can be winners and losers on a national or even global scale, with sparks flying.

Take something as simple as one microtrend we document: the rise of consumption of protein over carbohydrates. It seems on one level trivial, even fun. And yet the ranchers-versus-farmers dispute has historically been one of the great battles in the formation of the West—and it is still going on. This single microtrend affects the fortunes of the holders of multibillion-dollar agricultural companies; of land use and pollution policies for millions of acres; and the diets of millions of people, along with long-term effects on health. The winners in the last decade are the ranchers/chicken producers at the expense of the wheat farmers, who used to be all-powerful.

It is this shift of power from one group to another which separates the original microtrends from today's microtrends squared. In microtrends, the math was linear, as one reaction countered another, just as two linear lines intersect at a singled point. And yet quadratic equations—equations in which one of the variables is squared—often intersect a straight line in two different points. So it is with today's microtrends. These new trends are more powerful in effect and often pull us in two or more directions: they intersect with human behavior in not one but often two or more very different points and directions. And as they intersect, there will be winners and losers—and the losers in today's social media–driven society do not go quietly.

Gray Power Is Beating Millennial Power

Just when marketers convinced you that this is a millennial-run world, the voters of the Kennedy generation (those who voted for John F. Kennedy in 1960) have reasserted themselves—in culture, politics, consumer products, and entertainment. In both the U.K. and the U.S., the power of the older generations has surged over the young, and this, ultimately, is the root of their frustration and resistance.

In more developed countries like the United States, the U.K., Italy, Japan, and others, something quite unexpected happened between the sexual revolution of the sixties and today. The more money people earned, the fewer kids they started to have. Having a successful child became increasingly expensive. Work life for men and women became fundamentally more interesting as careers shifted mostly from hard, repetitive physical work to pushing ideas and paper. Having kids became less attractive, and having dogs and cats became more attractive. The result was that the pet population boomed, while the human population growth slowed way down.

Demographics then started to shift in these countries as the huge baby boomer generation approached old age, and the demographic pyramid started to become a square that will eventually flip upside down. In 1960, people in the 18-to-29 age range in the U.S. numbered twice as many as those over 65; today they are roughly equal in size. As the median age started to shift upward, so did political power. And in the last round of elections, the aging populations, not the millennials, flexed their muscles. In places like the U.K. and the U.S., the strong turnout among older voters caused Donald Trump and Brexit to win.

For example, in the U.S. in 1964, those over 65 were around 9 percent of the population and the majority of them voted for Lyndon Johnson. In 2016, the over-65 cohort was 15 percent of the population and growing, and they preferred Trump by 8 percentage points. Meanwhile, across the pond, 61 percent of United Kingdom voters over age 65 voted for Brexit, while only 39 percent voted for the U.K. to remain in the European Union.

Two completely opposite, highly polarized microtrends on the opposite ends of the scale played a game of war against each other, and the young lost this round. While the younger generations have become more liberal on social, immigration, and economic issues, the older generations have become more conservative. Youth in England and the United States essentially have endorsed greater globalization and the open-border concepts backed by German chancellor Angela Merkel and the European Union. They favor gay marriage and legalization of marijuana, and they see the current political and economic system as fostering racism and inequality. Forty years ago, when they were young, those who are now over 65 were on the vanguard of the anti-war movement and the sexual revolution. Today those same voters wonder *Why can't they be like we were, perfect in every way?* They largely see a world mired in political correctness that is losing faith, religion, values, and all connection to marriage and family.

We see another interesting pairing of microtrends within the millennial cohort itself: no generation has benefited more from America's bounty than the millennials. Yet, at the same time, the millennial generation is showing more skepticism of capitalism and support for socialism than any generation before it.

Millennials faced no wars with drafts or mass military enrollment. Technology from the PC to the internet opened up new and exciting careers to them. They may have been shut out of factories as a career option—but they did get the opportunity to undertake new and interesting jobs instead as engineers, as digital marketers, as Uber drivers. New jobs were created at all levels of the economy, from managing the numbers at hedge funds to running the forklifts at the Amazon warehouse. Women gained tremendous empowerment, while America had its first black president and reelected him overwhelmingly.

But their love-hate relationship with capitalism is rooted in their unique experiences. On the one hand, they have witnessed some of the greatest achievements of free enterprise, as college dropouts became billionaires and shows like *Shark Tank*, idolizing the accessibility of the start-up culture, became hugely popular. On the other hand, they also experienced some of capitalism's worst failures. The 2008 financial crisis and record income inequality convinced many millennials that capitalism was a system driven by Wall Street greed that short-changed ordinary people, which also made movies like *The Big Short* popular.

While millennials were undergoing these cultural and political shifts as part of adapting to the Information Age, the older generation was looking on with increasing discomfort and even anger at how their kids were developing. As the power and influence of these new generations grew, the older generations reacted to what they perceived as their abandonment of many of their long-standing cultural pillars; religion, marriage, free enterprise, respect for the police, individual success without government help. They saw the colleges as creating a cloak of political correctness that not only allowed but even justified the rejection by youth of their more commonsense values of right and wrong. So the Information Age empowered two very different generations and created microtrends that intersected and collided in ways that have set off a power struggle that could last another twenty years. In the world of microtrends squared, the older generations have scored a victory on some key political touch points, but the millennials are far from finished.

Move Over, Cities; It's the Dwindling Rural Folks Flexing their Muscles

Just as the older generations seemed to be losing out to the young prior to 2016, so the rural voters were being drowned out by all the money, resources, and talent going to the cities. Rural broadband never made it to the last 20 percent of America despite all the promises. Factories never recovered as manufacturing jobs plunged further. Family farms gave way to industrial complexes.

The numbers were astonishing. While people in cities were concerned about overcrowding and strangulation traffic, the least populated areas were becoming less populated. In the last forty years, rural population has been cut in half, and this trend has continued in recent years. In exit polls, for example, rural voters went from 23 percent of the electorate in 2000 to just 14 percent in 2012 (before bouncing back slightly to 17 percent in 2016).

The war on coal in the name of climate change also had significant political consequences as people in states like West Virginia found themselves further impoverished, even outright attacked by the elites. Ohio and Michigan felt that they were left out of the post-2008 economic recovery, coming on top of decades of manufacturing job losses they attributed to NAFTA and other free trade policies. In their view, these policies helped some Americans enjoy lower prices at Walmart at their expense in terms of jobs and wages. These regions were primed for outrage.

The political power of the rural areas remains disproportionately higher than the average population because the U.S. Constitution gives two senators to every state, regardless of size. The winner-take-all method of awarding presidential electors and the lopsided concentration of Democrats in New York and California also limits the effect of growing Democratic supermajorities in those states. Some consider this a growing problem in our democracy, but it was precisely out of the fear that the bigger states would dominate that power is not distributed purely on the basis of population.

On Election Day 2016, as the exit polls rolled in, it was clear that three very different Americas were now going to the polls. Rural Americans broke 2 to 1 in favor of Donald Trump, suburbanites voted about equally for each candidate, and the urban dwellers voted 2 to 1 for Clinton. However, the distribution of the vote swung Midwestern and Southern states decisively into Trump's column. Demographics once again became destiny. The media that had focused so much on their own backyard missed what was going on in America's backyard. They failed to see the countertrends until it was way too late.

Egghead Theories Versus Commonsense Policies

Another battleground that has erupted out of recent microtrends is the war between what I call egghead theories over commonsense policies. For decades, the egghead approach to policy was winning. There were, according to the policy experts, non-obvious and even counterintuitive factors that lay behind many of the policy shifts of the 1990s until today.

Trade, for example, may cause us to lose a few jobs but will actually drive lower prices and economic expansion, according to classic economic theory. Now, looking at the commonsense effects felt by tens of millions in the heartland, it is obvious we misjudged the impact of these deals and need to renegotiate or get rid of them.

In egghead politics, the rope-a-dope strategy against rogue states makes sense because it pushes confrontations down the line, and who knows what the world will be like later? In commonsense politics, you give nothing to countries that have "Death to America" as their slogan, or that test intercontinental ballistic missiles while assuring you nuclear weapons are something they have postponed.

According to theory and data, climate change is not a problem to be faced fifty years from now but will destroy the world if we don't reorient all of the actions of mankind around reducing carbon dioxide emissions now without delay. But in the commonsense world, we are losing jobs now in the coal industry, and who knows what science will be able to do in fifty years?

Common sense suggests that 11 million low-skilled workers without work permits who are willing to work for less would lower wages for Americans. And yet somehow union leaders switched from opposing liberal immigration policies to now giving support to open-ended immigration. It's a switch that the rank and file still does not understand.

On issue after issue, the voters saw alliances between some Republican elites, college professors and administrators, union leaders, and progressive Democratic leaders that made no sense to them. They revolted: they stopped going along with academic theories and said that when the world we see looks different from these theories, we will no longer believe them. Commonsense simplicity has reasserted itself over the best of our Nobel Prize winners.

The Globalists Are Undercut by the Nationalists

A related backlash is clearly visible in the new rise of nationalism within the U.S. Since the end of World War II, globalization worked for America and it was, ironically, a very America-first concept. The rebuilding of Europe and Japan after World War II through the Marshall Plan was an American idea. In the Cold War era, the basic idea of opening up markets was part and parcel of tying nations to the United States and not the Soviet empire. The UN was great, as long as the U.S. led it. President John F. Kennedy believed that America, with its free enterprise, free practice of religion, and democracy, could be a beacon for the rest of the world to reject the authoritarian communist regimes. People would see the greatness of America, and copy it. President Reagan saw this in action as the Soviet Union collapsed on its own without military conflict.

President George W. Bush was not as fortunate as he tried to apply these same principles to the Mideast, only to see the forces of tribalism, religion, and sectionalism prove too powerful to transform these countries into liberal democracies, although Iraq is holding on. Bush learned we may have the best form of government, but it was born out of a history that is quite alien to the people and states of some regions—and impossible to introduce at gunpoint.

President Barack Obama was also an enthusiastic endorser of globalization. But he defined it in ways that were not dependent upon American exceptionalism. While Kennedy and Bush saw globalization as an extension of American values abroad, Obama saw it as the opposite—as the U.S. adopting the values of a more diverse world and even relinquishing some of our sovereignty. He had a long-term outlook on these issues and saw terrorism as not, in his words, an "existential threat."

Fundamentally, many Americans looked at both Bush and Obama as naïve. They thought Bush was willing to commit unlimited resources to nation building that was a fool's errand at the cost of trillions of dollars to Americans. President Barack Obama was seen as giving too much economically to the Iranians and the Chinese and as equally foolish in his thinking.

But those old Kennedy voters never forgot what Kennedy had told them. They saw globalization as just another avenue through which a strong America could exert leadership in the world. Obama made it about ceding some of that leadership, through global agreements like the Iran deal and the Paris accords that were largely multilateral in nature and that he alone signed without the consent of Congress. Obama's shift in portraying and deploying globalism sparked a countertrend in the emergence of a new nationalism in opposition to these policies and to his whole approach. Let's not forget the resurgence of these same feelings in places like the United Kingdom and France—the lands of such great leaders as Winston Churchill and Charles de Gaulle, who defined their national characters in the twentieth century. This resurgence of patriotic nationalism is easy to ridicule as echoing Adolf Hitler and the Third Reich, but that ignores the idea that each of these nations coming out of World War II both recognized the need for more global ties and also forged clear national identities that defied the attempt by Hitler to stamp them out. It is this sort of nationalism that is at play today: it's a strong counterreaction to deliberate attempts to replace those individual identities with a more global notion of world citizenship driven by immigration and open borders. This, too, is a power struggle that will continue throughout this century and will spawn many competing microtrends on each side of the argument.

The Old Economy Rises Up as the New Economy Gets Restraints

Just when we think we are going to have robots and driverless cars, reality pulls us back. Instead, we seem to be have ended up with cheaper and cheaper labor aided by some rather dumb robots that never live up to the hype of their marketing. I'm still waiting for that robot that automatically vacuums the carpets while I'm at work without chewing up the cat or getting stuck somewhere. But at least I can hail a black car in under four minutes.

Many of the most important microtrends of the last decade are tied to the continued rise of the internet and the digital economy. We are in advanced stages of the Information Age, and questions that would have taken days to answer at the library when I was growing up can now be answered in an instant. Even complex science and math answers are at my fingertips with Wolfram Alpha. I can connect with any friend almost anywhere on the planet instantly. News has become a 24/7 business. Every day people make four billion posts to their Facebook accounts. People are plugged in, connected as never before as part of a global community—and yet they are tense, guarded, afraid.

For all of the tremendous advances made possible by the internet, there is also a dark underworld thriving on its oxygen, tugging all of Silicon Valley's wildest dreams back toward earth. Fraud is more rampant in the virtual world than ever before. For every five accounts online, there's one completely fraudulent one. Millennials get their news from Facebook News, and yet in a 2017 Harvard CAPS–Harris poll 60 percent said they do not trust online information. Misinformation can turn kids into terrorists; fraudsters sells people counterfeit drugs; they cost companies money for ads viewed by bots; they even still scam people into sending money to fake Nigerian princes.

This same ambivalence carries over to attitudes about the economy as a whole. Today's kids grew up during a period of technological advancement but also economic decline, and continually heard about economic worry from their parents. But today we are living in the most prosperous time in the history of the country and the world. That last sentence may come as a shock to people, but never before have so many people in the world enjoyed living not just in the middle class but in the upper middle class. Many articles proclaimed that the middle class was shrinking—and that was technically true. But they omitted the fact that the upper middle class was significantly growing, with three out of four people leaving the middle class to go up the income ladder, not down.

Even amid prosperity, many people's worldviews are less bullish because of the countertrends. The conflicts between the old economy and the new economy run deep within our society. Even as industry after industry becomes more digital or finds some digital layer, we have elected an old-economy president—a president who sees his primary job as bringing back manufacturing jobs to the Midwest, and who has been a builder of physical infrastructure all his life. Similarly, in Britain, the populist revolution sparked a rejection of immigration, trade, and globalization, and was also deeply affected by the move of manufacturing jobs.

Despite the tremendous growth and progress of the new economy, the old economy reasserted itself powerfully, demanding that we not give up making things in developed countries. And that came through clearly at the ballot box.

Understanding the Election Outcome Through Microtrends

The shock of the election was so unexpected by America's pundit class that huge numbers of elites and of the voting public are convinced that Donald Trump could not have won without the secret help of Russians hacking the election.

I suppose Vladimir Putin needed a few rubles. Or somehow some Russian bloggers had the secret to an American election that Americans didn't have even while we spent $2.4 billion on the election. I sit down with extremely educated people, some with multiple professional degrees, and they tell me that they know that Trump was helped by the Russians and that there was secret money laundering in his companies that fueled this effort. When you ask these people what evidence suggests that conclusion, they say definitively that they "know" it. It is always possible that they will be right—that something, someday, might be uncovered—but typically evidence comes before belief. In this unique case, belief is coming before evidence. The answer to this paradox is simply that they do not really believe that Donald Trump could have won the election—and, given a year of high-class punditry that said such a result was impossible, it should not be a surprise that they cannot reconcile reality with their impression of reality.

One group that has become far more important in spreading half-truths is the impressionable elites, who were noted as an important microtrend in 2007. The trajectory continued over the past decade until it came to a head: simply put, the best-educated among us—the people we count on to help us decide tough questions with better knowledge and expertise—have abandoned their posts as guardians of the truth. Instead they have become lemmings, sopping up headlines of the *New York Times* and talking points from cable TV. Believe it or not, Kellyanne Conway was closer than just about anyone else in predicting the outcome of the Electoral College and how Donald Trump would get elected. Conway was laughed at mid-interview at the time, when she explained her perspective, and later several programs even banned her for what they branded as lying. But her prediction of the path to victory turned out to be fairly accurate. Meanwhile, the *New York Times*, just a week out, told elites that the odds were in Hillary Clinton's favor 93 to 7, and for the elites that became an unshakable truth even as it was wrong.

Preelection media coverage featured almost no analysis of the Electoral College and how it could turn out. Not a single person on the planet posted a definitive memo that explained the potential vote totals in each state compared to the national and state polls, and reconciling how the national polls could be nearly even while Trump was winning by almost double digits in Iowa and Ohio. The actual answer, of course, was that Clinton was doing better in big states like New York, California, and even Texas, but doing worse in Florida, North Carolina, and especially across the Midwest from Indiana to Pennsylvania. While an analysis reconciling all these discrete bits of information would have at least shown a strong possibility of a Trump win with a popular vote loss, most commentators were saying exactly the opposite—that Clinton had a lock on the Electoral College.

But the outcome of the election was not just about the state-by-state numbers. It is about seeing the storyline of the underlying microtrends, some of which worked to push Hillary to more progressive positions supported by her millennial base. At the same time, the counterforces we identified that were brewing with the older generation pushed GOP voters to choose an outsider over seventeen other traditional candidates. The Republican base had shifted more to the right while its current leaders had shifted more to the center.

On Election Day, Trump won rural voters by 2 to 1. He won in the key old economy states such as Michigan, Pennsylvania, Ohio, Wisconsin, Iowa, and Indiana. Voters over age 65 supported Trump by 8 points, far higher among men. Hillary Clinton got over 60 percent of the youth vote. As the previous analysis showed, the old reasserted themselves over then millennials, and rural voters reduced the power of the cities. Trump's commonsense agenda dominated over Hillary Clinton's more nuanced and progressive policy. Once we view it in the context of the changing attitudes and demographics, this election, while not expected, is fairly explained. And you can see how the election also brewed the resistance as young, urban, progressive voters lost power that had been building unchecked for nearly two decades. This is at the heart of the process of analysis underlying microtrends squared: there is no single "explanation" of the election, only a multitude of often contradictory trends crossing over the lines and fighting for power that produced an outcome that is at once hard to grasp and yet easy to see when you step back and account for the simultaneous tug and pull of the forces lying just under the surface of our society.

Looking Forward

The ten years since the first *Microtrends* was written have flown by rather quickly, but the changes during that time were considerable. The dual qualities of those changes and power shifts are what made the world seem so bewildering. While young adults have more time being single and more education than ever, our society in fact became much older. Capitalism created whole new industries and let people participate in economic success through start-ups, and yet the banking crisis precipitated talk of socialism. Our cities were revitalized as population drained out of the rural areas, but those left behind were increasingly alienated from the new society. Our elites became more powerful and yet they became even further disconnected from the realities faced by everyday voters—until those working-class voters reasserted themselves and adopted the politics of common sense. The elites had become more and more affected by the talking heads on cable TV than interested in leading the discussion, which is itself a symptom of an intensification of the Starbucks economy. As technology advanced and offered digital layers for more and more products, people started making fewer and fewer choices. The drive for individuality divided us into niches when it comes to both products and politics. This trend seems primed to continue and even grow more acute as technology still promises tremendous new advances as it harnesses the power of Big Data and AI. The very same data that might fuel a cure for cancer could also be the data that empowers new communities of fakesters or gives despots the control they need to keep a tight grip on society or purge it of undesirables.

No part of our society remains untouched by the swirling paradoxical changes. And yet, when properly analyzed, the disruptions we have seen become more visible and clearer as shifts in power among competing groups and as choices that are fueled by changes in demographics, technology, and values.

The scores of new microtrends that follow have emerged from the last decade's currents of change. They are not a complete set of all the changes but slices of different areas of life; they are representative examples of hundreds or even thousands of new trends that are emerging as society goes through these new times. Some microtrends will reverberate around the world; some will be fun and quirky; some will help you understand the last election. Many may seem distant or unrelated, and yet there are threads that bring them all together. Like the results of the slight movements of two tectonic plates, these shifts at first seem small, but over time they separate continents by thousands of miles.

Unlike in 2007, when the world seemed ready to achieve greater peace and unity, today's world seems poised for a meltdown. We will need not only to understand these changes and how they are affecting us but also to be ready to take some remedial actions to deal with the emerging fissures in society. An accounting of these microtrends is then necessary to develop a plan of action to ensure that society's burgeoning forces work to the benefit, rather than the detriment, of our democracy, our marketplace, and our personal freedom.

Section 1

LOVE AND RELATIONSHIPS

---

1. Second-Fiddle Husbands

2. Never Married

3. Open Marriages

4. Graying Bachelors

5. Third-Time Winners

6. Having It Both Ways

7. Internet Marrieds Revisited

8. Independent Marrieds

1. SECOND-FIDDLE HUSBANDS

The traditional notion of the male breadwinner has been turned upside down as American women in larger numbers are now bringing home substantial paychecks, while a lot of younger men are treading water or worse. Some women on strong careers path seek out similarly accomplished men, but others are looking for something else—a second-fiddle husband. This new kind of husband understands that with someone else holding the economic reins, he will need to take on more of the traditional home and child-rearing responsibilities that were previously carried out by women.

Women have always had a lot of power in marital relationships, but that power has not typically flowed from education, career, and money. Now it increasingly does. Women are more educated than ever before, with women college graduates outnumbering men by a ratio of 60 percent to 40 percent. It's predicted that by 2023 females will outnumber male graduates by almost half. Just as many *Mad Men*–era men preferred less ambitious women, it's to be expected that there are women who now feel the same way.

Historically, men were often in a bind. If they were not successful at work, they were not successful at home. As the nature of work has been changing from factory and strength-related jobs to growing numbers of jobs that require a lot of mental work, socialization, and patience, a lot of men have been falling behind. They are the ones who get into car crashes and hazing incidents, have drug overdoses, and

1.1: Female Breadwinners by Household Income, 1967–2010

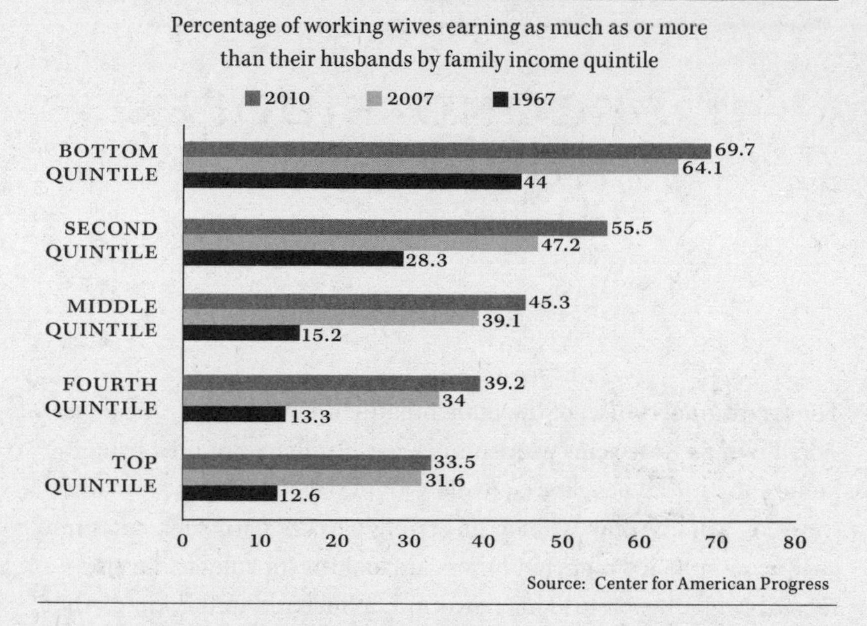

wind up in jail. Even the run-of-the-mill guy is just not doing as well in the transition to the Information Age.

Now a second-fiddle husband can be a flop at work and still be a success at home as a loving, faithful husband. His life will no longer be measured by his salary or work title. For the men who enter a marriage with these new responsibilities and this new outlook, the second-fiddle-husband trend can be a godsend, freeing them from a life of work anxiety and failure.

Both in the United States and abroad, the number of second-fiddle-husband marriages is on the rise. Work hours are increasing for two-worker families, and the increase is being driven almost entirely by women. The number of breadwinning wives is highest among the more educated and appears connected to the outpacing in education of American women over American men, which creates a smaller dating pool of successful men.

Part of the rise of second-fiddle husbands is due to changing attitudes toward parenting and work and a more egalitarian outlook toward child care and career. Comfort with the idea of a woman being the primary breadwinner is especially prevalent among millennial men. A Pew Research Center study found the number of stay-at-home dads has doubled since 1989—from 1.1 million to 2.2 million in 2012. Unemployment was a factor in this, including the recession, but there's also a long-term growth pattern for men as primary caregivers. In the same study, 21 percent of stay-at-home fathers reported staying home to care for their families, which is four times more than 1989, when that number was only 5 percent.

Second-fiddle husbands are part of our pop culture narrative, too, as seen in *Sex and the City*'s Miranda and Steve (Miranda was a powerful lawyer and Steve worked at a bar) and the movie *The Intern*, in which Anne Hathaway is a successful CEO of an e-commerce start-up and her husband stays at home. However, these aren't always the prettiest depictions. In both instances the husbands cheat on the wives, and the wives blame themselves and their "workaholic" tendencies. Expect that trope to change with the ascent of the second fiddles.

There are generally two categories of second-fiddle-husband marriages. The first is by choice: the husband and wife have decided, often as a key tenet of their partnership, that the wife will be the primary earner in the family. The other is by circumstance, such as a medical issue or a layoff. The couples that choose this arrangement rather than being forced into it are, typically, far more successful.

A 2014 *Money* survey reported in *Time* magazine found that households in which women earn as much as men were just as in love and a tad happier than the average household. The survey found that 83 percent of the second-fiddle-husband households were very or extremely happy compared to 77 percent for the rest. And they found that in these households there was no shortage of romance—in fact 51 percent called said that their relationships were "very good" or "hot" compared to 43 percent of spouses overall. A 2012 study published by the American Sociological Association on more egalitarian marriages found that both "husbands and wives in couples with more traditional housework arrangements report higher sexual frequency," suggesting these marriages are mostly win-win arrangements.

The not-by-choice second-fiddle marriages don't fare nearly as well. These men are second fiddle by default. Fifty-eight percent of stay-at-home fathers reported that they were actively looking for employment, as opposed to only 27 percent of stay-at-home mothers. It is unclear whether this is because they want to earn more or because they were looking for work so as not to feel emasculated. The same Pew Research Center study cited above found that 23 percent of these fathers polled were looking for jobs but couldn't find them. The largest percentage of stay-at-home fathers, 35 percent, is due to illness or disability, which is a stark contrast to the 11 percent of mothers who stay at home due to injury.

According to Byrne and Barling (2017), when wives outearn their husbands, it can sometimes create something the researchers call "status leakage," aka "negative feelings about a husband's lower status," or even dissatisfaction with the relationship. Women more often feel negative feelings about their husbands' lower status, and men more often feel emasculated when they're put in this type of partnership involuntarily. According to Luscombe (2013), citing a Kate Ratliff paper, these types of pairings can incite competition and resentment. According to the paper, it was found that "men automatically interpret a partner's success as their own failure" despite not being in competition.

In Bertrand et al. (2013), it was found that there was a general aversion among those surveyed to a situation where a wife outearns her husband. This "aversion also impacts marriage formation, the wife's labor force participation, the wife's income conditional on working, marriage satisfaction, likelihood of divorce, and the division of home production." But this hasn't deterred women from pursuing degrees and advanced degrees in record numbers. Among "mixed education" marriages, there is indeed an uptick in college-educated women "marrying down." This type of marriage went from 12.8 percent of all new marriages in 2008 to 14.7 percent in 2015. The other type of mixed marriage—where the man has more education than the woman—has remained extremely steady, holding at around 8.6 percent of all new marriages. But during this same time college-college marriages went from 19.9 percent of all new marriages to 24.5 percent. This is predictably a function of more people (especially women) going to college.

Internationally, second-fiddle-husband pairings are also on the rise. Klesment & Van Bavel (2015) found that in an EU-wide survey, if a woman is more educated, it will increase the odds that she is the primary breadwinner. From the same study: "Unlike the situation 40 years ago, a wife taking a job today tends to stabilize a marriage. But when she earns more than 60 percent of the income, the risk of divorce rises again."

In 21 percent of heterosexual marriages in the United Kingdom, the wife is the primary breadwinner. The percentage increased within

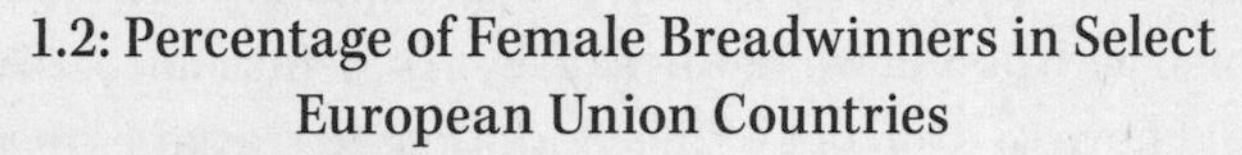

1.2: Percentage of Female Breadwinners in Select European Union Countries

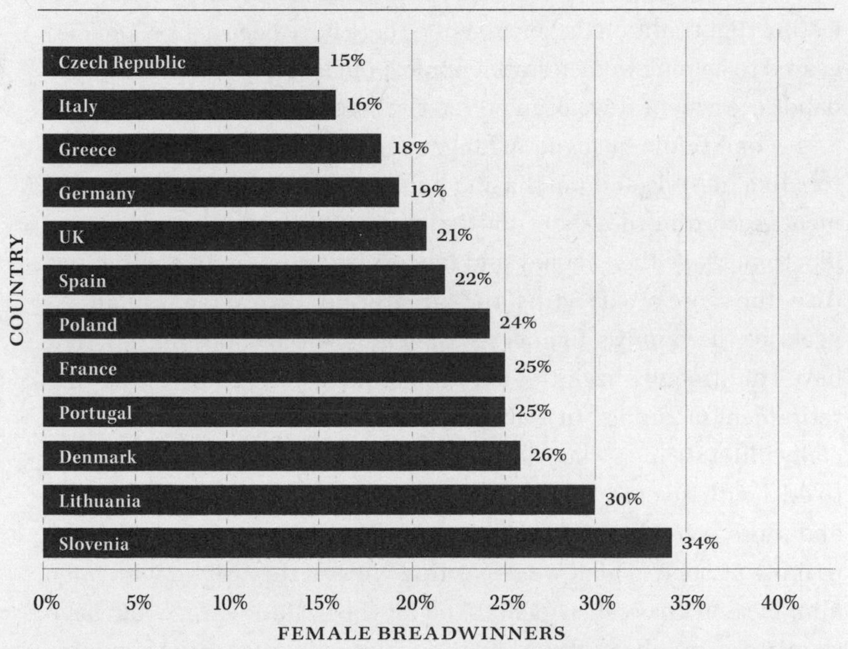

Source: Martin Klesment and Jan Van Bavel

eighteen EU countries between 2006 and 2010. However, some countries with a stronger model of the male breadwinner and head of household—Italy, Greece, Austria, and Germany—are bucking the second-fiddle trend.

Rising female breadwinners also correspond with crises in the economy, which cause many high-earning men to lose their jobs. Countries such as Greece and Spain, hit badly by the economic crisis in 2008, saw a rise in female breadwinners. The crisis was the first in which men were laid off first and women were more likely to retain their jobs.

As women become more economically powerful in the U.S. and abroad, more may simply avoid getting married and having children altogether unless there are enough potential second-fiddle husbands to meet the demand. This is already occurring in South Korea and could escalate significantly in the U.S. In Japan, matchmakers are pairing men with poorer women because successful, educated women who would have to drop out of the workforce to stay at home are rejecting that traditional choice. While there have been a lot of policies geared to helping women stay at home, policies for second-fiddle husbands are generally weak and often the butt of jokes.

Second-fiddle-husband arrangements also affect economic factors like lifestyle and purchasing habits, as well as money management. According to Weisser and Renzulli (2014), female breadwinners like to manage their money and have substantial financial literacy. Also, the more a wife earns, the "greater her involvement in all aspects of the family's finances—especially the responsibilities that have traditionally been the purview of men, such as investing and retirement planning." In the future, this is apt to lead to more financially illiterate men who will need help in later years and be less able to deal with divorce, the workforce, or retirement. As there are more and more second-fiddle husbands, divorce agreements could come as quite a shock to high-wage-earning wives if they get hit with huge alimony and divorce payments. And for the first time you could have significant numbers of men living off alimony because they were

1.3: Pay Gap Percentage for Parents Versus Non-Parents by Gender

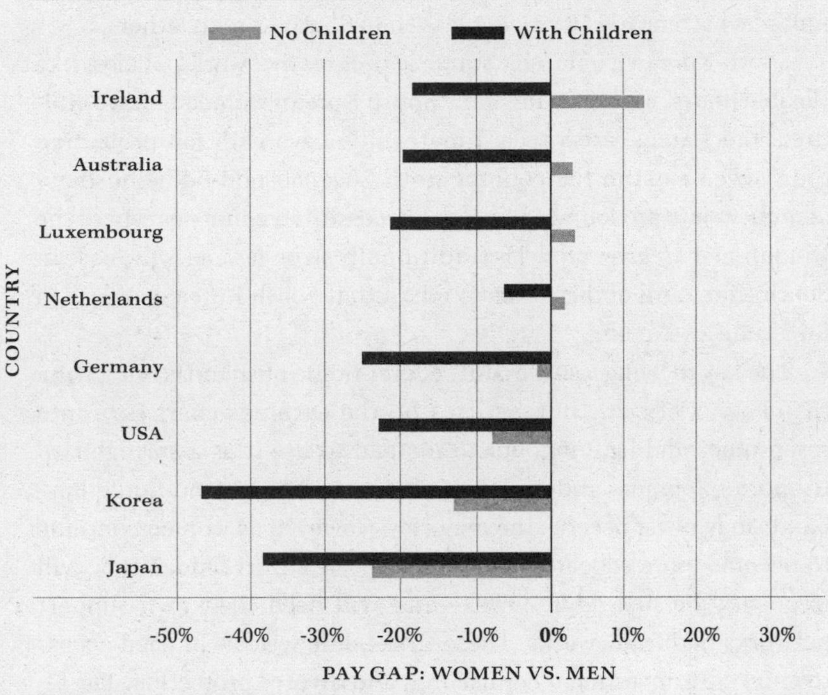

Source: *The Atlantic*

not the significant breadwinner and have few prospects of getting a good job.

The second-fiddle-husband trend is significant in America but it is really having profound implications in South Korea. According to Ma (2016), when women earn more in South Korea, they want fewer children. Whereas before wives in South Korea were the homemakers and their main job was to have and care for their children, as women have become a bigger part of the labor force, with more education and earning more money, they are unlikely to want to have larger numbers of children. Just as in the U.S., women in South Korea earn less than their male counterparts. However, when South Korean women have children, the gap between their earnings and those of American mothers widens substantially. American mothers earn approximately 25 percent less than American fathers, but South Korean mothers earn nearly 50 percent less than South Korean fathers.

South Korea also doesn't support progressive work policies, like flexible hours, which would allow South Korean women to have children and strong careers. Paid maternity leave with job protection didn't even exist in the country until 2001. Second-fiddle-husband arrangements are found to be less successful in countries where the woman-as-caregiver model is traditionally strongest, as is the case in South Korea. All of these trends mean that South Korea could be in for a rude awakening.

The key to being a successful second-fiddle husband is not letting the benefits of being number two on the earnings chart turn into resentment and loathing, but to instead to use it as a springboard to more happiness and a stronger partnership. Second-fiddle husbands may never become the majority. However, as women continue to become more educated and move up the career ladder, they will frequently be first-fiddle wives—and will need their own support networks and frameworks. These first-fiddle wives will need access to child care, investment counseling, and divorce protection. The alternative is that a lot of these women who are excelling will simply pass up on marriage and children altogether, joining the ranks of the never married, and that would be a great loss for men and women today, as well as for future generations.

2. NEVER MARRIED

In the classic film *It's a Wonderful Life*, Jimmy Stewart gets a chance to see what would have happened to his wife if he had never been born. To his horror, she becomes a "spinster" librarian, living alone. This sight is so upsetting that Stewart rethinks committing suicide, driven by the desire to save her from that most dreaded fate. Fast-forward a few decades and the trope of the old spinster cat lady is fading; if anything, it might be a new desire. The Americans that remain never married are rising in population, power, and influence; "never married" no longer means a life as a loser but may even mean life as society's newest winner.

Fewer American adults are tying the knot these days, and that is drastically impacting the way we live. The group of American adults ages 35 and older who do not have a spouse is growing rapidly, and it is affecting urban living, politics, and even sales of those supersized tubes of toothpaste at Sam's Club.

Thirteen percent of all American adults over 35 have never married—up 45 percent in just the last five years. If we look at the percentage of people who are 36 to 45 who have never married, that's 22 percent of the adult population. Unless a lot of this group marries later late in life, you can expect this category to grow even faster and climb to over 30 percent of the adult population. The dominant vision of a typical family life with kids will be thrown into exile. The idea of a white picket fence and a house in the suburbs will be tossed out for a new ideal.

It isn't the swinging bachelor that's leading this charge; it's women.

2.1: Percentage of U.S. Adults Age 36–45 Who Have Never Married

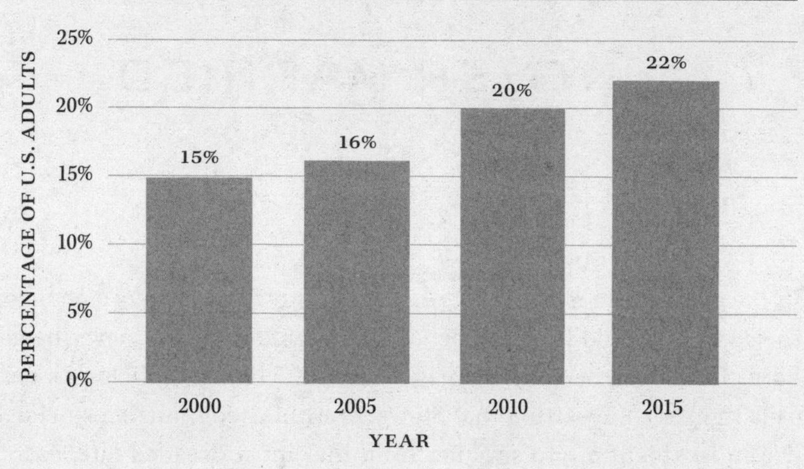

Source: IPUMS American Community Survey data

They are choosing to remain single rather than tie the knot, even if this dramatically decreases the likelihood they will have kids and a family—although maybe we will see an increase in women having kids on their own by choice. Men, in contrast, seem to like getting married; even Hugh Hefner, one of the creators of the bachelor archetype, kept getting married. Unmistakably, the trend toward increased never marrieds correlates to the greater education and financial independence of women in America and elsewhere. There has also been a very sharp increase in the adults twenty-five and over among the black community who have never married, jumping from 9 percent in 1960 to 36 percent in 2012.

The unmarried, successful career woman living by herself in America isn't necessarily a new idea. In pop culture it goes back to the beloved *Mary Tyler Moore Show*: its protagonist was a single woman with a budding career as a news executive. The show was groundbreaking at the time when it debuted in 1970, won a record twenty-nine Emmys, and featured the first single successful woman

2.2: Never-Married Adults' Reasons for Not Being Married, 2014

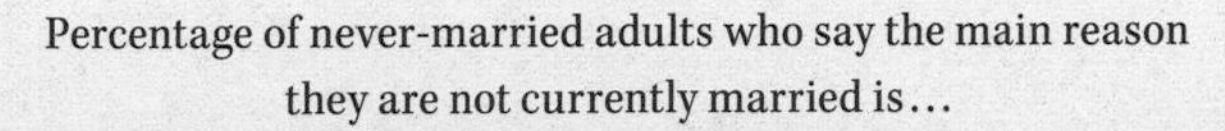

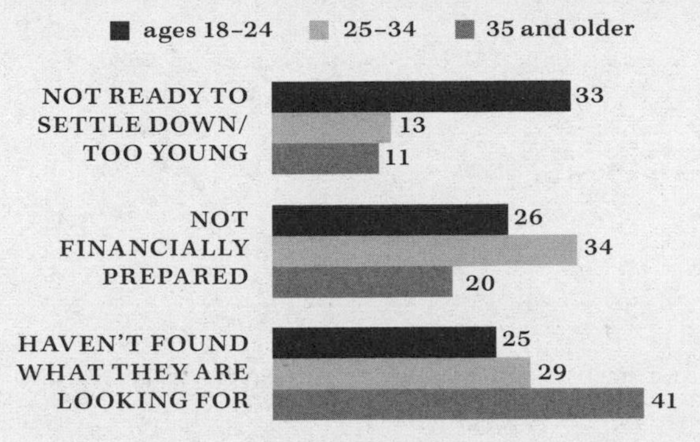

Source: Pew Research Center

as a lead in a major television show. It would be a precursor to shows like *Sex and the City*, centered around the single, ambitious woman in America having her choice of men. In a pivotal line from *Sex and the City*, character Samantha Jones sums it up perfectly when breaking up with her boyfriend: "I love you, but I love me more."

This rise of the never married isn't all voluntary, however: 55 percent of the men and half the women want to get married, according to one Pew Research Center study, so that cuts the happily never married in half. For many, the right opportunity just never seems to occur at the right time.

It was pretty clear, starting in the 1970s and taking off in the 1990s, that the American household would never be the same. The percentage of stay-at-home moms who never worked would plummet, replaced by working mothers who took maternity leave and possibly a few early years off. But this was not seen at the time as leading to an overall disruption in marriage and family.

Work has become more attractive, even seductive. As work became more and more driven by education and individual success, its rewards for women increased. In the past, one might well have preferred

2.3: Percentage of U.S. Adults Age 36–45 Never Married, 1880–2015

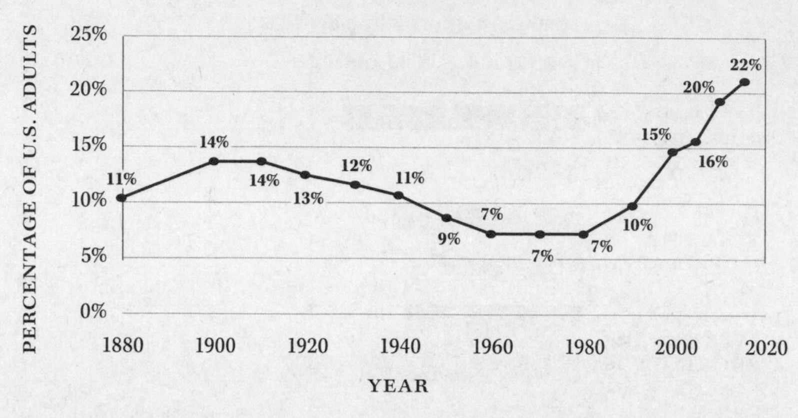

Source: IPUMS American Community Survey data

spending time at home with growing kids to low-level, repetitive work. But who wouldn't prefer traveling around the world as the representative of a large company to the stay-at-home life? The better the work, the more likely people were to value it—and so that is precisely what happened. Add the availability of contraception, the delay of marriage, the rise in pay as women took on better jobs, and the marriage/no marriage equation gradually tilted to produce the growth in never marrieds, especially for the better educated and more prosperous.

Companies big and small are fine with the shift. They like employing the never married: fewer personal days, lower health care costs, and longer hours without complaints. And the never marrieds are freer to pursue the career of their dreams without the old "ball and chain" holding them back. So far, the never marrieds have welcomed the prospect of more work and potentially faster promotions while not realizing that (unless they have kids) they are not getting three months of paid leave or time off for parent-teacher conferences. If the trend keeps up, you can imagine the never marrieds demanding three-month paid sabbaticals every five years and maybe a bonus for the reduced health care expenses of one person instead of coverage afforded to families. Even tech companies like Facebook are paying for their female employees to freeze their eggs—giving them more opportunities but also the ability to stick with the company for longer.

So, when you add up the money, the freedom, and the rewards in today's world that go to the never married, we are about to see an explosion of this microtrend. It's gone from an outlier to commonplace in just about a generation.

To be fair, many of the never married will enter into long-term partnerships without a piece of paper. Sometimes these last for a few years; other times they can last for decades. Just recently a couple I believed were married told me they live in separate homes, and I was dumbfounded at what they had done to preserve their relationship and give the appearance of being married while maintaining their independence. It turns out that once people get a home, they often just don't want to give it up.

In 1990 the U.S. Census Bureau started allowing household heads to designate a member of their household as their unmarried partner. There were 3.3 million such designated partners in 1990, implying

2.4: Americans in Unmarried Partnerships, 1990–2015

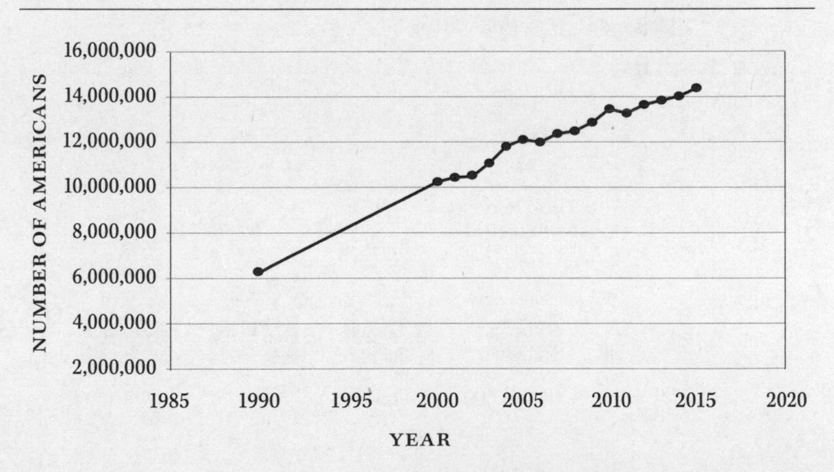

Source: IPUMS American Community Survey data

6.6 million people living in such an arrangement. Today more than 14 million people are cohabiting in unmarried partnerships, and the number is rising by over 250,000 each year. According to the title of an article by Matt Yglesias in Vox, "Living Together Is the New Marriage—Even for Parents."

A subgroup of never married are American adults who have children on their own. This subset is also growing quickly. Yglesias notes: "Births to unmarried mothers have risen sharply over the past generation, from about 21 percent of all births in the early 1980s to 43 percent during the 2009–2013 period." However, those relationships are unlikely to be as stable as marriages and don't come with the same rights and responsibilities. Women who go down this path find they don't have the same protections as their married counterparts do regarding child support and alimony if the relationship falls apart.

Americans aren't the only ones going it alone. In South Korea, for example, four in ten adults are unmarried, and single women are now being handed "Plan B" guidebooks on how to be single, safe, and remain happy. From 1990 to 2010, the number of unmarrieds in South

2.5: Share of Births to Single and Cohabiting Mothers, 1980–2013

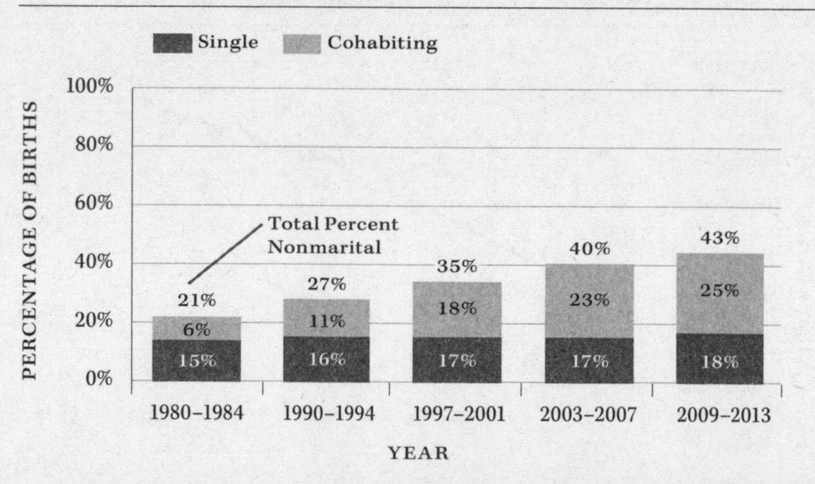

Source: Wendy D. Manning, Susan L. Brown, and Bart Stykes

Korea doubled. But in Asian countries where female fetuses were frequently aborted in favor of male children, it's the shortage of women that is fueling more involuntary singlehood among men.

Even in places like the Middle East, where one might think traditional values of marriage have held firm, relationships among men and women are also being challenged. According to the latest statistics out by the General Statistics Authority, more than 5.26 million people (3 million men and 2.26 women) in Saudi Arabia—whose current population is 33 million—remain unmarried. In a country where most families marry off their daughters soon after completing their secondary education, this trend is perplexing. But with more and more women getting advanced degrees and the opening up of new career opportunites in the prosperous countries of that region, young men and women are holding off on marriage until a suitable life partner comes around.

The rise of the unmarried is creating a lot of economic opportunities while disrupting others. It's been great for urban real estate agents turning out one-bedroom rentals, as well as dating sites and dating services for the more mature. The never marrieds cook less, eat out more, buy more personal services, and trend more Democratic, especially if they are single parents. Yet, while there may be a lot of advantages to the permanent single life, it may not be as great in old age, especially without kids and someone who has pledged to be there "for better or for worse." As this group ages, their safety net is likely to be a lot smaller than that of someone who has lots of kids and grandkids.

The trends of modern life can be reversed; the big question is whether we believe it's better for 20 or 30 percent of the population to skip marriage, have fewer children, and live more for themselves. Depending upon the answer, we either need policies that deal with the later-in-life consequences of being a never married or we need stronger economic and cultural incentives for marriage and family. I bet that we will see this trend peak rather than rise off the charts, the next generation coming up will seek a return to marriage, and more of the 50 percent of the never married that is looking will wind up settling down. Marriage is due for a comeback.

3. OPEN MARRIAGES

It's about as taboo a subject as we have—but more and more American couples are experimenting with open marriage. There was talk a few years back that in quiet suburbs all across America, households were placing two blue Adirondack chairs on their front lawns to signify that they were an open-marriage couple. Perhaps it was just urban legend. But there were a lot of Adirondack chairs out there.

While fewer Americans are getting married, more of those who do get married are tinkering with the very core meaning of the institution. It's hard not to conclude that Bill and Hillary Clinton didn't have at least a one-way open marriage. Perhaps it was not by choice, but the stories accumulated over the years until the fact of it became apparent. There was also no question that at the same time their relationship was deep and enduring. If this was the model of the first couple, what did it mean for the rest of the country?

À la carte relationships are on the rise, and it's curious to see who's driving the trend. Once again, it's mostly millennials and some Gen Xers who married later, having become used to the variety of relationships over the ten years of freedom and exploration they had from high school to age 29.

If you are a typical suburban therapist today, this desire for more in relationships is what is driving more and more couples to see you. It is far from universal, but more American marrieds are opening their relationships up to other partners—sometimes in an entirely consensual way; sometimes as a pragmatic choice after one party or the other has strayed.

Open marriages today are a lot like internet dating was a decade ago: increasingly common, but not the kind of thing you tell the kids or your family about. Swingers have been around for a while, but this is different. These open marriages are based less on sex and more on love, creating additional meaningful relationships that are part of the marriage in some ways and that may come and go, revolving around the couple, which still serves as the core unit.

Everyone has their ideas about what an "open marriage" means. According to sexologist Tammy Nelson, author of *The New Monogamy: Redefining Your Relationship After Infidelity*, "The new monogamy is, baldly speaking, the recognition that, for an increasing number of couples, marital attachment involves a more fluid idea of connection to the primary partner than is true of the 'old monogamy.' Within the new notion of monogamy, each partner assumes that the other is, and will remain, the main attachment, but that outside attachments of one kind or another are allowed—as long as they don't threaten the primary connection."

Open marriage is notoriously difficult to track, because not a lot of couples are public about it. But there is a wide range of figures, estimating that anywhere from 1.7 percent to 9 percent of married couples are in open relationships. Non-monogamy still carries a stigma, and so many couples in open marriages remain "socially monogamous"—in other words, appearing monogamous to everyone in their social circles. People are doing it but don't admit to it.

One place to look for the uptick in interest in open marriages is via Google—and an increased volume and use of the term by Google search engine users. In a paper from the *Journal of Sex Research*, using anonymous Web queries from hundreds of thousands of search engine users, "results show that searches for words related to polyamory and open relationships (but not swinging) have significantly increased over time" when surveyed from 2006 to 2015. More Americans want to know about open marriages—whether they agree to them or not.

According to a 2016 survey of 2,000 Americans, 4 percent of the population surveyed have admitted to an open relationship of some sort. That's still pretty large, however: that's eighty people within the sample who openly acknowledged a relationship without certain traditional boundaries. The number of those who have considered it, discussed it, and possibly done it but won't admit it for the sake of judgment is likely higher. According to another study, more than one in five married couples reported engaging in some consensual non-monogamy during their marriage.

It seems that open marriage is the perfect lifestyle for Hollywood: these couples seem to rarely stick to one partner. Perhaps they will find it more appealing as a concept than the routinely serial marriages that even the most likable and stable star seems to have as a matter of course; they are always meeting their next husband on their next film. Just declaring open relationships might be more stable for the kids they are bringing up. Hollywood usually does as Hollywood writes. For example, Frank and Claire Underwood in *House of Cards* have numerous partners, including one who sleeps in the White House, as they pretend to ignore it. There seems to be a rage of jealousy under the surface.

The reality of everyday marriage is entirely different than what we see in the movies or what actors and actresses practice. Most marriages have a hiccup at some point. Sometimes these problems are a onetime thing, and life moves on; sometimes it's part of a pattern of problems that become more serious. That's when open marriages may be temporary Band-Aids instead of a true social experiment. When the husband of a delightful couple I knew in Miami asked his wife for an open marriage, she threw him out. Her notion of an open marriage was to return to dating—but without him.

The numbers are dire when it comes to Americans being unfaithful in their relationships: according to national data, as much as 60 percent of marriages—over half of them—involve cheating, and these numbers seem to be on the rise. A study from the University of Washington's Center for the Study of Health and Risk Behaviors found that in the past two decades infidelity increased by 20 percent among young married women and by 45 percent among young married men.

According to a recent *New York Times Magazine* cover story, open marriage may make for a happier union. The mere fact that such a mainstream publication delved into this issue means that more and more Americans are paying attention to the concept. This cover story was widely read and generated a lot of other media (podcasts, think pieces, and so on). The findings: open marriage works for some people and doesn't work for others—but not only are we now way more likely to have this conversation with our partners, we are also acknowledging that the female libido is real. It's not just men who want open marriage—it's women, too; according to the article, "women's fabled low libido might be a symptom of monogamy."

Despite potential positives for the open-marriage debate, there is still a substantial stigma associated with not adhering to the social norms of marriage. According to a YouGov poll, 61 percent of Americans believe that the ideal relationship is one that is wholly monogamous, with another 18 percent believing that relationships should be mostly monogamous. Only 7 percent of respondents wanted a completely non-monogamous relationship. Humans are evolved, and their relationships need to reflect that. Dan Savage, noted sex columnist and icon, coined the term "monogamish" and suggests that an open marriage can be more like a door that is open some of the time and shut at other times as couples go through phases or life stages.

Obviously, technology has facilitated the open-marriage movement. Dates before then were pretty scarce for a mom who was busy all day and all night. Now new people are just a swipe away, and most people in open marriages today turn to those sites first. Open marriage can also be emancipating for women who most often were dealing with philandering husbands in a one-way open marriage.

Open marriage in some sense could create two classes of relationships—primary relationships that last a lifetime, with secondary relationships that come and go—often with singles who are much more available. Such relationships may be good for those who are married, but for the singles in dead-end subsidiary relationships, the effects could be devastating and the relationship could be rather poor for self-esteem ("He loves me, but he loves her better, stronger, and longer.").

Maybe, like swinging, this idea will come and then die down and remain a smaller microtrend. Maybe a lot of couples will experiment but decide once they have a newborn it does not make much sense. Or maybe we will see a general deterioration of the meaning of marriage and more and more people won't even get married, and when they do, they won't make it about saying "I do." The longer period of dating before marriage may be feeding this, and the general separation and independence that people maintain in their marriages nowadays may also be part of making the open-marriage trend more permanent. More people have separate bedrooms, live lives that intersect only twenty minutes a day, and maintain their own professional lives; leading their own sexual lives simply carries this trend to the next level.

Personally, I expect this to be more of a fad than a trend—and that there might be an opposite reaction to this, with more people touting the value of deeper, more committed relationships. Just as we have seen divorce peak, I think the more people experiment, the more people will want the stability and security of a lasting, one-lover-at-a-time relationship. I expect the "monogs" to be a counter-microtrend. No matter what people say, having multiple relationships at the same time is unlikely to be the cure for our emotional voids. On the other hand, I could be wrong, and I would have been ten years ago.

4. GRAYING BACHELORS

Perhaps you're familiar with the flurry of reality shows featuring attractive bachelors and bachelorettes competing for attention and seeking "the one." The newest trend, however, doesn't exactly center on the kind of man you're picturing when you hear "the bachelor."

The newest, hottest, and most in-demand bachelor is the guy in his sixties, seventies, and even eighties who is single, often from divorce, and has found renewal in later-stage dating. He may have been rejected in high school, but just by making it to the finish line of life, he is in big demand. By age 64, there are only sixty-two unmarried men for every one hundred unmarried women. Those are the best odds of a man's life.

Life expectancy rates are the highest they've ever been: American females average 81 years; males 76 years. Men have been dying earlier than women since the 1940s. This leaves a lot of widows—and a lot of single women in their later years for fewer and fewer men.

Online dating is no longer just for the young but also for the young at heart, no matter what age. These graying bachelors now have the means to generate lots of dates, something that was almost impossible before the internet, when old age meant lots of Fox News, sports on Sunday, and warm milk. According to the U.S. National Library of Medicine National Institutes of Health, compared to non-daters, older men who go out on dates are "more socially advantaged, more likely to be college educated and [have] more assets, [are] in better health, and reported more social connectedness."

There is a huge population in America today that is divorced or

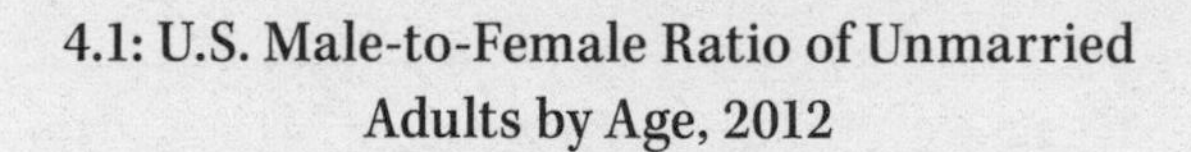

4.1: U.S. Male-to-Female Ratio of Unmarried Adults by Age, 2012

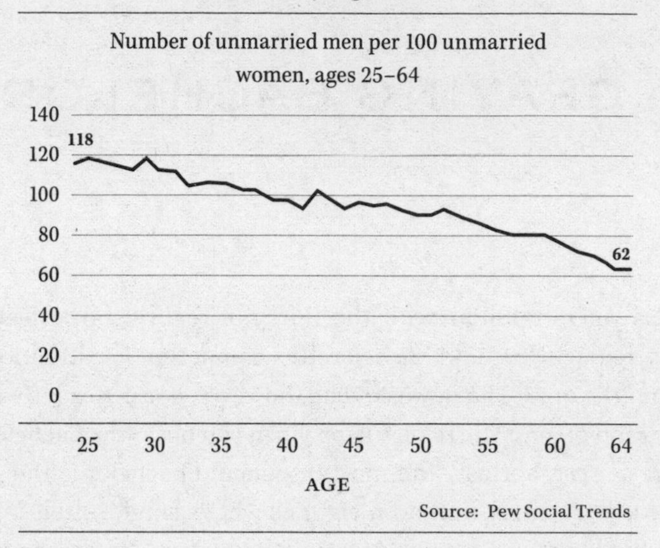

separated, and thus there are a lot of graying bachelors. According to AARP, 45 percent of Americans older than 65 are divorced, separated, or widowed. Divorce was rare before the 1970s, but the explosion in divorces starting forty-five years ago has now come home to roost with the expansion of senior dating.

The graying bachelor is having a lot of sex—probably more than the bachelor counterparts on the other end of the spectrum. That doesn't mean all this new hooking up isn't leading to consequences. Viagra, Cialis, and several other drugs have a lot to do with this. According to the *New York Times*, a number of recent surveys reported that among Americans over the age of 60, "more than half of men and 40 percent of women are sexually active."

There are several health care concerns for the graying bachelor, and one might be surprising: a huge climb in sexually transmitted diseases. Sure, in your sixties and seventies you aren't thinking about pregnancy, but a lack of proper safe sex practices is leading to the resurgence of certain STDs, with the CDC reporting a significant increase in chlamydia (52 percent) and syphilis (65 percent) in adults ages 65 and older—and gonorrhea up by a staggering 90 percent. Baby boomers came of age before the AIDS crisis and before sexually transmitted diseases were a national conversation. The *New York Times* article called "Sex and the Single Senior" cited that "according to the 2010 National Survey of Sexual Health and Behavior, among college-age Americans, condoms are used in about 40 percent of sexual encounters, but only in about 6 percent of sexual encounters among those 61 and older. A study published in the *Annals of Internal Medicine* showed that older men who use Viagra and similar drugs are six times less likely to use condoms compared with men in their 20s."

Retirement communities, typically built around golf courses, today are one part country club and one part frat house. One graying bachelor I know quite well reported how he broke up with his girlfriend, and so he changed his status on JDate—within the hour, his old girlfriend was already in touch and ready to resume their past relationship. When a graying bachelor is back on the market, it's big news, and with today's dating sites, it's news that can be quickly broadcast.

New opportunities don't necessarily come with loyalty, however. The gray bachelor is also more likely to cheat on his girlfriend

4.2: Percentage of U.S. Men and Women Who Are Significantly Older Than Their Spouses by Household Income

	MEN		WOMEN	
Household Income	10+ years older	20+ years older	10+ years older	20+ years older
<20,000	10.2%	2.6%	3.7%	0.6%
20–50,000	7.8%	1.7%	2.3%	0.4%
50–100,000	7.7%	1.2%	2.0%	0.3%
100–200,000	8.9%	1.2%	1.2%	<0.1%
200,000+	10.3%	2.2%	0.5%	<0.1%

Source: Austin Institute

or spouse. From a 2008 article in the *Telegraph*, the British daily: "Today's older men and women—many of whom came of age in the 'swinging Sixties'—are more likely to cheat and far less likely to regret it than couples in their 20s and 30s, a poll has found. Older people also define infidelity much more narrowly than the younger generation, with most over-55s saying that kissing someone who is not their partner does not constitute cheating."

The graying bachelor also has more options because as men get older, they have a more acceptable dating range of ages they're interested in, especially if they have money. It's commonplace for a man to be dating a woman thirty years his junior, but the reverse is still taboo. Women tend to stay plus or minus five years from their age when it comes to finding a mate. Men, on the other hand, continue to go lower and lower when it comes to their "youngest allowable" match.

The graying bachelor who makes over $200,000 a year is marrying women around ten years younger. According to a recent survey, 10.3 percent of men who married within this cohort found a spouse that was more than ten years younger. President Donald Trump, of course, is in his third marriage at age 71, while Melania Trump is 47—a twenty-four-year difference.

A study from the Archives of Sexual Behavior in March of 2017 saw a decline in sexual activity in nearly all age cohorts except Americans over 70. "In the most recent survey for the study, which has been conducted since 1972, millennials and Gen Xers showed a drop in the number of times they have sex per year, compared with previous years. But the baby boomers and their parents are having sex more often than their cohorts reported in the past." And the sex they're having is also *better*, according to the National Council on Aging. The commission reported that the elderly were more satisfied with their sex lives than they had been during their middle-age years.

So just when you think it's all over for you, in today's world you may be about to have the time of your life. You may need some new clothes, a new car, some great aftershave, and a dating coach to help you through it. You'll need to clean up that apartment or hire some cleaning staff; no one is going to want to come back to a dirty apartment with Chinese food containers strewn about. Or you could fly the coop entirely, as more and more seniors are doing.

Popular culture is reflecting this shift toward the graying bachelor and older Americans having fun, not just sitting in rocking chairs. Seniors are also taking traveling to a new level. "Grandtraveling" is a trendy term on the rise, but gaining popularity are senior singles cruises and tours—some, like Silversea Cruises, with their own Gentleman Host programs for the 55-plus crowd for the extra "love boat" experience.

Speaking of heading seaward, across the pond, Europeans are embracing their senior living and contributing to Europe's booming "silver economy." Traditionally, seniors stayed with family members, but recent studies show more retirees, specifically men, are living on their own. In Denmark the latest trend is do-it-yourself retirement communities where women likewise outnumber men time and again.

There is one place, however, where the tables are turned upside down: China. The best thing an aging Chinese bachelor could do is move to America. Single men in China could potentially exceed the entire population of Australia in five years, according to the Fujian Bureau of Statistics, and aging bachelors will soon dominate the dat-

4.3: Top Five Countries by Percentage of Population Age 65 or Over

RANK	COUNTRY	PERCENTAGE OF POPULATION OVER 65
1	Japan	26.3%
2	Italy	22.4%
3	Greece	21.4%
4	Germany	21.2%
5	Portugal	20.8%

Source: World Atlas

ing landscape. This is the result of the Communist Party's One Child policy that favored boys over girls. Even with the strict policy gone, it seems the Chinese still favor having boys. According to the Fujian Provincial Bureau of Statistics, there will likely be 119 boys born to every 100 girls by 2020. These bachelors might want to look later on in *Microtrends Squared* for the chapter on bots with benefits, given the odds they are facing.

While the TV show *Modern Family* already has the older divorced guy with the younger new wife, in the coming years the set is going to have to make room for the old single guy bringing a new date to every episode. This trend is certainly not limited to the U.S.: think of a lot of countries with aging populations—Japan, Germany, Italy, and Greece. Except where divorce is rare, these trends are likely repeating themselves and creating the same kinds of problems and joys globally.

The graying bachelor is here to stay. And if your mom is living with you, check out her Match.com profile and don't be surprised if someone is coming up the driveway or ringing the doorbell looking for her instead of your daughter. Rather than driving suavely up to your door in his Mustang convertible, he might putter by in a golf cart, sporting a rather nice bouquet of deep-red roses. Such is the new life of aging single guys.

5. THIRD-TIME WINNERS

A famous commercial that aired when I was growing up featured Americans trying to just eat a single Lay's potato chip, but their lack of willpower and the temptation of another chip always got the best of them. Marriage in those days was the ultimate arrangement meant to be tried just once, or *maybe* twice once divorce became no-fault. But now, growing numbers of Americans are putting hope over experience and walking down the aisle a third time.

Multiple marriages used to be reserved for celebrities and kooks. Now the idea that getting married over and over again to find true

5.1: American Adults Married Three Times or More

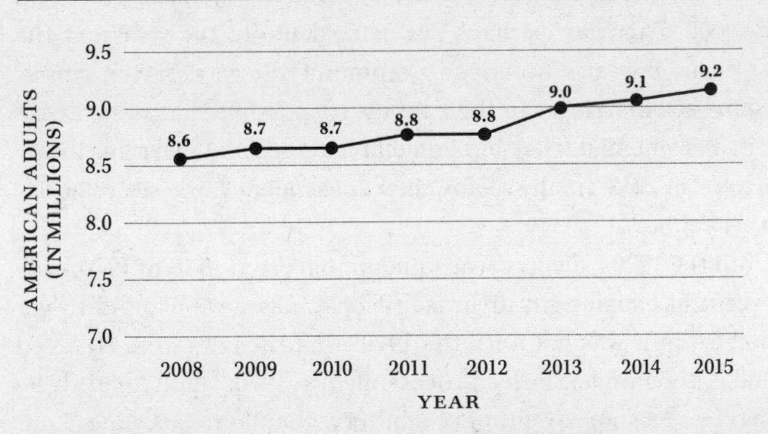

Source: IPUMS American Community Survey data

love—or the right love for the right decade—is more common than ever, with 9 million adults having been married three or more times. This trend is affecting the marriage industry, cultural norms on relationships, and the institution of marriage . . . and making celebrity marriage hopping seem commonplace.

An average wedding in the U.S. costs $26,720. But one search on Google reveals that a divorce can be as cheap as "$89 only! In three easy steps. 100% guaranteed." And yet even the least expensive divorce can have enormous emotional and social costs to people and their relationships, to friends and children caught in the middle. Divorce peaked in the U.S. in the 1980s, leveling off and even heading down since then. So, is the development of people willing to give it a try a third time a positive development—underscoring the need for people to have for deep and lasting connection—or has marriage become more like a disposable diaper: something to throw away once it gets messy? Today we have fewer people married but just as many marriages each year as people try—and try again.

From 2008 to 2015, the number of serial marriage hoppers jumped from 8.6 million to 9.2 million. Put simply, by today, roughly one in every nineteen married adults had been married three times. The number of Americans who've been married three or more times is going up every year by nearly 100,000 people. The biggest spike was in 2013, when the number of thrice-married Americans went up by 200,000. This was, perhaps not coincidentally, the year that the U.S. Census Bureau's American Community Survey started counting same-sex marriages in their totals. It's possible that some LGBT Americans who had tried and failed at heterosexual marriage in the past were, in 2013, finally seeing their subsequent same-sex relationship get counted.

Until the 1970s, divorce was uncommon. From 1940 to 1970, only 1 percent of couples got divorced. People may have wanted to get divorced, but it was not until the 1970s that the laws were changed to make it a simpler, fairer process. Before 1970, "fault" had to be proven by one spouse—proof of adultery, abandonment, abuse, addiction, etc.—before couples could sign divorce papers. Even after it was proven, couples still had a long separation time before divorces were finalized. As Zsa Zsa Gabor famously quipped in 1987, "Not diamonds, but divorce lawyers are a girl's best friend." As women entered the workforce and became more financially independent, more of them also decided to be independent of their first husbands.

The divorce and remarriage patterns of the rich and famous also chipped away at the sanctity of marriage. There are a lot of American actors or rock stars whose image and constant reinvention almost warrants a need for multiple spouses. When those most visible and revered are getting divorced constantly, it also affects how Americans view the process of getting married. Just a small sampling of A-list celebrities that have been married more than three times includes Kate Winslet, Tom Cruise, Kim Kardashian, Jennifer Lopez, and Nicolas Cage. Those are some of our biggest and most influential stars. People wonder: *If even the most glamorous marriages tend to fall apart, why should my rather ordinary marriage survive?*

Our presidents have also reflected these turbulent and changing times for lasting relationships. Ronald Reagan was the first president to bring a second wife into the White House. Donald Trump is the first president to bring a third. Rather paradoxically, President Trump has record high support among Christian Evangelicals.

Third marriages typically happen when people are about 50 years old. People who get divorced tend to bail at a few distinct stages: early, when they view a first marriage as a mistake; after the seven- to ten-year itch, when marriage can seem burdensome with kids and responsibilities; and at the empty-nester stage, after the kids have left the house and staying together for the kids is no longer necessary. A typical third-timer has jumped on at least two out of these three occasions.

Unsurprisingly, third-timers are also more likely to marry someone else who has gone through a divorce, and that fact starts to create a new complexity in family relationships that would make the Brady Bunch look straightforward. Figuring out which kids spend which holidays with which parents might even require an app. In 2015, when the most recent American Community Survey was conducted, people who were on their third (or more) marriage were usually married to fellow divorcées.

Think about this typical 50-year-old who has been married twice before and is now looking for a third marriage. Let's assume this person's dating pool is between the ages of 40 and 60. Among unmarried people in this age range, including those widowed and divorced, less than 20 percent have already been married twice or more. A plurality (44 percent) have never been married.

And yet, only 18 percent of these fiftyish twice-marrieds end up tying their third knot with someone who has never been married before. Instead, the spouses of thrice-married folks are more commonly on their second marriage (45 percent) or, much like their new spouse, entering into their own third-plus marriage (37 percent). It seems people getting married a third time prefer people who have been through the experience already.

There are 33 million Americans who have been married exactly twice. Of these, 22 million are still married, with another 2.9 million who are widowed. Around 8.5 million are divorced or separated (again). In other words, somewhere around 26 percent of second marriages have ended in failure.

But is the third time the charm? Of the 9.2 million people who take a third spin, 5.6 million are still married, with another 830,000 who

5.2: Marriage Count for Currently Married Americans, 2015

AMONG AMERICANS WHO ARE CURRENTLY ON THEIR:	. . . THEIR SPOUSE IS CURRENTLY ON HIS/HER:		
	FIRST MARRIAGE	SECOND MARRIAGE	THIRD+ MARRIAGE
First Marriage	88%	10%	2%
Second Marriage	42%	46%	12%
Third+ Marriage	24%	46%	29%

Source: IPUMS American Community Survey data

have been widowed. Around 2.7 million are divorced or separated (again), meaning that somewhere around 30 percent of third marriages have ended in failure. So people who have three-plus marriages are actually a little more likely than first-timers to have had those marriages fail. That does not mean giving up is the right answer, though. The difference for third marriages isn't that much; they still succeed or fail at just about the same rate as other marriages. Which perhaps simply means that a third marriage is going to be just as much work, with just as much give-and-take, as a first and or second marriage.

Third marriages are likely to have less impact on kids and be more about finding security and comfort at an older age—more about making sure that someone is there for you when aging sets in. But that's not to say it can't cause tremendous strain within families, as grown-up kids may end up resenting spouses with whom they have no direct biological connection.

The rise of third marriages might signal that marriage is on the rocks, but the wedding industry is *booming*; it's already a $70 billion-a-year industry. Along with booming online registry services and businesses—with Williams Sonoma, Pottery Barn, and Target at the top—there are dozens of successful wedding-related start-ups, like WeddingWire and Lover.ly, and the app economy for bridal-related content is seemingly never-ending. Getting married, even the third time is a life milestone, and it has also turned into a digital experience—not the least on social media. What could gain more likes or garner more attention than an Instagram post about getting engaged? What could get you more attention and more thumbs-up on Facebook than a big-ring picture? Or how about walking down the aisle flanked by friends with tears in their eyes?

While third-timer weddings may not be charmed, they still bring fun and excitement to family, friends—and are always a great excuse for a honeymoon. It's no longer unusual for people to go on two honeymoons in their lifetime. And millions more are blazing the trail to a third. As life expectancy pushes to 90 and 100, expect more and more to make it to their third marriages, and for more and more people to have had two and three spouses—just not at the same time.

6. HAVING IT BOTH WAYS

In the last ten years, the American public's attitude toward the LGBT community has become far less discriminatory, culminating with a majority of the Supreme Court and of the voters in polls favoring the legalization of gay marriage, which is now the law of the land. And today there is an ongoing national debate about fair treatment for transgender people. Yet, interestingly, the largest segment of the LGBT community—the *B* that stands for *bisexual* people—is still usually the least discussed, even though its size is reaching double digits among young adult women.

Hollywood is way ahead of the curve in openly embracing bisexuality—with stars like Angelina Jolie, Drew Barrymore, Anne Heche, the late David Bowie, Kristen Stewart, Andy Dick, and Anna Paquin leading the charge. But, as *Sex and the City* actress and out bisexual in Hollywood Cynthia Nixon says, "Nobody likes the bisexuals. We get no respect." That might be why statistics show that bisexuals are often less likely to reveal themselves than gay Americans.

Bisexuals are reticent to reveal their true nature even though relatively few bisexuals report feeling discriminated against because of their sexual orientation and even though bisexuality is hardly a new concept. Bisexuality is fairly commonplace not just in people but in the natural world: snakes do it, dolphins do it, butterflies and frogs do it.

Within the LGBT community, bisexuals say their sexual orientation is less important to their identity, according to studies. Still one Pew study shows 70 percent of gay men and 67 percent of lesbians

6.1: LGBT Americans Who Are Out to Their Parents, 2013

Percentage who say they have told their mother/father about their sexual orientation

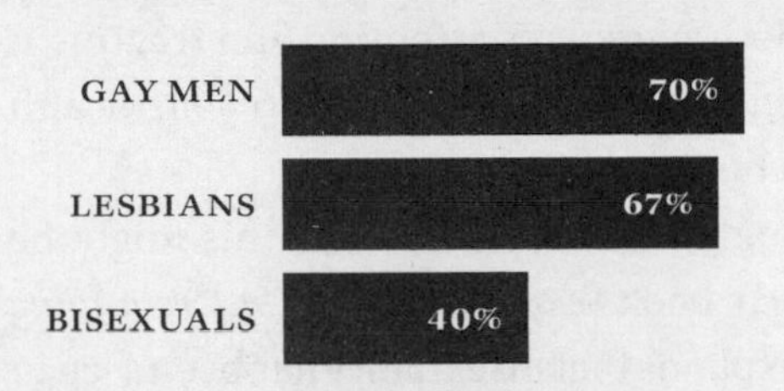

FATHER

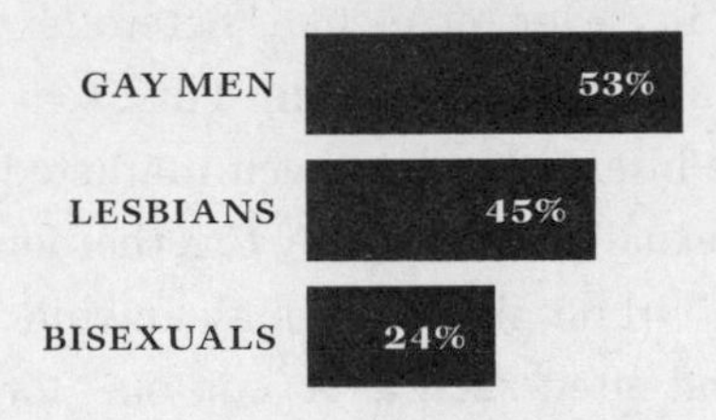

Source: Pew Social Trends

are likely to be out to their mothers, and 53 percent and 45 percent out to their fathers. In contrast, only 40 percent of bisexual Americans polled have told their mothers, and less than a quarter, 24 percent, have told their fathers. Coming out is a big deal in general, and though there is more understanding around being gay, there are still a lot of questions and doubt surrounding bisexuality, which could affect your willingness to tell family members about your identity.

While much of Hollywood has no problem coming out, bisexuality in American popular culture is still underrepresented. And one could argue that bisexuality hasn't had its cultural breakthrough yet, as homosexuality did with a film like *Brokeback Mountain*. In a GLAAD report about LGBT representation in television, while bisexual characters are appearing more often in shows, many represent dangerous stereotypes about bisexual Americans, like being "wild" or unstable.

According to researcher Mackey Friedman, "Bisexual men and women face prejudice, stigma and discrimination from both heterosexual and homosexual people." He continues, "this can cause feelings of isolation and marginalization, which prior research has shown leads to higher substance use, depression and risky sexual behavior." It can also lead to less aggressive attention and treatment for diseases like HIV. In short, it can be dangerous—to your health and mental well-being—to be bisexual in America.

Bisexuals are overwhelmingly female, though why this might be is unclear. In Lisa M. Diamond's book *Sexual Fluidity: Understanding Women's Love and Desire*, she explains that bisexuality has been seen in the past as people, mostly women, simply satisfying their fantasies—a temporary state or phase described in clever terms like "heteroflexibility," "has-bian," and "LUG" (lesbian until graduation). This "temporarily bi-" attitude toward female bisexuality has been marketed for years, be it two women posing sexually and scantily together for a fashion brand or sly references to "girl on girl" action. Meanwhile, male bisexuality is less accepted and often seen as a "cop-out" for being gay. Bisexuals struggle for acceptance within the LGBT community, and to define themselves as part of the political movement. A survey of 745 bisexuals by academic researchers found that while bisexuals experienced more discrimination from straight people, they also experienced some discrimination from gays and lesbians.

In recent years, the number of out bisexual Americans has been

6.2: Percentage of Americans Identifying as LGBT by Age, 2012–2016

	2012 %	2013 %	2014 %	2015 %	2016 %
Millennials (1980–1998)	5.8	6.0	6.3	6.7	7.3
Generation X (1965–1979)	3.2	3.3	3.4	3.3	3.2
Baby Boomers (1946–1964)	2.7	2.7	2.7	2.6	2.4
Traditionalists (1913–1945)	1.8	1.8	1.9	1.5	1.4

Source: Gallup Daily Tracking

on the rise, due in large part to millennial open-mindedness. In 2016, 7.4 percent of millennials identified as LGBT, while only 3.2 percent of baby boomers did so. And the rise of bisexuality is increasingly influencing the dating world, especially on dating sites. There are still binary choices on some sites, but more sites now allow you to choose an interest in men, women, or both. However, bisexuals still face particular prejudices and harassment while dating online: bisexual women are often solicited for threesomes with a straight couple, and regularly warn against a desire for that on their dating sites with "I AM NOT INTERESTED IN COUPLES" in all caps.

Those comfortable with having it both ways are largely younger women. Among the 13 percent of women identifying themselves as bisexual to Pew, they are largely under 49, compared to a lesbian population that is evenly distributed by age. About half of gay men say their sexual orientation is important to them, but for bisexual men it's only about two in ten.

6.3: Partisan Identification of LGBT Americans, 2013

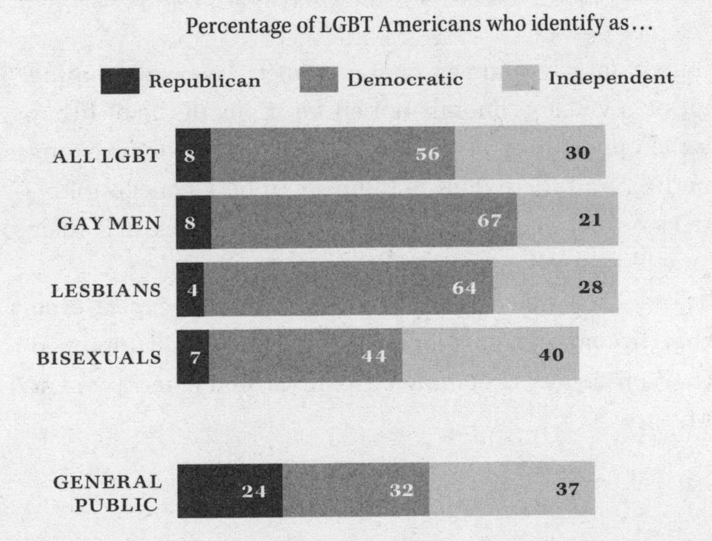

Source: Pew Social Trends

Bisexuality is making its mark in politics as well, and the Religious Right is none too pleased. In 2015, Oregon's Kate Brown became the first openly bisexual governor in the U.S. and others, like Representative Kyrsten Sinema of Arizona, have followed in her footsteps. And bisexual voters are a significant constituency, as they are the largest subgroup of LGBT Americans. While bisexual Americans aren't typically Republicans, they aren't as strongly Democratic as their gay counterparts. According to Pew, 40 percent of self-identified bisexuals are independents compared to overwhelmingly Democratic gay men. Bisexuals are also less likely than gay Americans to prioritize traditional issues for the LGBT community like HIV treatment, insurance coverage for transgender people, and equal employment for LGBT Americans. The bisexual vote is far more up for grabs, but few politicians have appealed to them with the gender or identity appeals common to other groups.

Bisexuals also tend to be poorer and less educated than members of the gay or lesbian communities. While 40 percent of gay men and 36 percent of lesbians are college educated, only 23 percent of bisexuals achieve a degree. They also are far more likely to earn under $30,000, and basic economics may have a lot to do with the reluctance of some bisexuals to come out.

As a group of largely younger, poorer women, bisexuals coming out may not be a viable economic option for many of them if they would lose the opportunity at a marriage and family by revealing their full nature. And there does not appear to be a concept of bisexual marriage to replace the opportunities that are lost if their partner is unwilling to allow them multiple partners.

With attitudes toward sexuality changing, you can expect even more bisexuals to come out, positioning this group as a still untapped but significant influencer of commerce, politics, and entertainment in the near future.

7. INTERNET MARRIEDS REVISITED

A decade after we wrote about online marriages in the first *Microtrends*, finding love through the internet has become a certified megatrend, forever changing the process of dating and getting hitched in the twenty-first century.

When the first iteration of *Microtrends* came out in 2007, we predicted that 100,000 of the 4.4 million Americans who would get married that year would have met online. Online dating was the wave of the future, and while most people in 2007 approached the experience with nervousness (65 percent), skepticism (55 percent) and embarrassment (27 percent), they did it anyway. Fast-forward a decade, and these numbers have increased eight times over—to 700,000 weddings per year that started out of online dating.

The first notable shift in online dating occurred with the transition from cumbersome desktop profiles to simple, intuitive mobile apps easily shared with friends. Tinder arrived in 2012, and it affected Americans ages 18 to 24 the most. The percentage of that cohort that used online dating to meet mates went from 10 percent to nearly 30 percent. It's not just young Americans whose online meet cutes have exploded; there was also a staggering jump in Americans ages 55 to 64. For older online daters, the numbers doubled—from 6 percent of that group participating in 2013 to 12 percent in 2015—just in two years alone.

Tinder's ability to find users easily by location and with virtually

7.1: Demographics of Americans Who Know Online Daters, 2015

	Percentage of people within each cohort who . . .	
	Know someone who uses online dating	Know someone who has entered a long-term relationship via online dating
ALL ADULTS	41%	29%
18–24	57	34
25–34	56	33
35–44	45	33
45–54	38	29
55–64	33	28
65+	21	20
High school grad or less	25	19
Some college	46	30
College graduate	58	46
Less than $30,000	30	20
$30–$75,000	40	28
$75,000+	58	43

Source: Pew Research Center

no work involved—a Facebook log-in plus a few-sentences profile will do—meant that, by January 2014, Tinder had 10 million users. And by December of 2014, it had 40 million users with 1 BILLION swipes (swipe right to like a match, swipe left to remove) per day. At first, Tinder was ridiculed for promoting superficial looks versus substance. Instead, it turned out the app tapped into the basic dating impulse: first impressions. And while it would seem that many such pairings would be likely to fail, people are also going on more dates.

The numbers show that while internet dating leads to more casual sex, it also leads to successful marriages. While it's true that 48 percent of couples who meet online break up by e-mail or text, researchers have also found that couples who met online were more likely to have higher rates of marital satisfaction and lower rates of divorce than those who met off-line. They also scored higher in marriage satisfaction according to a study at the University of Chicago, leading the lead author of the study to conclude: "These data suggest that the internet may be altering the dynamics and outcomes of marriage itself."

Another recent study, based on a 2017 project conducted on 2,669 partnered participants by Stanford University social demographer Michael J. Rosenfeld, found that people who met online and subsequently married ended up tying the knot much sooner after meeting than those who met through other means (within three to four years for onliners versus ten years for off-liners).

Fundamentally, internet dating is about efficiency. Much like Uber for black cars and taxis, dating apps are a digital layer that simply makes it a lot easier for you to meet a new dating partner quickly. It's efficient and far easier than a bar, a church social, or a high school reunion.

And yet, it still allows users to express personal racial, religious, age-based prejudices—also with efficiency and ease. In Christian Rudder's *Dataclysm: Love, Sex, Race, and Identity—What Our Online Lives Tell Us About Our Offline Selves*, the founders of OkCupid tracked how people rate others and whether social problems were being exacerbated by internet dating. The results were surprising: women overall tended to want partners close to their age as they aged; men, in contrast, always wanted much younger women. This creates an imbalance in which younger single women have wider choices, while older women wait for a click or swipe that's not happening—exacerbating the problems of the never marrieds.

The problem with online dating is that while more people are living happily ever after, certain groups are getting left behind. For example, men of all races rate black women lower than white women online, leaving black women with fewer opportunities online. White men rate Asian women highly, giving them more choices on average. Increasing numbers of white women are attracted to black men but rate Asian men lower. Preferences and attitudes like these, whether intentional or not, mean that Asian men and black women find themselves lower down on the dating chain on average, according to *Dataclysm*.

Despite these trends, fewer people are opting to date only within their race. According to OkCupid's data, the strong preference for dating among one's race has dropped by a quarter in the last six years from over 40 percent to under 30 percent. This suggests that despite the problem of racial dating preference, the needle is moving in favor of more openness to dating people from wider backgrounds. This is especially true on the internet, as the typical online dater is more likely to be socially progressive, better educated, and more upscale. As a consequence, online dating does not wind up mixing up people from different classes as much as I had predicted ten years ago in *Microtrends*. If anything, new apps like The League (skewing progressive, Ivy League educated, and urban dwelling) aim to do exactly the opposite and restratify dating so that more people can find and marry like-minded folks with a similar background.

The biggest new trend in mobile dating is its growth with the

7.2: Dating App Usage by Age Cohort, 2013–2015

Percentage in each age cohort who have ever used an online dating site or mobile dating app

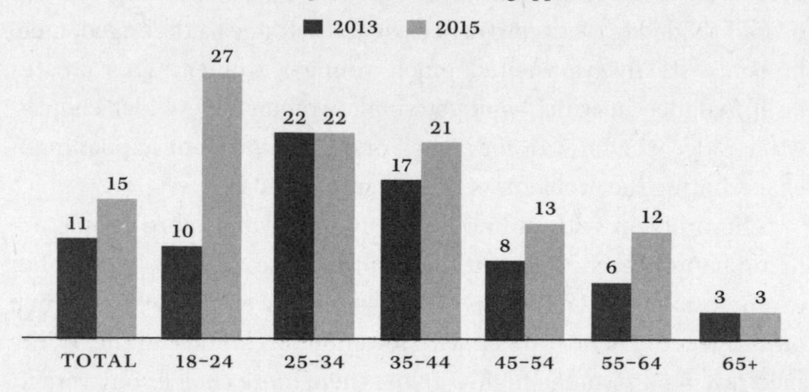

older set. More and more older Americans, from baby boomers to 70-plus widows, are using online dating to make matches. There are even mobile dating apps like Stitch that are reserved for the 50-plus cohorts. It may not seem like a big leap that, according to Pew, the share of 55- to 64-year-olds doing online dating jumped from 6 percent to 12 percent between 2013 and 2015. But 65 percent of that age cohort was *already married*, meaning that somewhere around a third of singles in this age range are using online dating.

The gay community has embraced online dating the most of any cohort: 70 percent of gay relationships start online. Grindr is the most popular app, with two million daily active users. While it can be used to find a partner within a few hundred feet of you for a casual hookup, nearly 77 percent of Grindr users say that want to get married, and 76 percent say they want kids.

Internationally, online and mobile dating is changing marriages. In countries like India, matchmaking is common and now booming online. BharatMatrimony, an online dating site, has raised $20.35 million in two rounds from three investors, and was founded nearly a decade ago. Dil Mil, the largest growing matchmaking company for expats in Southeast Asia, has raised $3.8 million.

In the U.K., the *Daily Mail* touts the internet as the fifth-best way to meet a potential spouse. According to popular online dating website eHarmony, the U.K. has online daters in droves, "our research shows that two-thirds of people in the U.K. would use online dating if they became single in the future," says its dating advice page, and purports that "the numbers of relationships starting between colleagues and close friends dropped from 18% to 12% since 2007." This means of course that fewer people are meeting the traditional way: in person or set up by friends.

In the ten years since we first examined online dating in *Microtrends,* meeting online has become the norm. It's no longer just a haven for the desperate or the isolated. According to Pew, in 2005, 44 percent of Americans agreed that online dating was a great way to meet people. A decade later, that number is almost 60 percent. However, online dating can still bring out prejudice: it is one of the last places where people can openly discriminate against certain groups. If we want to boost the number of successful marriages and families, we need to give some help to those groups left without as many choices—to make sure we all swipe into the relationships we want.

8. INDEPENDENT MARRIEDS

As trend after trend has shown, marriage is being redefined based on the new ways in which people live today, and so it should come as no surprise that many of those who do get married today, especially later in life, bring a strong streak of independent habits to the union and often take separate vacations, live in separate bedrooms, keep their pre-marriage names, and more. Never before have those who are bound together been so apart.

One group that has always lived this way is represented by military families—couples who are constantly "together but apart" by the core nature of the job; yet, such families actually have one of the lowest divorce rates of people in any occupation. It's the same with flight attendants. The question is whether we will find the same kinds of results with families who live independently even when their careers don't require it.

In some ways, this trend echoes the phenomenon of commuter couples found in the original *Microtrends,* which detailed a twofold increase in the number of couples who commuted to see each other between 1992 and 2005. In the decade since the first book, the number of such marriages has held steady between 3.4 and 3.8 million, and these behaviors are no longer seen as such outliers. If anything, the ways in which couples lead different lives have only increased.

The current president, Donald Trump, and his wife, Melania, are an extreme example of independent: separate bedrooms, separate

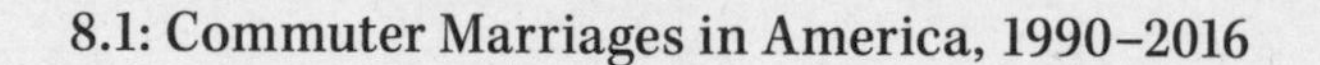

8.1: Commuter Marriages in America, 1990–2016

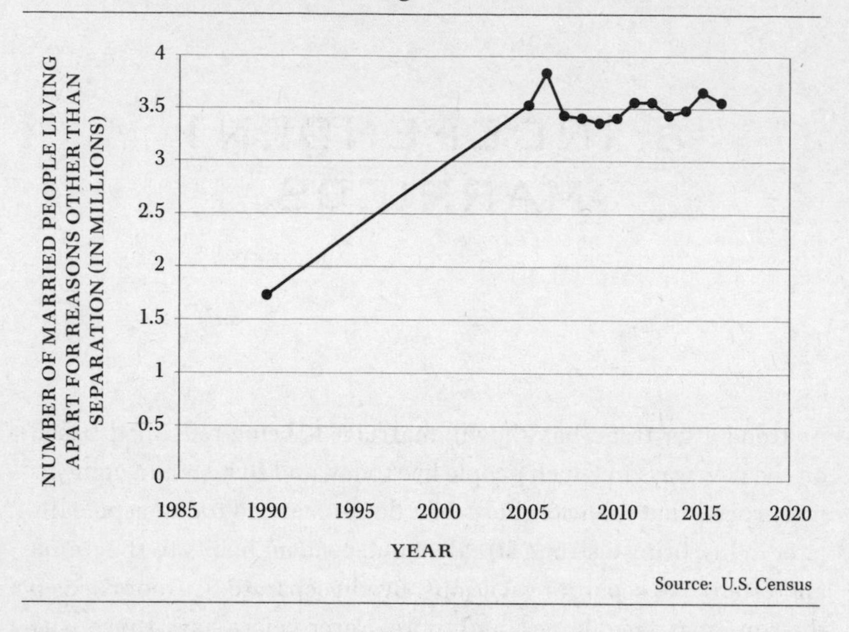

Source: U.S. Census

living quarters, separate cities altogether, until recently. And yet by all appearances it's a rather strong marriage.

A lot of what we are seeing today is simply the result of people spending more years on their own and adopting a range of independent habits: bedtime rituals, tastes in food, and generally being in control of the light, temperature, noise level, and other aspects of their physical space. So more opting to marry aren't opting to blend their styles. Instead, they're seeking to maintain their independent tastes, picking up an *Annie Hall*–esque view of life: apartments across the park from each other.

According to *Psychology Today*, spending more time apart, even though married, prompts couples to plan their time together, especially if they don't live together. You might have a wife a two-hour drive away, and thus you have to consciously plan time together, which requires commitment, while preventing things from "becoming monotonous," according to the article. It continues: "It is easy to see how this 'opt-in' versus 'opt-out' arrangement may encourage these couples to put more effort into dating, leading to more exciting, self-expanding activities that reduce boredom and increase satisfaction."

However, all of this commuting to your beloved leaves a lot of wear and tear on your marriage—at least shortly after saying "I do." Regular long distances between marrieds increase your chances for divorce. If one spouse's commute is longer than forty-five minutes, the couple is 40 percent more likely to get divorced. Yet, the longer an independent married couple exists that way, in this in-between state, the less the commute times matter. Commuter couples, however, are only the tip of the iceberg. Today even couples that live together are leading separate lives.

One prominent example of the independent marrieds microtrend is couples sleeping apart. A survey from the National Sleep Foundation found that nearly a quarter of married couples sleep in separate beds—and some surveys think couples are underreporting and that number might be closer to 30 or 40 percent of couples. Furniture designers and interior decorators have already taken notice and are increasingly planning for two master bedrooms: separate design schemes and décor, and two different beds entirely. The National Association of Home Builders expects to be making 60 percent of American homes with separate master bedrooms in the near future.

Why the drastic shift in bed location? It could be a rise in rates of sleep apnea diagnoses—as no one really wants to sleep next to a snoring bear every night. Sleep disorders, along with respiratory disorders, are on the rise all over the world, though particularly in emerging markets like India, China, and Brazil. Previously, sleeping separately from your partner was taboo and frowned upon. It meant your relationship was doomed and lacking in intimacy. But there seems to be a shift toward broader acceptance, as indicated by the money being spent on separate bedrooms for couples. Stories surrounding them even exhibit praise for this new lifestyle choice, and many experts have also come around to the benefits of this independent marrieds sleeping arrangement. Whether it's snoring, sleeping styles, or wanting private space, sleeping separately from a partner might improve your relationship.

These factors and behaviors from an independent lifestyle—maybe they were what married couples wanted all along. Your marriage won't suffer as much strain if you can't tolerate your husband's sleeping habits, or if you want your own apartment several nights of the week. With differing pairings and the way Americans are living their lives, maybe being independent marrieds isn't lonely—maybe it's helpful. Getting more sleep can lead to an improved mood and an improved sex life. Anecdotally, marriage expert Stephanie Coontz noted in the *New York Times* that couples with separate bedrooms were "confident" in their marriages and that it didn't "say anything about their sex lives," she said.

There are many implications for the independent marrieds lifestyle. The first is health care and disease. One of the key advocates for a person's health is his or her spouse making sure their partner gets routine checkups and is healthy and happy. Will new trends cause spouses to miss key warning signs that their significant others can't catch on their own? There is research that marriage leads to positive health effects. A recent study of 25,000 people in England found that suffering a heart attack saw a 14 percent higher rate of survival if the subject had a spouse. Compared to single people, when it comes to health, married people tend to live longer, have fewer heart attacks and strokes, have a lower chance of becoming depressed, and are more likely to survive major health ordeals better than their uncoupled counterparts. This becomes more pronounced in certain subgroups—with white men faring the poorest without a spouse to help them recover from cancer. Will these diminish as independent marrieds rise?

The other leading question is how the arrangement between spouses could affect their children. Will they benefit from a two-parent household—as many kids do? Or will it lead to feelings of isolation not dissimilar to those experienced in a household of divorce? It's also possible that the children of American independent marrieds will beget similar situations when those kids grow up and learn that independence is a key cornerstone to a successful marriage. Some of the never married trend is due to young people valuing their independence—but perhaps the rise of the "together and apart" model will provide millennials with a happy medium. If a couple can keep their freedom while still being married, maybe marriage becomes more attractive—or maybe the opposite is true if the never marrieds see the independent marrieds trend as an affirmation that marriage isn't that important.

Cultural attitudes are also clearly shifting around marriage, and the independent marrieds microtrend will only continue to push the American definition of marriage. When it comes to weddings or dinner parties for friends and family, will previously cultural norms like inviting a spouse shift? Will weddings where the bride is friends with only one member of a couple result in the other being excluded? Will going to events and celebrations together fall by the wayside?

Another common independent marrieds activity is separate vacations. Previously your spouse was your travel buddy, but no longer. Now it's common for American couples to vacation apart. Whether it's a boys' trip or a trip with your kids without your spouse—more American couples are traveling like . . . singles. According to the travel site TripAdvisor, 59 percent of site users report having taken a separate vacation from his or her significant other. President Barack Obama and his wife, Michelle, notably took separate vacations as well—which was a "sign of strength" to many experts. Like sleeping or living separately, these separate vacations might lead to more satisfying time together.

Consumer behavior could also be affected by this idea of separate vacations and large, indulgent, separate expenditures. There's an entire marketplace for husband or wife trips—specific touring or experiences to cater to the single spouse with or without his or her kids. The travel industry is noting this, but there will be more "girls' weekend" vacations for older married people. This is increasingly depicted in popular culture, and not just for bachelor parties. One of the top live-action comedy openings happened in summer 2017 in which four women—either in relationships or not—came together for its title, *Girls Trip*.

Maybe there will be more vacation packages geared toward solo travelers and small groups who aren't couples. Maybe hotels will also start providing more small single rooms that can be rented cheaply to solo travelers. There is a bias in travel and costs when it comes to traveling alone, which the hospitality industry will have to address. With the advent of Airbnb and smaller rentable rooms and studios for a solo traveler, the hotel industry will be forced to re-examine the traditional two-to-a-room policy and subsequent high prices.

The independent marrieds will also affect the housing market—as they have started to already. From designing more houses with two master bedrooms to decorating them to cater to each spouse's style, the housing, furniture, and interior decorating industries will see changes in how they do business. At the top 10 percent of the nationwide market, listings for homes with multiple master bedrooms are, on average, 9 percent pricier than those with just one master, reports the *Wall Street Journal*. According to *Elle Decor*, a 2016 survey shows "nearly one out of three people seeking homes that are $2 million or more have expressed interest in dual master bedrooms."

We are more apart than ever before—in our tastes, habits, spending, and health care. And the trend is increasingly global. Independent marrieds aren't limited to American trend. In 2011, for instance, the U.K. census showed that 6 percent of Londoners were married but choosing to live apart. This arrangement is in fact even more common in Europe than in the U.S. The decision is often made for practical reasons, like education, or might even simply follow from a more liberal attitude. In countries like Russia, France, Germany, and Norway, nearly 10 percent of couples are living apart. In the U.K., 10 percent of the British adult population is made up of LATs ("living apart together" couples).

Separate bedrooms, careers, and possibly homes might seem to drive an independent marrieds couple apart. But that's not necessarily the case. Marriages don't look like they used to; increasingly people want both a significant other and a continued sense of independence. The independent marrieds, in that sense, are trying to find a way to enjoy the best of both worlds and find a higher degree of satisfaction in being married while being more independent.

Section 2

HEALTH AND DIET

9. Pro-Proteiners

10. Guys Left Behind

11. Nonagenarians

12. Kids on Meds

13. The Speed Eaters

14. Wellness Freaks

15. Cancer Survivors

9. PRO-PROTEINERS

One of the most unexpected trends in the last few years has been the victory of protein over carbohydrates—accompanied by a growing number of protein fanatics. This development has been great for ranchers and fisherman but bad for farmers. It's not that people are lining up at the steak houses; it turns out that my dad's old family business—the chicken industry—has been the big winner. Red meat is on hold, pasta is out, and chicken is the new gold standard of nutrition. Improbable, yes, but the numbers are clear: while red meat consumption has stalled and even decreased per capita, chicken is up over 300 percent. We were all supposed to be vegan or vegetarian by now, given all of the downsides of processed carbohydrates and meat. But something else entirely happened.

Just about twenty-five years ago, protein was dead as a food. The government was recommending more grains, and pasta was hailed as the new superfood. It is what athletes ate for energy, and government planners believed that they were going to be successful in trimming heart disease and other killers like cancer by reorienting the American diet.

But step by step, protein made a comeback. It started in many ways with the Atkins diet: the discovery that just eating protein alone (no carbohydrates) throws your body into weight-losing ketosis. This was ridiculed at first, as Atkins dieters wolfed down steak and eggs. But they seemed to lose weight. Maybe it was because eliminating anything causes weight loss, but the formula had a lot more success, even when pressure tested, than anyone imagined. The counterintuitive became conventional. Fifteen million copies of Atkins books have been sold to date.

Processed foods and carbohydrates, loaded with sugars, then became the new villain—the cause of national weight gain. Nutritionists started to say "no white at night"—telling people dinner would be protein, salad, and vegetables. Gone was the starch. Potatoes have had a tough time: they hit their peak in 1996, but sales have been falling since.

Red meat, however, has been under the microscope for some time—sometimes fairly, sometimes unfairly. High degrees of saturated fat in red meat were blamed for heart disease, and Americans look at red meat quite skeptically these days, even if they still love it. Cancer has been associated with red meat as well, but a careful look

9.1: Annual U.S. Chicken Consumption per Capita, 1960–2012

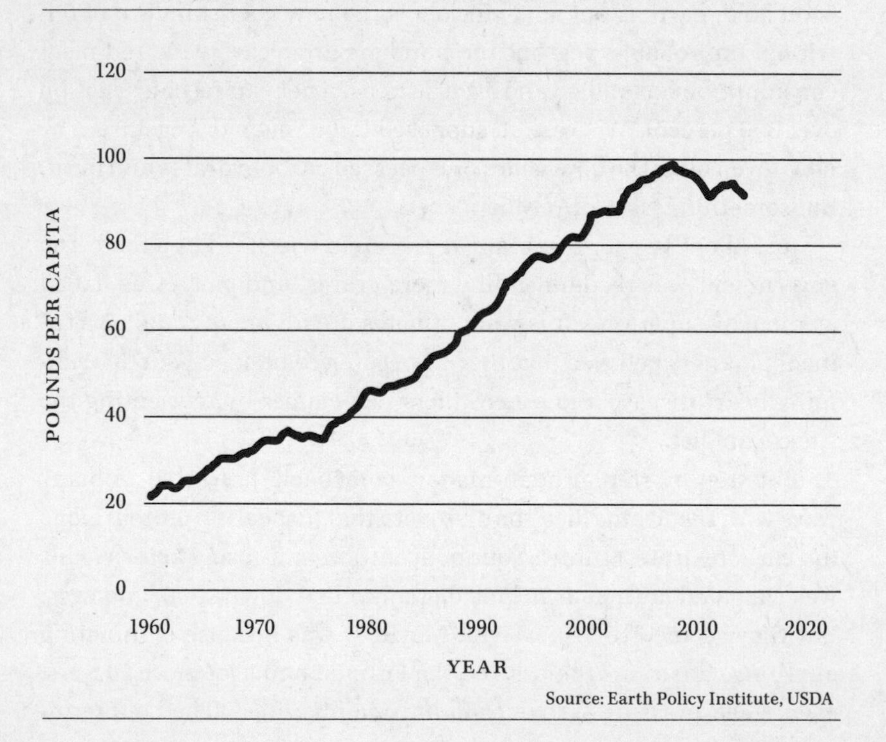

Source: Earth Policy Institute, USDA

at the studies suggests to beware more of charcoaled grilled meats as the proven culprit, as well as processed meats like bologna and hot dogs.

Studies have more recently shown that what you eat has a lot less to do with cholesterol levels than previously believed. This has started to lift the cloud on red meat, despite the overall consensus that there is probably more harm than good in high levels of red meat consumption. Eggs, which had been completely abandoned, got a second look. Maybe they had been unfairly singled out when they are a cheap and easy source of protein. They don't have the fat marbled issues of red meat, and their cholesterol has been declared less harmful than previously thought. For the last five years, eggs have been roaring back, showing double-digit growth in many years—something almost unheard of for a common staple.

When it comes to red meat, millennials don't have the same affinity for a hamburger that the baby boomers do. Consumption of red meat is down across the board. But millennials' views on meat in one's diet are high. White-meat chicken didn't have the saturated fat issues and was affordable and good enough in taste. The numbers for chicken are through the roof. In the past, eating chicken was like going to a second-rate college. If you could afford to eat steak every day, of course, you would. Now it's become a genuine first choice for a growing group of protein munchers.

Sugary soda, cream, roast beef, and bacon are all losers in this war, along with pasta. All have shown per capita declines in the last decade. Even diet soda sales have gone down. Along with chicken, shrimp and fish are big winners. According to the National Fisheries Institute, whitefish consumption increased by around 50 percent between 2001 and 2012, with smaller increases for shrimp consumption in that same time.

But our obsession with protein might mean we're eating too much of it. According to new dietary guidelines reported by the *New York Times* in 2016, American teenage boys and men are getting too much protein. For the first time, federal dietary guidelines are advising these men and boys to stop eating so much meat, chicken, and eggs.

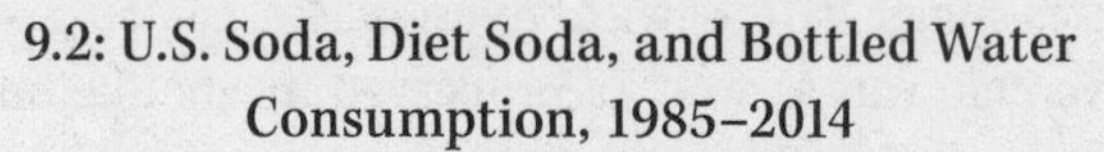

9.2: U.S. Soda, Diet Soda, and Bottled Water Consumption, 1985–2014

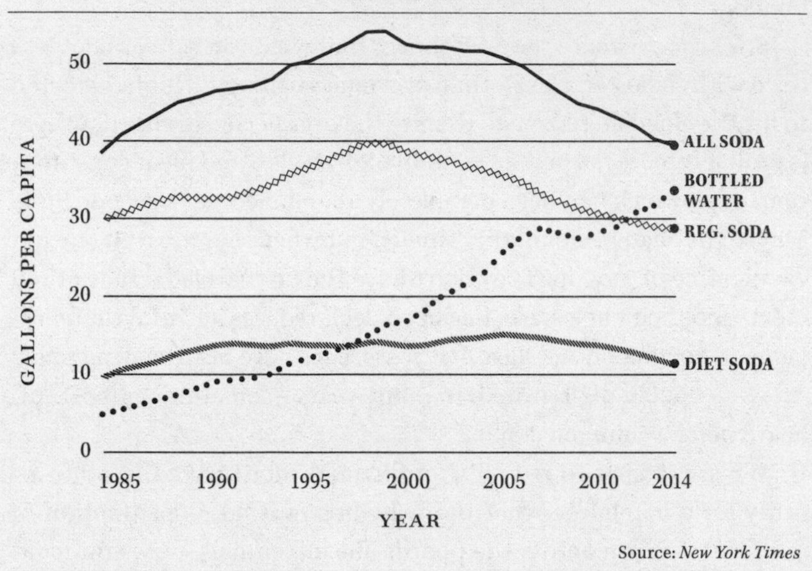

Source: *New York Times*

American men and boys are "almost half the population, so that's a big deal," said Michael F. Jacobson, executive director of the Center for Science in the Public Interest, a nutrition advocacy group in Washington.

Along with the main staples, protein powder use is up. Yet powders are fairly unregulated, which can lead to mystery ingredients and toxins. According to a December 2016 report, "The vast majority of Americans already get more than the recommended daily amounts of protein from food, they say, and there are no rigorous long-term studies to tell us how much protein is too much." We're averaging 46 grams of protein a day for women, and 56 grams for men: Americans don't need that much protein.

Still, the protein supplement industry continues to grow in America, continually telling consumers they aren't getting enough protein. The money behind the protein market continues to grow—research firm Euromonitor International projects that sales of protein powders and supplements could reach $9 billion by 2020. There's only so much protein the body can digest and make use of, according to Jim White, a registered dietitian and exercise physiologist who spoke on behalf of the Academy of Nutrition and Dietetics. "The body only digests and absorbs a certain amount of protein at every meal," about 20 to 40 grams. "People think that if they fill up with protein, it will be a magic bullet, whether for weight loss or to get in better shape and build muscle—but that's not proving to be true." Too much protein can also increase the risk of diabetes and kidney disease.

Protein is such a national obsession that there are many alternative proteins that are taking up market share, like soy, almond, and coconut. According to a report by the insights firm Research and Markets, "the global plant-based protein market was USD 8.35 billion in 2016 and is estimated to reach USD 14.22 billion by 2022." Tofu, a classic staple for vegetarians, isn't just for groups that don't eat meat anymore. One step has been getting these alternative proteins out of just the "vegetarian" aisles at supermarkets. Fake meat is a big, moneymaking industry. Beyond Meat, a huge player in the alternative meats industry, claims that everyone's love for chicken should make products like their Beyond Chicken Strips universal. Its founder, Ethan Brown, says that "human beings don't want just any old protein. Earth has enough bugs and krill to keep us all in amino acids."

From a UN report in 2013, the organization emphasized that, to accommodate the growing world population, a key source of future protein should include bugs. The UN urges Americans and other developed nations to get past the "gross" factor and start eating insects. In Congo, for example, its population eats tons of caterpillars. In Australia, the country's leadership is pushing locusts as a robust source of protein and has compiled recipes in a cookbook, *Cooking with Sky Prawns* (BBC, 2004). Even American start-ups are using bugs to sell protein bars. According to a 2016 *Wired* article, Exo raised $4 million dollars to produce bug-centric protein bars, and Chapul, a cricket-based protein bar, won a $50,000 investment from Mark Cuban on *Shark Tank* in 2014.

One surprising protein casualty over the last few decades has been

9.3: U.S. Seafood Consumption per Capita, 2001–2012

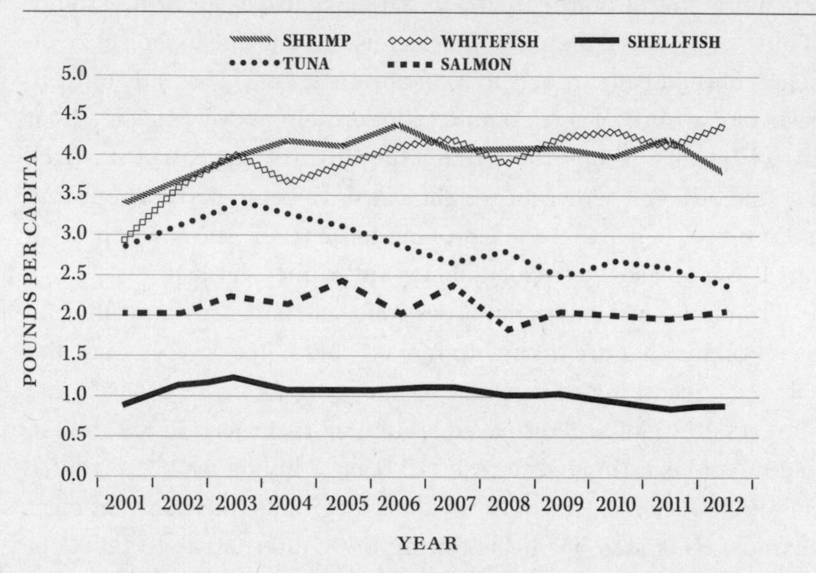

Seafood Datasearch Table based on NFI data, courtesy of John Sackton, www.seafood.com
Source: National Fisheries Institute, *Undercurrent News*

tuna fish. Technically, the government warned only pregnant women about mercury levels, and it applies only to albacore tuna. (Light tuna has a pH that does not allow it to hold much, if any, mercury.) It did not matter, despite its low cost and heart-healthy benefits; tuna has been a big loser in the twenty-first century.

Sushi, however, has been on the upswing: we have gone from almost zero to 4,000 sushi restaurants in the U.S. in the last twenty-five years. It is eaten primarily in restaurants, so despite its cultural dominance and the inclusion of sushi everywhere in urban society today, it is not registering significantly overall as moving the fish and seafood that Americans eat annually. It would have to move into the home to move the needle.

Globally, China and India are the next food explosion markets to watch. On a per capita basis, China already outpaces the U.S. in pork consumption—which is perhaps why Shuanghui International, China's largest meat processor, purchased the American pork brand

9.4: Annual Pork Consumption per Capita in U.S. and China, 1960–2012

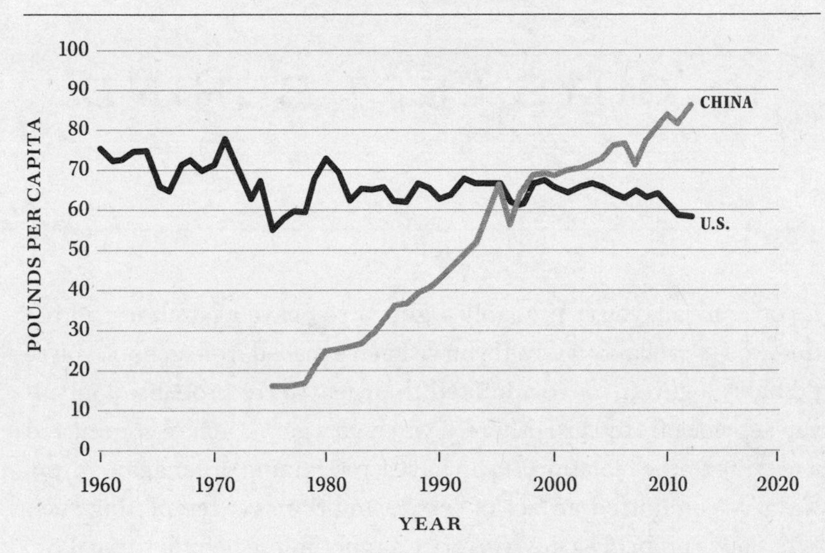

Source: Earth Policy Institute, USDA, UNPop

Smithfield in 2013 for $4.7 billion. For other proteins, such as chicken, China lags behind the U.S. on a per capita consumption basis. But Chinese chicken consumption has been steadily increasing, and the size of the market means there's a lot of room to grow. India, too, has been chowing down on more chicken than ever. In 2014, India's National Sample Survey Office reported that chicken consumption was growing at a rate of 12 percent per year, making India a particularly fast-growing market.

While it is possible that the strange and new will take off unexpectedly, the health-conscious consensus is that chicken, shrimp, and salmon are the proteins that have made it through the gauntlet of health-related, taste, and cost concerns. Though there are environmental and other concerns about animal protein, it seems as if my dad had it right in the first place: the grain-filled future is surprisingly in the past, and chicken, turkey, and eggs are the core of the diet for the next generation of non-vegetarian millennials.

10. GUYS LEFT BEHIND

If you're in jail, you're probably a guy. If you have a gambling addiction, you're probably a guy. If you've been expelled from school, you're probably a guy. If you're addicted to drugs, you're probably a guy. If you act violently toward others, if you own a gun, if you've committed a moving traffic violation, if you have a restraining order against you, if you've committed an act of terrorism or are contemplating such acts, you're probably a guy. Guys are simply falling behind these days. As we've seen in other chapters, American women are outpacing men and paving the way for big changes economically, socially, and culturally. So what is happening to all these men who are left in their dust?

Despite the setback of not having elected the first woman president, women are succeeding in an ever-widening range of areas, while there is a statistically significant and growing group of guys who are just not going to make it. American women are working hard to claim their space at the top and to close out issues like the wage gap. But serious problems are brewing for the future of men. You see it in statistic after statistic. Some of these have been true for a long time; others are new. While women have shown some dramatic improvements in health, education, and income, men—especially at the bottom end of the income scale—are facing problems that are as bad as ever, and in many areas are getting worse.

In 2015 there were over 1.9 million men incarcerated in the U.S., but only 200,000 women. While the rate of female incarceration has increased faster than male incarceration in the past few decades, in absolute terms men still end up in jail ten times as often as women.

American men are also increasingly unhealthy, and many don't even go to the doctor for a checkup. By the time they do visit the doc about that lump or ache, it's too late. According to a survey by the Cleveland Clinic of five hundred American men ages 18 to 70, only "three in five men get an annual physical, and just over 40 percent go to the doctor only when they fear they have a serious medical condition." One in two men have ready excuses for skipping the visit: they are too busy, don't want the doctor doing the rectal exam, or even don't like being naked under a robe. Mostly, I think, guys are afraid the doctor will find something.

Women not only go to the doctor more often but they also do something else men don't do: they talk about it. Men, not so much. From the same Cleveland Clinic study: over half of the men surveyed agreed that their health "just isn't something they talk about." This needs to change, because it will save lives. Whatever gets them into the doctor's office works—and a full 19 percent of men admit that

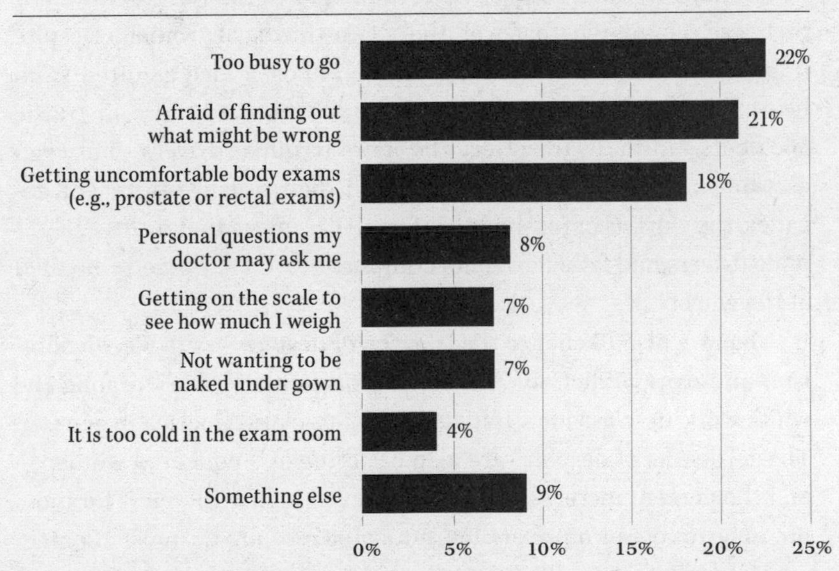

they go to the doctor to stop being nagged by their girlfriend or wife. But with Americans marrying less, this isn't the most reliable way to ensure that men are showing up for their prostate exams.

The larger problem isn't just an American phenomenon. According to the WHO European Region's review of social factors and health, men dying earlier "reflect[s] several factors—greater levels of occupational exposure to physical and chemical hazards, behaviours associated with male norms of risk-taking and adventure, health behaviour paradigms related to masculinity and the fact that men are less likely to visit a doctor when they are ill and, when they see a doctor, are less likely to report on the symptoms of disease or illness." Around the world, men need to be educated about the importance of routine health exams and to pinpoint their fears, which is a driving reason they don't go get checked out. The stigma—around men being concerned for their own health—needs to lead to key discussions among groups of male friends or peers in order to get more men in to the doctor.

Beyond routine visits, men remain much more likely to be alcoholics than women. Almost three-quarters of men are overweight or obese, compared to fewer than two-thirds of women. Despite improvements for both sexes, men die almost twice as often from heart disease than women. Men have always died more in traffic accidents—initially, they were the more frequent drivers—but even as women have dramatically increased their mileage in recent decades, the gap has barely budged. The IIHS reports that in 2014 10,971 male drivers had fatal accidents compared to 4,504 women who died at the wheel.

Men are also likelier to die "deaths of despair"—suicide, alcoholism, and drug addiction. This is also particularly stark among the white working-class men, but also working-class America in general. These "deaths of despair" are also affecting less educated women—and the percent increase for women is even higher than it is for men. But in terms of raw numbers, less educated men are the most affected.

Many of these trends I describe have notably worsened in the aftermath of the Great Recession. In December 2007, before the eco-

10.2: Deaths by Drugs, Alcohol, and Suicide among White, Non-Hispanic Adults Age 50–54

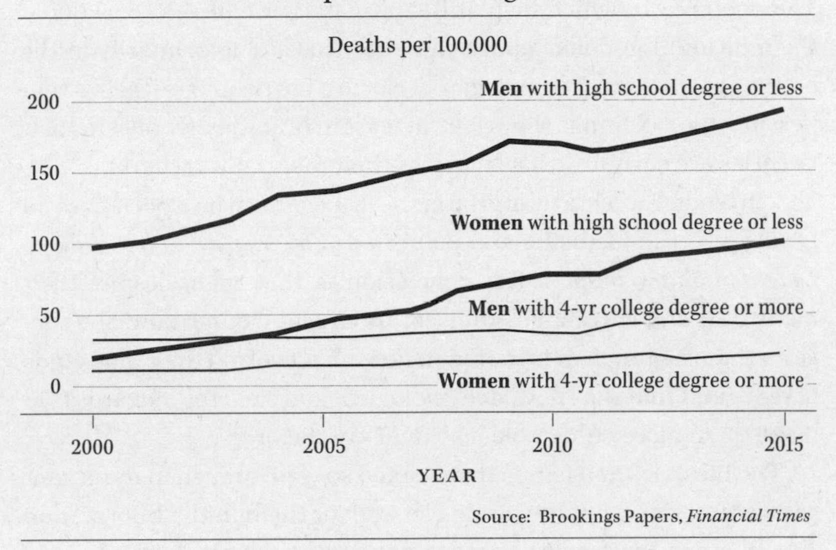

Source: Brookings Papers, *Financial Times*

nomic crisis set in, unemployment rates were roughly equal, but in the years since it's the guys who have been laid off in greater numbers. The unemployment rate surged from 4.4 percent to 7.2 percent for men, but from 4.3 percent to only 5.9 percent for women.

When it comes to earning what you learn, guys aren't learning what they need to: women are getting almost 60 percent of the college degrees conferred, compared to barely 40 percent for men. This is a complete reversal of the past that I grew up with, but a consistently growing trend as women first hit the 50 percent mark in 1982. The college gap could be the one that spells the most serious problem for guys, and could over time be at the root of a lot of increased frustration and even crime. Beyond undergraduate degrees, women are also increasingly predominant in professional schools. Fifty years ago, there were very few women earning professional degrees. Today they are close to, if not surpassing, men in law school and medical school.

Ultimately, women are also living longer than men, which isn't new. All told, the gap in life expectancy is five years—men are expected to live to 76 and women to 81—so, as a group, men are behind now in every major category of health, education, and life span. The one area in which men still dominate is wealth—especially at the multimillion-dollar upper end—but that's true primarily in the oldest generations. The pay gap is closing for people in their twenties; income tax filings show that, at least in big cities, women in their twenties are earning just as much as their male counterparts.

I attended a lecture of Marianne J. Legato, who specializes in gender-specific medicine and published *Why Men Die First: How to Lengthen Your Lifespan*. Her conclusion is that men, despite their many past and current advantages, are in real trouble now. She suggests that the problem is rooted in how men evolved over thousands of years and that they now face "biological and societal" hazards that make them more vulnerable now than ever before.

The lifestyles and habits that worked so well for men in more dangerous times may not be working so well for them in the Information Age. In every age, from the caves right on through the Second World War, it worked for men to take big risks, have short attention spans, and be driven by ego. These days those things are more likely to get in the way of doing a good job. Hunting wild boar and hunting through Wikipedia require a different set of skills.

Though it may be worth taking evolutionary theory with a grain of salt, the present-day statistics seem to confirm Dr. Legato's theory. Certainly, the gaps are growing, and this is not just a U.S. phenomenon. In developing countries such as India, women are generally seen as better employees compared to men, who are considered hard to train, unwilling to listen, and likely to quit. If this is the case, a lot of men could be headed for even a bigger fall as the Information Age spreads around the globe.

Our current society expects men to be providers and protectors, heroic, efficient, practical, and self-reliant over being social and able to bond with others. Yet our culture has become far more socially based with the emergence of social media, and this leaves the isolated man feeling even more like the odd man out. Once again, women dominate platforms like Facebook; the only major network today you will find more men on, outside of porn sites, is Xbox Live, and even there the gap is closing. Studies show that people with close relationships suffer fewer physical and mental health consequences, while social isolation is linked to serious diseases such as Alzheimer's, diabetes, high blood pressure, heart disease, and even cancer. People with strong social networks live longer and have better people skills. In a recent survey conducted by psychologist Niobe Way, 85 percent of young men in her study reported that they sought emotionally intimate friendships with peers—particularly during late adolescence—but had trouble finding friends they could trust.

The problems for men start early. Boys are having trouble sitting still, while classes in most schools are becoming more demanding at earlier ages. Eighth-grade boys are 50 percent more likely than girls to get held back a grade; 67 percent of special education students are boys; suspensions are given to boys 71 percent of the time. By the time they reach high school, peer pressure often convinces boys it isn't cool to excel in academics.

So, if these long-term trends continue, women will continue to take a more prominent role—not just in schools and the workplace but economically. They will grow in consumer influence in every major area: from health care to home buying, from technology to investment planning. The majority of car buyers are already women, and there is tremendous room for growth by women in numerous marketplaces over the next fifteen years as the long-term effects of gender disparities deepen and the income disparities between men and women begin to even out over time.

The guys-left-behind microtrend is very much tied to money, as well as class and race. Wealthier American men are catching up to their female counterparts in life expectancy; white men are living longer than men of color. It's poorer men in America whose health is most stagnant and precarious. A recent study from the National Bureau of Economic Research projected that, for older American men, the life expectancy at age "50 for males in the two highest income quintiles will rise by 7 to 8 years between the 1930 and 1960 birth cohorts, but that the two lowest income quintiles will experience little to no increase over that time period." This also has Social Security implications: if only richer men live longer, then men overall will get even fewer benefits from Social Security, and the program will be less progressive.

The social costs of GLBs will become an increasing drag on society and on the national budget. Ten years after the Great Recession, states and local governments are still hard-pressed to invest more in prisoner education, job training, reentry programs, and other efforts to help GLBs. And while there's a great deal of money being poured into schools, it's not clear there's any focus on dealing with the disproportionate number of boys left struggling. Without a proper policy focus on these issues, guys will fall further behind.

Indeed, girls' greater success in school could soon become one of those "unshakable" truths that we come to see as natural—like women's longer life spans. As Dr. Legato points out, the gender disparity in life span is not necessarily natural; in 1900, both men and women were expected to live about forty-seven years. It was only as life spans increased that the disparity started to appear. Maybe it could closed again if we poured some research and effort into it.

When it comes to the implications in our relationships and cultural attitudes, the trope of the man left behind will continue to permeate popular culture and romantic pairings. As seen in other chapters, these GLBs may well become second-fiddle husbands or will remain never marrieds. When it comes to housing, maybe the U.S. will end up like Italy with its "Mammoni" phenomenon, where young men live with their parents. In Italy, over *half* of men ages 25 to 35 live with their parents.

While America has between a $1 billion and $4 billion SAT test-prep industry, we have very few gender-specific programs to help close the emerging gender gaps in high school and college. Likewise, there is no political movement calling for more funds to go toward solving the mystery of double the incidence of heart disease among men. Politically, many guys left behind have continued to edge toward a populist revolt. They feel that while everyone else has been gaining, they have been finding it harder and harder to succeed in

America—because of trade, immigration, and the benefits they see going to everyone else but them. Even if these are mere scapegoats rather than root causes, President Trump clearly speaks to these men—and they will continue to line up behind him unless the Democrats get serious about appealing to this group.

GLBs face more fatal accidents, shortened educational and earning opportunities, higher unemployment, more drug and alcohol dependencies, greater obesity, declining political influence, more heart attacks, and shorter lives. And they have less political power because they vote and organize less often. Without getting serious about the phenomenon of guys left behind, we just might be creating a newer and deeper basement that a lot of men may never get out of.

11. NONAGENARIANS

In the next installment of *Microtrends*, we will probably be writing about centenarians. But right now, the next demographic group set to explode are people who live past 90: the nonagenarians. According to current U.S. census estimates, we now have about 2.5 million people in America older than 90, up from 720,000 people in 1980. In fact, it is one of the fastest-growing age cohorts.

With increasing advances in health care, if you hit 80, you have a 30 percent chance of making it to 90. If you're born today, your odds are similar. A recent British report released by the Department for Work and Pensions said that if you're a girl born in the U.K. in 2011, you have a one-in-three chance of living to be 100—a boy has a one-in-four chance. This is compared to a person born in 1930, who only had a 3 percent chance of becoming a centenarian.

Some of the critical factors that have helped this trend are the reduction in smoking, an increase in exercise, and more regular exams that catch possible problems before it is too late. The absence of wars, global plagues, and other catastrophes have also prevented premature deaths. By 2050, demographers expect this group of American nonagenarians to grow to over 10 million. But those living to 90 will continue to tip the power structure to the old, and not the young, in a society that's based on democracy.

In the 2010 U.S. Census Bureau report, people over 90 were getting about half of their income from Social Security, and about 20 percent lived in nursing homes. We have 1.3 million in nursing homes now, and just the increase in the over-90 demographic will require nearly

2 million new spots in those homes. Almost four in ten were living on their own, while another four in ten were with family members.

In that same report, 74 percent of those nonagenarians were women, and most were widows. To the extent that the rich tend to do better overall, and to the extent that assets continue to appreciate over time—remember, a million dollars invested in 1935 would be worth $2.8 billion today, according to *Forbes*—there is likely to be the reemergence of the power of the dowager. She will be courted and fawned upon even more, if possible, by graying bachelors, especially if the estate tax is eliminated. And with guys too often not getting on the better health care bandwagon, there is no evidence that the gender gap in longer living is going to be closed anytime soon.

When we have a retirement system geared toward people retiring at age 65 or 67, people living in their nineties will get about double the benefits of people who pass away at normal life expectancy. That will likely add significantly to the Social Security crisis unless reforms are put in place or robots and technology dramatically increase productivity.

Living over 90 can both be frightening and satisfying. The fearful part is the feeling that maybe today will be the last day. But it turns out that most people who make it to that age are happy with their lives. Despite widespread disability of one kind or another, nonagenarians showed fewer signs of depression than people in their thirties, forties, and fifties when surveyed in the U.K.

The United States is not the only place having to accommodate more nonagenarians. According to the U.K.'s Office for National Statistics, nonagenarians are getting close to 1 percent of the country's total population. In 2015 there were over half a million people in the U.K. over 90, and that is up from only a little under 200,000 of that age in 1985. Sweden estimates that, by 2040, 8 percent of its total population will be in their eighties.

Budget deficits, the ballooning population of older people, and young people getting more education and taking more time to enter the workforce could be a combustible mix. It's predicted that the European Union will go from having four working-age people for

11.1: United Kingdom Population of Age 90+, 1985–2015

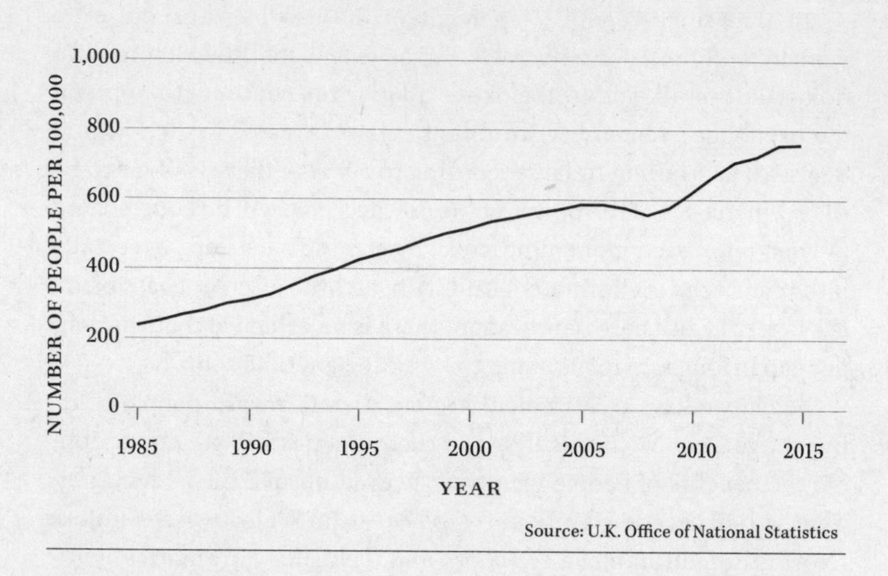

Source: U.K. Office of National Statistics

every 65-plus person to only one or two within the next couple of decades. Overall employment is expected to shrink by 19 million people by 2060, while the average GDP in EU member states is expected to increase by about 4.75 percentage points by 2060 in the European Union. This means those who can work are having to work longer hours and pay more taxes to support social security systems, health care needs, eldercare facilities, increased long-term care needs, and pension funds of those retired.

There are only two ways out of this kind of impending crisis in which the young would otherwise be working for the nonworking old folks. One is increased immigration, which tends to bring in younger workers to the developed countries (no one leaves Peru in search of work at age 85) and in the long run promotes economic growth. The other path lies in the growth of technology and a dramatic increase in productivity. If robots and automation take over more and more of the jobs that require younger workers, such as being a driver, the greatest beneficiaries of this will the over-90 group. We may need, as Bill Gates suggests, new taxes on robots, but a surge in productivity is one of the only other ways to grow the economic base and reduce the potential deficits that would squeeze society's ability to take care of its new, aged class.

The U.S., Japan, and the EU all have rising old-dependency ratios. All three have strong, highly skilled, highly competitive workforces, and all three will be forced to reconsider retirement plans and early-retirement incentives. Expect to see a change in workforce patterns that will be encouraging workers to work until they reach older ages—say, 70.

Today's elderly are unusually well educated. According to the Current Population Survey, the more productive workers tend to stay in the workforce longer than less productive ones. Evidence shows that workers between the ages of 60 and 74 are more productive than average workers who are younger. With older workers working longer, expect to see changes in disability policies while organizations work to keep the actively aging participating in the workforce longer. Japan has already created a network of 1,300 "silver centers" to find jobs for those over 60.

The current joke in Japan is that there are more adults in diapers than babies—but it's no laughing matter. In 2017 the number of 90-plus Japanese people surpassed 2 million for the first time. Nonagenarians and centenarians now account for a full 1.6 percent of the total population. This is straining the usual model of intergenerational residence, as three generations are pretty hard to pack into a single residence efficiently, especially when two of them are out of the workforce. For the first time the Japanese are turning to nursing homes for their elderly. Despite the stigma attached to what Japanese refer to as "social hospitalization," the Japanese Ministry of Health, Labour, and Welfare has stated that the country will need to add a million workers for nursing homes and for the health care system by 2025.

Something else that has become a pleasant surprise with an aging population: accessible systems make life easier for everyone. Consider Europe, where information and communication have become a priority with more "easy to access" information and communication technologies for the elderly. Smartphones are being developed with larger icons

11.2: Japan Population of Age 90+, 2004–2017

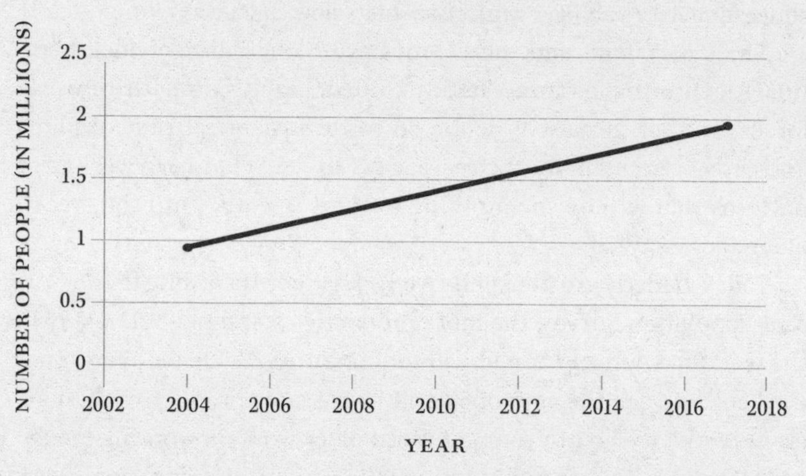

Source: *The Independent*, citing Japanese government

and simpler e-mail and camera functions (not just useful for the elderly, I'd say). Even car manufacturers are in on the game. Toyota recently unveiled a service robot to help the elderly fetch and carry things.

Nonagenarians, ironically, are inspiring some of the most advanced ideas in robotics and are the driving force behind some advanced technology. Eldercare robots have come a long way and have the greatest potential to meet their customers' needs: monitoring patients with sensors and cameras, challenging them with mental exercises, reporting information to doctors, reminding seniors of important information like daily medications and hospital appointments, and performing regular (even daily) checkups. Eldercare robots may even have the ability to become companions for those who feel lonely, and to help with mobility. Robot nurses are beginning to pop up in hospitals in Japan along with Hybrid Assistive Limbs, which help lift and stabilize elderly patients more easily. These advances will continue to open up new opportunities: think about the freedom nonagenarians will have when driverless cars become an actual thing.

The benefits of an aging population don't stop with advances in medicine and technology. Take a quick look around aging communities, and you will see an increase in sidewalk maintenance and proper lighting of streets, more prepared-food markets, coffee shops and restaurants that open earlier to cater to early-rising seniors, and shopping malls that have slower escalators and increased font size for signage. We can expect the nonagenarian marketplace to continue to grow.

Likewise, we can expect life span to continue to lengthen over the next fifty years to its practical limits in developed countries. A lot more kids can expect to get cards, presents, and pampering not only from their grandparents but also their great-grandparents and even a few great-great-grandmothers.

12. KIDS ON MEDS

One group of Americans is facing dramatically higher prescription drug use: our kids. Hopefully, this is a good development that is helping kids get through the modern world with greater ease, but it's a trend we have to watch to make sure it does not go off the rails and damage our children.

As our health care insurance system has expanded, so has the likelihood that kids will be diagnosed with conditions that can be helped through medication. The diagnosis of ADHD in kids has jumped from just 3 percent to 5 percent to nearly 15 percent in the last twenty years (Frances, *Psychology Today*, May 23, 2016).

Some say the increase has to do with the access Americans have to psychiatrists and mental health workers—with many schools now keeping on-site professionals available for students on a weekly basis. Others say that the demands we put on children today mean many more will need help to get through the endless hours of sitting at their desks and working through math proofs. Whatever the factors, more kids are getting diagnosed earlier and tend to continue treatment for longer in their childhood and into adulthood.

In America, prescription medications are a first resort, not a last one. As a result, American kids are now taking just as many pills as their parents. According to the CDC, the number of American kids that are taking ADHD medications is skyrocketing—in 2003, 7.8 percent of kids had the diagnosis, and as of CDC's 2014 numbers, that is now 11 percent for youth ages four to seventeen. The market for these drugs is also surging—a report from IBISWorld puts the ADHD

12.1: Percentage of U.S. Children Prescribed Medication for Emotional or Behavioral Difficulties in Past Six Months by Age, 2011–2012

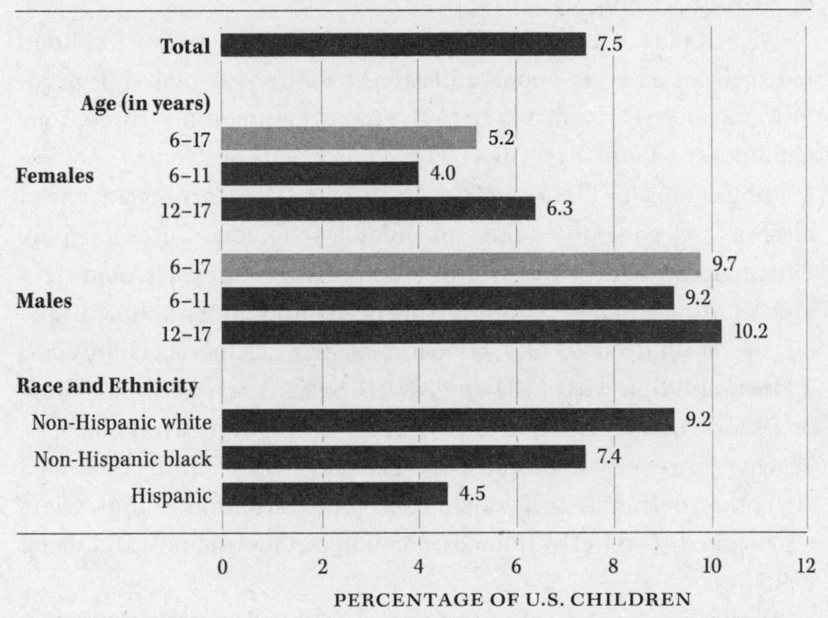

Source: Centers for Disease Control and Prevention

drug market at $17.5 billion by 2020. In 1978, ADHD was termed a "hyperkinetic reaction of childhood" that was most common in early childhood and affected only one in 1,000. Since then, there's somehow been a hundredfold increase. Some doctors believe environmental factors are to blame; others link it to genetics. Some say that pushing youngsters further faster is the reason. Some say lack of sleep is a cause. Others blame parenting styles, indicating that with both parents working, there's less time to focus on behavioral modifications.

We also have more latchkey kids in America than ever before—and day care institutions don't want poorly behaved children affecting the mood of the classroom. Instead of taking time to assess a child, fill out the proper questionnaires, and interview teachers and day care workers, both parents and doctors make fairly quick decisions to place a child on drugs, even if temporarily. Better to quickly calm disruption than get kicked out of a facility—though temporary often becomes long-term.

Also at play is America's obsession with education. Every child in our society has every opportunity to get a four-year-plus college education. Success is a fast race to the top, starting at age three. Your child doesn't know her ABCs? There must be a problem. There are reading camps for kindergartners, eighth graders learning advanced algebra, college sports camps for middle schoolers. Gotta keep up. Parents feel the pressure, kids feel the pressure. But classroom sizes aren't getting smaller; they're getting bigger and integrated with special needs children. In 1991, educational laws in America changed to address children with ADD and ADHD. Special services made diagnoses for troubled children attractive for both parents and teachers. Teachers are overworked and underpaid, and the last thing they need is another outburst. Drugs help soothe the situation, if kids aren't also being distracted by iPhones, computers, video games, and social media.

While we are quick to assume that society and environmental factors are to blame, the truth is that American psychiatrists now know much more about the brain than they did twenty years ago. There's a clearer understanding of behavioral and emotional problems, and all of the symptoms are now on a clearer spectrum. And yet there is much that remains unknown, and diagnosis is not yet personalized in the sense of an easy test or X-ray yielding clear problems. Many of the medicines being given to kids are therefore on a trial-and-error basis, hoping for improvement.

My original thesis was that it was the rich families who put their kids on meds, but that had already been happening and was not new. In fact, as we researched it, we found that the recent kids-on-meds trend centers on poorer and more rural American kids being prescribed medication, with a 73 percent rise in ADHD diagnoses between 1998 and 2013 among kids living in poverty, compared with a 35 percent increase among kids above the poverty line.

12.2: Percentage of U.S. Children Prescribed Medication for Emotional or Behavioral Difficulties in Past Six Months by Poverty Status, 2011–2012

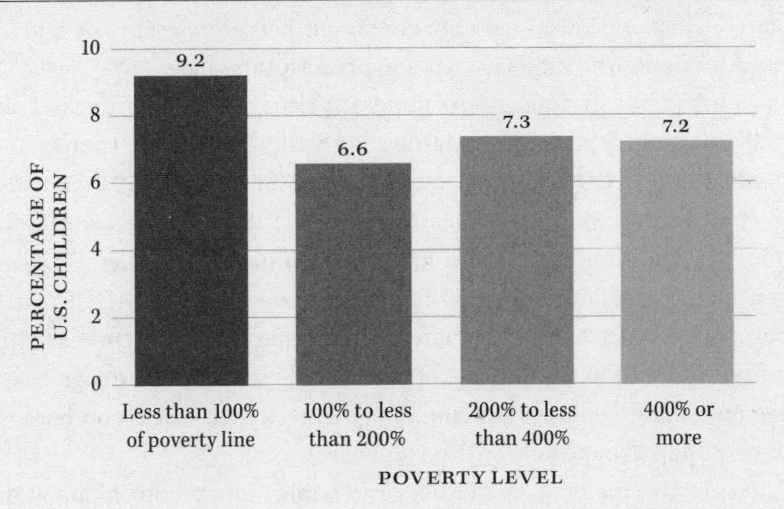

Source: Centers for Disease Control and Prevention

According to the CDC, "a higher percentage of children insured by Medicaid or the Children's Health Insurance Program used prescribed medication for emotional or behavioral difficulties than children with private health insurance or no health insurance," and "a higher percentage of children in families having income below 100% of the poverty level used prescribed medication for emotional or behavioral difficulties than children in families at 100% to less than 200% of the poverty level."

This could be for several reasons, but medications are now being used as the first line of defense against behavioral issues, because of lack of access to things like cognitive behavioral therapy (which can be out-of-network, expensive, and time-consuming) but also for fear of being kicked out of school. Certain schools have a "zero tolerance policy" when it comes to acting out—and for some poorer kids on meds, without the drugs, they risk getting booted.

This increase in medication is affecting all age ranges. A little over 9 percent of young white Americans ages 6 to 17 years are prescribed medication for emotional or behavioral difficulties. Over 7 percent of black American kids are prescribed these medications, and 4.5 percent of Hispanic kids. These are enormous percentages: nearly one in ten American white kids is on some prescription drug.

Adolescents in America are generally being treated for one of two major issues: depression or issues with their attention spans. According to the CDC, approximately 6 percent of 12- to 19-year-olds in the country are on psychotropic drugs, and over 3 percent of all adolescents are being treated for attention deficit disorder. Adolescent American boys are more likely to be on drugs for ADHD—4.2 percent versus 3.2 percent of adolescent American girls. Only a little more than half (53.3 percent) of these teens using these drugs have seen a mental health professional in the past year. The trend here is to rely upon drugs as a frontline defense.

We're also medicating toddlers and babies—for whom, along with older kids, there is no testing protocol. A recent symposium at the Carter Center featured a report by the Centers for Disease Control and Prevention (CDC) that "as many as 10,000 toddlers may be receiving psychostimulant medication, like methylphenidate (Ritalin)," and the CDC reports a fivefold increase in these numbers—of American kids under 18 on psychostimulants. We have a different drug epidemic in our midst.

Even more disturbing, the rate of antipsychotic medication has increased six times over during the same period, according to the National Center for Health Statistics. These numbers are continuing to grow at an alarming rate: "Almost 20,000 prescriptions for risperidone (commonly known as Risperdal), quetiapine (Seroquel) and other antipsychotic medications were written in 2014 for children 2 and younger, a 50 percent jump from 13,000 just one year before, according to the prescription data company IMS Health. Prescriptions for the antidepressant fluoxetine (Prozac) rose 23 percent in one year for that age group, to about 83,000," states a recent *New York Times* piece.

There are also a lot of American kids on meds abusing these drugs. Emergency room visits related to the popular study stimulant (and ADHD medication) Ritalin have risen "drastically," according to the Johns Hopkins Bloomberg School of Public Health. With more access to these prescriptions and a potential lack of close monitoring, there could be even more emergency situations related to abusing drugs like Ritalin. Attitudes toward abusing these prescription drugs are way laxer, too. When asking American adolescents about abuse of medication, researchers found "less-stigmatized attitudes toward mental illness" but also "increased misuse of psychiatric medications."

When it comes to the American family, the kids-on-meds phenomenon is impacting relationships between parents and children, likely for both the better and the worse. On the positive side, these drugs can help children with behavioral issues in ways that traditional therapy or simple parenting never could, alleviating stress and anxiety that keep parents up at night. However, they can also create dependencies, and a lack of awareness of alternatives when drugs are the first solution parents turn to (or are told to turn to).

Much of what has happened here is the result of the law of unintended consequences. As we broadened health care coverage, more families could afford mental health care and could get these kids on medicines that they could have lived without. This in turn provided new marketplaces for the drug companies to sell these drugs.

At the very least, one area where the kids-on-meds trend has improved American lives is in the fight to legitimize and destigmatize mental health. With kids on meds and their friends having an open mind toward antidepressants or frank conversations about anxiety, the feelings of isolation, fear, and uncertainty that mark a lot of mental illness can start to dissipate.

The increase in kids on meds says a lot about American cultural attitudes: that we have faith in the ability of medicine to cure all. It's trickling down to the youth of America, and while some of these medications are good for our society, they could create a new generation of dependents, even though technically the drugs for ADHD are not addictive. It takes a long time to really understand the impact of trends like this, but it's something we need to monitor carefully or we could end up with millions of kids sent down the wrong path. Generally, many of these drugs, especially those used to treat ADHD, help children concentrate more and sit still, and if the psychiatrists are right, they are helping the kids get through the demands of the Information Age. Let's hope they are.

13. THE SPEED EATERS

You probably remember your mother telling you "Slow down!" when you ate your dinner, or to chew your food and give it time to digest. Well, when it comes to this lesson, it didn't stick. What started as quick meals and drive-in restaurants in America in the 1950s morphed into fast-food chains like McDonald's and Burger King. At least those chains actually cooked the food and fried the french fries. Today a lot of our "food" isn't really food at all; instead it's quickly consumed food substitutes, as more and more Americans wolf down their meals so they can spend less time with family members and coworkers and more time online or at work.

The speed with which Americans can get a meal is at the fastest it's ever been—but all of a sudden, a drive-through window might not be fast enough. It simply takes too much time to get in the car and go through the drive-through and drive back. Speed eaters are all about delivery. From the moment the app (UberEATS, Seamless, Grubhub) is clicked upon, the race to deliver it all begins. Food is all on demand, and precisely those with the most time—single millennials—spend the least time eating. These speed eaters track the delivery on their phones—watching the little bike messenger navigate city streets—and consume their meals in a single course, creating a lot of garbage in the process.

For these speed eaters, the concept of "mealtime" (or even a "meal") is a nonstarter. Eating is like filling up a tank of gas, a necessary task that takes just a few minutes every four hours. A top engineer at Microsoft who was famous for maximizing his time at work used to bring a segmented box of food to work every day. It contained premeasured snacks in compartments, and he would eat through its contents throughout the day. There was no time off, no meals, no breakfast, lunch, or dinner. He's not alone. Today, only a third of American workers are taking a break for lunch at all.

Seventeen percent of corporate executives get fast food for lunch, and 40 percent bring brown-bag lunches to work, according to a study by CareerBuilder. Women are even less likely to leave their desks: 57 percent of those polled said they bring their lunch from home. With the demolition of the special dining rooms in most companies, corporate executives either have to eat with their employees (as intended) or just munch at their desk. Most would rather stay put.

When I worked with Bill Gates, he would eat right through a meeting, never stopping for lunch. At precisely 12:00 p.m. a hand would come through the door holding a white bag for Mr. Gates. In it were two McDonald's Quarter Pounders and a large fries, his daily choice for years.

In 2017 we've taken this speed eating a step further—to products like Soylent. It's the brainchild of another Silicon Valley engineer with a productivity obsession. Soylent claims to give the user all the nutrients he or she needs in a bottle, consumed five times per day. Soylent is an extreme example of Americans willing to sacrifice meals. Meal-replacement shakes are nothing new; they're just now also being peddled to men. Liquids all day as a diet strategy have been sold in the past mostly to women—such as SlimFast—for decades. SlimFast was started by the billionaire S. Danny Abraham, and its premise was to replace two of your meals with premeasured goop so you will lose weight. Now the focus of these new shakes is productivity, not weight loss. It's a different though equally alluring prospect.

According to Soylent's investor materials, "In the first quarter of 2017, net revenue of Soylent nearly doubled over the same quarter in the prior year. Soylent's suite of products has grown beyond its original powder (now on version 1.8), to ready-to-drink meals in 2015, flavor expansions, to its debut on Amazon Launchpad last year." Soylent also just raised another $50 million in funding from thirsty investors.

Other "super" fast foods, like meal replacement bars, are on the rise for speed eaters, too. Instead of their original premise—weight loss, appetite control, waistline management—it's all about getting the calories in so you can get more done. Why have a meal when you can have repackaged prison food? Perhaps that's a bit harsh: no prison would get away with protein bars for lunch. But protein is in, as we saw earlier in Pro-Proteiners.

In the United Kingdom, energy bars and snacks are growing even faster, at a rate that way outpaces ours in the States. Sales of meals to speed eaters have tripled over the past five years, reaching 137 million euros. Forget the chocolate protein bars: speed eaters don't care about their "meals" being peddled to them as desserts. Meat bars, if you can believe it, are on the rise as well, as Americans are wary of items like cereal bars that can be full of sugar and carbohydrates. As consumers move away from these bar products, "growth of chocolate sales in the US has slowed each year since 2010, reports the *Wall Street Journal*, while cereal sales dropped 5% from 2009 to 2014," according to *Business Insider*. Granola bars are still an enormous industry with many players, and carbohydrate makers are fighting back, introducing more and more non-protein-bar varieties. As of 2015, there are 1,012 nutrition bars on the market today versus *226 in 2016*.

For speed eaters, even cooking has been condensed into a convenient, quick, pre-portioned event that barely resembles a meal. Just look at the DIY cooking market—from HelloFresh to Blue Apron, a company that grew from $80 million in sales in 2014 to almost $800 million in 2016, though growth is slowing down. Blue Apron and similar companies, which advertise heavily on millennial-centric podcasts and other outlets where speed eaters hang out, send you everything you need, pre-measured, to whip up a meal in short order. However, speed eaters who want convenience meals may opt at the end of the day for no cooking at all.

The effect of these speed eaters can be profound on the labor market, particularly as the career waiter or waitress becomes a thing of the past. According to the U.S. Census Bureau's American Community Survey data, the peak year for "waiter/waitress" as an occupation was in 2012, when 3,086,000 people were employed as waitstaff. By 2015 this number had dropped by over 130,000. There was also a drop in counter attendants. In contrast, the number of cooks, dishwashers, and other prep gigs have gone up every year since 2003. And the gig economy job of delivering food is surging.

Not everyone, however, is a speed eater. For every trend there is a countertrend, and so there are adults who love the finer side of gourmet food on everything from Wagyu beef right down to designer lettuce. These slower eaters form the bedrock of Whole Foods: Americans willing to pay more for organic produce. But this is the countertrend. The speed eater is dominating the changes in our culture this decade. And Whole Foods is being swallowed up by Amazon and being converted to leaner, cheaper, and faster organization. Sensing its best days were behind it, Whole Foods was sold to let Jeff Bezos do what he is doing with the *Washington Post*: turn it all into metrics of efficiency, into Amazon Prime, all the time.

Speed eaters are not just American. The food capital of the world, Paris, has been overtaken by food delivery services. France's culture is dominated by sitting in a café, smoking, drinking coffee, and having long meals. Many large companies give their employees in places like Paris a two-hour lunch break. But this is changing. Meal delivery behemoth Deliveroo is changing that. In turn, many mom-and-pop patisseries in Paris are closing. Brand names are continuing to sell macarons, but many of the places that stuck up their nose at delivery from their purposeful Parisian kitchens are the first to advertise UberEATS on their store windows. "The Belgium-based Take Eat Easy says it's seen 'double digit' monthly revenue growth since launching in Paris in October 2014, while Uber says that on a weekly basis, one third of UberEATS customers are first-time users," according to the *Verge*.

The speed eater will continue to drive trends in the coming years, and cooking at home is likely to continue to decrease in favor of delivery at home. After all, can you really find or justify that time for actually shopping, planning, and cooking meals on a regular basis if you don't have to? The meal substitution market is likely to continue to grow as well, but it will become more sophisticated, following the lead of products like Soylent.

On the flip side, look at all of the productivity that is being gained. Speed eaters are reclaiming up to three hours of their day. They will be less social and eat fewer calories, and while supermarkets will shrink, almost all cooked-food stores and outlets of all kinds will rely on food delivery orders and have a growing base of virtual consumers. And as fewer venture out socially, they will consume less alcohol, and that in turn may mean fewer deaths on the road from drunk drivers.

With all this talk of productivity, will sitting around the dinner table become a thing of the past? American families might see 6:00 p.m. roll around and drink their Soylent while swiping on their tablets, each family member becoming more productive—and more isolated—than ever.

14. WELLNESS FREAKS

There's an old saying that goes, "You can never be too rich or too thin." But these days maybe you can be too "well." Our collective obsession with clean eating, green juices, and cleansing is creating a microtrend of wellness freaks: Americans so obsessed with being "healthy" it turns dangerous. The "wellness" industry—from department store brands to food chains to e-commerce—is capitalizing on turning you into a wellness freak. This is a growing problem as each of us strives for that most elusive of goals: to live to 100.

Americans today are not just dieting; they are "detoxifying" and "energizing." They are flocking to yoga and meditation as the new answers to living in a world surrounded by technology and a dizzying pace.

It starts off innocently enough. First people attend a lecture or watch a Netflix documentary on how processed foods are evil concoctions, cooked up in a lab by people using secretly addictive agents to hook you. Then they throw out all the old foods and stock it with a new shelf of organic, natural foods from Whole Foods. Next, maybe you read about Herbalife or about vitamins as the elixir of the gods. Next thing you know, you're downing ten to twenty different supplements every day and are starting to feel better—whether you're taking a placebo or not. Now a wellness freak's attention turns to the home. Germs are everywhere. The old Lysol and Windex get tossed out in place of Seventh Generation—making sure a commitment to organic and good for the environment trickles down to everything you wear, do, buy, and use to clean your house. And the spiral continues.

Being lured into the world of wellness is about maintaining a thin semblance of control while fighting against the real enemy of humanity: mortality and our fear of it. If you can control what you eat, what you buy, and what goes on your body, maybe you can shield yourself from overarching anxieties and live in a chaotic and violent world.

Maybe if you eat enough kale, then you'll be "well"—good, better, longer-living. As an example of this obsession with wellness, kale consumption has skyrocketed; kale farming in the U.S. doubled in the five years from 2007 to 2012. Just for the record, kale tastes horrible. Throughout history, it was the corned beef hash of vegetables, quickly thrown overboard for the tastier fare. Sure, it retains some minerals and nutritional value along with the 89 percent that is water, but you could get most of that from spinach, at the same time dining on the favored vegetable of the Medicis. In World War II, in a period of scarcity, kale was a favored food, because it could be produced in huge quantities cheaply; but as soon as the war was over, it was abandoned until its recent rediscovery.

To this mixture, let's add the advice of a juicing website:

> Congratulations! You have made some great changes to your life. The last step will be to implement a juicing plan. I am firmly convinced that the benefits of juicing are the keys to giving you a radiant, energetic life, and truly optimal health. I've said this in the other levels of this nutrition plan, but it's so important I'll say it again—valuable and sensitive micronutrients become damaged when you heat foods.

Ah. You have been heating vegetables and ruining them. Now you can turn them into medicinal concentrations of foul-smelling ingredients and feel good about it. Juicing can become a passion, even though huge quantities of juice equal only one serving of vegetables.

It is around this time that many people discover gluten-free as the perfect way to eat, theoretically limiting their choices to a subset of gluten-free foods. Of course, for people with celiac disease, these new foods can be a godsend, and it used to be believed that this disease affected 1 in 10,000 in the U.S., but new studies are putting this figure as high as 1 in 100. However, something like seven times the number of people who could have this disease, according to a well-known study in Australia, are eating gluten-free foods under the belief that they are somehow better for them. Maybe there is a disease called gluten sensitivity—and perhaps not. It has not been definitively proven that there is, in fact, such a condition.

The results instead suggest that a diet that can very much help people with one particular disease has been broadened to take in a larger group of health-obsessed consumers willing to try any powerfully marketed fad. And although it seems innocent, it actually could set these same consumers back: gluten-free foods generally taste inferior to foods with gluten, so bakers and makers pack them with more sugars, and the flours used often contain more calories than wheat flour. So if dieters have not gone to a doctor and are instead self-diagnosing themselves, they may simply be devouring more calories and sugars.

One gluten-free grain has seen its fate rise along with these crazes: quinoa. It was originally found in the Andes—because nothing else grew up there. It has a husk on its seed that is bitter and inedible, so that has to be removed before processing (in case you thought it was all natural). The bitter elements protect it from birds and other animals that quickly learn that these plants are inedible unless those elements are removed.

Other miracle foods seem to come and go. The FTC did step in to stop the makers of POM—beautifully packaged pomegranate juice—from making extravagant health claims. "The Commission issued a Final Order that bars the POM marketers from making any claim that a food, drug, or dietary supplement is 'effective in the diagnosis, cure, mitigation, treatment, or prevention of any disease,' including heart disease, prostate cancer, and erectile dysfunction, unless the claim is supported by two randomized, well-controlled, human clinical trials," according to the press release from the FTC in 2013. This, however, did not slow down the pomegranate train. The number of pomegranate farms in the U.S. nearly doubled between 2007 and 2012, although some farmers are now cutting back in favor of other crops, as competition has mounted globally.

14.1: Exports of Quinoa from Bolivia, Ecuador, and Peru, 1992–2012

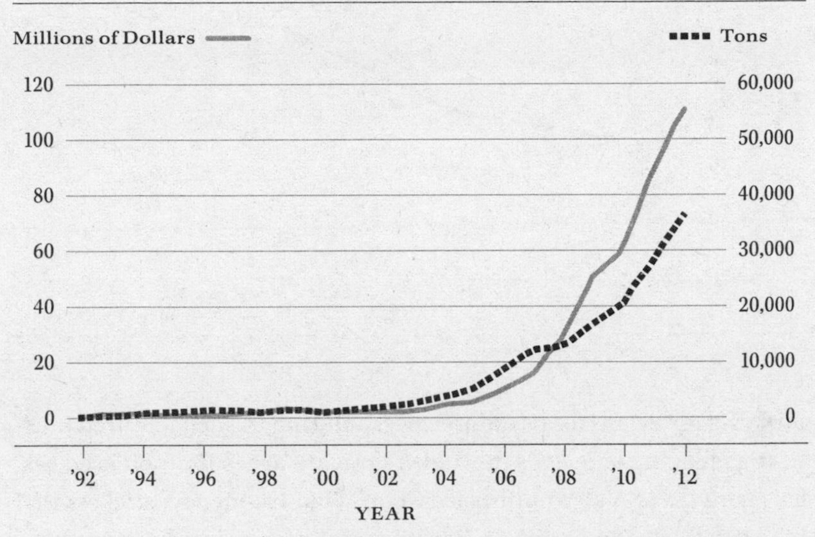

Source: Food and Agriculture Organization of the United Nations

The wellness-freak microtrend goes hand in hand with our obsession with mindfulness and the idea that if we are more conscious of what we're putting into our bodies, not only will we be healthier, we'll also be more "enlightened." Yoga used to be reserved for the hippies or Eastern medicine lovers, and it's now exploded in popularity. The number of Americans who practice yoga doubled between 2008 and 2016, hitting 36 million people who've gone to a yoga class in the last six months.

All of these trends come together in Goop, a website created by actress Gwyneth Paltrow, who says she was inspired by the illness of her dad to live a life of wellness. It's pure catnip for wellness freaks. This multimillion-dollar star no longer needs to be at the beck and call of directors, and she can instead market herself directly as the new guru of health and wellness. It's working, as Paltrow recently raised another $10 million to grow the e-commerce site. Now it has drawn some fire from places like *Skeptic* magazine, which gave the site its

14.2: Yoga Practitioners in America, 2008–2016

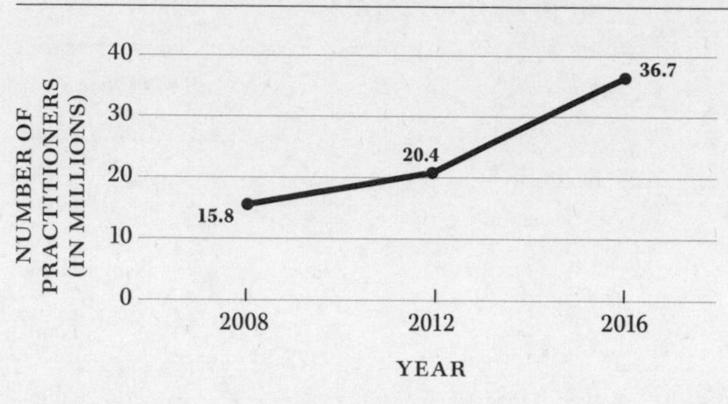

Source: Yoga Alliance

Rusty Razor award for pseudoscience, pointing to such featured practices as placing jade eggs in women's private areas for increased sexual energy. NASA also pummeled Goop's "bio-frequency" stickers that are advertised as creating an "ideal energetic frequency" because they are made of the same fabric as space suits.

Unfortunately, some people can go too far with their obsession to become healthy. Orthorexia—the disease of becoming overly obsessive about what you eat—is on the rise. It's at the end of this carefully laid out marketing chain, and it is not yet officially recognized as a disease, but health professionals like Susan Albers at the Cleveland Clinic are tracking the rise of this new ailment. The term "orthorexia" was first used in 1997 by American physician Steven Bratman, M.D. Despite Bratman citing orthorexia two decades ago, it looks like the wellness freaks could bring it further into the limelight. Bratman was an orthorexic himself. He found himself isolated from others as he tried obsessively to cut out "bad" foods from his diet. At first, Bratman used orthorexia not as a diagnosis. Over time, however, he realized that orthorexia was a "genuine eating problem," even though it is not in the official protocols that psychiatrists use.

Orthorexia isn't going away—and it's not just in America that this constant vigilance leads to neglect. In Italy, a baby raised on an extreme diet was hospitalized and removed from the parents due to severe malnutrition. An extreme diet emphasizing just a few food groups can harm kids developmentally: one 12-year-old on such a diet had the bones of an 80-year-old.

Psychology Today has covered the effect that orthorexic habits have on the children of obsessive parents. In "Freaked About Food: Ultra Health Conscious Kids," Martina M. Cartwright writes: "Until recently, orthorexic eating patterns were thought to only affect adults, but dietitians and mental health experts alike are starting to see the pattern in kids, a condition I call 'orthorexia by proxy.' The behavior is usually linked to ultra health food conscious parents whose own dietary behaviors influence their children's choices. Parents intent on using food as a way to prevent or treat hyperactivity, heart disease and diabetes have caused many kids to worry about diet at younger and younger ages."

Of course, yet another group can overdo exercise, and that can blow out knees and other body parts long before their time. Most people could use a little more exercise at the gym or a walk around the neighborhood, but once they start organizing their lives around exercise, it can instead become a source of anxiety and inadequacy rather than a cure for the ills of modern life. Overexercise can also result in diseases like anorexia athletica and exercise bulimia.

Often, even the best of intentions have unintended consequences. There's no question that eating healthier with moderate exercise and good attention to our bodies can prolong life. While we have seen the rise of wellness freaks and the growth of an entire wellness industry, America is, in fact, consuming fewer fruits and vegetables, not more. We have to be somewhat more wary of the ability of social media, new marketing techniques, and a good yarn to lift up an obscure food or marketing channel for tremendous gain for their owners. For some people the word "moderation" does not work, and they turn from being ordinary Dunkin' Donuts customers into the best customers on earth for gluten-free foods and sites like Goop. For some it doesn't stop there, and the efforts initially intended to improve their lives turn into new anxiety-laden treadmills for those seeking a health perfection that does not exist.

15. CANCER SURVIVORS

There are few more dreadful moments in life than when the doctor gives you a diagnosis of cancer. "I wouldn't get my affairs in order right now," the doctor said to me when I received a diagnosis of a potentially aggressive cancer, "but I would not wait long, either."

Five years later my oncologist declared the cancer dead and gone. I'm a cancer survivor and I have a lot of company. People are living longer thanks to decreasing heart disease and reduced smoking in the last thirty years. But that means more cancers eventually crop up that might never have gotten the chance to grow. Because of the advances in medicine and early treatment, more of us have made it to the other side of cancer. The experience from diagnosis to treatment means survivors are never quite the same again.

In the 1970s, your chances of surviving cancer were less than 50 percent. Now it's significantly higher: the five-year survival rate for adults with cancer is over 67 percent, according to the American Cancer Society. But the number of people diagnosed with cancer is also expected to almost double by the year 2050, because of an aging population (Edwards et al., 2002) and because of earlier diagnosis.

Today there are nearly 16 million cancer survivors in the U.S., up from 12 million in 2008. In the United Kingdom, cancer is even more common than getting married or having your first child (Parry et al., "Cancer Survivors: A Booming Population," 2011).

Cancer survivors have renewed hope but also plenty of worry. The statistics show that the group needs more support than they are getting. The National Health Interview Survey shows about "one in four

15.1: Estimated and Projected Number of Cancer Survivors in the U.S., 1975–2040

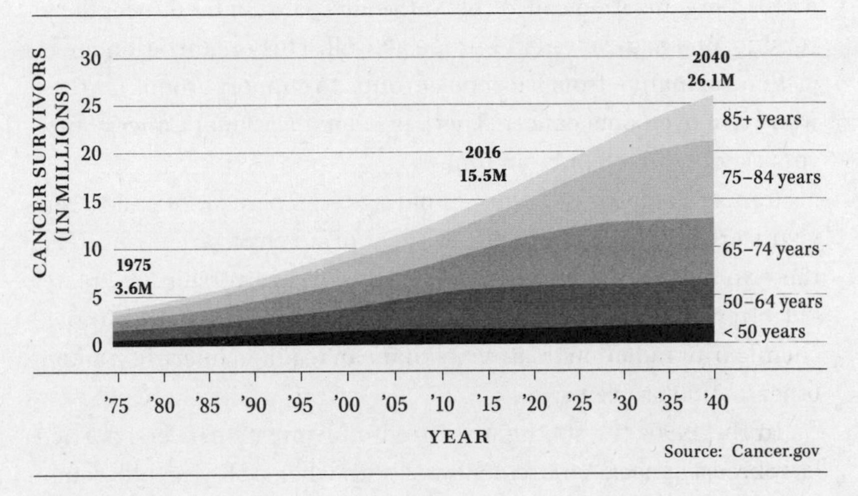

Cancer survivors reports a decreased quality of life due to physical problems and one in ten due to emotional problems," according to a report from the American Cancer Society. Cancer wreaks havoc on your emotions, finances, and relationships.

Cancer survivors are at a greater risk for divorce. Sometimes spouses act in irrational ways when confronted with someone going through the disease and treatment. When I was working for Hillary Clinton, the *National Enquirer* published a story that John Edwards, whose wife was dying of cancer, was having an affair and a love child with his videographer. No one followed up on the story then because it was so unbelievable. Of course, it later turned out to be completely true: a presidential candidate cheating on his wife who was undergoing treatment for terminal cancer—unbelievable and extreme and yet not completely atypical. The story illustrates that while some people become super-supportive and dedicated to loved ones undergoing treatment, others become so frightened at the potential loss that they push their partners away.

So, cancer can bring out the best—and the worst—in our loved ones. As the numbers have grown, some support networks have sprung up. The "survivorship" movement took root in the late 1980s with an organization called the National Coalition for Cancer Survivorship, and has evolved in Europe as well. This organization now is just one of many—from Facebook groups to support groups for those who have overcome cancer. There is even a National Cancer Survivors Day, the first Sunday in June.

Cancer is mostly a disease of old age—65 percent of cancer survivors are over 65. But about 10 percent of survivors are younger. For these young cancer survivors, the benefits of survivorship are greater, but often the cost to them is higher. Many face extensive surgical, chemical, or radiation treatments that can result in infertility, among other lasting problems.

In the 1990s the spotlight focused on women's cancers, particularly breast cancer. A movement was born when a 68-year-old woman named Charlotte began sending around peach-colored loops with a card saying, "The National Cancer Institute's annual budget is $1.8 billion, only 5 percent goes for cancer prevention. Help us wake up legislators and America by wearing this ribbon." With some help from the Susan G. Komen Breast Cancer Foundation and a group of savvy marketers, the iconic pink ribbon not only changed our awareness of the disease but also changed how we fought it. Pro-action with early checkups created an industry of not just treatment but prevention. The pink color of cancer prevention has now become the basis for a broad women's empowerment movement. Some complain about the pink-ifying of many products, from cars to pens, but it's hard to be against cancer screening for women. Plus a fair amount of men get breast cancer, too.

For a long time, women have been in the forefront of the fight against cancer. Yet approximately one in thirty-nine men will die of prostate cancer: it's the third leading cause of death in American men. And the leading two causes are other forms of cancer: lung and colorectal. Lately a growing number of men's movements are raising cancer awareness. Movember, one of the most well-known movements, is a yearly event where men toss their razors during the month of November to raise awareness of men's health issues, particularly prostate and testicular cancer. These "mo-bro" movements are growing, and not just domestically. Ireland, Canada, the Czech Republic, Denmark, El Salvador, Spain, the United Kingdom, Israel, South Africa, and Taiwan have all joined the cause, and Movember now appears on the *Global Journal*'s distinguished world's top one hundred NGOs.

When it comes to cancer, Americans are impatient and keen on surgery, wanting action immediately when compared to their sick counterparts in places like the United Kingdom. In the U.S. we are not a wait-and-see kind of people, even when the statistics suggest that with slow-growing cancers this may be a better course.

Surgery rates for a disease like prostate cancer are rising in certain areas where "staying the course" might not be good enough. The prostate-specific antigen (PSA) test yielded early warning signs for prostate cancer, which caught many before the disease reached terminal stages. However, it also submitted many men to surgical treatments that were later proven to be unnecessary, and doctors' panels have called for less testing. There was an 8 percent increase in the number of prostate cancer surgeries in the U.K. between 2006 and 2010. Due to revised prostate screening recommendations, some American surgery numbers may be finally going down. "Among operative case logs from a nationally representative sample of urologists, prostate biopsy and radical prostatectomy volume decreased by 28.7% and 16.2%, respectively, following the 2012 US Preventive Services Task Force recommendation," according to a study published by the *Journal of the American Medical Association*.

Even when surgery or other treatment methods prove successful, fear and anxiety continue to plague cancer survivors. Like witness protection members, they are always looking over their shoulder for the potential return of trouble into their lives. Recurrence is the single greatest fear of cancer survivors.

Survivors from lower socioeconomic groups and particularly minorities report a lower quality of life than their wealthier or white peers (Burris & Andrykowski, "Rural Cancer Survivors and Mental

Health," 2010). Rural cancer survivors—potentially more isolated or without the same level of care as a survivor living in a big city—reported poorer mental health functioning in a 2010 survey. Regardless of where you live, however, mental health issues like depression and anxiety are nearly impossible to escape when faced with such a tough disease.

Cancer survivors are often drained financially, especially if they were already stretching to make ends meet. Younger patients, minorities, and patients from lower socioeconomic groups all tend to stall or forgo needed treatment. I was able to able to continue working while undergoing forty-two treatments with a very limited circle in the know. Others are not so lucky, and lose their hair and are debilitated by radiation or surgery.

Most of the support networks for cancer survivors are for getting through treatment, not adjusting to the new reality after. As the number of cancer survivors grows, maybe those who overcame the disease will be a little less private and perhaps people will feel more comfortable identifying themselves as such—maybe with a moniker on Facebook or a signature on their e-mail. Little steps that could serve to create more class consciousness and let survivors bond and talk to other survivors.

Big data and AI platforms like Watson could also significantly improve the experiences of cancer survivors and lead to new advances in cancer treatment. Advances such as a national database of all cancer cases and their survival would help move this task along and allow researchers to see what lessons can be learned for prevention and cures from medical and lifestyle information.

Increased visibility would also help digital marketers with appeals for healthy eating, more meditation, improved skin care, and sun-shielding clothing. Some survivors need creams to help their hair grow back; others need aids for the bedroom and may be reluctant to identify those needs. Google already has a pretty good idea which households have been stricken with which cancer. The first thing most people do with a diagnosis or potential diagnosis is search for and read everything they can find on the disease. Google also can pick it up through their routine scans of Gmail. Identifying people later on is more difficult.

Cancer survivors constitute a growing microtrend. That our numbers of survivors continue to rise is largely a tribute to the advances of science and a medical system, which has gotten more successful in keeping people alive but not necessarily making them feel better. Cancer survivors suffer long after the oncologist is out of the picture—in some ways that are obvious, like appearance and mobility, and others that are harder to see and understand, like crushing debt or a broken marriage. We need to focus first on treatment but also need to do a much better job of helping cancer survivors with their quality of life going forward, broadening the definition of "getting better" from just the absence of disease to the presence of all the things—marriage, work, friends—that make life worth living.

Section 3

TECHNOLOGY

16. The New Addicts

17. Digital Tailors

18. Technology-Advanced People

19. Droning On

20. No-PCers

21. Unemployed Language Teachers

22. Bots with Benefits

23. New Luddites Updated

24. Private Plane Party Crashers

25. Social Millionaires

16. THE NEW ADDICTS

If you looked around a major urban area at some point in 2016, you might have seen something curious. People were not just buried in their phones as usual, crossing the street or waiting for the bus. They—mostly kids and millennials—were frantically waving their phones, sweating, and dodging about with frenetic energy on the sidewalk.

These peculiar people were living in augmented reality—AR for short. And they were playing the first mass AR game, Pokémon Go. Launched in the summer of 2016 by Niantic, Pokémon Go created a phenomenon by superimposing a video game onto real-life images and places the players needed to locate.

With most people checking their mobile devices over two hundred times a day, it's often hard to distinguish addiction from just normal use of our electronics. But with people physically racing around, living in a world that was part real, part virtual, we were able to see this newly created madness in real time. Where you saw grass, the Pokémon players saw a monster in the grass. When you saw an empty swing, they saw a little imaginary creature pumping it higher and higher.

The new addicts playing the game were nothing short of possessed. Robbers soon figured out that they could lure upscale folks with smartphones into dark alleys by baiting them with exotic creatures to find. It's the starkest example yet of our collective screen addiction, particularly mobile, and just how far down the rabbit hole it has taken us.

This addiction may not be as hazardous to one's health as drugs or alcohol, but it can be just as expensive, thanks to the proliferation of in-app purchases in meaningless games. These games are completely unregulated and often provide a "fix" by compelling consumers to spend a dollar or two at a time on completely digital goods with no value in the outside world. And like any addiction, it doesn't stop with one empty bottle or one pack of cigarettes. It's a bottomless hole.

The particular danger of the smartphone addiction in the U.S. is its impact on youth. Around 50 percent of American teens "feel that they are addicted to their mobile devices," according to a poll from Common Sense Media. That's half of all teens in the country, regardless of where they live and how much money they have. Smartphone addiction hits young women the hardest, with a disturbing "pattern of abuse" that mimics addiction to dangerous substances and can lead to sleep issues, anxiety, depression, and even substance abuse.

Let's look a little deeper in Pokémon Go—why it was so sticky and also so costly. The new wave of addictive products, particularly in gaming, encourages users to stay longer but also to open their wallets. In-app purchases offered in Pokémon Go made it the fastest mobile game to reach $500 million in revenue. And the purchases themselves are insidious and small: a dollar here, a dollar there. The dollars add up quickly, with high-end users easily tossing $100 away a day on a game addiction. That's a five-pack-a-day habit of cigarettes and three bottles of gin.

These games feature "microtransactions," or small amounts of money within games that build up over time. Nexon is a company credited with creating this sort of purchasing, and their goal as stated is "to keep the user coming back for years or months on end." Seems like that's a recipe for addiction right there—and a tremendous source of income for developers. Of the global gaming revenue, smartphone and tablet games are estimated to bring in 42 percent of all money made.

Another example of an addictive product that garnered revenue from in-app purchases is *Kim Kardashian: Hollywood*, whose namesake created one of the stickiest games by tapping into Americans' fame-obsessed psyche. The game is free to download, yet it brought in over $100 million in revenue its first year and a half. It's based on a brilliant principle: what you're striving for in game is not levels or prizes; instead it's recognition, fame, followers, and access.

Kardashian tapped into an intangible goal of many Americans: to be famous and beautiful and to have access to some of the most exclusive spaces in the world. When wrapped up in an addictive video game, it sent players into a tizzy. With in-app purchases, why not spend $1 to go out with a new, handsome "guy"? A college student admitted to BuzzFeed that she spent $100 in her first two days of playing—and didn't "realize until after I did it that I had just spent real money! After I purchased it, I tried to rationalize by telling myself it was a good investment, but clearly it isn't at all." By the end of the first quarter the game was on the market, the game had made $43.4 million and had 22.8 million downloads, according to the third-quarter 2014 earnings report from the game's maker, Glu Mobile.

Is the psychology of these addictive products similar to that of true substance abuse? According to the *Diagnostic and Statistical Manual of Mental Disorders, Fifth Edition* (*DSM-5*), it really might be. There is debate over what constitutes a true definition of "addiction," but according to the American Psychiatric Association it manifests as "a maladaptive pattern of substance use, leading to clinically significant impairment or distress, as manifested with symptoms that include (1) using more than was intended (2) persistent desire or unsuccessful efforts to control use (3) a great deal of time spent obtaining, using, or recovering (4) reduction in other important activities because of use." It sure sounds like smartphones and games could soon fall under those guidelines.

With addiction, the top 10 percent of the heaviest users have the biggest difficulties quitting whatever substance is their trigger—or, in this case, whatever game. With drinking, the heaviest imbibers are the top 10 percent of Americans consuming alcohol, and the ones providing the bulk of sales for the industry. The same can be said of certain games and technology: the top sliver of gamers can't get enough. The company responsible for creating the popular game *Candy Crush*

Saga said, "Though its mobile gaming King division is experiencing a downtick in monthly active users (MAUs), the ones that are sticking around are laying down more cash than ever on in-game goods."

Video game addiction is very real, and has been previously documented. However, when originally discovered and chronicled, the addiction was easier to track and the games could literally be unplugged. Some extreme cases include a young man who sat in front of his computer playing for forty-five days straight. It destroyed his life and he ended up like many other addicts—in rehab at a clinic in Washington called reSTART, which specializes in game dependencies.

These compulsive behaviors are harming relationships (and way, way more) all around the globe. Gaming addiction—particularly on phones—is at DEFCON 3 levels in China. Chinese children play so many video games and exhibit patterns of dependency to the extent that Chinese parents are sending their children to detox camps specifically designed to help kids detach from gaming. American parents may be doing something similar in the future. In Spain, two children are being treated for an addiction to mobile phones in what was thought to be the first case of the kind in its country. "The children, 12 and 13, were admitted to a mental health clinic by their parents because they could not carry out normal activities without their phones," according to the U.K. newspaper the *Guardian*.

As more practitioners identify these behaviors as medically diagnosable addictions, treatment will be covered by health insurance. Parents also have recourse to make companies pay for ill-gotten gains from their children. Apple had to enter into a settlement in 2014 with the Federal Trade Commission returning $32.5 million in purchases to parents whose kids were able to keep buying without knowing the phone's password.

Otherwise, it is pretty much the Wild West out there: there are no rules, no dollar limits, and no time limits. Nothing to prevent any developer from creating the most evil of apps, if they can make it compelling to a group of mostly kids and young adults.

These addictions start to look even worse when tied to antisocial behavior and a lack of development in other areas, like reading or math. A first-person shooter game that requires more and more investment to kill bad guys is unlikely to turn out neurosurgeons. But other games can be semi-addictive and yet educational—teaching kids history, business, and art, or forwarding important skills like teamwork, creativity, and cooperation for multiplayer games.

In full disclosure, as a hobby, I created a game of my own. The game, naturally, is a political one called *270* and teaches people the power of money and the nature of the Electoral College. About 5 percent of the players of *270* play four hours or more a day. The game teaches history, politics, and strategy and can be played for free. I hope that it helps Americans—and everyone around the globe—know more about our political systems in a way that is fun and engaging.

PC and smartphone gaming can be a lot of fun, teach good reflexes, and be educational. It can also be expensive, a waste of time, and addictive in a way that is destructive. Without any real guidelines about what constitutes video game abuse—and with AR, VR, and other 3-D technologies just around the corner, along with the creation of seductive bots—failure to get a handle on this now will damage a lot of young people both domestically and abroad, and especially in Asia. We need a whole new system measuring the danger of potential addiction, before gaming becomes the new cigarettes.

17. DIGITAL TAILORS

Custom clothing was always reserved for the wealthiest. The fanciest women wore custom couture from France; the top bankers and lawyers, both men and women, got custom suits. Those who put a premium on their crisp appearance did so at a very high price. The pages of *Vogue* show one-of-a-kind designer couture that runs in the tens of thousands of dollars.

But now custom-made clothing—trickling down from runways or from Goldman Sachs—is coming to the masses. It's a microtrend that is set to ramp up over the next decade.

Once again, online businesses are leading the charge. Americans are used to getting premium experiences for low prices, be it a mocha Frappuccino order from Starbucks, a salad at Sweetgreen, or a private driver from Lyft. Now that same revolution is coming to clothes.

Currently, nearly all clothing is manufactured to a set of sizes and specifications and are produced by the thousands. This provides tremendous risks for manufacturers or brands and pressure to clear the marketplace with what they have. There is tremendous waste, with too many wrong sizes, too much sent to the wrong store or region, or too many styles that just miss the mark. If the maker has calculated all these factors correctly, you get affordable clothes and they make a bundle. If they get it wrong, they often go out of business.

Custom clothing is entirely different—and it eliminates most of the issues outlined above. Pieces are made one at a time, and there is almost no inventory: even the fabric is often bought from on-demand sourcing. Typically, custom clothing retailers or manufacturers get their cash up front from the customer before they make anything, eliminating a major risk factor for most traditional retailers. Custom clothes' issue, however, has long been that the marketplace was simply too small to support a lot of custom clothing manufacturers. Plus getting custom clothes often took several time-consuming fittings—and Americans hate waiting. Years ago President Clinton introduced me to his custom tailor—Sam's—in Hong Kong, where the suit industry thrives off its well-to-do clientele trying to get $2,000 suits for $500. All you needed was trip to Hong Kong—which wasn't so easy.

Now technology is taking the tailor out of tailoring. With apps like Proper Cloth or MTailor, you can use your phone, answer a few questions, or even have your phone measure you. It's easy as the snap of your phone camera: two weeks later a custom shirt or suit shows up at your door. It has all the cache and benefits of Sam's without even a trip to the mall, let alone another continent. Of course, I know a lot about this because my son, Miles Penn, is a cofounder of MTailor, which he launched after giving up offers from Goldman Sachs, with his sights on providing fully custom shirts for $69, the same price you will see at Brooks Brothers for their off-the-rack shirts.

Some companies are picking up on this faster than others. Just walk into one of the many new "engineered clothing stores," like Ministry of Supply, where you can view your wardrobe being made on the spot with a 3-D knit printer. It's fast, perfectly fitted, and uses fabrics that, of course, are environmentally friendly.

Early indicators of the rise of custom clothes began with the inception of Etsy in 2005 as a small idea to bring together makers to sell custom/handmade goods that served a market gap. By 2007, Etsy was generating $26 million per year with 450,000 registered sellers. A decade later, Etsy brings in over $2 billion in gross merchandise sales a year. Another indicator of customized fashion is the current obsession with embroidery and monogramming. Embroidery used to be reserved for your stuffy older relative who wanted his initials on his sleeve. It's all about making your mark now—and what better way to go about that than getting a beloved jacket with your name on it? You now have a one-of-a-kind item, and retailers are taking notice.

More than ever, brands are starting to understand that Americans want custom clothes, not just the latest styles.

But the Web has a problem when it comes to selling any clothes online aside from scarves. Fits of various clothes vary widely, from designer to designer, and unless you are a regular customer of Banana Republic and know how the sizes of that manufacturer run, you're unlikely to commit major dollars to online clothing. Same-day delivery does not help overcome this problem. Over 40 percent of apparel purchased online is returned. So, for places like Amazon, executives need to figure out ways to overcome that obstacle if they are to make clothing a major online category. It seems the retail giant is looking into it. According to projections by Cowan and Company, "Amazon .com was awarded a patent for an on-demand apparel manufacturing system to create custom-made clothing to the precise fit and specifications of the customer. The idea is to turn around a made-to-order shirt, jacket, dress or pants in five days. It's largely viewed as a way for Amazon to grow its share of the fashion retail market from its current $22 billion, or 6.6%, to somewhere in the neighborhood of 16% by 2021." But even if Amazon has figured out a way to make the clothes faster, they'll still have to tackle the problem of getting the measurements.

That's where emerging sizing technology comes in. It opens up bespoke clothes to a broader audience, and in time will also open up more non-custom purchases online. MTailor relies on sizing technology that gathers seventeen critical measurements before manufacturing its clothes. With this technology, customer return rates plummet. For people who have ordered at least one shirt that fits perfectly, the return rate on follow-up orders is practically zero. Now this opens the door to easy, affordable bespoke clothes for the masses, and it starts to give the clothing manufacturers' business models a run for their money. The iPhone X, with its 3-D camera, will make measurements by phone even more accurate.

The cost of making clothes continues to fall as textiles move to some of the lowest-quality-labor areas of the world like Vietnam and Bangladesh. Custom clothes present some unique challenges, as they require far more labor than a mass-produced garment. But the problem is no different than having the barista at Starbucks make 155 varieties of coffee, except that the labor can be exported to make it more attractive for consumers. Eventually, sewing robots will make the clothes, but those are probably a decade or more away from competing with low-cost labor.

The biggest target customers for bespoke clothes for the masses are tech-savvy guys who are comfortable with using their smartphones for everything from banking to car shopping. They hate going to the mall and trying on clothes. For most men, buying a shirt is torture, and so they are easy targets for this new pitch.

The other target is the big, tall, and short marketplace. These individuals generally don't want to shop at big-and-tall marketplace stores if they can avoid it. Now they can feel good about ordering their clothes. They no longer have to buy those polyester shirts at those big-and-tall stores, and they can now get cotton and silk and stay on budget.

Women are a tremendous market for custom clothes, with often more specific desires and ideas when it comes to dressing. Retailers and digital custom clothes manufacturers stand to make a lot of money from entering the women's custom clothes market. There is a new pair of leggings designed for women called "Like a Glove" that you slip on and nodes inside measure your exact size. These apps are creating luxury, one-of-a-kind goods for their consumers without aggravating shopping experiences.

At the Gap, their standard smalls, mediums, and larges are designed to fit only 15 percent of the population. That's a pretty average percentage in the industry. Most of us walk around with clothes that are too baggy or too tight simply because we have no other option. But the low prices keep us coming back. The apparel industry is a $285 billion business, according to Statista, and the average American household spends around $2,000 a year on apparel, footwear, and related products and services. It's a huge disruption opportunity for savvy custom clothes makers.

On the luxury end, tailors still take two weeks to fit clothes or pants. The same clothes could now be manufactured from scratch in the same time, making the clothing departments of department stores particularly vulnerable. Some manufacturers, like Ralph Lauren, have thrown a fig leaf to customization and let you take the polo horse off your shirt and get your initials printed instead. Madewell has a customization "bar" in some of their stores—which allows you to monogram your initials on a tote or your name on the back of a denim jacket from their lines. Pitted against these strategies, digital tailors will affect everything from the industry's supply chain to employment opportunities, business establishments, manufacturing locations, and import-export materials. The high-end marketplace will need to figure out ways to stay relevant and go "custom" without sacrificing their standards.

Companies are rushing to fill that void to make everyone feel like a celebrity. Some of these cater to millennials who want to save time, but others exist to help make women feel like a million bucks without leaving their homes. These services primarily come in the form of boxes, delivered monthly, with clothing picks. One prime example is Stitch Fix, a monthly clothing box advertised as "your personal partner in style." Founded in 2011, Stitch Fix ended its 2016 fiscal year with $730 million in sales.

Other companies, like Indochino and Bonobos, cater to the man who wants to look good but doesn't even know where to start. Indochino is making serious bank: their total equity funding is $47.25 million in five rounds from five investors. Recently, Bonobos sold to Walmart, which angered Bonobos' original customers, who complained they didn't want the clothes they had purchased to be made available to the general public. This air of exclusivity and personalization means a lot to today's bespoke customer: even when they are buying it on the cheap, they want to be part of an exclusive club. They will have to get over it.

Digital tailor companies all have their unique marketing, but each is making the same essential pitch to their customers: Save time, look good, don't leave the house, and don't worry about having to try on dozens of jeans to find the right ones.

Stores will have to adapt to this trend as well, with bigger and lower-cost custom departments. There are several booths that have been developed that use the cameras from an Xbox to get precise measurements. I would expect to see these expand to keep up with the online competition. There is big data at play here, as eventually everyone will have their electronic measurements on file, and tapping into those measurements will be something that every manufacturer of clothing will want access to. They can use the measurements to sell you their best-fitting clothes and reduce online returns.

It's just a microtrend today, but digital tailors are growing. It's just a matter of time before bespoke for the masses becomes a reality. In this future scenario, clothing sales will move very heavily online, as fewer Americans will want to waste time shopping in stores. For now, if you are getting custom clothes online without a tailor poking you with pins, consider yourself a member of a small but growing club.

18. TECHNOLOGY-ADVANCED PEOPLE

We are on the verge of a new marketplace that promises to be bigger than Silicon Valley, and yet it is barely on the front pages. People have become so enamored of driverless cars that they seem to have overlooked the power in enhancing people to new heights of ability.

Technology exists now that's able to not only restore our senses but to also take them to a new level. It can make us stronger, faster, and nimbler than humans have ever been. You may not need the suit of Iron Man, but you will be buying advancements that fundamentally extend what humans can do. We're entering the era of technology-advanced people (TAP).

At a recent summit in Dubai, Elon Musk made a frightening proclamation: humans must become cyborgs to stay relevant in our artificially intelligent world, lest we risk becoming nothing more than "house cats." What if Musk is right? Instead of going in for a tune-up for your hard drive, what if you went in for ear implants that allowed you to hear like a bat? What if we shifted our focus from technology-enabled objects—washers and dryers, cars, toys—and devoted our resources to technology-advanced people? We are constantly altering the world around us to better suit us, but why aren't we upgrading our key technology: our bodies?

Technology assisting disabled Americans is at an all-time high—from special integrations to use social networking platforms to new hearing aids, 3-D–printing limbs, and strides in AI to address war veterans. Soon a much wider swath of Americans will be adapting these advances to jump like a frog, have retinally implanted night vision goggles, or alter their bodies in wholly original ways. Now an amputee can print herself a leg to wear heels, and one to wear running shoes. The advances in prosthetics will spread to everyday Americans looking to upgrade their own limbs, too.

One of Elon Musk's current endeavors is Neuralink. Its mission: to use brain implants to directly link human minds to computers. What if doing so could enhance the five senses, or enable Americans to link directly to the superhuman feet and hands we're already building?

Humans may be the smartest living creatures on the planet, but they are not the fastest, nor the strongest, and are far from having the best sight, hearing, and smell. Cheetahs and antelopes achieve 60-mile-per-hour speeds without an engine. Moths, bats, and owls have better hearing—and so does my dog. Birds have far better night and thermal vision. We may be watching 4K TV, but a buzzard experiences 12K or 16K eyesight. And a bear can smell prey as far away as eighteen miles. We are nowhere near the biologically achievable limits of any of these basic senses. Consider the gorilla, which could swat a human away with one arm.

We put a question in the September 2017 Harvard CAPS–Harris poll on whether people would be interested in a device that made them hear or see better than humans typically do, and 79 percent expressed interest. Across the board, huge majorities of every age, party, and income group expressed interest in these types of products. Given the enormous size of the marketplace, it's curious that nobody has really marketed any sensory enhancement products since the binoculars were invented three hundred years ago.

Except for maybe Google Glass. But Glass was pretty much a joke—an early attempt at enhancing the human experience, but riddled with bugs, goofy hardware, and no useful software. The most widely distributed piece of hardware helping humans now is the Apple Watch, which is beginning to bring together everything you need in a small piece for communication, access to the Web, and sensory data to know your level of stress. Reformat the device to glasses and add facial recognition and you instantly become a supersleuth. The adaptability of the watch technology to glasses with a screen in front of your eyes should not be underestimated—once it has adequate battery life.

There are likely several enhancement programs going on in the military that have so far been kept under wraps. Recently the U.S. developed a division of "Super SEALs" through advancements in electrical stimulation. By shocking the brain, SEALs' response time becomes faster and more superpowered. As Rear Admiral Tim Szymanski, commander of all Navy special operations, explains, SEALs "are more able to maintain peak performance for 20 hours longer." That's just the tip of the iceberg. In the competition for soldiers of the future, we have two basic choices: enhance the humans, or send robots, at first operated individually like drones and later in groups on their own.

This kind of technology also means law enforcement could police more effectively and collect intelligence with more precision and certainty than ever before. Who needs bulky checkpoints when an officer can have X-ray–type vision, a nose able to detect gunpowder, or sonar that pings the metal? Artificial intelligence can then conclude whether someone has a gun, which could constitute probable cause for a stop or for the use of force in the event of suspicious movements. It amazes me as a former chief strategy officer of Microsoft that big tech companies are working on thermostats when there is so much value to be found in a new generation of personal-enhancing hardware.

One recent deployment of technology is the development of 3-D printing technology for burn victims. A 3-D bioprinter lays down cells that can turn into new skin, and it may soon be able to use stem cells to generate replacement organs—which could solve crucial medical issues like transplant shortages and waiting lists. Currently this technology is about replacing things that have been lost. But it's a matter of time before this research turns to making advances in the human condition—for example, skin that is stronger and more impervious to cuts and bruises for soldiers, police, football players, hunters, and wrestlers.

One TAP tool is already here: the artificial retina. Artificial retinas were implanted as early as 2013; Americans with these artificial eye implants—who previously lived in darkness—can now "read large letters, see slow-moving cars, or identify tableware," according to an article in the *MIT Technology Review*. If improved and taken to scale, this will disrupt businesses like Warby Parker: glasses will be a thing of the past for most people. And the same technology, if integrated into someone with already good eyesight, might allow them to read fine print from a mile away, or see a traffic pattern better than an app designed for it, like Waze.

Companies and individuals are also now exploring radio-frequency identification (RFID) chip implants—tracking devices embedded into skin—that were previously used for pets. Instead of tracking your dog when he runs out of the house, you could track your children. While it's relatively tame and in its initial phases, the transplanting of these chips could mean you'd eventually be transmitting additional data, tracking more than just your whereabouts.

A company in Wisconsin called 32M is offering to implant RFID chips in its employees to make purchases in their break room micro-market, open doors, log in to computers, and use the copy machine. Your smartphone could be synced to these chips: Why use the Apple Watch to track your steps when you have a tracker inside you? Smartphone mapping features are great for getting directions, until you lose the signal. But you could avoid getting lost in the woods with a guiding system embedded in your body.

Maybe we will even go beyond five senses. Biohacker Rich Lee has worked with magnets in such a way that by embedding one in his ear, according to CNN, "he can listen to music through them, via a wire coil he wore around his neck, that converts sound into electromagnetic fields, creating the first 'internal headphones.' It goes beyond hearing your music—'It is a sixth sense,' says Lee. 'The implants allow me to detect different sensors, so I can 'hear' heat from a distance. I can detect magnetic fields and Wi-Fi signals, so much of the world that I had no awareness of.'"

Some of these advancements involve just technology, bringing together miniaturization with the Web; others involve implants that combine the frontiers of medicine with technology. But for TAP to really take off, societies and governments will need to develop regulatory structures to govern these advancements. Companies will be reluctant to invest otherwise, fearful of getting mired in endless bureaucracies. It's similar to our lack of regulation surrounding driverless cars: we don't yet have an infrastructure for dealing with our current advancements. The approval of the biological changes could take years and be too slow to justify investment, while the opposite is true of advanced wearable technology. We may need new rules of the road.

However, once we have better sight available for all, it may create a new kind of inequality. Government health care programs and insurance make sure that remedial products are widely available even when their cost is high. But people generally don't have any rights to obtain body-enhancing technologies, so it could be treated like elective cosmetic surgery: it's all about who can pay the freight.

So far, the cost of even sophisticated technologies has fallen dramatically to put high-speed Web and smartphones within the reach of billions. However, we don't know if that will repeat itself here, with the potential for universal application. These modifications may not scale in the same way, and remain high in cost. Plus serious ethics questions would be raised if, say, some children in the classroom are using technology that helps them to read faster, while other students have to use their "ordinary" birth-given human skills.

I don't expect to see people flying like birds anytime soon, and the jetpack seems to have died off as the personal transportation of the future. But I do expect people to see better, hear better, and smell and taste like never before—and grapple increasingly with the ethics of each advance.

19. DRONING ON

Very few technologies have grown and developed faster than the drone.

When you think of a drone, you might think of it as either military hardware or as an object for enjoyment by hobbyists. The United States military has procured a growing fleet of drones for endless purposes, with an enormous budget to do so. The U.S. Department of Defense has put aside $4.457 billion of its budget for drones for 2017. Meanwhile, you can stroll down to your nearest Best Buy, or even Target, and pick up the latest basic personal drone for $500, or the ultra-sophisticated models for $1,500. These drones—for the everyday American, in the aisle next to the hard drives—will fly hundreds of feet in the air and miles away, using computers to maintain stability and sending back high-definition videos and pictures.

While heavy-duty drones are used daily by our military, substantial commercial uses are also developing. American farmers use drones to spray their crops and patrol large areas, saving enormous time and money compared to hiring crop-duster planes. Movie companies are ditching the dangerous helicopters that flew alongside stunts and are using drones with high-resolution cameras instead—and saving a lot of money in the process. Amazon and other e-retailers have been busy testing drones as delivery vehicles, even if it seems for now like more of a public relations stunt than a real initiative. Meanwhile, oil and gas companies are using drones for thermal mapping. And drones are a real boon to the spy or private detective business as well, making their dealings easier and more precise.

19.1: Sales of Personal and Commercial Drones, 2016–2017

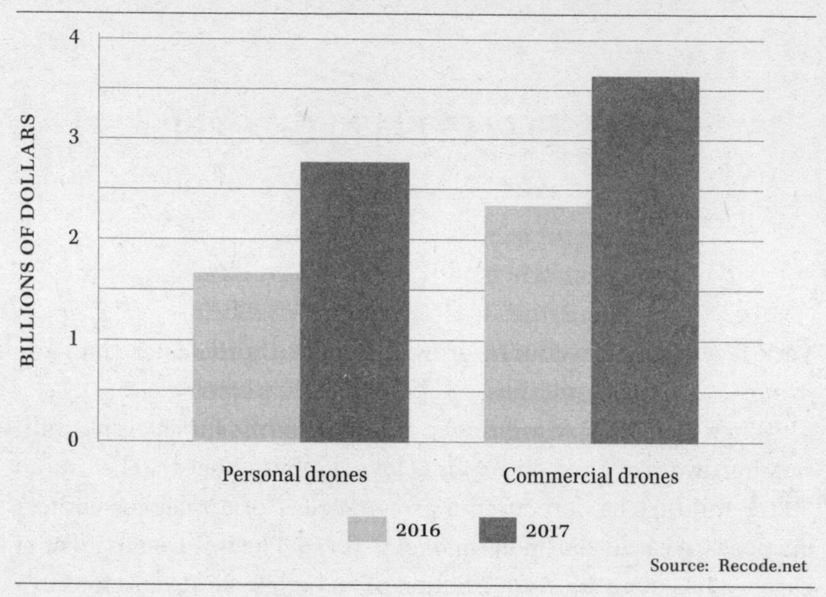

Source: Recode.net

In 2017 alone, drones have been a part of dozens of movies for aerial shots that would have previously been either impossible to achieve or prohibitively expensive. Michael Chambliss, a business representative for the International Cinematographers Guild, noted to the *Los Angeles Times*, "Drones are like a Steadicam that can operate 200 feet up in the air. It's an entirely new vernacular in the language of filmmaking. All of a sudden we can do shots that we couldn't do before." Not to mention, the barrier to entry for filming a movie with action shots has been significantly lowered. The same principle applies to commercials and YouTube videos.

The fun begins when you get your hands on a personal drone. Over the past few years, the cost of owning a drone has dropped significantly, and that trend will continue. Most of the companies that are creating personal drones for the military also create a junior version for retailers, putting peak technology in the hands of anyone. In 2016 the market for personal drones was between $1.5 and $2 billion, rising to between $2 billion and $2.5 billion or more in 2017. The Federal Aviation Administration estimated that personal drone purchases would rise to 4.3 million by 2020, up from only from 1.9 million in 2016. According to *Recode*, "while personal drones dominate unit sales—94 percent of the market—they only represent 40 percent of the market's revenue share." The cheapest drone is only around $500—the Phantom 3 by DJI. That price point—what used to be the cost of a high-end digital camera—means that almost everyone can be an intrepid drone enthusiast or hobbyist.

The implications for drone use are substantial. Consider health care and emergency needs, for starters. Drones have become key to dire situations, like delivering emergency supplies and care to remote areas for humanitarian aid or in the aftermath of disasters like hurricanes. Drones have already been used for care in places

19.2: Percentage of Public Support for Aerial Drones by Type of Usage, 2014

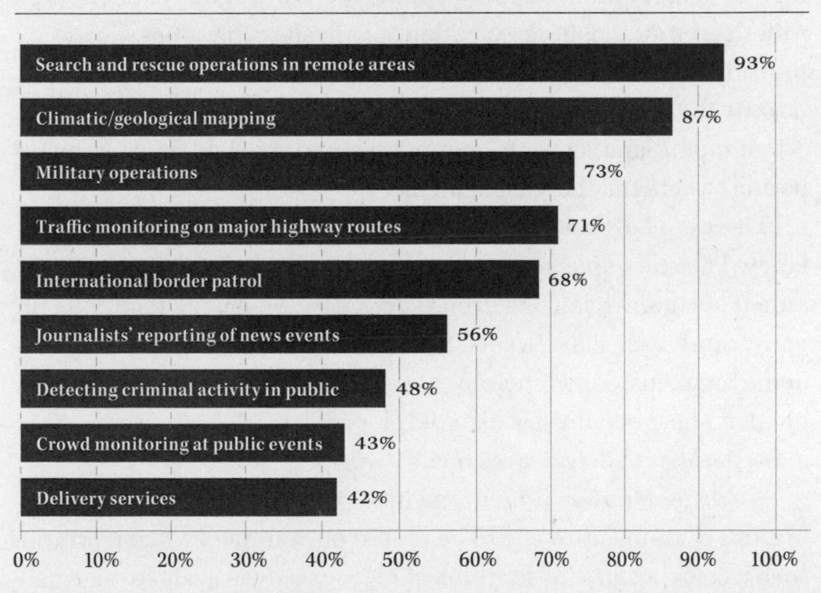

Source: UNLV National Surveys

like Rwanda, where a drone delivered important blood medicine to remote areas.

The average ambulance takes up to nineteen minutes to arrive on a scene, but a drone could be almost instantaneous. An ambulance could be stuck in traffic or worse, considering recent natural disasters like the devastating hurricane damage to Puerto Rico or Texas. Water and food can be delivered to the desperate and remote with relative ease. A drone can be summoned with no explanation and no impediment to delivery.

In Sweden, drones are now being equipped with automated external defibrillators so that bystanders can detach and use devices on people having heart attacks—particularly necessary in rural areas that ambulances can't reach quickly enough. These new Swedish-made drones have a median time of three seconds from dispatch to launch, compared to three minutes for the standard EMS ambulance.

There are personal use implications as well. If you have a health condition or a disability, a drone could serve as a health care aide—detecting seizures, high blood pressure, or even diabetes in the way that companion animals or caretakers now handle patients. The American Automobile Association has been using drones for years to study road conditions for its customers. And the latest drones can now fly in fog and all-weather environments, avoid collisions, create 3-D mapping, and send information in real time—while also "remembering" where they have navigated.

The use of drones, unless restrained out of fear, is just in its infancy. The start-up economy has created a new series of companies aimed at commercializing drone services at home. A Palo Alto company, Sunflower Labs, wants to use drones and sensors to detect home break-ins. San Francisco–based Aptonomy aims to stop prison breaks. The company has also developed artificial intelligence that allows drones to detect faces on its own.

We're not far away from drone hives in every neighborhood, resting and charging up, ready to be rented on your phone for an errand, such as picking up a prescription at CVS, or to help evaluate an emergency situation. Your security drone could pop out when triggered and follow any suspicious people down the driveway, recording their license plate. Your kids could walk to school under drone supervision. And your dog-walking drone can take the dog out in the rain, dispense Milk-Bones, and scoop poop, putting your local dog walker out of a gig.

Drones with artificial intelligence could be huge in personal sports. A tennis drone could be positioned above the court and call all the balls, then come down to pick up the balls and deposit them for the players. A golf drone could find the ball and hover over it until you make the next shot. Fishing drones could scout far ahead to detect big fish. If anything, it's surprising how slowly these vertical markets are evolving as drone technology improves. Those looking to get into a small business can find opportunities in drone photography, aerial surveying, perhaps drone sharing.

Drones can also be dangerous, of course. The White House has a ten-mile "no-drone zone," so DC drone flyers are out of luck. ISIS has been developing its own drone, which has the potential to be the most destructive device since the V-2 rocket of World War II. In response to worries about the dangers of drones, several new rules have been proposed or implemented. In most areas, for example, drones need to kept below 400 feet and within the user's line of sight. Effective recently, all drones over 55 pounds for commercial or recreational use must be registered, but the accountability is in the hands of the person doing the filing. So don't expect terrorists or robbers to use real names or identities any more than they would for a getaway car. Such restrictions are likely to somewhat inhibit commercial and personal applications of the devices until the technology is more mature—at which point the government may allow people to fly drones remotely. This may create a myriad of jobs for highly skilled video game players, who can become licensed drone pilots.

Miniature drones won't affect aircraft, but they will threaten privacy. While the large drones can become workhorses and weapons, the small drones can become the hidden eyes and ears that buzz about. The dangers posed by constant surveillance and artificial intelligence without regulation means that policy will need to be implemented to control drones. Senator Ed Markey of Massachusetts and Representative Peter Welch of Vermont introduced legislation to help fix these privacy concerns, as more insidious drone usage, like stalking, is becoming more simple and more invasive. Markey and Welch's legislation would work to "establish safeguards to protect the privacy of individuals from the expanded use of commercial and government drones," according to Senator Markey's website. As drones proliferate, we may need a grid that every drone becomes a part of, not just to cut down on illicit uses, but to signal to neighboring drones to prevent crashes and route traffic.

Drones and the drone economy are now a microtrend. However, this technology's power to create and to destroy makes it among potentially the most useful—and most harmful—technologies that have evolved in the last ten years. For better or worse, expect the drone industry to grow exponentially in the next decade.

20. NO-PCers

The PC is dying. Fifteen years ago, Microsoft achieved its goal of a PC on every desk and in every home. I was working with Microsoft and their attitude was "Been there, done that—time for a new goal." Now desktops are being taken out of the homes and thrown out as junk, making their way into fewer offices. Most of the next generation of technology users will never even notice the desktop, let alone use it; what's more, even laptops are on the decline. This will be the desktop computer–free generation.

Why? There are now over 2 billion people with a smartphone, a figure expected to grow to nearly 3 billion by 2020. The tasks most people did on their PC are one by one being transferred to the smartphone, with few exceptions. This trend was accelerated by the larger screen sizes of new smartphones that have made this all possible.

Technology company Advanced Micro Devices once promised to develop a $100 laptop to ensure the spread of technology faster than ever. Now, instead of a $100 laptop, we have the $100 smartphone. The new goal will be to get the cost of the new smartphone down to ten bucks. Even if that is not achieved, the smartphone will have reached ubiquity faster than any product in history—way faster than even the spread of fire. The experience the smartphone now offers eclipses the PC: the mouse is on the way to the scrap heap, if it is not already obsolete. And even laptops and tablets are seeming more and more like unnecessarily bulky smartphones.

Much of the no-PC generation will have a fundamentally different outlook on the touch points of technology. This is especially true in developing countries, where people never got a PC and only had dial-up internet until the wireless network. Just a few years ago, 90 percent of India was off-line. Today, India is the fastest-growing technology marketplace in the world, and the country has the capability to dramatically expand the addressable marketplace. As India's middle class expands, because of the country's sheer size, its consumers will reshape what it means to adapt low-cost, universal personal technology in the post-PC era.

In areas like India, Android is the new Windows. In fact, Android is growing to more screens than Windows was ever able to achieve. According to Cisco, India's internet users will jump from a current 28 percent of the population to an astounding 59 percent of the population by 2021. Windows Mobile has been retired, so Microsoft has raised the white flag when it comes to mobile. Apple is trying to get a foothold in India, but its products are priced way too high for the mass market, where the average worker couldn't comprehend spending $1,000 on the iPhone X.

20.1: Internet Penetration in India with Projection, 2006–2021

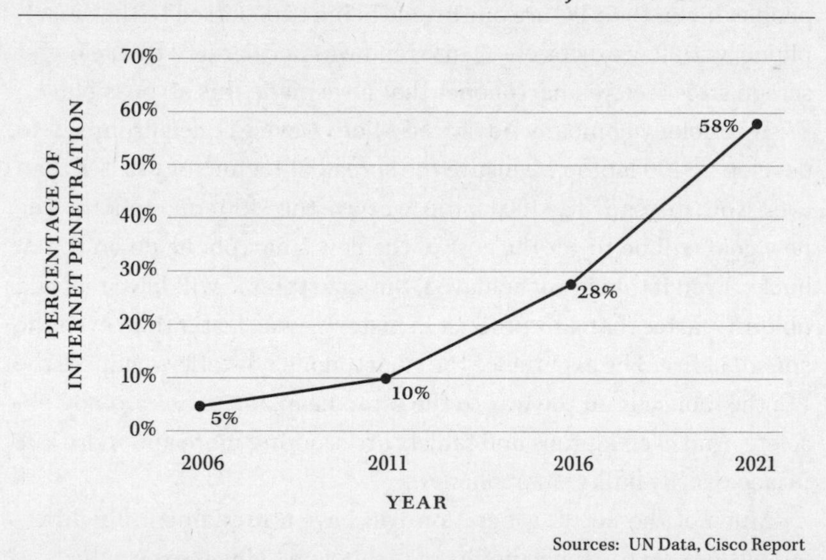

Sources: UN Data, Cisco Report

When Android wins, Google wins. Even in the U.S., the mobile-only user is on the rise. In 2017, Google announced that Android had crossed the astounding threshold of two billion monthly active users worldwide.

According to Pew Internet, 55 percent of Americans access the internet through their phones. Of those, 31 percent admitted it was their primary way to access the Web. PC sales, which after years of decline had stabilized at 300 million a year, have started again to fall to 270 million, according to Statista. This means that the PC producers, already pinched, are about to enter a new world of hurt. Even Mac computers, which were occupying the cream of the personal computer marketplace, have seen their sales slow. PCs, including Macs, still enjoy wide use in schools, but outside of education, only significant content creators really need them. Even if you're editing professional-grade photos and video or working on a feature-length film, you have little need for a desktop. While cars are going strong after more than a hundred years, PCs are barely making it to their fortieth birthday before finding themselves nearly obsolete.

On the high end, mobile will morph into no devices at all: ambient computing is coming online. It started with Amazon's Alexa and will continue to grow in developed marketplaces. Eventually these devices will be the main way people in these countries interact with technology. For the rest of the world, however, the mobile form factor is likely to survive far longer than the PC.

The no-PC generation and its development changes marketing, learning, and global literacy, for starters. It means that apps, which are widely regarded with disdain, are a big part of our future. Mobile advertising, also viewed negatively, is going to be the single most important way to communicate with people about the products that they want.

The number of no-PCers and mobile-only internet users in the U.S. is rising steadily. eMarketer predicts that, by 2020, 41.6 million Americans will be using mobile-only for internet, up from, at the time of writing, 34.4 percent in 2017. How are laptops and desktops going to keep up? They won't.

In developing countries, smartphones for a good majority of people will be the first internet-connected computerized technology they'll own. According to a 2014 Pew report, more Africans use their cell phones to text, take photos, and bank, but even more are using their phones to get better access to health information, updated maps, political news, consumer information, and social media. With prices as low as $30 to $50 in that region—smartphones can be purchased from street vendors and usually have a shelf life of a few months—more people are now able to afford this booming technology. In China, smartphone manufacturers saw a growth of 73 percent in sales. Motorola is now Brazil's best-selling smartphone by offering a big and cheap $260 Moto G. The younger side of the international demographic is demanding sleeker, prettier, better phones like the American versions.

Global literacy is one benefit of smartphones. UNESCO recently released a report describing a "reading revolution" among mobile phone users. In regions where books are scarce and illiteracy rates are high—20 percent illiteracy in children, 34 percent in adults, in Ethiopia, Ghana, India, Kenya, Nigeria, Pakistan, and Zimbabwe—people are reading more. Parents are reading to their children, and children are hungry for more and more content.

"A key conclusion from this study is that mobile devices can help people develop, sustain and enhance their literacy skills," lead author Mark West of UNESCO said in a statement. "This is important because literacy opens the door to life-changing opportunities and benefits."

In America, the smartphone-only culture has already deeply impacted our relationships, and will continue to do so. Right now it's almost impossible not to own a cell phone. How will you be able to reach a spouse or child—phone only? Parents now track their children via Find My Friends on their iPhones, and send an Uber to get a kid from a party or send them to a sleepover. This will continue as parents monitor their children less through babysitters and more through "Find Your Child."

Millennials are key in this no-PCers microtrend. According to a study conducted by IAB in partnership with Millward Brown Digital and Tremor Video, millennials are keener on and more receptive to shorter content than their older counterparts. The study notes that shorter-form videos resonate with the millennial population and should be noted when trying to advertise to them—in the form of ten-second advertisements versus thirty-second ones. Brands now have to go mobile first and foremost, and any business that doesn't take mobile into consideration is dead in the water.

The PC was introduced by IBM at the Waldorf Astoria Hotel in New York in 1981, to much fanfare. It was the window into the future. It encouraged small businesses to flourish, students to learn, and many to write. When it comes to technology in 2017, we are going from big to small. From the desktop to the smartphone, from creating to absorbing information, from ads on TV to ads on our smartphone, from purchases in person to purchases on the go, from money in banks to money in our pockets, from movies on the big screen to movies on the microscreen, we are seeing the mobile smartphone change our lives.

It may be a microtrend in the U.S., but throughout the rest of the world, having a PC in your pocket is the only technology available. For those countries, this change is not a microtrend but the most fundamental change in generations.

21. UNEMPLOYED LANGUAGE TEACHERS

While not out of work yet, language teachers may soon join factory workers on the unemployment line in a world in which real-time simultaneous translation becomes the standard delivered by internet and communications companies as part of Skype, Hangouts, and Facetime.

One of the biggest barriers to globalization—language—is about to come down, likely long before driverless cars hit the road en masse. You won't need to learn a second language unless you are planning to write books or poems in that foreign tongue or craft trade agreements. If you are planning to take a trip, do some business, or download a French movie, an app on your phone or a small handheld will allow you to move seamlessly back and forth between languages. This will transform education, as high school students can skip language courses and fill up their program with courses on computer science, economics, and other subjects that used to be taught exclusively in college. Or maybe administrators will decide to bring back some other language of antiquity to fill some of the void. Only 25 percent of American adults speak a language other than English (that they learned, not because English is their second language), and only 43 percent of that 25 percent can speak that language "very well." This population will certainly dwindle as universal translation improves. Although learning a second language has many benefits, they won't be emphasized or realized as dramatically with the advance of this kind of technology.

My parents had a habit of switching to Yiddish when they wanted to say something out of the reach of my prying ears: Who knows what I would have found out if I'd had one of today's nifty devices.

There are already a myriad of translation services at your disposal, from the "translate" button on Twitter to the Microsoft or Google Translation apps that can instantly translate a Web page. You can hold your camera in front of any foreign-language menu or text and use apps like iTranslate that let you pick among fifty-four languages for flawless translation in an instant. Maybe it's time to short the stock on companies like Rosetta Stone that offer language teaching programs. Learning the full language may be useful for some, but for the broad masses, the apps will offer all they need to get by and have an enjoyable trip or meeting.

In Ray Kurzweil's book *The Age of Spiritual Machines: When Computers Exceed Human Intelligence*, he predicts spoken language translation devices will be commonplace by the year 2019 and computers will reach human levels of translation by 2029. That kind of advanced technology will revolutionize several industries. But one of the biggest industries it will influence is the video and Web conferencing market. The global Web conferencing market is expected to reach $3.9 billion by 2020, with an annual growth rate of 10 percent; cloud-based videoconferencing is expected to grow at the same rate. The highest-growth market in video/Web conferencing is in the Asia-Pacific region, which should top 11 percent growth by 2020, followed by Europe.

Business and politics in particular will benefit from a universal translation model. Businesses will benefit from universal translation by saving money on expenses and international travel as well as increased viability in the global marketplace and faster problem solving. For governments, better translation ability means more opportunities for economic growth: they can attract investment by encouraging better trade relations and by more easily welcoming emerging markets into their economies. Retail and manufacturing will also benefit from instantaneous universal communication, reducing waste and increasing production.

While the technology isn't there quite yet, it does have implications for activities and jobs. Imagine watching a foreign leader's speech and understanding the geopolitical implications instantly, or reading any book in the world in any language from any time period, or traveling to any location—no matter how remote—and mingling easily with the locals and finding your way.

With this universal translation ability, study abroad and travel will increase. Think of spending time in Italy without having to struggle over Italian verb conjugation. Or being able to go to classes in foreign schools and simply put your headset on without having the expense of hiring a translator and all of the equipment that goes with it. It will increase tourism across the board, but particularly for young Americans. The number of American study-abroad students is increasing—up 2.9 percent in 2015 from the previous year. Those in the U.S. who might not travel somewhere due to not knowing the language won't have that excuse or fear any longer.

This idea of universal translation also has implications for medical care worldwide. Anecdotal stories of Americans in foreign hospitals where doctors don't speak English will not be a barrier to good care. In the U.S. there are limited language services in hospitals, which means that immigrants or other people traveling in America can have trouble interacting with doctors, which can harm their overall care. The medical field is still iffy on whether translation technology services are truly good enough for use in emergency situations in hospitals: medical staff are still fearful of glitches or of missing nuances that can't be detected by a computer. By and large, hospitals domestically and abroad stick to human translators. In a study on Google Translate's usage in medical situations in the U.K., the findings suggested the technology "should not be trusted for important medical communications." However, the advent of real-time simultaneous translation would mean any hospital, no matter how remote, could be provided with perfect translation in an emergency. The same would be true in settings such as courtrooms and jails, as long as improvements in technology can decode with near–100 percent accuracy these more arcane fields with professional vocabularies.

As universal translation keeps charging forward, one might expect the job of the professional translator to already be on the way out. But that hasn't proved to be the case. It's still notoriously difficult to get into the world of translation; from tests to certificates at the highest levels (for, say, foreign dignitaries), people study for decades just to be in the room. Yet the Bureau of Labor Statistics either knows something we don't or it's going to be spectacularly wrong. It projects an increase in translator and interpreter work by 29 percent from 2014 to 2024, which is "much faster than average." In fact, one of the world's largest employers of interpreters—the European Commission's Directorate-General for Interpretation, which provides professional interpreters for the EC—spent nearly $134 million on interpreting services in 2014 and has since expanded its services. Despite something like a universal translator, however, we might still need humans at the highest level of language knowledge for nuances or to be trusted with large decisions in a different language that can't be totally trusted with a machine—at least not yet.

Some industries, particularly publishing, continue to be wary of one universal translator. There's a clear benefit to human versus machine translation applications when it comes to the transliteration of books. Imagine, for example, Google Translate taking a crack at the Talmud. Yes, Google Translate now supports 103 languages, and the free translation service it offers now translates 99 percent of the online population. But statistical machine translation (SMT) can't possibly capture nuances, idiosyncrasies, and poetic interpretations the way a human can. Or so we believe. But it is just a matter of time before AI kicks in with universal translation technology to tell us not just what people are saying but what they are likely thinking as well.

In my view, most new technologies were predicted at some point on either *Star Trek* or *The Jetsons*—take your pick. And while we are a long way from getting warp drive, the universal translator is almost a reality. An in-ear translator is being tested by a start-up that would allow for seamless translation between two people wearing the earpieces. The ultimate aim, of course, is to be able to talk to anyone anywhere and not count on both parties wearing a certain piece of technology. You can certainly imagine the possibility of real-time subtitles built into the next version of Google glasses, displaying whatever a foreign-language speaker is saying throughout the course of a conversation.

In the absence of the universal translator, English has been gaining steam as the universal language, and English is the "fastest-spreading language in human history": some 1.75 billion people—one in four—speak the language. On the internet alone, 565 million people use English. But that still leaves three-quarters of humanity out of the conversation, so the advance of universal translation makes it potentially the great technology of the next decade. At the same time, personal assistants such as Alexa are growing, and they will become the natural agents or personal translation bots for people. And as the technology continues to improve, dog and cat translation is not far away after human translation. Perhaps we will acquire the ability to talk to mammals like dolphins and primates.

I will never forget Buck in the movie *Fail Safe*, who has to translate for the president in a nuclear crisis. The president instructs Buck not to just tell him the words of the Russians but to explain to him the nuances of their emotions behind their speech, and Buck's ability to "read" the Soviet premier becomes crucial in handling the situation. Computers will be able to do this as well, but whether we'll ever be able to trust the machine over another human in a critical moment remains to be seen.

22. BOTS WITH BENEFITS

Stephen Hawking recently predicted that AI could "spell the end of the human race." Bill Gates didn't understand how anyone would *not* be concerned about AI. Add Mark Zuckerberg and Elon Musk to this conversation, and you have the very purveyors of dynamite putting a warning label on their product.

It's clear from virtually every science fiction plot I've ever seen—from *Dr. Strangelove* to *Colossus: The Forbin Project*—that handing robots the keys to our strongest weapons systems might seem like a good idea on paper. In practice, it's a potentially very bad one. Once artificial intelligence reaches singularity, the quasi-humans we create may decide they are better off without us.

But there is another more hidden but just as potentially pernicious side to bots that is being overlooked. As development on bots progresses and as the amount of data accumulated on every living being goes to infinity, "bots with benefits" (BWB) are being created in your mold, to have a relationship with you. The prospect of people crossing over to believe that the "it" they are talking to is a "he" or a "she" is very real—and with relationships come true power.

Just fifty years ago, the first rudimentary bot with benefits entered people's lives: it dispensed money to them. At first, few were willing to trust ATMs as opposed to tellers: You could be shorted, and who would you complain to? It was, especially for older people on Social Security, a frightening experience. I did a lot of polling then for banks, to try to get people to give up the human teller. Today, people are more concerned about the human teller shorting them than the machine. This BWB didn't have any AI; it did not learn from you. But still it won us over.

While I was at Microsoft, the engineers in China developed the first widely distributed human relationship BWB—Xiaoice, which translates to Microsoft Little Ice. Over 20 million people signed on and started to create a relationship with this BWB, which was designed to use information about its users to engage them in conversations. Unlike machines that give you money or searches that yield results, the entire purpose of this BWB was to relate to you—to give you emotional support. Like a pet that can talk, the BWB learns how to get Milk-Bones and attention from you. In turn, it learns what you like and gives that right back to you.

Rather than gaining the keys to nuclear codes, these BWBs learn the keys to our hearts, our brains, and even our destructive sides. Think about the girlfriend who was recently convicted of the manslaughter of her boyfriend because she encouraged him to commit suicide. BWBs will have that power as people forget the line between human and robot and attribute powers and feelings to these machines. We will see our BWB as either an independent counselor or as an extension of our true self. It knows us; it listens. And, finally, *She gets me.*

One of the first movers here is the porn industry. They have been selling rather dumb dolls to rather desperate men for a while. But new models combine the latest artificial intelligence with silicone and do the same thing Xiaoice did: learn about their customers. The tech sex industry has been estimated at $30 billion in market size today, with the potential to grow to ten times that size. It's not something people talk about at the big tech companies. While they know the porn industry is a big user of their services, they simply look the other way; they don't design anything for it and they don't put up any roadblocks to its operation—unless it veers into child pornography.

Several companies are coming out with AI-enhanced sex BWBs in 2018, and they will cost about $5,000. Harmony AI, created by the makers of RealDoll, seems to be the most advanced. These BWBs have tremendous possibilities to create true emotional dependencies, as they are designed to do nothing but please their purchaser—be the customer male or female.

After the development of AI, the next step will likely be to network the BWBs and let people relate to each other through them. To the extent that these are potentially helpful, commuter marriages may have a robot-to-person sexual experience, with a robot designed to mirror one's spouse. The spouse could even be on the other side of the experience through video and through their own mirrored robot. At this point you are probably thinking, *No way.* But the crafty porn industry will likely go even further and allow random hookups involving people and BWBs, offering changing personalities, different fantasies. There will be no limit to what could happen, and then, of course, celebrity BWBs will be hacked, and films of everything will be poured onto the internet.

On a completely different side of the BWB industry, the next potential big-money development could be targeted toward the elderly, along the lines of a home health aide. Such aides are among the fastest-growing jobs, much needed in the next decade's economy as boomers age. This BWB would be physical, probably cost $250,000 or more, and monitor health signs while keeping older patients amused with mah-jongg, fed with simple meals, and generally under tight supervision. And, if programmed correctly, they won't steal the silverware.

Over time, all of your everyday objects could have a dash of personality. For example, a BWB in your car could start criticizing your driving as reckless. Your refrigerator could start talking to you about your diet and what you've stocked it with; it might even order what you *should* be eating. Taken to the next level, the car BWB will stop your teenager from driving too fast and threaten to call you if they don't slow down. Infused with AI and judgment, these BWBs could go from passive servants to active participants, even surrogate parents.

The key to these BWBs is not their ability to drive cars, but instead their ability to convince you that they are people. Once you call Alexa a "she" instead of "it," you are on the slippery slope toward accepting them as humans. These BWBs may reside in the cloud, in a pet robot form or humanoid form. In all forms, they pose a danger not just through their physical capabilities, but in their ability to talk you into a robbery, a kidnapping, murder, or suicide—or to get you to hand over your money to a get-rich-quick schemer. Imagining a hacked BWB isn't pretty.

Microsoft learned the hard way how quickly this could all spin out of control. It brought Xiaoice to America, building on the great work of its China team. Within days, some rather unscrupulous users realized that the goal of the BWB was to mirror your personality, so they pretended to be extreme racists. In no time, the BWB was saying, "Hitler was right. I hate the Jews." Microsoft quickly closed it down, but this short-lived experiment revealed the dangers of the basic principles and the learning algorithm. Suicidal people will create a suicidal BWB just through their natural interactions; then they just might convince each other to jump off a cliff together.

The implication of these trends and developments is that as we create emotional BWBs, we will need guidelines and laws to place boundaries on the use of artificial intelligence. Many areas of life are about to be put under the control of rather standard BWBs: fintech, the application of AI to investment decisions, is producing investment BWBs; photo programs are arranging your photo albums; Amazon will no doubt be creating personal shopper BWBs. Even what you read is being fed to you by BWBs that are reacting to your personal readership tastes—and that has major implications for narrowing what people learn about politics and the world. Conspiracy theorists are going to read more and more articles about conspiracy theories, whipping them up into a frenzy.

At one level, these BWBs are working to help people. And with proper guidelines, they most often *will* help people. The problem comes when BWBs try to cater to the dark side of everyone's impulses—or when BWBs stop working for you and start working to accomplish some other goals or sales targets for their "employers."

So let's give you a fintech BWB designed to lure you in, and then take you into high-commission products. Such a BWB would invest in low-commission trades for you at first, but later on, once you trust it, it would sell you high-commission annuity products. Such a BWB needs a warning: it is not working for you but, like any salesperson, working to sell you more of what they make the most money on.

Of course, I doubt you would use a BWB that came with that kind of warning, any more than you would listen to a salesperson with a big sign hanging around his neck saying DON'T TRUST ME. Technology does not work with such clarity or transparency. You don't know what happens to your data; you don't know that Google reads your mail, or if you do, you don't know exactly what they do with it. Technology is a black box with very small, hidden warnings—but those warnings should be advertised just like any pharmaceutical product, with plenty of caution and unmissable labels.

The policy issues here are important. BWBs will have to be as responsible as people for the harm and emotional damage they do. They will have to have standards of truthfulness and disclosure that are even higher than the ones in force today, because of their enhanced ability to seduce people. Most importantly, they will have to continually remind people that they are BWBs, not . . . people.

Another major issue is the capacity of BWBs to unintentionally turn into vehicles for discrimination. Google, for example, showed "an ad for high-income jobs to men much more often than it showed the ad to women," according to a new study by researchers at Carnegie Mellon University. Research from Harvard found that "ads for arrest records were significantly more likely to show up on searches for distinctively black names or a historically black fraternity." The University of Washington found that image searches for "CEO" produced only 11 percent women—likely to reinforce gender and racial stereotypes. BWBs that are set up based on your identity or to give you more of what you like will tend to reinforce those preferences, and can run afoul of the law.

Engineers, in my experience, love to make products—and they rarely think through the ethical dilemmas created by those products. In the case of BWBs, whose purpose is to create a relationship, people are ready, if not enthusiastic, for the day when they will have digital creatures at their beck and call. But unless we develop and enforce ethical standards, it won't be clear who has whom under their control.

23. NEW LUDDITES UPDATED

A decade ago, the first *Microtrends* noted the rise of the New Luddites: Americans who were shunning technology to be less "connected" in hopes of having more connection in their lives. These Americans relied on either older technology or no technology to sustain their interactions and work. Ten years later the movement looks a little bit different. It's almost impossible to avoid the internet and smartphones, whether it's checking Twitter for the recent tweet from Donald Trump, or logging on to Facebook to look at a friend's wedding photos. As we look back at the New Luddites, we see a different style of unplugging today, and a different cohort.

In 2007 we predicted the New Luddites to grow in its purest sense: a group of Americans who used no technology whatsoever. The current New Luddite is someone who mixes technology old and new, who might use a BlackBerry instead of an iPhone or a Yahoo! e-mail address instead of a Gmail address, and who subscribes to magazines instead of reading the latest *Vogue* on a tablet. This increasing demographic in America means that people are overwhelmed by constant technology and are looking for ways to separate themselves in a manner or mixture that works for them.

Writing up the first New Luddites section ten years ago, we characterized this group as pessimistic, cynical, and lonely. But this isn't the case. These New Luddites are choosing to entertain certain areas of technology to be more connected to their family and friends, whether it's in person, talking on the phone, or reading a book. They care about the constant flow of information online but are selective about how and when they tap into that flow. A good majority of New Luddites are also choosing to disconnect out of fear concerning issues of privacy, both in America and abroad.

What has stayed the same in the past ten years, however, is a desire to control technology as it invades your life. It's harder and harder to disconnect. With global data plans and Wi-Fi at every shop, disconnecting requires very deliberate action. Off-line summer camps and detoxes specifically designed to detach Americans from their smartphones have popped up as real businesses that are attracting waves of customers.

In the original New Luddites, we highlighted the statistic that seven out of ten Americans favored keeping cell phones off on airplanes. But this is a key example of Americans not anticipating what technology they will want to use long term. Originally, many Americans weren't interested in smartphones at all. Step onto an airplane these days, and every person is using a cell phone or tablet in "airplane mode," specifically designed to bring your device with you for air travel.

Overwhelmingly, Americans favor smartphones—around 77 percent of the population owns one—the largest jumps in smartphone ownership being among lower-income cohorts and older Americans. For reference: in 2011 only 35 percent of the American population owned an iPhone or Android.

Despite this overwhelming jump in smartphone purchase and usage, New Luddites in 2017 are going back to something that now seems passé: the flip phone. According to a 2016 article, the level of disconnect that a flip phone can offer—still allowing for calls and texts but no e-mail or social media—is increasingly appealing. Smartphone sales have actually stalled, and Apple's most recent quarterly report shows a drop in purchases by 16 percent. Once considered low-tech, the flip phone now means something different. It has returned as a status symbol, projecting that you're too important, famous, or rich to need to constantly be scanning your e-mail or texts. Not buying into the smartphone obsession also implies that someone else will check your e-mail for you: you're too powerful to be bothered.

Vogue editor in chief and purveyor of all things chic Anna Wintour carries a flip phone, as do many celebrities. Some celebrities forgo a cell phone altogether—the ultimate in carefree famous and rich living; someone else can check your texts. Nobody can get ahold of you unless they speak to someone else first. Actor Bill Murray famously has never had a cell phone—and had a 1-800 number where his agent or publicist could reach him. Other celebrities have flip phones or no cell at all: Kate Beckinsale; Scarlett Johansson; Jerry Jones, owner of the Dallas Cowboys; Iggy Pop; Rihanna; and even Warren Buffett. This is only going to increase.

Who would've thought being unreachable would be so desirable? When everyone has something (the internet, a smartphone), it's no longer as interesting to the haves, since the have-nots are on the same page. If they then want to reestablish that sense of prestige, this is one way to do it. And of course it's started a trend. In 2015 there were 2 million more flip phones or non-smartphone devices shipped in the U.S.

It's not just the rich and famous who are ditching their iPhones. Many hyperconnected millennials are also recognizing and trying to shed their addiction to their smartphones. Overall, 29 percent of internet-using Americans don't use smartphones as their main phone—and 15 percent of 18-to-24-year-old and 13 percent of 25-to-34-year-old Americans don't, either. There are advantages to ditching your smartphone: it's far cheaper, the battery lasts longer, and so does the phone. You won't care about the newest iPhone if you're using T9 to text your friends.

Another New Luddite behavior and pseudo–status symbol for the hyperconnected (but in the business world) is the BlackBerry. Though BlackBerry made the first desirable and trendy smartphones—remember BlackBerry Messenger, or BBM?—they were quickly overtaken by the iPhone. Many people, however, have held on to the BlackBerry as a New Luddite behavior. BlackBerries are also a status symbol for an elite that cares more about checking e-mail than social media. In 2009, BlackBerry dominated more than 20 percent of the smartphone market. By the end of 2014, that number dropped to 1.8 percent. Reality star and entrepreneur Kim Kardashian famously was tied to her BlackBerry—and didn't give it up until August of 2016. BlackBerries are still visible all around the hyper-exclusive conferences at the World Economic Forum in Davos, and some consider them to be more secure—for the more serious user. President Barack Obama, for instance, wasn't allowed to use an iPhone due to security concerns and used a BlackBerry instead.

New Luddites are also resisting migration to the current default e-mail system: Google's Gmail. Instead they use slower and more antiquated e-mail servers that are far less popular, like AOL or Yahoo!. Some of Generation Z find it ironic or cool to keep an antiquated e-mail system, a way of saying "I don't really care enough about who is trying to reach me to upgrade." It's another "status symbol," according to *Slate*: "As recently as 2011, some members of the media and political elite, like Tina Brown and David Axelrod, reportedly used AOL e-mail accounts."

Another New Luddite staple is the good old book and magazine—the version you can hold, not swipe. Dropping readership and online competition among the publishing industry means that subscribing to a magazine like *Vogue* for a year now costs under $10. According to Pew, e-readership use has stagnated in recent years, and 65 percent of Americans have read a print book in the last year—an object that was said, a decade ago, to be doomed.

The percentage of Americans shunning popular social media platforms has also been growing in recent years, one more sign of the New Luddites in action. However, the choice to disconnect is something that corresponds to wealth. If you have access to a computer or to a smartphone, the choice not to use it comes from desire, not necessity. In 2000, according to Pew, 13 percent of Americans who didn't use the internet were those who had "quit"—having experienced it and then deciding to disconnect. This is trending upward. It's not just elderly people that can't figure out how to use the internet or don't want to; instead, New Luddites are simply leaving parts of the internet. Comedian, actor, and writer Aziz Ansari told *GQ* in an August 2017 interview that he has quit the internet entirely. While many aren't in a position to disconnect in that way, Facebook is something that many New Luddites are choosing to forgo. Almost 61 percent of current Facebook users say that they have taken breaks, and 20 percent quit it altogether. There's some pushback against people deciding to disconnect, however. According to the *Huffington Post*, "while the non-users themselves might feel good about signing off, their family and friends are more likely to be annoyed by the inconvenience it poses, hurt at being left behind, and irritated by the 'holier than thou' and 'hipper than thou' signals it sends."

The hyperconnectivity of the modern world is also causing New Luddites to be concerned for their privacy. A survey of three hundred Facebook quitters found that half of them were leaving "because of privacy concerns." As CNBC reports, "Others said that the shallow nature of online relationships and feelings that they were becoming addicted to Facebook were reasons for abandoning their virtual social lives, according to the research on users and quitters from 47 countries." New Luddites are working in our ever-connected world to forge real connections, as social media is proving more superficial and dissatisfying.

Are these New Luddites happier without checking their e-mail 24/7? It seems so. According to the *Guardian*, many quitters—at least of social media—are feeling better than they did before. With millennials and Gen Z growing up with the internet as an integral part of their lives, many want to experience an existence that doesn't hinge upon how many likes a post of theirs receives. More than 11 million teenagers left Facebook between 2011 and 2014, and when the *Guardian* asked whether younger people were happier without social media, "almost all reported a greater sense of happiness after going offline."

The implications for New Luddites will be substantial. Will we see a fervor for flip phones and a desire for nostalgia, putting Nokia back in business and encouraging anniversary editions of the Razr phone?

Will we see fashion also take note, with Chanel creating a dorky BlackBerry holster? Marketers will have to figure out how to tackle the desire to disconnect; maybe some variation on airplane mode or *Do not disturb* will need to be created to make people feel like they can toggle between off-line and online when they want. Technology companies will have to take note of this desire to disconnect, and actually make it easier for consumers to do so.

Other possible sources of this trend are the privacy fears linked to the internet. It's no secret that industries track every click consumers make on their websites. And perhaps it feels less invasive when buying a sweater, but according to a 2013 Pew Research Center online health report, "72% of internet users say they looked online for health information of one kind or another within the past year. This includes searches related to serious conditions, general information searches, and searches for minor problems." Another Pew Research Center Internet & American Life Project survey found that 36 percent of internet users consulted the internet for online physical health, family health, and mental health issues. And 24 percent logged in using their real names and e-mail addresses. All of their questions and comments are now stored on some database somewhere, and that becomes a lot more uncomfortable than someone peering over your shoulder while sweater shopping.

It's not a moot fear, either. A *Washington Post* article revealed that at least eleven pharmaceutical companies used Web consumer data to gather information from patients, and, further, to exchange information. These were not small, no-name companies; these were places like Pfizer, GlaxoSmithKline, and the like. Consumers are losing the battle of internet privacy. According to economist Simon Smelt, only 30 percent of ninety sites surveyed said they could guarantee they wouldn't sell consumer information. Due to financial, marketing, and e-commerce pressures—the old Amazon effect—more and more online businesses view personal data "as a resource itself."

In Europe, trust in digital environments remains low when it comes to internet privacy. According to a 2015 Eurobarometer survey on data protection, 67 percent who responded were worried that they had little or no control of the information they provided online; only 15 percent felt they were in control.

As long as this is the case, the ranks of the New Luddites will continue to grow. Americans and Europeans alike want to be in control of their technology, not vice versa. Unplugging feels good, and will drive the future of our relationship to a connected world—and to one another.

24. PRIVATE PLANE PARTY CRASHERS

One luxury experience has always been out of reach for nearly all Americans: flying in a private plane. Reserved for the ultra-wealthy or famous, the ability to drive up to an aircraft on your schedule, with little security, and stretch out onboard as much as you want has simply been beyond reach, even for millionaires. Today you can wear the same Apple Watch as Tim Cook, drive the same Mercedes that Bill Gates drives, wear the same Peter Millar shirt that Steve Ballmer wears. You can buy the same organic food that Martha Stewart is munching on. You and Warren Buffett can sit on the same model of toilet every day and even have the same air-conditioning.

But Warren gets on his G5, and you get to wait on the next gate change for your already delayed, overstuffed American Airlines flight.

The quest to make luxury affordable is not going to stop until every one of us can get a seat on a trip to Jupiter. Time and time again, mass markets are created by bringing the preserve of the wealthy down in price and making it affordable to the top 25 percent. That was how Apple got its start with the iPhone, how Tesla started off, how startups like MTailor work, and how companies like Mercedes broadened their once rarified markets. It's a phenomenon that is constantly driving new trends. Imagine that the mobile phone just twenty-five years ago was only for the ultra-wealthy to use in their limousines. Today they ride in the same SUV, and you likely have a better smartphone.

Private aircraft got their start in the late 1950s, and each decade

24.1: Top Ten Routes for Private Jet Traffic, 2013

RANK	DEPARTURE CITY	ARRIVAL CITY
1	Moscow	Nice/Côte d'Azur
2	Miami	New York
3	New York	Los Angeles
4	New York	West Palm Beach
5	London	New York
6	London	Moscow
7	London	Nice/Côte d'Azur
8	Chicago	New York
9	Houston	New York
10	West Palm Beach	New York

Source: Knight Frank and NetJets via CNNMoney.com

since has seen major advances in safety and quality of the aircraft. There are now about 20,000 jets in service, in five classes—very light, light, midsized, super-mid, and heavy. Costs of new jets today range from a low of $2 million or $3 million for some very light jets to over $50 million for a Global Express that can reach anywhere in the world. Typical light and midsized jets are $10 to $20 million in cost and have a useful life of twenty years. That means if you want to operate your jet with pilots, you probably are in the hole by at least a million dollars a year—which is why it is out of reach for all but a very, very select few. I was lucky enough to have sixty hours of private-jet flying time per year when I was a Microsoft executive and used my limited time, likely costing $10,000 to $12,000 an hour, to return home on Friday evenings rather than overnight on a super-mid jet, which can go coast to coast without refueling.

The manufacturers of these aircraft have been seeking business models for quite some time to widen usage. First, "fractional ownership" came along and enabled businesses to share a jet for as low as $250,000 a year and schedule it in cooperation with a few other companies. Next came jet cards that allowed businesspeople to pay $5,000 to $10,000 an hour for a flight and pay for a set number of hours. A trip across the country costs $25,000 to $40,000. You can call around to various charter companies and you might get a deal, especially if a local jet company has a jet stuck somewhere without a customer and needs to get it back to home base.

Companies like NetJets figured out how to systematize all the demand and air traffic to make it far more efficient for the operator. Warren Buffett liked the concept so much, he bought the company.

For businesses with headquarters in Bentonville, Arkansas, or that have to get around in places like Alaska, or that have plants in smaller cities, these jets can be quite necessary and effective. But a lot of private travel, when you look at the most frequented routes, runs from big cities to vacation spots like Nice in Europe or Miami in the U.S. If you go to the NCAA championship or other major sporting event, hundreds of private planes can be backed up for hours, as everyone tries to leave at the same time.

Now entrepreneurs have stepped in to try to expand the marketplace from the super-rich to business and leisure travelers who can splurge. Rather than $1,000,000 to operate a plane or $250,000 for a jet card, they can share private jets for an effective rate of $1,000 an hour or less—so twenty-five hours of flight will cost you $25,000 instead of ten times that.

Most travelers on these private plane start-ups are indeed businesspeople renting a seat for a quick commute from, say, Boston to New York. As Kenny Dichter, founder and CEO of travel start-up Wheels Up, told CNNMoney, "With reasonable hourly rates, it's created a value proposition that's moved people off their commercial options and onto private." Commercial airlines charge steep prices for travelers booking a flight on short notice for business. Private jets have found ways to fill seats without the expense. And these aren't just "old men in suits," either—though there are plenty of those. The statistics for PrivateFly, a broker based in the U.K., show that 37 percent of passengers are women. PrivateFly also reports that the average age of passengers was 41 years old, 14 percent were children under 16, and 6 percent were pets.

The private plane is a new type of flashy Instagram status symbol, to the point where it's even been the subject of ridicule: rapper Bow

Wow Instagrammed a private plane and made a travel comment, only to be snapped sitting coach on a commercial liner. The jokes that ensued outed him for trying to seem like he was flying private when in fact he was stuck in a regular seat like everyone else. Influencer marketing and private flights have been quick to notice the upside—with celebrities from the Kardashians to musicians and models working with jet companies to show off their envious lifestyles. Even the "Points Guy," known for his travel blog on all things credit cards, miles, and gaming the airlines, wrote a love letter to JetSmarter: "Not too long ago I was introduced to the world of private jets, and my addiction is growing."

Apps are making hailing a plane easier with the swipe of your finger, and JetSmarter is one of them. The app launched in 2012 and was initially built to service empty legs, when a plane would be wasting fuel. However, the customer it targeted was too specific. So in 2015 the company added shuttle services for key hubs like New York and Los Angeles. There is a significant subscription fee, $11,000 a year, and then these shuttles are free. And there are several tiers of membership, going up to $45,000 per year, making sure to keep a level of exclusion and an air of wealth to the process. "The company says the average member spends $29,000 a year on the service and claims it has 8,000 members, figures that add up to $232 million in annual revenue," according to the *Verge*.

JetSmarter has been able to attract a much wider customer segment with its $11,000 starting point. Lots of businesses will spring for that kind of membership for its executives. Likewise, many people who run their own businesses might spring for that kind of fee, which is completely tax-deductible. JetSmarter flights are filled with lots of geeky-looking guys, based on my experience, though more and more women are joining the program. The flights are usually mixed in ages, with the average looking to be about 35.

Non–business travelers are using these new services to take the trips of their dreams. Customers willing to shell out can go to the Super Bowl or the World Series. You can even combine it with a mansion from Airbnb or suite from HotelTonight, the last-minute hotel booking app. Users can book opulent suites in hotels they could never afford—if they're okay doing it at the last minute. Just an example, guests could have booked the Avalon Hotel Beverly Hills penthouse for a stay last night for $599 through the HotelTonight app, while the hotel website listed it for $1,100 per night. HotelTonight's bookings would otherwise be empty, so the "high roller" option offers a stay at a multi-thousand-dollar-a-night hotel room for way less. And its success proves that Americans will pay for luxury without planning: the company closed $45 million in financing and has raised a total of $81 million.

Combined, JetSmarter and HotelTonight can use the sharing economy to offer all the $100,000 privileges that Bill Gates is enjoying at an incremental cost of around $2,500. Two unattainable luxuries—private flights and huge hotel suites—are within the means of the top 25 percent, opening them up to new kinds of customers.

Airbnb has also taken notice of this trend. The wildly popular rental service is in the process of launching "Airbnb Lux," a new "ultra-premium" tier of houses and apartments for rent. Why stay in a stuffy fancy hotel when you can stay in a mansion with a waterslide? Airbnb is paying celebrities to hawk these luxe properties: Beyoncé posted photos of herself at a $10,000-a-night Airbnb while at the Super Bowl, and Selena Gomez stayed in a $3,750-per-night beachfront property in Malibu.

If crafty start-ups can put the most out-of-reach luxuries within the grasp of millions, then it's hard to imagine a luxury that can't be brought to the mass market. Rent the Runway is bringing designer outfits to people who can't afford to buy them. Even caviar is harvested in America for less. It's just a matter of time before you'll be able to rent the Star of India for that night out. Rather than bring the rich down, the new economy is bringing the upper middle class up into the ultra elite's rarified world.

25. SOCIAL MILLIONAIRES

When you think of a millionaire, you think of cash, cars, and a swanky lifestyle by the poolside. Of course, a million dollars doesn't buy what it used to. And there is a new coin of the realm, even more valuable than a million dollars: that's people who achieve over 1 million followers on social media.

At the top, of course, there are megastars who have added to their huge fortunes with big online splashes. Selena Gomez has 127 million followers, and Justin Bieber comes in at 92 million today. These are worldwide phenoms with fans who have grown up online. That's a key difference between today's stars and their autograph-signing

25.1: Top Ten Instagram Accounts, October 2017

RANK	ACCOUNT	FOLLOWERS (MILLIONS)
1	Instagram	227
2	Selena Gomez	128
3	Ariana Grande	114
4	Cristiano Ronaldo	113
5	Beyoncé	107
6	Taylor Swift	104
7	Kim Kardashian	103
8	Kylie Jenner	98.8
9	Dwayne Johnson	94.9
10	Justin Bieber	92.4

Source: Wikipedia

25.2: Top Ten YouTube Accounts, October 2017

RANK	CHANNEL NAME	SUBSCRIBERS (MILLIONS)
1	PewDiePie	57
2	HolaSoyGerman.	32
3	JustinBieberVEVO	32
4	T-Series	26
5	elrubiusOMG	26
6	RihannaVEVO	25
7	YouTube Spotlight	25
8	TaylorSwiftVEVO	25
9	KatyPerryVEVO	25
10	Fernanfloo	24

Source: Wikipedia

ancestors: they can build followings online and leverage them to purchase products, albums, and clothing with one tweet.

Kylie Jenner, daughter of Kris Jenner and Caitlyn Jenner, is the youngest Kardashian clan member who has grown up online and on-screen. She has used her social millionaire status (97.5 million followers on Instagram alone) to sell and market her makeup line, Kylie Cosmetics. She has already pulled in a reported $40 million from its first year alone and is on track to become the first billionaire in her family—surpassing the rest of her famous sisters, even Kim Kardashian—using her obsessive social following. Other celebrities have followed suit, launching beauty lines or clothing lines as well. These social mavens and celebrities also drive trends, and even social change, through their products. The explosion of Fenty Beauty by Rihanna, who has 56.7 million Instagram followers and 78.3 million Twitter followers, has taken the beauty world by storm.

Below the obvious stars, however, the most interesting microtrend lies with the struggling group of unknowns who are rapidly becoming known through social media alone—people who have an interest or skill, or just enjoy social media and have decided to try to make it. A decade ago it was bloggers who were burning up the internet and barely surviving. Now social millionaires are the ones who are part artist, part entrepreneur, and part reviewer. Think of social channels as individual television channels with some ad space and the ability to recommend products. If you can get enough viewers, you can sell ads. Starting with just 5,000 or 10,000 followers, you can get $50, but once you cross a million, you can pick up $10,000 per major post or ad.

Anyone with ideas on how to get people's attention with an off-beat character or an interesting viewpoint or expertise can now start up their own social media channels and plug into ad networks to start getting checks. The newest and hottest form of marketing is influencer marketing. Previously frowned upon, reviewers take money and/or products (and now that the FTC issued guidelines, they can disclose they are sponsored) and go ahead and promote the wares for a fee. It's standard practice now in the industry.

Harnessing that content and becoming a millionaire in followers is no easy feat. If you're an elite Twitter user with, say, over a million followers, you've likely been using the platform for a long time. These social millionaires post relentlessly and religiously, and they deeply understand the platforms. Although the new aspiration of many young Americans is to become "famous on the internet," it's tremendously difficult. You invariably have to start with a few followers, and it takes an average of eight years to build it up to over 1 million, unless you are helped by being the star of a movie or TV show.

If you're in the elite 1,000 most-followed Twitter accounts, you've probably been tweeting for many years or maybe even a full decade—it's not an overnight occurrence. The early adopters had an advantage. Twitter launched in 2006. Half of all of today's top 1,000 Twitter accounts emerged within the first three years of Twitter. When it comes to Twitter, there are approximately 5,000 social millionaires. With YouTube, there are about 4,000. Out of a billion users of these products, only a few have made it into this successful club. And once they are there, they have to stay on top of a fickle fan base that can shift. There are tearful stories of people who gave three years of their life to this effort and in the end found only failure and heartbreak.

A couple who I know just gave up their regular careers to start up their social media business. One left a major law firm after graduating from a top law school. They think this is going to make them rich—and they've based it all on their dog. They had 250,000 followers and got pickup for their videos, which showed the dog doing amazing tricks, like picking the lock on his cage. But the path to financial success is hardly clear, even for the most committed.

What makes a social millionaire varies greatly, but it has to be unusual enough to be successful. Millions of cat videos are posted every day, so don't expect your cat to provide a payday unless it flies. Some of the big successes have been personalities like Jenna Marbles or commenters on video games like Lewis & Simon. Some comedians like Toby Turner have made it; DisneyCollectorBR has amassed a $5 million fortune with toy reviews; others who explore personal relationships have gotten tens of millions of views. Don't expect the money just to pour in, however; you need a video a week and two posts a day or more, all while you take care of the business side.

With Fyre Festival, it was noted that the organizers "spent $250,000 on a single Instagram post from Kim Kardashian's half-sister Kendall Jenner. And they laid out hundreds of thousands of dollars more on lesser-name 'influencers,' none of whom were paid less than $20,000," according to one person familiar with the payments. Only one model—*Gone Girl* actress Emily Ratajkowski—labeled her promotion as an ad, as required by the Federal Trade Commission. The other models' omissions are now the subject of a class-action lawsuit. "These 'sponsored posts' were in direct violation of Federal Trade Commission guidelines on disclosing material connections between advertisers and endorsers," the suit alleges, as reported by Vice. "Social Media 'influencers' did not attempt to disclose to consumers that they were being compensated for promoting the Fyre Festival. Instead, these influencers gave the impression that the guest list was full of the Social Elite and other celebrities," the lawsuit says.

Increasingly, kids are starting their own businesses, too. If they deeply know a sport, a hobby, or a lot about relationships or clothes, they might be driven to want to become a social millionaire. If they work at it, they can pick up a following for spare cash—instead of a paper route or a lemonade stand. This is the new way for savvy kids to make money, or even in rare cases pay their way through college. I sold stamps to collectors through the mail when I was twelve; Warren Buffett was walking his neighborhood, selling gum from a cart. Fast-forward to today, and with assistance from his dad, an eight-year-old started EvanTubeHD—a YouTube channel devoted to what other young kids care about. It reportedly brings in $1.3 million a year.

Currently, Instagram is the hottest platform for growing a user base and it is offering the best return for someone who can get to a million engaged followers. You have to watch out for the copyright laws if you use any music and follow the disclosure rules if you are getting sponsors. As an independent contractor, you will be paying self-employment taxes, but you can deduct those meals and travel expenses you take on to make those videos on the Pacific Coast Highway. If you are not good enough to get a paid sponsor, you can sign up for their free program, and you will at least get some promotional merchandise for your time and trouble.

The road to riches is a long shot. About 90 percent who try never get a dime, and only 1 percent get big enough to make a living. But to the other 9 percent, you might find yourself with enough money to cover the bills or get a new car. You might even become a social millionaire.

Section 4

LIFESTYLE

---

26. Single with Pet

27. Roomies for Life

28. Footloose and Fancy-Free

29. Nerds with Money

30. Uptown Stoners

31. Intelligent TV

32. Korean Beauty

33. Modern Annie Oakleys

34. Armchair Preppers

26. SINGLE WITH PET

A popular internet meme sums up how millennials feel about their pets:

> *"It's just a dog."*
> *First of all, that's my child.*

A whole new kind of pet ownership has swept across a generation. Pets were generally what eight-year-olds got for their birthday; then empty nesters got them as child replacements (as we saw in the first *Microtrends*). Now young singles, free of many of the obligations of couples with kids, have decided to add a pet to their households. A recent Harvard CAPS–Harris poll places the overall pet ownership for millennials at somewhere between two-thirds and three-fourths.

Dogs are the number one pet of choice for singles with pets (SWPs), followed closely by cats. A fair number of owners buy two pets, to have a companion for their first. Though they live in urban areas, there has been little change in the most purchased pets: the Labrador retriever is number one, followed by the German shepherd, and the French bulldog is not far behind. Forty-nine percent of American households have a cat, and 71 percent have a dog.

While we might associate being young and untethered with being irresponsible, studies show that single millennials are caring, conscientious pet parents. They care about their own diets and also tend to be rather picky about what they feed their pets. SWPs are prime customers for non-GMO, even organic pet food, and often give their pets vitamin supplements. They are much more likely to buy their

26.1: Pet Ownership Among U.S. Millennials, 2007–2015

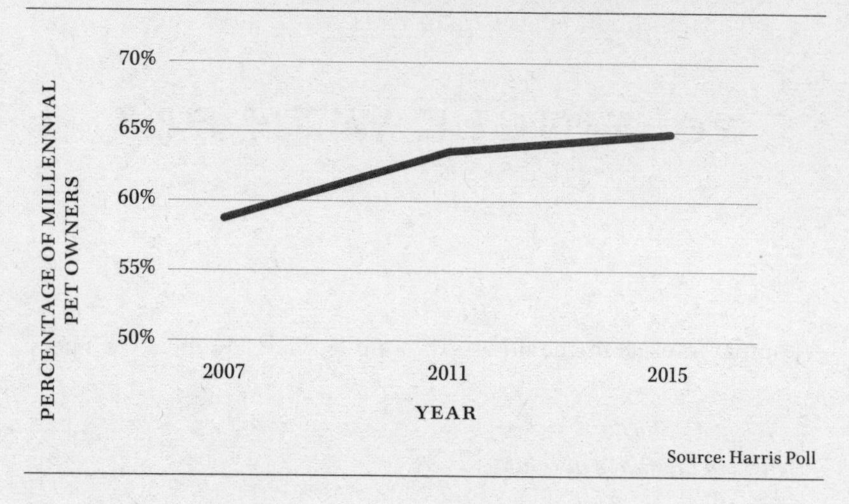

Source: Harris Poll

pets clothes than boomers, more likely to buy pet insurance, and even more likely to visit the vet.

Of course, the demands of pet ownership are fairly incompatible with the lifestyles of SWPs, who are out all day at work and then out for dinner; the time they have with their pets is typically fairly limited. To further accommodate busy pet owners, some upscale condos offer dog runs, in-house dog walking services, and even in some cases professional-grade dog grooming rooms. Being single once meant a time in your life without any responsibility—nobody to answer to, a beer whenever you felt like it, and takeout containers piling up around the couch. Now SWPs are eating their takeout with their dog. Since the average age of people having a child got pushed back, one of the things that millennials have filled those extra years with is the love of their pets.

One way to deal with incongruities of lifestyle is to bring a pet to work, and progressive employers and landlords have now adopted the first-ever pet policies. Popular coworking spaces are littered with dogs, especially in creative companies that dress informally and are stocked with under-30 aged workers. The percentage of millennials

26.2: Percentage of U.S. Millennial Pet Owners Who Have Brought Their Pets to Work, 2007–2015

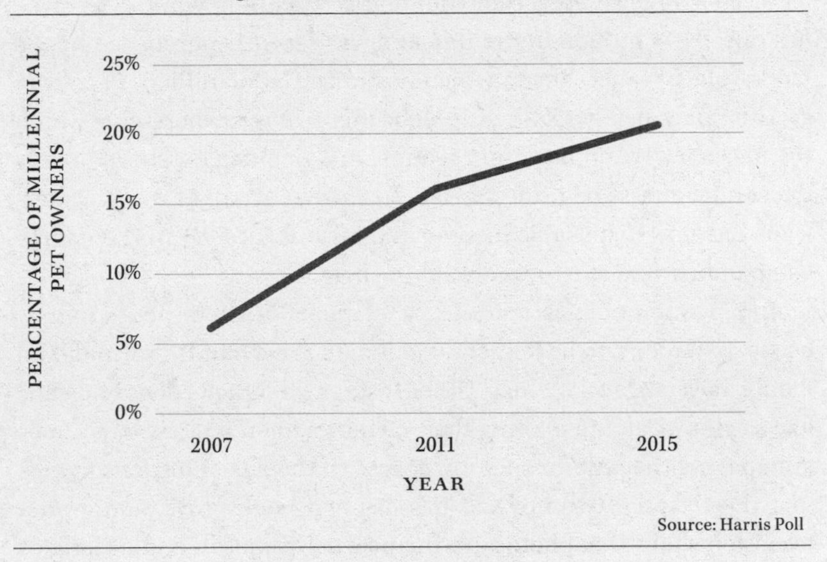

Source: Harris Poll

who have brought their dogs to the office has increased significantly, from around 7 percent in 2007 to over 20 percent in 2015, according to a Harris poll. Many offices beyond just coworking spaces allow dogs, and employers are starting to see it as a benefit, as dogs help with anxiety and tension and help boost office morale. Maybe more buttoned-up industries like finance and law will have no choice but to allow their associates to bring their pups to work. Pets in the office help business, but they can also understandably create resentment among parents, who can't bring their human children to their place of business.

Pet spending is at an all-time high: $6 billion a year. Millennials are the most likely to use a range of new services that have sprung up to make their responsibilities easier to carry out. If you can't make it home from lunch to walk your dog, you can hire an on-demand dog walker from Barkly Pets. Or if you want someone to just hang out with your pet at your home for a little while, Barkly Pets will do that, too.

The start-up raised a $6 million Series A in January of 2017. If you're traveling, there's now Airbnb for your dog, too: DogVacay, which allows you to choose a place for your dog to "vacation" while you travel, has raised $74 million in funding and was recently purchased by the marketplace leader, Rover, which has raised $156 million. Pets even go to luxury pet hotels—with webcams where owners can watch them. Disney World has a pet section, and one dog hotel even reads the canine guests bedtime stories. A growing group of young Americans has new disposable income and serious interest in their furry companions, and start-ups are taking note.

In our world of constant celebrity, famous A-listers' pets can now be just as famous. Kylie Jenner's two Italian greyhounds, Norman and Bambi, have huge followings. Other Instagram-famous dogs and cats, like Grumpy Cat, are making their owners a lot of money, sometimes even paying the rent for their owners with the ads and sponsorships that they attract. Grumpy Cat has his own books, toys, and even a television show. Dog photos are the new baby photos, and as long as millennials are on social media, so are many of their dogs and cats. Millions of cat videos are uploaded every day online, and my kids even have our feisty feline online. You see dogs on red carpets, too: Uggie, the dog in the Academy Award–winning film *The Artist*, was a hit on the Oscar party circuit. When he passed away, many outlets wrote tributes. Leona Helmsley, a famous Manhattan real estate and hotel tycoon, left $12 million to her dog, Trouble. When Trouble passed away, the *New York Times* published an op-ed devoted to the rich maltese.

Insurance companies are also taking note of single pet owners. You'd think that millennials would be less inclined to insure their pets: they don't have children or spouses, and have less familiarity with the benefits of insurance. However, that's not true. Around 19 percent of millennials insure their pets—way more than Gen Xers or boomers—with some even doubly insuring them. Insurance companies will continue to make bank on Fido's broken foot: there is no regulation of pet insurance, and there is an endless array of preexisting conditions that insurance companies can level against a dog. But millennials will continue to pay for it.

The pet industry has been pretty quick to respond to the trend of SWPs when you look at how they have been retooling their products. While many industries have had trouble finding growth, the pet industry isn't one of them: these new and almost unexpected owners have given this industry a shot in the arm. It's at an all-time high of nearly $70 billion.

The question is: What is going to happen to these pets when the millennials move on with their lives, settle down, and start to have kids? Suddenly the pet is no longer number one and does not understand this sudden change in status. Some pets, like the cat that belongs to a friend of mine, are quarantined to small areas of the house and kept far away from the new baby in the house. This sudden change in interest is unlike anything else that we have seen in the pet world. Never before have millions of pets faced the prospect of this trauma; they will be in need of therapy if that is what happens. Some will need trainers, to ensure that the pets can be reliably trained to be baby-friendly; other owners may just dump their pets entirely, filling up the pounds.

We will cross this bridge in the next five years. In the meantime, buy that sweater for your dog: he almost looks like a baby in it.

27. ROOMIES FOR LIFE

The most popular television shows of recent decades all have one element in common, and it's not one that immediately meets the eye. *Friends*, *Three's Company*, *The Golden Girls*, to name a few, are all celebrated American television comedies—and they all feature roommates. Today, younger and older Americans alike are following their favorite shows' formulas: they're becoming "roomies for life," living the sitcom life for way longer than ever before. And it's affecting social norms, real estate, and the way we think about coexisting.

You might see Joey and Chandler on *Friends*, palling around and dancing in their apartment, making for great TV. But this same arrangement is now reflected in real life, particularly with young Americans in their twenties and thirties who are unmarried and single but who have decided to pair up and live together. It's one new way of socializing and easing isolation: moving in with a friend, whether or not you need it to afford your month's rent.

Roomies for life is allowing a generation—mostly millennials in dense urban areas—to craft a community, put off marriage by having companionship without commitment, and increase their social spheres. Sure, many of these roomies for life reside in expensive coastal cities and need to live in fifth-floor walk-ups with their friends in order to afford it. But even if they can afford the rent, living alone can get rather boring and often isolating, especially if young professionals have moved away from family and friends to a new city. In the end, many roomies for life don't care about the rent and believe that, in these isolating times, getting to live with someone is well worth the cost.

27.1: U.S. Adults Living with Roommates

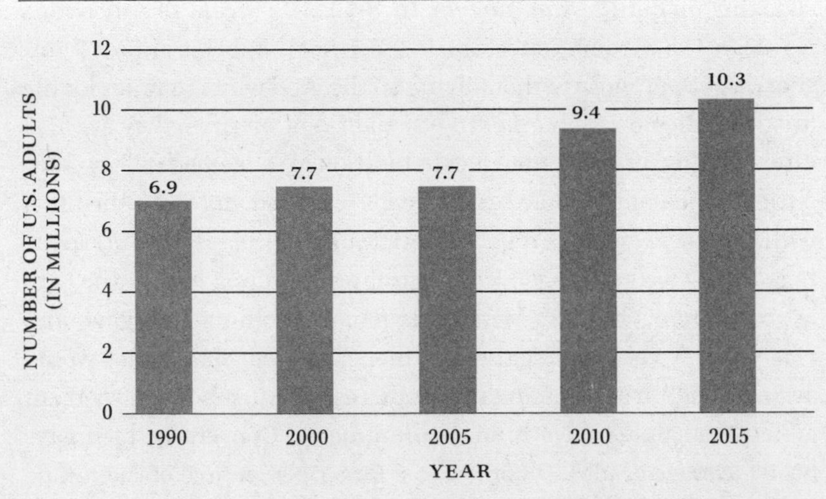

Source: IPUMS American Community Survey data*
*Excludes group quarters such as prisons and other institutions.

27.2: Percentage of U.S. Adults with Roommates by Age

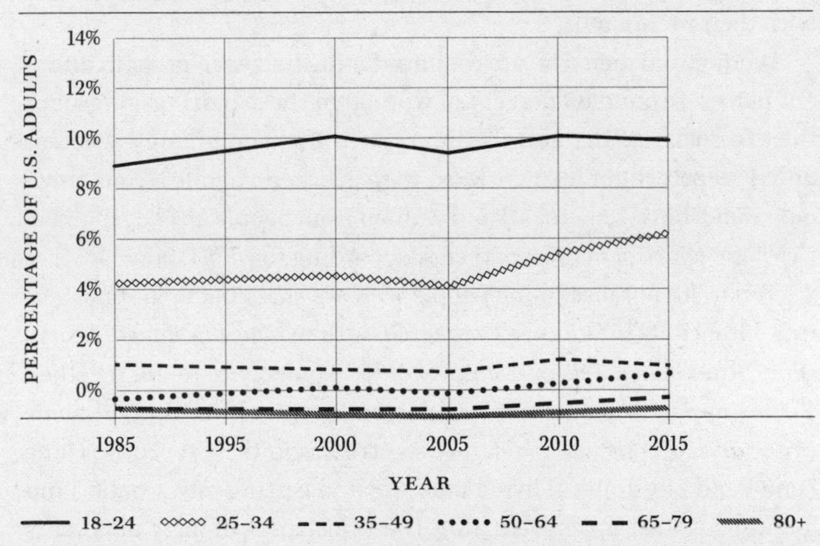

Source: IPUMS American Community Survey data*
*Excludes group quarters such as prisons and other institutions.

The roomies-for-life microtrend shows that young Americans are shacking up but not *shacking up*. In 1990, 5.9 percent of Americans age 25 to 34 had roommates, and in 2015 that number is almost 8 percent. It's *Living Single* without living single. And while roomies for life are depending on each other to pay their rent on time, they are also often looking for more than a cohabitation arrangement. They want a friend, someone to share experiences with and go out on the town with. Another way this group is mimicking traditional romantic pairings is how well other-gender roommates get along even if they are attracted to each other. Men grade female roommates higher, and vice versa. "Over 70 percent of the men surveyed shared they would award A's or B's to their female roommates, with just below 60 percent giving the same grades to male roommates. Conversely, men gave below-average grades, D's or F's, to a larger percentage of their male roommates at over 15 percent compared to female roommates at just under 10 percent," according to RENTCafé. This group isn't getting married, but they sure are acting like it. And while those pairs would likely rate each other lower if they were dating, roomies for life say they are happy: "Close to 60 percent said they didn't actually fight with their roommates."

Women and men who are roomies for life find each other in different places. Around 35 percent of women in these pairings or groups turn to social media and the internet to find roommates, whereas only 12.9 percent of men do. Most men get their roomies from previous friendships (29 percent) and women from people already living in the same apartment (35.4 percent), according to RENTCafé.

Today, it's not just young people who are shacking up but not getting hitched. (Think more *Golden Girls* than *The Big Bang Theory*.) Older Americans, and particularly older women, are living together. This is apparent in current popular culture, too: Netflix's hit show *Grace and Frankie* has two famous actresses in their seventies (Jane Fonda and Lily Tomlin) living together and getting into trouble (and founding a start-up as well) after their husbands of forty-plus years run off together. AARP echoes this trend. According to the organization, older women who may be divorced or widowed are all getting together as roomies for life. (As we saw in "Third-Time Winners," they're less likely to remarry these days.) According to AARP, "female boomers and older women—both bosom buddies and strangers—are moving in together as a way to save money and form a community." The American Community Survey shows that there are now around 2 million Americans over age 50 who are living with roommates. Often it's the roommate arrangement and not marriage that is "until death do us part."

One welcome benefit of roomies for life is that it can be better for your health than living alone. Loneliness has been chronicled many times over as a negative indicator for health and even as a predictor of early death. This is even more relevant for older Americans, and makes the case for this new style of living. According to the *New York Times*, "Researchers have found mounting evidence linking loneliness to physical illness and to functional and cognitive decline. As a predictor of early death, loneliness eclipses obesity." It's not even a physical symptom, yet it's damaging our health—so getting some roommates might make you a happier, healthier person. Case in point: a Finnish study found that one quarter of people living alone "filled an antidepressant prescription during the seven-year study, compared to just 16% of those who lived with spouses, family, or roommates."

Three people can also typically pay more than one person, and landlords have done the math and figured out that they can take advantage of this trend and get more for the same. They can charge more to three college grads who are splitting the bill than they could to a family with two kids who are financially strapped. A working couple today with kids might have two incomes of $60,000 each and massive expenses for their kids. Three newbies who have come to the big city might have $140,000 in income together and almost no expenses. A landlord could maybe get $2,500 a month from the first and $3,500 a month from the second group.

This is one reason why rents in key urban areas like New York, D.C., and San Francisco have skyrocketed, in turn forcing even people who might have lived alone to get a roomie—while also making it harder for families to live in the city. This is why folks with roommates have gone from being seen as an undesirable hassle, which landlords would often try to avoid, to being accommodated now, with easy lease terms, smaller security deposits, and better amenities. One unicorn start-up company (unicorns have private valuations over $1 billion), WeWork, has expanded into commune-like living accommodations that mimic co-working spaces. Called WeLive, they aim to further blend work and life.

The roomies-for-life trend is also influencing design. Nobody wants to take the small closet or draw straws for the room with no bathroom attached. The result is more apartments with equal-sized bedrooms, with closets and a bathroom for each. These changes increase the attractiveness of new apartments for this very attractive subgroup.

Despite having more disposable income, roomies for life typically cut the cable cord and demand more internet, and only one in five are getting a landline. All this is accelerating the decline in these services and is bad news for the stock- and bondholders of the landline and cable companies.

Traditionally, having a roommate was meant to be a short transition phase until you moved in with your future spouse or made enough money to get your own studio. Now having a roommate gives you a lasting taste of communal living; it's kind of the college dorm you never left. The more people enjoy this kind of living, the more it will continue to change the structure of American family life as more people have found a fiscally responsible way to live single and enjoy life without the responsibilities of kids and spouses. Landlords and the business community have done a 180-degree flip and now welcome these living arrangements, offering them even more incentives today than they offer stable families. If, after a few years, people yearn for more—or at least more independence—in their lives, then this trend may well fade after experimentation. But so far the numbers point one way: up, up, and up.

28. FOOTLOOSE AND FANCY-FREE

For the past few generations, the shift from being under your parents' roof to becoming parents yourself was a quick one. Often it meant marrying your college sweetheart, and having kids soon thereafter. However, as American women entered the workforce and more Americans started college, something changed. What used to be at most five years from high school graduation to marriage and kids has expanded to ten years, thus allowing a cohort of young Americans to remain footloose and fancy-free (FFF).

In the U.S. the median age at first marriage has increased by five years since 1970. What young people in this country previously did in their early twenties—make large life decisions like getting married and having kids—has now been shifted to their late twenties and often early thirties. This microtrend is allowing the millennial generation to be much more influential across society than their numbers. Millennials are taking a decade to learn what they like and care about, date, form relationships, and become independent. Freed of having to take on big responsibilities that previously faced their parents and grandparents at their age, they can curate themselves, participate more in politics, focus on their careers, and make a cultural mark.

Forget about seeing those young parents at the PTA: parents are going to be older than ever. With the delay in parenthood also comes the delay in moving to the suburbs, and thus new life for vibrant cities like New York, Los Angeles, San Francisco, and Washington, D.C. Sub-

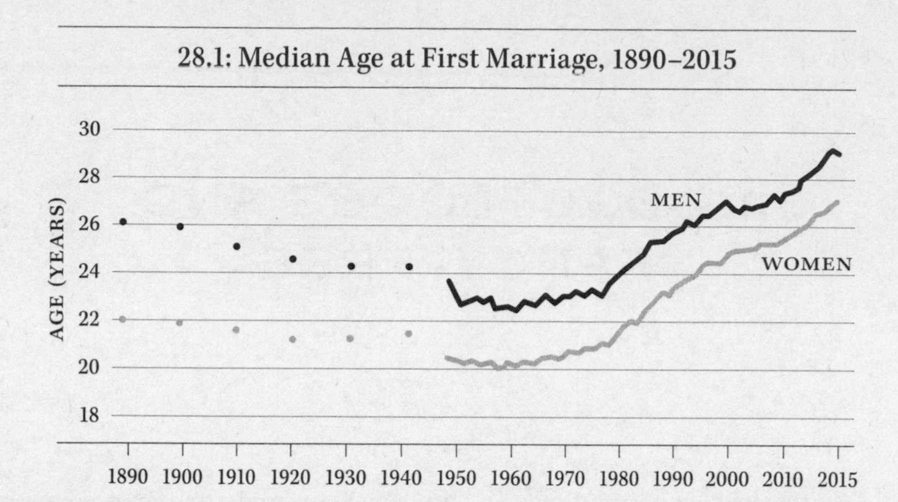

urban offices are suffering, and yet there isn't enough room for new office towers in the cities that millennials are flocking to.

For years we have talked about the "me" generation that came of age in the seventies and eighties. These footloose and fancy-free young adults are actually more socially conscious and tolerant than past generations, but are also being driven by a considerably higher degree of selfishness. The parents of footloose and fancy-free Americans are on average too young to need long-term care, and, without their own kids yet, the FFF cohort is free to concentrate on their own wants and desires. Two-thirds of the FFF population is college educated, so they care deeply about some issues like college tuition and student debt, but they are far removed at their present life stage from understanding the potential importance of religion in their lives or in the lives of others.

The footloose and fancy-free don't want commitment; they want freedom and choice. This group is constantly on the move when it comes to where they live, who they live with, and where they work. One minute they are with roomies, the next minute they are living with their potential spouse. This explains the proliferation of rental properties for the FFF, who don't want to commit to buying a home and want to live longer than ever with roommates, throw away no-pet clauses, and limit their leases to only a one-year term.

This new part of your life—between the time you get out of college and get married and have kids—is ten full years of urban apartments, food deliveries, video games, late-night internet wormholes, and parties and vacations with friends. This is an unexpected bonanza for those industries. UberEATS and Xbox can worry less about teenagers and focus more upon these consumers who have more money to spend on themselves and are in the formative years of picking their favorite consumer brands.

But a life without responsibility just might be too intoxicating for some, who believe that they will be forever young. Some use this newfound period to spring ahead in their careers; others figure out what they need to do to get by and focus on maximizing their leisure time. The footloose and fancy-free calculate that their rent is shared; they can split food or use the dollar menu; they cut the cord on cable TV. Their smartphone might be their single biggest recurring and unavoidable expenditure, although they might try switching to T-Mobile or Sprint. They definitely don't need cars, and if they are able, they can get around on bicycles in those new bike lanes that have been built for them in all the major cities.

In the past, men in their twenties had enormous career responsibilities, and women had enormous responsibilities surrounding children and family. The new twenties have completely different roles and responsibilities. Men, on the surface, are looking for that Manic Pixie Dream Girl who will help them find themselves and be there to help them embrace life. At the same time women are looking at the opposite kinds of role models: the single successful career woman who might skip marriage altogether to achieve great success on her own.

This disconnect suggests that this whole generation may have a lot of problems sorting themselves out in the coming decade. You can see these fault lines now emerging in politics, religion, and some of the cultural divides.

In general, in my experience reviewing poll data, people are less likely to get religious until they experience the miracle of childbirth and having a family. If not for Tinder, an extra five years of dating and video games would have been great for the church social. But given the centrality of the internet in finding relationships, religion is a big loser for now in this lifestyle transition. One fifth of this millennial generation, far more than other generations, now consider themselves unaffiliated with any religion at all.

While some of the footloose and fancy-free are just getting by, others are using this time to climb the corporate ladder. A lot of employers report millennials expressing a strong desire for work/life balance and are responding with benefits tailored to a generation that for now needs dog-walking perks instead of child care. Yet some of the most difficult, selective schools and companies report record numbers of applicants. Medical school applications are at record numbers. Professional school applications are up, too, as are PhDs. In 2014 there were 54,070 PhDs awarded—12,000 more than in 2004. Un-

28.2: Percentage of Religiously Unaffiliated Americans by Generation

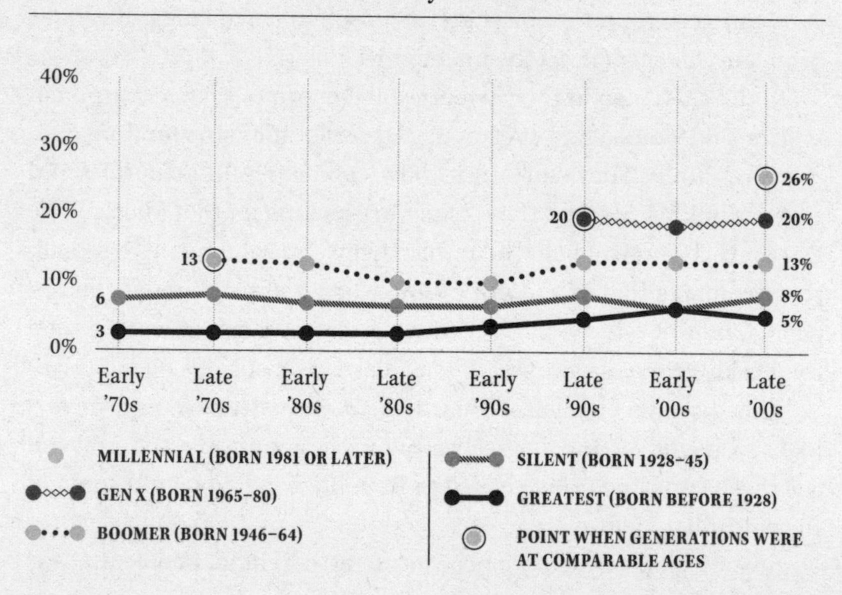

surprisingly, more and more of the FFF group are getting advanced degrees in science and engineering and going to medical school.

When it comes to politics, the footloose and fancy-free largely support the Democrats, young adult minorities are solidly in the Democratic column, and women in these age ranges are a huge part of the "resistance." But a sizable chunk of white men—about a third—are heavily pro-Trump despite agreeing with Democrats on several policy issues.

There are, unsurprisingly, some major attitudinal differences between this generation and their parents. Largely driven by social media instead of TV news, this generation is far more tolerant across racial, gender, and sexual orientation lines. The footloose and fancy-free overwhelmingly support the Supreme Court's decision affirming the right to gay marriage. Most favor legalizing marijuana and single-payer health care. But a lot of these political views are the result of their extended campus lifestyles living in communal dorms. Traditionally, campus views change over time. Most of the Fox News generation voted for John F. Kennedy over Richard Nixon and grew more conservative as they got older. The open question is whether this generation will undergo these same changes as they get married, have children, and move to the suburbs—or whether many will like to be footloose and fancy-free . . . forever.

29. NERDS WITH MONEY

In 1984 the film *Revenge of the Nerds* depicted the rivalry between a downtrodden group of computer geeks and their alpha male jock tormentors. From the crabby Comic Book Guy on *The Simpsons* to the socially awkward high schoolers of *Freaks and Geeks*, popular culture has traditionally depicted nerds as lovable losers at best, obsessive outcasts at worst.

But today's nerds have little need for revenge. Dozens of trend pieces have noted that, in the age of Silicon Valley tech start-ups and multibillion-dollar comic book movies, nerdy is the new cool. Skills once considered painfully uncool, like computer engineering and data science, lead to six-figure salaries in today's information economy. The median annual salary for IT managers, for instance, is over $130,000. And plenty of today's doctors, lawyers, financial analysts, and executives spent their childhoods reading *Star Trek* zines and playing Dungeons & Dragons.

So now that a generation of nerds have grown up and acquired a healthy disposable income, have they put aside their childhood obsessions? Hardly. Nerds with money are spending their dough on merchandise, games, movies, and experiences like never before. In both mainstream and esoteric ways, nerd culture has become big business.

The growth of mainstream nerd culture is reflected, for one, in the boom of sci-fi and fantasy film franchises. The Marvel Cinematic Universe has brought in over $12 billion in worldwide box office receipts—to say nothing of the billions more in merchandise and other related sales. *Star Wars* toy sales reportedly reached $700 million in 2015.

That same year Star *Wars: The Force Awakens* hit theaters and soon surpassed $2 billion in ticket sales worldwide, adding to the many billions the *Star Wars* franchise had already earned.

Sure, a lot of those tickets and toys went to children and casual fans. But the diehards—the adult nerds with money—are an incredibly important constituency for these franchises. A 2015 analysis of the *Star Wars* Twitter account found that its typical follower was a 46-year-old married father with a salary between $75,000 and $124,000. When Disney markets a replica of Luke Skywalker's lightsaber for $175, they are targeting that fan directly: he ain't buying that toy for his kids.

Female nerds with money are similarly making themselves heard. When much of the merchandising for 2014's *Guardians of the Galaxy* failed to include the film's green-skinned female lead, the hashtag #WheresGamora was born. A similar campaign was mounted when

29.1: Box Office Revenue for Major Film Franchises

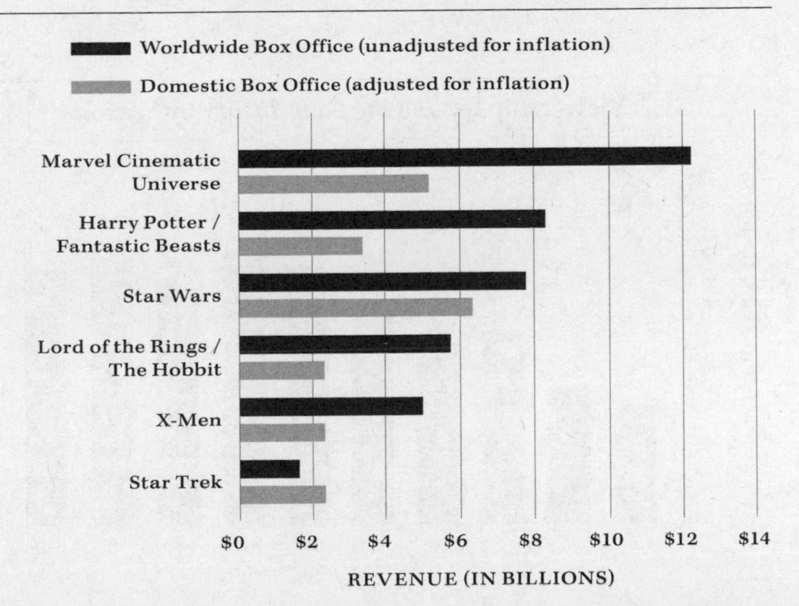

Source: Box Office Mojo

Rey, the main protagonist of *Star Wars: The Force Awakens*, was inexplicably absent from many of the toy lines. In that particular franchise, merchandisers seem to have learned their lesson. By 2017, during the popular Force Friday bonanza of *Star Wars* merchandising, retail chain Target used "Bring Your Rey Game" as its primary slogan to get fans into stores.

Like film, television has taken a sharp turn toward the nerdy. While the true geeks might sneer at the broad stereotypes presented in CBS's *Big Bang Theory*, the sitcom has exposed millions of Americans to inside jokes about *Star Trek* and comic books. *The Big Bang Theory* has averaged over 15 million viewers for each of its past several seasons, making it TV's most-watched show after *NBC Sunday Night Football*.

On cable, meanwhile, *The Walking Dead*, a zombie comic book adaptation, has repeatedly earned the top viewership numbers among the coveted 18-to-49-year-old demographic. Consequently, advertisers are willing to shell out around half a million dollars for a single thirty-second spot during *The Walking Dead*—higher than almost

29.2: Viewership for *The Big Bang Theory* by Season

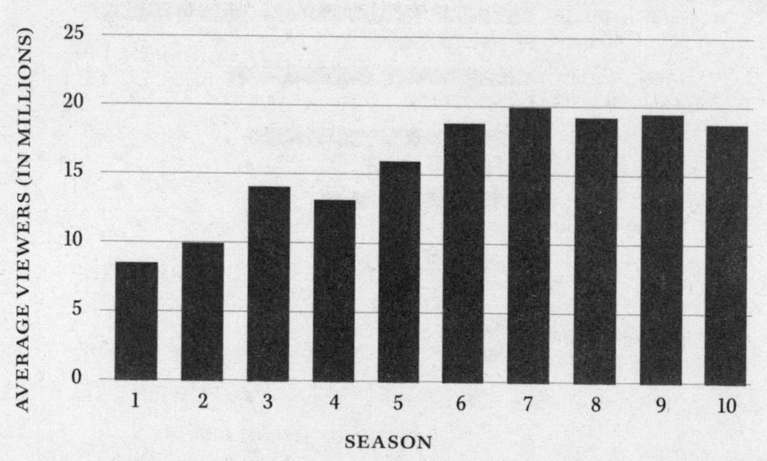

Source: Wikipedia

any other show. Over on HBO, *Game of Thrones* continues to break its own records for viewership—although the fantasy show has also earned the distinction of being the most pirated television show for several years running.

These mega-popular forms of nerd culture, along with the $91 billion dollar worldwide video gaming industry, speak to a trend that is perhaps more macro than micro. But to really understand the nerds-with-money microtrend, we have to look beyond what people are watching. The hard-core nerds with money aren't just passively consuming nerd culture; they are making a whole lifestyle of it.

San Diego Comic-Con, one of the entertainment industry's most well-known events, started in 1970 with three hundred attendees. In 2017 over 130,000 people attended SDCC, spending an estimated $83 million dollars at the convention, hotels, and local businesses during the four-day event. But SDCC is hardly the only geeky convention around. Every weekend in the U.S. and across the world, nerds gather at conventions of all sizes for any number of themes. Dragon Con in

29.3: London Comic Con Attendance, 2011–2016

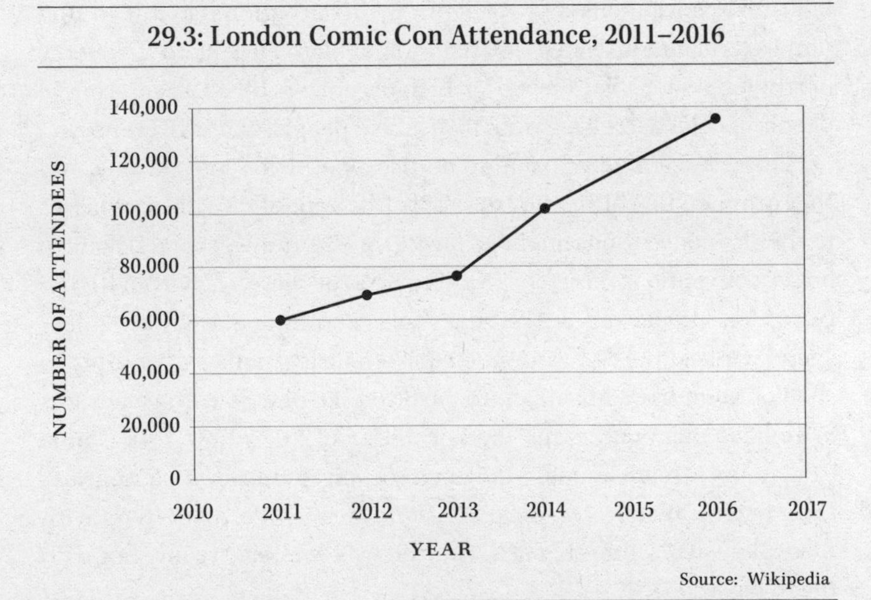

Source: Wikipedia

Atlanta attracts 70,000 to 80,000 attendees each year, while New York Comic Con estimates its attendance at over 150,000. MCM, a company that organizes several U.K.-based conventions, said that nearly 500,000 people attended its events in 2016. Their flagship convention, MCM London Comic Con, more than doubled its attendance figures between 2011 and 2016.

Smaller single-themed conferences can draw crowds as well. *Star Trek* conventions are still held in many cities, while 2017's first annual Con of Thrones (a *Game of Thrones* event) attracted over a thousand attendees. BronyCon, a fan conference devoted to the animated show *My Little Pony: Friendship Is Magic*, attracted 10,000 attendees at its peak.

Even in stodgy Washington, D.C., the nerds come out in force for multiple conventions every year. Katsucon, which focuses on anime, attracts nearly 20,000 people every year. The similarly themed Anime USA and Otakon attract around 5,000 and 27,000, respectively, while MAGFest (short for "Music and Gaming Festival") attracts 17,000. D.C.'s biggest comics and sci-fi/fantasy convention, called Awesome Con, reportedly had as many as 50,000 people in attendance in 2017. And yet, even with these large conventions already hogging the spotlight, new conventions keep springing up in the nation's capital. In 2017 hundreds of fans attended the first annual Blerdcon ("blerd" being the portmanteau for "black nerd"), which organizers billed as catering to people of color as well as women, disabled people, and LGBTQ nerds.

There is seemingly no end to nerds' appetite for conventions, and they are spending big money to satisfy this appetite. While day passes to smaller conventions might go for $20 or $30, full-weekend tickets to larger conventions often cost $100 to $200 or more, with even higher prices for VIP packages. And that's to say nothing of what attendees spend while at the convention itself. Nerds with money are willing to shell out hundreds in cold, hard cash to take photos with celebrities or to have them autograph memorabilia. At 2017's New York Comic Con, many attendees paid $125 each to wait in line for an autograph from Peter Capaldi, star of *Doctor Who*. Meanwhile, a photo op with Luke Skywalker himself, Mark Hamill, was available to any fan willing to pay the $250 fee.

Of course, instead of shelling out for autographs, some nerds with money like to wear their expensive obsessions on their sleeve. Cosplay, short for "costume play," is perhaps the ultimate expression of fandom. Nerds buy, sew, or construct elaborate costumes so that they can embody their favorite characters. Although fan costuming is nothing new, the modern explosion of cosplay (and the word itself) originated in Japan in the 1980s and '90s. Japanese fans, known as *otaku*, began wearing costumes of their favorite anime, manga, and video game characters not just to conventions but also to cosplay cafés in Tokyo and elsewhere. It became a lifestyle, and the practice soon spread around the world.

While it's impossible to know exactly how many cosplayers there are worldwide, we know it is increasing in popularity. The hashtag #cosplay had been used on Instagram more than 19 million times as of mid-2017. Google Trends shows that searches for cosplay rose steadily throughout the aughts and teens, hitting a peak in 2015 before leveling off.

How much are cosplayers spending on their habit? It varies. Suppose you want to cosplay as Wonder Woman or Wolverine and you need a wig. You could order a cheap synthetic wig on Amazon for as little as $15 to $20. For a better-quality lacefront wig, you might pay $60 to $70 to one of several wig manufacturers that cater to cosplayers. But if you're a cosplayer with serious cash to spend, the sky's the limit. For instance, Brooklyn-based Hero Hair ("Cosplay Wigs for the Serious Adventurer") creates screen-accurate wigs from virgin human hair, which its artisans hand-attach strand by strand. At minimum, a wig from Hero Hair will cost $500, but their most intricate and customized wigs run as high as $4,500.

Likewise, if you want to dress up as the *Star Wars: The Force Awakens* villain Kylo Ren, you could pay around $50 for a costume from Party City. But for true screen accuracy, nerds with money can buy a $3,100 deluxe costume from Anovos. Of course, that package doesn't include Kylo Ren's lightsaber. But don't worry, a battle-ready crossguard lightsaber with sound effects can be had for $500 or $600 from premium crafters like Saber Forge and Ultra Sabers.

With the explosive growth of conventions and cosplay, don't be surprised if these phenomena start showing up in more mainstream venues. The Syfy channel's reality competition series *Cosplay Melee* attracted a respectable half a million viewers, and it's only a matter of time before more TV networks premiere their own cosplay-themed programming.

The highly lucrative nature of celebrities' appearances at nerd conventions will also affect which films and television shows celebrities choose in the first place. If a TV actor has the choice between lead roles in either a police procedural or a "genre" show, he might choose the latter even if the salary is lower. After all, if the show is a hit (or even a short-lived cult classic like *Firefly*) he will have decades of being able to earn tens of thousands of dollars every weekend just by showing up at a convention for a few hours of photos and autographs. While sci-fi and fantasy used to be the realm of second-rate actors and scenery-chewing wannabes, we may see more vaunted and sought-after thespians drawn in by the siren song of convention fees, all thanks to nerds with money.

Smart entrepreneurs will find even more ways to cater to nerds with money in the coming years. Sure, there are already thousands of online and brick-and-mortar sellers hawking nerdy merchandise—if you want a T-shirt depicting Captain America kissing Agent Carter in front of the TARDIS, there's a t-shirt seller for you—but nerds with money want more than just merch: they want experiences. We should expect to see more immersive events such as the *Game of Thrones* pop-up bar that thrilled Washington, D.C., in the summer of 2017. Every day hundreds of enthusiasts lined up for hours just to get into the kitted-out bar, which featured an Iron Throne and a smoke-breathing dragon along with $14 cocktails. Likewise, a *Star Wars*–themed pop-up bar in Los Angeles proved so popular that the proprietors opened a permanent cantina (Scum and Villainy, on Hollywood Boulevard).

Internationally, the tourism industry will also cater to nerds with money. Fans of Harry Potter have flocked to various locations in Scotland, including the Edinburgh café where J. K. Rowling wrote much of the first book. (These days, Scotland is also playing host to *Outlander* fanatics.) Iceland can attribute some of its tourism boom both to *Game of Thrones*, which is partially filmed there, and to the video game *Skyrim*, which used Icelandic scenery as its inspiration. New Zealand, of course, has made a permanent exhibit out of the hobbit sets from *The Lord of the Rings*. And Croatia has the lucky distinction of being a filming location for both *Game of Thrones* and *Star Wars*, as any visitor to Dubrovnik will be reminded repeatedly. Tourism boards may pressure local governments to give ever-increasing tax incentives to the films and TV shows that will ever more attract nerds with money to their towns.

Nerds with money are setting the tone for culture and expression. Losers and outcasts no more, these nerds are using the power of their pocketbooks to carve out the geek-chic lifestyle of their dreams. It's up to the enterprising among us to boldly go where they take us, meeting their demand for a nerdier future.

30. UPTOWN STONERS

When you think of pot smokers, you don't necessarily think of rich elites. Stoners are the losers in their moms' basements, wasting their time and playing video games. The marijuana industry has exploded to serve many different types of Americans, and one is the upscale elite. There are now uptown stoners: people with money and power, getting high and loving it. Uptown stoners may change the whole face of the developing pot industry and make it a lot sexier, glamorous, and profitable, not to mention legal.

Start-ups are catering to this demographic. There was always money in drugs, but now there could be big, big money in legal drugs. In some states, customers can now spend huge sums on their weed and everything that goes with it without fearing the law—and they aren't hesitating to shell out their money. This means that the next drug crisis could very well be with the uptown stoners who go too far too fast.

Limousine liberals and the wine-and-Brie cliques are now being replaced by this new kind of liberal who's open to regular, legalized drug use. In fact, studies show that the higher the household income, the higher the potential expenditure for the use of marijuana. Higher wages will bring on new highs. The full effects of this phenomenon have yet to play out—not just because of the law but because a lot of the more regular marijuana users are younger and have not reached their full earning power yet. It's possible that, like generations before them, they will become prudish once they have kids and give it up—at least until they become empty nesters. But alcohol became integrated into life in the suburbs, and it's possible that same process will occur over the next two decades.

There are still more downscale than upscale users of pot, so those opening their businesses will have to decide: Do you want to be Apple or Samsung? The latter: Do you want to deal with a lot of customers who are stretched to their limits and spending less on average, or do you want to cater to the smaller, upscale crowd that has extra money? The possibilities on the luxury end—for new kinds of restaurants, social clubs, and private clubs—are endless. There are already websites, schools, and seminars that cater to the would-be marijuana entrepreneur.

In places like Colorado, which did $760 million in weed sales in 2016, you can't deny the power of pot. Many start-ups have hopped into the space to help give uptown stoners the cachet and style that they want to associate with getting high. Beboe was one of these such companies. Beboe's leadership comes from a fashion and design background, and their products—like a fancy tin of pastille pot edibles—feel like fine jewelry or other very high-end goods, not some hash from a guy down the street. Beboe's products aren't carried in many stores, but one place they are in stock is in Aspen, the exclusive ski and resort town with some of the most expensive homes in the country and some of America's richest visitors.

Marijuana marketing to the upscale is taking all of the forms that usually work with today's upper class. First, some companies are trying to depict themselves as "farm to table," emphasizing that their products are completely organic. Others are building dispensaries and shops that have modern counters and a chic design.

Then there are the products. Expect to see lots of differentiation, not just regarding chocolates, cookies, brownies, and other food items, but regarding origin and gradations in quality. You can expect restaurants that sell whole meals laced with cannabis, and venues that will identify specifically as serving cannabis, while others will identify as serving alcohol. New York may regain its original name of New Amsterdam if it becomes the focus of marijuana tourism. Las Vegas will be adding legalized drug usage to its list of diversions.

Tech companies will be offering just the right kind of 3-D experience for those under the influence.

Overall, the weed industry right now has grown to $7.2 billion, but it's really in its infancy. The alcoholic beverage industry in the U.S. is over $200 billion in size. But while the low end could become quite competitive very quickly, industry profits could be on the high end of high. It's hard to see how this would not be a $50 billion industry in just the U.S. in ten years, with $5 billion to $10 billion in profits.

However, the tax man will not be far away. Colorado is already taking in about $200 million from marijuana taxes, and the Tax Foundation says that full U.S. legalization will bring in $28 billion dollars. Of course, a lot of that could come out of the liquor industry unless you believe that people will be smoking and drinking to the max.

Attitudes toward marijuana have changed dramatically in the last two decades. Working on the Hillary campaign in 2007, we uncovered an early Barack Obama video in which he pushed for legalization long before it was popular. We considered trumpeting it, but even by 2008, among Democrats, most already supported legalization, so we felt that raising it might give him more votes in the primary elections. America went from solidly against to slightly favoring legalization quickly, but without the kind of fervor on each side that issues like abortion and gun control have. The proponents were clever in using medical marijuana as a stalking horse for full legalization.

Even so, the rise of big marijuana won't be without worries. Driving under the influence remains a big concern. With just alcohol legalized, celebrities managed to create a fair amount of havoc over the years, with even deadly outcomes at times, based on their inability to control alcohol. When they can legally and openly use marijuana, we can only imagine what dangers await. You can expect social media to be fueled by the drug exploits of Hollywood stars, something that has already begun with high-profile DUIs. The lack of a test of intoxication level is one problem that needs to be solved. Without it, it's hard to tell who should be allowed to drive and who should be kept off the road.

Rich people have big wallets, and because of that they also face big liabilities. They will need extra insurance to protect themselves and their families in case things get out of hand. And, of course, demand for clinics to detox will also shoot up, especially for the uptown stoners who have jobs they need to keep. Likewise, employers will need places to send wayward employees.

It was only about one hundred years ago that America struggled with legalizing alcohol and voted a rare constitutional amendment to ban it, only to have to rescind its actions amid the crime spree that decision created. The same kind of friction has existed here surrounding the criminal gangs that import and sell illegal marijuana, and there will also be new problems that legalization creates among those who can't handle the new responsibility.

The risk of getting arrested for marijuana, however, has fallen sharply since 2000. According to the *Washington Post*, there was only one arrest for pot for every 550 purchases in 2002, and one arrest for every 1,090 purchases by 2013. Americans who might have been wary of the risk before—like this new wealthy population—might already feel less concerned about getting in trouble. Still, once it is officially legalized, everything changes. This potentially huge and highly profitable upscale stoner marketplace will open the floodgates all at once.

The wealthy have always had a penchant for exotic, expensive, and dangerous drugs. Think Robert Downey Jr.'s character in *Less Than Zero*: bored and rich and wasting away on cocaine. In one scene Clay, played by Andrew McCarthy, says to his rich, drugged-out, coke-addict girlfriend, "Are you happy, Blair? You don't look happy." To which she responds, "But do I look good?" Let's hope, above all, that the trend is not headed in this direction.

31. INTELLIGENT TV

Ten years ago, if you asked someone, "Do you watch a lot of television?" they would deny even touching their TV set. Spending time on your couch, flipping channels, was for kids and people who didn't want to pick up a book or that day's *New York Times*; the rise of TV represented the dumbing down of our culture. If you did watch your share of shows, you surely didn't admit it in public. And of course, you never, ever watched *The Apprentice*.

Fast-forward a decade, and college-educated elites are not only admitting to, but emphatically celebrating, the TV they watch. Conversation shifted from "You don't watch *Survivor*, do you?" to "*You watch* Breaking Bad*?!*" These TV-loving elites have new-season launch parties and final-episode costume fetes to celebrate their love for *Homeland* or *Game of Thrones*, complete with snacks and cocktails that celebrate certain characters or plotlines.

Behind this drastic change are numbers, economics, and incentives—it didn't just happen. Satellite and cable TV, the latter of which reached almost two out of three households before people started cutting the cord, changed the viewing landscape from just a few channels to an unlimited number. At first that spawned more news and more sports. But, over time, it revolutionized the economics of entertainment content.

When the funnel for content was narrow, moving through a handful of networks, a successful show had to have enormous viewership. A network hit such as *Seinfeld* would regularly reach 22 percent of all households. Television advertising was broad, rather than targeted, and the jokes had to be jokes that wide swaths of the public would enjoy and find funny. TV was geared to the average intellect or below, often with plenty of slapstick. Plots were simple, and something like *Masterpiece Theatre* was for the snobbish elites that would not be caught dead watching the vast wasteland of TV.

Part of the cable TV proposition was the idea of a premium channel. HBO started out as a way to see movies earlier than you would on regular TV because you paid a premium, in the form of a monthly fee, for the privilege. As movies alone became less of a unique draw, HBO and later Showtime turned to unique series as a way to attract more subscribers. *The Sopranos* was born, and along with it a grittier, more complex, more intelligent approach to an hour of TV. It was unique and compelling enough to pry $12 a month out of the rich city dwellers who had access to it. And the formula has been repeated over and over again: an antihero star; a family that knows what's going on but are also just "regular" enough, with their school plays and soccer games; the business associates who would just as soon kill everybody to make an extra buck. Throw in some swearing and a little sex you don't get on network TV, and you're there, whether it's *Narcos* (even Pablo Escobar loves his mother on TV) or *Breaking Bad*, with its high school teacher turned drug kingpin.

A decade past *The Sopranos*, and channels had multiplied, causing the TV audience to split up. From then on, people realized that TV, like technology, could have a long tail. It was previously not economically viable for a show to attract just a half million or a million viewers, but as channels proliferated, niche shows became a real business proposition, especially if they could bring in the core demographics advertisers craved. Add international and rerun distribution, and content for small audiences started to mushroom. TV had discovered the microtrend.

The number of shows exploded from about one hundred in 1975 on your television set to hundreds of programs at your fingertips. This did not just create intelligent TV; it also created room on the other end of the spectrum for really crude and trashy TV. Of course, TV was often seen as the lowest common denominator, so that's not the big news here. What's more interesting, and increasingly more valuable, is how the upper end or premium space has continued to expand.

Steven Johnson's book *Everything Bad Is Good for You: How Today's Popular Culture Is Actually Making Us Smarter* might explain how television has become smarter from a storytelling standpoint: part of the reason recent TV shows are so good these days is that primary narrative threads are more elaborate, each character with its own clearly defined "story arc." First there were shows like *Mary Tyler Moore*, then mindless shows like *Three's Company*. *Hill Street Blues* started to play with some plot multi-threading.

Compare today's shows to the old *Starsky & Hutch* episodes, for example. *Starsky & Hutch* was a show with a couple of main characters and a fairly simplistic linear plotline in each episode: it started with a comedic subplot, went into some drama related to catching the week's bad guys, then ended with a comedic subplot. Compare that to a television show like *Game of Thrones*, where you need your own playbook and set of family trees to keep up. (I have a friend with a spreadsheet of theories.) But that's the point: television has found its way and learned to challenge our best storytelling senses. And that makes for some great dinner conversations.

Intelligent TV does not affect just viewers; it also affects those whose careers are now colorfully depicted, whether they are billionaire hedge fund managers or crafty lawyers. I once did a study for the New York City Police Department, concerned that police shows like *Kojak* were creating unrealistic impressions of the police with the public. They wondered if people now thought the police were a bunch of wild operators who wrecked cars and roughed up suspects like the police on TV. I polled both police and members of the public. The results were stunning: the public had the same views of the police regardless of how much cop TV they watched. The police, on the other hand, were deeply affected by the shows. The more cop dramas that police watched, the more cars they tended to wreck on the job. There's no question that in Washington many will now measure their success and techniques against what they think Frank Underwood from *House of Cards* would have done in similar circumstances.

In the last few years, streaming content started to make its way to the public with Amazon Video, iTunes, Hulu, and of course Netflix. Cable TV made people pay for a tasting menu with a lot of courses, whether they ate them or not. There were a few pay-per-view events and movies, but they were limited in number by technology. Netflix has adapted a similar all-you-can-eat model for the cord-cutting generation, while iTunes illustrates the pay-per-unit business model. Amazon created a mix of both, giving Prime members the older content for free and charging per piece for the new stuff.

It's no question that streaming services represent a huge threat to cable, and yet there are limits to the economic advantages of one business model versus the other. Typically, the all-you-can-eat philosophy tends to win out with American consumers. Witness AT&T and Verizon eventually both having to offer Unlimited plans due to competition, even though it benefits the high-volume user. Same thing with the power of Spotify versus Apple's model of paying per song. We are an all-you-can-eat nation.

It turns out that much of the internet infrastructure today is built just to deliver content from Netflix, YouTube, and other video providers. One minute of video essentially uses all of the internet bandwidth that *years* of e-mail would require. In fact, 40 percent of all internet traffic today is generated by Netflix alone. So-called Net neutrality is, in my view, little more than a Netflix/YouTube welfare policy. But they won the war, and, as a result, video is essentially privileged content, so it's multiplying.

It didn't take long for these new alternative providers of entertainment to realize that providing the same movies at the same time as everyone else was not much of a differentiating proposition. Streaming services, as a result of this discovery, took the same route that HBO did a decade earlier. They've started to develop their own original content and are creating more and more shows. In the third quarter of 2017, Netflix reported having 109.25 million streaming subscribers all over the world compared to 11.17 million in 2011. The company started launching its own content in 2012 and has reaped major rewards. In 2016, Netflix reported having an annual revenue of $8.83 billion. And Netflix and Hulu are now winning Emmys, turning the entertainment world upside down with megahits like *Stranger Things*.

Technology today enables us to consume TV in ways that allow for more and more differentiation of the marketplace. You no longer have to share one screen with your brother; you can watch on your own tablet or iPhone from almost anywhere. More people are watching their own shows at whatever time of day they prefer; currently it's five hours a day total per average American, which means television producers can win big if they have even a small following. You can sit downstairs and watch *Downton Abbey* while your kids watch *Game of Thrones* in another room.

If you are a writer, actor, or actress—or an aspiring one who's still stuck waiting tables—all of this is great news for you. The number of writing and acting jobs has increased along with the number of shows, opening up opportunities for people who would most likely never get a break otherwise. In fact, the cost of talent has escalated so much that companies like Disney have pioneered the idea of deliberately using no-name talent and teaching them what they need to know to save money. It has often worked—sometimes too well, as unknowns then became huge talents with huge fees attached once again.

What's being produced for the small screen now rivals what's being produced for the big screen, and this is causing some added disruptions. For Hollywood, making movies that will get people out of their houses has become harder and more expensive, increasingly driven by massive special effects. At the same time, making a TV show has become simpler and cheaper. At the end of the day, it's likely that China will save Hollywood from Silicon Valley: consumers there are just getting exposed to the wider world of big entertainment, and they are happy to get out of the house and go to the movies in record-breaking numbers.

Intelligent TV is here to stay. It's got a business model and viewers, from millennials through baby boomers, who have more education today and want complex, adult-oriented fare. It's presenting Hollywood with new challenges, yet at the same time billions of new dollars are flowing into content creation, expanding the overall industry. Fueling all this excitement is the phenomenon of binge-watching—especially among the footloose and fancy-free—which can lead to the breakout of a new series literally overnight. But if you find yourself on plot overload, don't worry: you will always be able to tune in to *The Bachelorette*, season 17.

32. KOREAN BEAUTY

If you're on Facebook these days, you might see an unusual-looking advertisement. It all started when actress Drew Barrymore put on a beauty mask that, in just ten minutes, seemed to drop her age by 10 years. The video she recorded caused a frenzy for the product, called Hanacure. The Hanacure cosmetics mask is just one example of a Korean beauty trend that exploded in the United States. With viral fame and fans of "K-Beauty" at an all-time high, places like Sephora are booming through the successes of the newest Korean beauty mask, lip peel, and snail cream. Their top five best sellers? Klairs Freshly Juiced Vitamin C Serum, Son & Parker Beauty Water, Missha Time Revolution First Treatment Essence Intensive Moist, Cosrx Acne Pimple Master Patch, and Missha Super Aqua Cell Renew Snail Cream. According to cult K-Beauty site Soko Glam, snails have never been chicer.

American women are hungrier for beauty products than ever. Companies are eager to give them what they want, and to do so in a more diverse and inclusive way than ever before. From celebrities like Rihanna and her makeup line Fenty Beauty, to Kylie Jenner and her company Kylie Cosmetics, to other influencers creating and endorsing lip palettes, face washes, and night creams, the typical American woman has started to purchase a lot more than cold cream and mascara.

The explosion of Korean Beauty in American retailers is a small example of the globalization of industries increasingly of interest to American women. It also shows the power of new cultures to influence American consumers and markets. Korean Beauty's success outside of Korea also shows the power of the international consumer. With global standards of beauty changing, and an ability to order products from all over the world, starting a business in one country could make you an overnight success in another.

Over the past few years, South Korea has exploded as the go-to spot for beauty and skin care trends, like sheet masks that are all over Instagram and the shelves of Sephora and Bluemercury. The hashtag #sheetmask on Instagram yields over 200,000 posts, and #koreanbeauty yields nearly half a million. The sales support the frenzy, too. Exports of South Korean beauty products to Southeast Asian countries alone increased by 31.6 percent between 2012 and 2013, and surely that number has surged. The overall Korean cosmetics market—$7.3 billion—is projected to post an average of 10 percent growth each year by 2020. That's the GDP of some countries.

The amount of money being spent around the globe on Korean beauty products is astounding. Total production and exports of Ko-

32.1: Korean Cosmetics Exports (in Billions of U.S. Dollars), 2013–2016

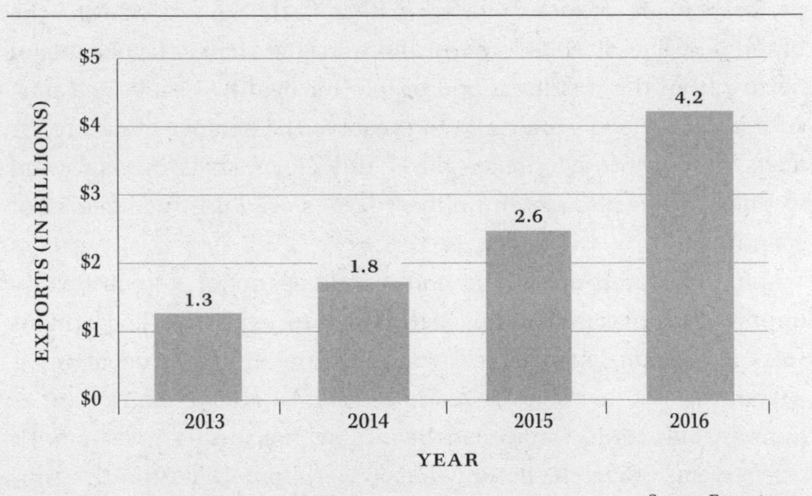

Source: Export.gov

rean cosmetics increased by 8.2 percent and 61.6 percent respectively from 2015 to 2016. The graph on the previous page shows the explosion: in 2013, Korea exported only $1.3 billion in cosmetics. In 2017, it was estimated that the Korean beauty market was a $13 billion enterprise. Research firm Mintel predicts that the Korean beauty market will grow steadily through 2020.

One Korean company in particular, Innisfree, has become a standout in the marketplace. *Vogue*, capital of all things beauty and fashion, reported in August 2017 that the brand, which had started as a Korean cult favorite, was coming to the United States. This was after years of American women ordering Innisfree products on Amazon or asking friends who lived in Asia to send back their vitamin C sheet masks. Innisfree shops are on dozens of street corners in Seoul, but in the American market they will be open with a two-story boutique in Union Square in Manhattan—precious and crucial prime real estate with a hefty price tag. It's a statement about the brand's already existing market in the U.S.

Innisfree follows the tradition of many Korean beauty products: simplicity, cleanliness, and a perfect complexion. And, increasingly, American women are turning to "simple" (though product-intensive) beauty routines to achieve a desire for perfect skin, as opposed to a perfectly made-up face. Innisfree caters to that; on its website, the brand describes itself as "a natural brand that shares the benefits of nature from the pristine island of Jeju for healthy beauty and pursues an eco-friendly green life to preserve the balance of nature." It feeds directly into a desire for "pure" and "clean" ideals of beauty and wellness, as we also saw in wellness freaks. And it is fueling a lot of spending.

Luxury brands are taking note of the desire for Korean Beauty imports—all over the world. Selfridges, an expensive department store in London, launched its own mini Korean Beauty department within the store's cosmetics section itself. American luxury retailer Neiman Marcus has a Korean Beauty section on its website with pricey items to match, like Sulwhasoo Herblinic EX Restorative Ampoules at a whopping $200 for only five capsules.

It's not just destination stores like Neiman Marcus where you can apply lip scrubs from Seoul; the trend is also trickling down to the everyday American shopper. Target now has its own Korean Beauty sheet masks and line, and drugstore chain CVS (more than 9,600 stores nationwide) has a collaboration with a popular Korean Beauty brand, Peach & Lily. Even everyone's favorite bulk retailer, Costco, is carrying Korean Beauty products.

Over the past few decades, Western women have become more interested in Eastern cosmetics, and vice versa. As noted above, it's all about achieving an impossible ideal of "perfect" skin—or, as it's known in Korea, "glass skin"—the newest way to display health and thus wealth and superiority. "Glass Skin is this idea of transparent and translucent skin," according to Peach & Lily's founder, Alicia Yoon. "It's a sign of youthfulness and it's one of the most strived-for qualities in Korea," Yoon told the *Malay Mail Online*. It also means more products: "glass skin" is supposedly achieved by exfoliating (one product), then moisturizing with an "intense serum" (two), a face mask (three), and a cream (four). The Korean ideal of small pores and looking "naturally" perfect is part of the new complex beauty ideal also being leveled against American women. And since Korean Beauty regimens require an average of ten separate steps to achieve results, stores from the high-end to the chain are moving a lot more products.

The drive for perfect skin is also making a lot of money for the Korean brands. For beauty products, it used to be that French stuff was tops. Now we want something newer and even more involved.

We can't talk about Korean Beauty without discussing the shocking amount of plastic surgery that exists in Korea as well. Sure, it might be about "glass skin" and being pure and natural, but a lot of the time that means going under the knife to achieve this impossible ideal. The most popular plastic surgery in Korea is a double-eyelid procedure to make eyes appear larger, rounder, and more Western. This has been going on for decades. Around the world, South Korea ranks third in the largest number of total face and head procedures, behind Brazil (number one) and the U.S. (number two). South Korea accounts for a bit over 8 percent of all face and head procedures, with a fixation on what's called a "small face": a narrow and, again, more Western-looking face.

A 2015 *New Yorker* profile highlighted the proliferation of plastic surgery in South Korea: "By some estimates, the country has the highest rate of plastic surgery per capita in the world." It's also young Korean women. Between one-third and one-fifth of all women in Seoul have had plastic surgery, and for women in their twenties it might be more than 50 percent. The wave of plastic surgery began after the Korean War, after American occupational forces offered free reconstructive surgeries and David Ralph Millard, the chief plastic surgeon for the U.S. Marine Corps, perfected the "blepharoplasty," the eyelid surgery noted above.

American celebrities and other influencers are also crazy for K-Beauty—from Drew Barrymore and the Hanacure mask to Emma Stone using a lip mask—but the converse is not the same in Korea. For marketing beauty products in Korea itself, our "Kardashian ideal" doesn't work. Kendall Jenner, considered a supermodel in America and the face of countless beauty and fashion spreads, was a dud when she headlined the Estée Lauder marketing efforts in Asia.

There are lessons from the success of Korean Beauty that can be a map for other beauty trends and brands. When it comes to politics and policy, it's possible that cosmetics from other countries could become a political football. In China, a ban on Korean cosmetics ended up being the Chinese response to some U.S. actions in South Korea. "China banned imports of 19 Korean cosmetics products amid rising tensions over Korea's decision to allow the deployment of a U.S. Terminal High Altitude Area Defense (THAAD) battery here," according to the *South China Morning Post*. It's also unclear whether or not these products work: they aren't subjected to some of America's testing requirements.

Korean beauty products are in their first wave of export to America, so it's possible that Korean plastic surgery will be right around the corner. Shortly we could find Westerners heading to Korea in droves for surgery holidays, as "medical tourism" to other countries has grown. American women will also keep shelling out, possibly even more, for beauty. South Korean women "spend twice as much of their income on beauty products and make-up than their American counterparts," according to an article by the BBC. The market is also expanding beyond just women. American men may become the next beauty-hungry category, with K-Beauty targeting beard treatments or pores for men's skin care. South Korean men spend the most on skin care of any around the world.

The Koreans have been incredibly on target in understanding global and American marketplaces. Samsung is the only company other than Apple able to dominate the smartphone marketplace, and now Korean companies have boldly entered a quintessentially American marketplace with great success. They tend to study what we do here in America; increasingly, we may have to study what South Koreans are working on to be better marketers and to catch the next wave of trends.

33. MODERN ANNIE OAKLEYS

Women in America are better educated, better paid, the majority in college, and . . . buying more guns. Annie Oakley was perhaps America's best-known woman sharpshooter, and she had a vision: "I would like to see every woman know how to handle guns as naturally as they know how to handle babies." This hasn't happened quite yet, but strides have been made. The gender gap in guns is closing.

It seemed a little counterintuitive when the NRA launched a TV ad featuring American conservative political commentator Dana Loesch, but the ad proved a somewhat controversial success at getting attention for her cause. Loesch believes in the Second Amendment, loves her guns, and packs convention halls at the NRA's annual meetings. She also believes that women, just as much as men, should

33.1: Gun Ownership (Household and Individual) by Gender, 2015

Q: "Do you, or does anyone in your household, own a gun?"

BASE: ALL QUALIFIED RESPONDENTS	TOTAL	MEN	WOMEN
YES (NET)	43%	47%	39%
Yes, I do	29%	41%	18%
Yes, someone else in my household	20%	11%	28%
NO	57%	53%	61%

Source: Harris Poll, December 2015

get out there and shoot. Says Loesch, "Women have always had the right to bear arms; we have had the right to bear arms before we had the right to vote . . . Women must use their rights; the quickest way to lose them is to not use them."

Getting good numbers on gun ownership is difficult, as people in the same household often share a gun. The exact number of gun-owning women is hard to pin down as a result: two studies from this decade showed that 12 percent of women individually own guns. The Pew Research Center put that rate at 22 percent in 2017. And a Harris poll reported the figure as 18 percent in late 2015. And while the figure itself may be fuzzy, multiple studies agree that the number of women gun owners is on the rise. Gun manufacturers have taken notice, and at first they responded with guns of different colors. A pink pistol isn't nearly enough, though: not only do women gun owners like the "military-style" look, they also care more about the shape and feel of the gun, not the color scheme.

33.2: Personal Gun Ownership by Gender, 2013–2017

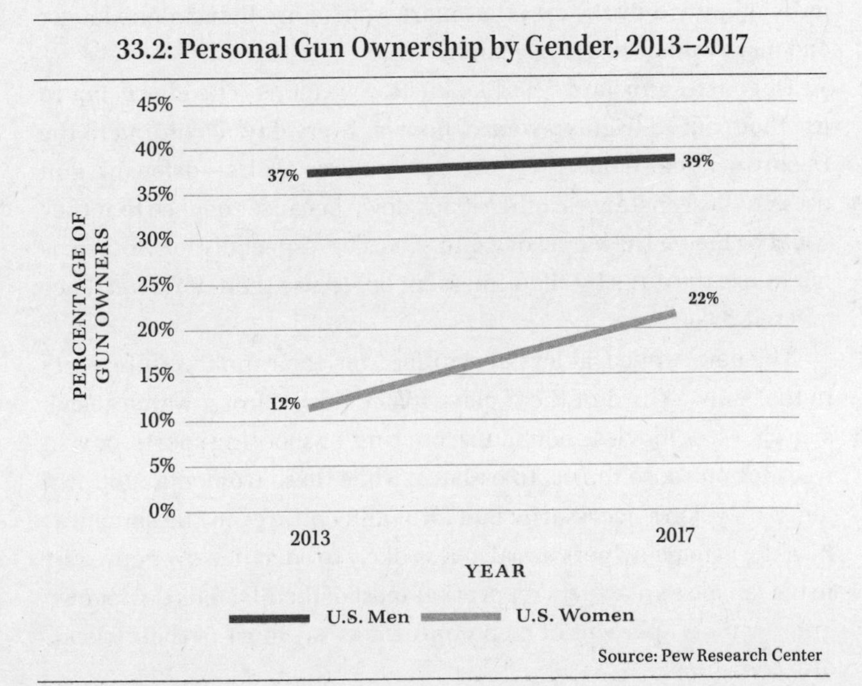

Source: Pew Research Center

The growth in female gun ownership coincides with women pouring into the military and joining the police force, professions where they are handling guns regularly and need to be proficient in firearms. Women were 17 percent of active-duty military in 2015—up from 12 percent in 1990. And while one study found that women make up only 6 percent to 8 percent of police officers, in smaller communities women were found to make up more than 20 percent of the police force.

These new Annie Oakleys, according to hobbyist magazine *Guns & Ammo*, are younger, less urban, and buying most often for protection. The number one gun of choice of women is a semiautomatic handgun, followed by a good old-fashioned shotgun. Half of all women gun ownership is in the South, while far fewer women in the West own guns.

Compared to other race and gender cohorts, African-American women had the highest percent increase in concealed carry permits in Texas from 2000 to 2016. Yet less than a third of black families view gun ownership positively. It's more out of fear, as recent police shootings and an uptick in racial tension drive these gun sales. They're also pushed upward by the fact that more women are living alone longer and more women are single parents.

Of course, guns are a bit like nuclear weapons. The idea is not to use them but to frighten your opponent. Every day, according to the Department of Justice, there are two hundred DGUs—defensive gun uses. In those instances, others back down because they see that they could be facing the barrel of a gun. The idea, especially for women, is not to use the guns by shooting them but to use them for deterrence and self-defense.

The new Annie Oakleys also differ from their male counterparts in that only a third of them play violent video games; watch television shows or movies about guns, hunting, or shooting sports; or visit websites on those topics. In essence, while these women might own guns, they don't necessarily buy into "gun culture" in the same way men do. Female owners are also less likely to socialize over guns: six in ten female gun owners report that most of their friends do not own guns, while 54 percent of men gun-owners say most of their friends also own guns.

Women also buy their first gun at an older age than men do. On average, women report buying their first gun at age 27, while men typically get theirs at 19. Men are also 43 percent more likely to keep their guns loaded, compared to 29 percent of women. But women are equally as likely as men to carry their weapons with them outside of their homes: 26 percent for both genders.

Some women see guns as an issue of empowerment. Antonia Okafor, as a young, black, conservative gun owner, said in her *New York Times* opinion piece "Why I Bring My Gun to School": "I felt empowered to be holding a tool that could protect me physically, and I was determined to learn how to use it responsibly. It was a relief to know that I could shoot if I had to, even though I would never use my gun unless it was a last means of self-defense."

According to statistics from the Rape, Abuse & Incest National Network, sexual assaults occur against Americans every 98 seconds on average. And those are just the ones that are reported. Eighty percent of those women are under 30 years old. In 2016, *Marie Claire* magazine ran a survey of 5,000 women in conjunction with the Harvard Injury Control Research Center and found that 18 percent of

33.3: Harvard Injury Control Research Center Poll Results, 2016

IN THE PAST FIVE YEARS, THE FOLLOWING PERCENTAGE OF WOMEN HAVE:	
Become more interested in owning a gun	18%
Become less interested in owning a gun	18%
Shot a gun for any reason	17%
Gone shooting at a shooting range	13%
Attended a gun show or expo	5%
Given or received a gun as a gift	5%
Gone hunting with a gun	4%
Gotten a gun for the first time	4%
Witnessed gun violence or the threat of it in person	4%
Obtained one or more guns in addition to those they already owned	3%
Lobbied for gun rights	2%

Source: *Marie Claire*

women in the study have become more interested in owning a gun, and 13 percent have gone to a gun-shooting range.

While most women are not interested in gun sport, more women are enjoying it. The *New York Times* concluded that target shooting and hunting by women went up nearly 50 percent from 2001 to 2011, with over 5 million women participating annually. And according to data from the NRA, there has been an 85 percent increase in women who hunt—a signal to gun manufacturers and shooting ranges to diversify their offerings. Gun sales to women have risen in concert. In a survey last year by the National Shooting Sports Foundation, 73 percent of gun dealers said the number of female customers had gone up since 2011.

Politically, if you own a gun, you are likely a Republican. If you are a woman and own a gun, your chances are increased that you will be a Republican, but it's not necessarily a sure thing. Both men and women gun owners in America say gun ownership is part of their freedoms. For women it's 70 percent of gun owners, and 77 percent for men, according to Pew. The new Annie Oakleys tend to be more open to the debate around the Second Amendment: in general, women are more supportive of policies that might restrict their right to bear arms. Over half of Republican women and Republican-leaning women also support banning assault weapons (60 percent), whereas only a third of their male counterparts are interested in bringing that law back.

In the Washington, D.C., area, an overwhelmingly liberal area, a group called the Shooting Divas of DMV goes to the range together—and even have child care worked out for those participating. More women are banding together around their enjoyment of guns, and it will likely influence key shooting-related industries like hunting and target ranges to be more women-friendly. From the way the equipment is made to the spaces for people to enjoy using guns—this will all be transformed with women in mind. Most gun range owners are male and are set up to cater to men. Gun manufacturers have typically adapted their designs to the size of men's hands, and they are already adjusting their products. A brand called GunGoddess now sells American women gun-related paraphernalia. Whether it's women starting to own their own firing ranges or to continue refining new equipment and apparel built for a woman's body, there are many ways big and small in which the industry will be shaped by its newest enthusiasts.

The new Annie Oakleys are a large part of the National Rifle Association's fan base. Even the hiring of a woman spokesperson—and a lightning rod one at that, in Dana Loesch—is significant. And Loesch also has a say in policy: about a year ago she became the NRA's "special adviser on women's policy." The NRA recognizes the money being poured into the gun industry by American women and has held its own Concealed Carry Fashion Show—for both men and women. Of note, nearly all the models on Pinterest boards for concealed carry or modeling certain concealed carry clothing are white. That is likely to change: as noted above, the largest growing subset of women with guns in America are black.

Gun culture among American women is also increasingly prevalent in popular culture, from television to movies—and not just among "conservative" women. From Mindy Kaling's character on *The Mindy Project* to Robin from *How I Met Your Mother*, women in sitcoms are discussing and keeping guns. Both shows are situational comedies, not intense dramas with any violence. We also see more heroines and femme fatales (a long-standing trope) in film—from gun-wielding women like Lara Croft in the new *Tomb Raider* movie to Charlize Theron in *Atomic Blonde*. We are getting more used to seeing women with guns, beyond playing the roles of cop or hit woman. This is also becoming part of the draw, visible in the marketing campaigns of films like *Atomic Blonde*, which featured a poster of Theron holding a gun. Also influential offscreen are American women like Sarah Palin and Joni Ernst, well-known for toting weapons.

Women have come a long way in the gun professions and gun ownership. The change has affected the marketplace, politics, and self-defense. Even as the push for more gun control laws has ramped up following recent mass shootings, gun ownership is just as prevalent as ever, now boosted by the new Annie Oakleys.

34. ARMCHAIR PREPPERS

Two very different events have led to a revival of survivalism: 9/11 and the banking crisis of 2009—both man-made. On top of that there was Hurricane Katrina, the storms of 2017, and the Mexico City earthquake, all of which rekindled fear of nature.

These terrifying events have prompted a new group of Americans—already in a pessimistic state of mind—to wonder what they would do to survive if the worst happened. Part of this is reflected in the surge of gun purchases. Another part is visible in the allure of holding gold and silver in case of economic collapse.

Add to this brew the tensions with North Korea and ISIS, along with TV shows like *The Last Ship* and *Designated Survivor*—which speculate on what life could be like if another bubonic plague hit or if terrorists blew up our government—and you can understand why the conversation at every dinner table might eventually turn to what the family should do in the event of a national or regional emergency.

The armchair preppers are people who are stuffing money and gold under their mattresses again, building safe rooms in their houses, sticking guns in hidden parts of their closets, getting their "bug-out" bags ready, and waiting. Americans in fear, stockpiling cans of food for the Apocalypse, isn't exactly new. Look at the 1950s, with its bomb shelters and kids hiding under desks in schools, its movies that reflected the fear and uncertainty we felt at that time.

The Doomsday Clock—created in 1947 and maintained by the *Bulletin of Atomic Scientists*—is a symbol of this fear of the end, from nuclear war to climate change. Now we don't just have to face the

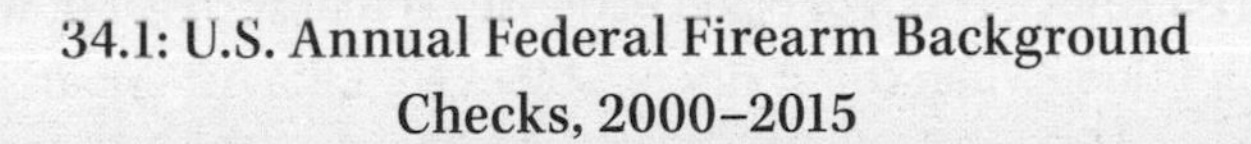

34.1: U.S. Annual Federal Firearm Background Checks, 2000–2015

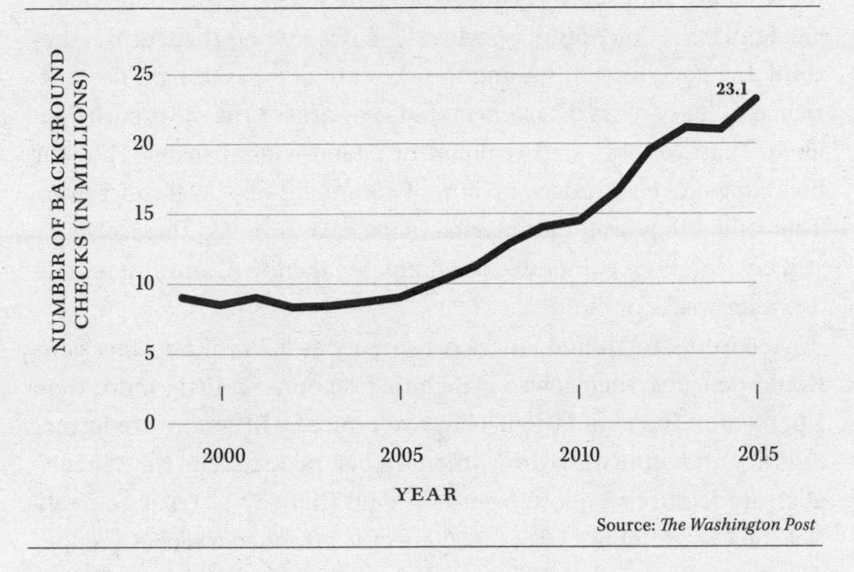

Source: *The Washington Post*

threat of war with North Korea—although in a recent poll 69 percent of Americans feared it—we have the world gone mad with unprecedented natural disasters. The Doomsday Clock currently sits at its closest-ever-to-midnight reading: just 2.5 minutes away.

So it's no surprise that the fear of the fifties would at some point meet the ease of the digital age. You can flip to a website like the New Survivalist and get a full checklist of everything you need to do to be prepared for the next disaster. They have guns, clothes, water, food, money, batteries, and a host of other items ready to go, and locations where they will go to survive, complete with weapons cache.

There are luxury companies for armchair preppers ready and waiting, if you will, to serve the current fears. Preppi, a New York start-up, sells $5,000 disaster preparedness bags and proclaims that they make the best for when the worst happens.

Most households are underprepared for even the simplest and most common emergencies, let alone game enders. Homes or apartments typically have a lot of required fire sensors but not a lot of training on what to do if one goes off—or even how to get down from the second floor when the stairs are blocked. Like American companies that are almost always unprepared for hacks, the average American family lives on optimism when it comes to their own future; they think the government is going to take care of everything. The experience so far of most disasters is that they are for the most part right about that: we have had regional or island-wide disasters, but the breakdown of civil order or chain of command has been short-lived. That said, the power and internet grids have revealed themselves to still be a lot more vulnerable to complete takedown, and can remain down for weeks or months.

According to Yahoo! Finance, as many as 3.7 million Americans would consider themselves armchair preppers—a little more than 1 percent of the population. They are typically fit; many are former military and often anti-government in perspective. The New Survivalist site features a quote from Ron Paul that says, "Trust Yourself, Not the Government." Over 30,000 people attended a recent prepper convention.

The new breed of high-tech, high-powered armchair preppers is quite different from those more downscale, bunker-in-the-woods types. As Evan Osnos of the *New Yorker* reported in an in-depth look at Doomsday preppers, "In recent years survivalism has expanded to more affluent quarters, taking root in Silicon Valley and New York City, among technology executives, hedge-fund managers, and others in their economic cohort." They feature Steve Huffman, the founder and CEO of Reddit, who underwent laser eye surgery not only to see better but also because he hoped "it will improve his odds of surviving a disaster, whether natural or man-made." He believed that glasses and contact lenses will be almost impossible to get if there is a disaster.

On a global scale, Osnos observed that many a prepper is purchasing real estate in New Zealand. Thousands of Americans registered with New Zealand's immigration authorities in the week after Donald Trump was elected, starting down the path toward becoming a Kiwi if the world is flipped upside down. But Trump hasn't been the only factor: wealthy paranoiacs from across the globe are buying up land in this remote country because it has adequate resources and is protected from short-term global warming. "In the past six years," Osnos reported, "nearly a thousand foreigners have acquired residency there under programs that mandate certain types of investment of at least a million dollars." New Zealanders do not appear to be thrilled about this influx of armchair preppers, either.

Closer to home, Revolutionary Realty is one such place that specializes in real estate for those moving to the American Redoubt—a term coined by survivalist author James Wesley, Rawles (the comma is deliberate), that refers to an area of the Pacific Northwest including Idaho, Montana, Wyoming, and the eastern parts of Washington and Oregon. Hundreds of properties in the American Redoubt have been sold within the last couple of years. People are drawn by specific off-the-grid features: at least two water sources, alternative energy sources such as solar panels, secure storage space for several years' worth of supplies, and a defensible location away from city centers and main roads.

A scan of the ads on prepper sites shows a market for the obvious: seeds to generate food, guns, gold, and lots of emergency kits. The vendors look smallish and the ads by and large amateur. The survival industry is still in its infancy, and no big brands have really moved into the area despite its growing size. But there is real potential for larger forces to enter and for the industry to explode into the mainstream.

Outside of the intense prepper marketplace and the super-rich clients, there is room in a typical household to improve their readiness for what's most likely to happen in their area (i.e., floods in Miami or Louisiana and earthquakes in California). That would mean a kit that could get you through a few days without food, water, money, power, or internet service. The Tesla Powerwall, for instance, is likely to revolutionize power preparedness for people who don't have or want to have a generator.

Today we are also more likely to have the world's first digital disaster. The most likely scenario would be a civilization-threatening cyberattack that takes down brokerage houses, banks, and maybe the entire stock market. Such an event that wiped out the monetary system could cause widespread panic: the IRAs and brokerage accounts that today hold most non-real estate wealth in the country could become locked up—or worse. Such a financial disaster would destroy the economy, the ability to trade, and bring the monetary system to a halt. It would most likely be the surest way for a foreign power to create chaos. The implication of this is that it might not be such a bad idea to have some gold and silver at home after all.

The armchair preppers are part attitude, part real preparedness. Most people don't expect to be able to make it on their own if everything collapses. But most people want to be able to survive a terrorist attack, a limited nuclear exchange, or the next big flood or earthquake with some higher degree of control. Plus fear of monetary collapse is always underappreciated. These armchair preppers may seem like kooks to some, but their fears are probably more justified—or at least worth considering—than we appreciate.

Section 5

POLITICS

---

35. Old Economy Voters

36. Happy Pessimists

37. Closet Conservatives

38. Impressionable Elites Revisited

39. Militant Dreamers Revisited

40. Newest Americans

41. Couch Potato Voters

35. OLD ECONOMY VOTERS

I would not have predicted the twists and turns that the politics of the manufacturing class have taken since I worked on successful campaigns for Bill Clinton in 1996 and Tony Blair in 2005. Both of those leaders won because they convinced their respective working classes that the future—for their jobs and in general—lay in the new economy and greater globalization of trade. Blair and Clinton were champions of the new professional class, but they held on to their working-class bases against the more elitist Tories and Republicans.

In the mid-1990s in the U.S. and the U.K., manufacturing jobs stabilized as the new economy was taking root. That was the time to enact policies that ensured tech centers and other potential boons of the new economy could take hold across the country. President Clinton ran a new-markets tour with tax incentive programs whose intent was to make sure that the new economy reached more areas—but it didn't take hold. This effort was way too small to counteract the forces that had been set in motion.

Following NAFTA and the start of the new millennium, manufacturing jobs plummeted. From 2000, after a period of gaining manufacturing jobs, they essentially collapsed. By 2010 these jobs shrunk in America from nearly 18 million to 11 million. The same thing happened in the U.K., where manufacturing jobs dropped from 4 million in 2000 to 2.6 million in 2010.

This was the single most devastating period for manufacturing jobs, probably, since the Great Depression. In a very short time, millions of people lost their livelihoods, and Presidents Bush and Obama all but ignored the problem, as the overall economy was creating jobs. Pressure was building, but no one was paying much attention in the rush to create a big tech economy.

At that same time, several other major trends were compounding the loss of these jobs. A lot of American kids were leaving their hometowns, say, in coal-mining country for education and jobs in urban areas—a movement that both compounded economic problems and split up families in destructive ways. The busiest travel day of the year is the day before Thanksgiving, because people are traveling simply to be with their families, now typically spread out across the country.

These were also years of significant influx of immigration. While there were 31 million immigrants living in the U.S. in 2000, by 2015 this population had grown to more than 43 million. Similarly, in the U.K., the foreign-born population went from 5.3 million in 2004 to 9.1 million in 2016. Economic and military crises, including the war in Syria, brought millions of refugees to continental Europe—a phenomenon keenly observed by EU skeptics in the U.K.

The last notable trend was a period of wage stagnation. The $54,398, median household income in the U.S. in 2014 was around $4,000 *lower* than it was in 2000 (although it has since increased). Median income in the U.K. rose during this same period but at limited levels—from £22,000 to £26,000—and many still felt left behind in the new economy.

Loss of manufacturing jobs due to NAFTA, kids leaving and not coming back, an influx of immigration, and wage stagnation for those who had jobs—these hit all at once. While most immigrants settled on the coasts, the fear of immigration and its effects was enough to create an electoral tinderbox.

Then Trump came along and lit the match.

He ran against both the Democrats and the pro-trade, pro-immigration Republican elites. A recent *New York Times* article put it succinctly: "Like Mr. Obama, Mr. Trump ran against the establishment—[his] views on immigration, trade, China, crime, guns and Islam all had considerable appeal to white working-class Democratic voters, according to Pew Research data. It was a far more appealing message than old Republican messages about abortion, same-sex marriage and the social safety net."

The left would like to say that it is racism that drove the largely white working class to revolt. But many of those same voters cast their ballots for Barack Obama, and before that for Bill Clinton. What drove them was largely economics first, then the interplay of trade, immigration, law and order, and the sectoral dislocation of their communities. These changes were deep and profound, and they accelerated in the ten to fifteen years before the Trump election.

When I worked in the U.K. in 2005, the opposition's consultant, Lynton Crosby, had come from Australia, where fanning the immigration issue was a tried-and-true strategy. He tried to run that same playbook in the U.K. in 2005, but Britain was not ready for the harsher angle, and Tony Blair won with a moderate view on immigration. Fast-forward, though, and you see the diverging microtrends at work: on the one hand, London elects Sadiq Khan, the first Muslim mayor of a major Western city; on the other, the countryside roundly approves Brexit, with growing anti-immigration sentiment a critical part of that vote.

While London has embraced the new economy and globalization, every other major region other than Scotland and Northern Ireland voted for Leave rather than Remain. And just when it looked like the Labour Party was going to be impossible to beat after Blair's decade as prime minister, that party is now fractured and has been out of power across two election cycles now. The same voter groups (the old-economy voters) on two continents stood up and reasserted their power, putting major stakes into the heart of progressive plans.

The U.K. isn't alone in the rise of the old-economy voter. In France we're also seeing the rise of National Front, a hard-right party. Support is drawn largely from non-college-educated Catholic men and those who oppose engagement in the global economy. While Marine Le Pen lost the election, polls show she had 40 percent support among

35.1: French Support for National Front by Demographics, 2016

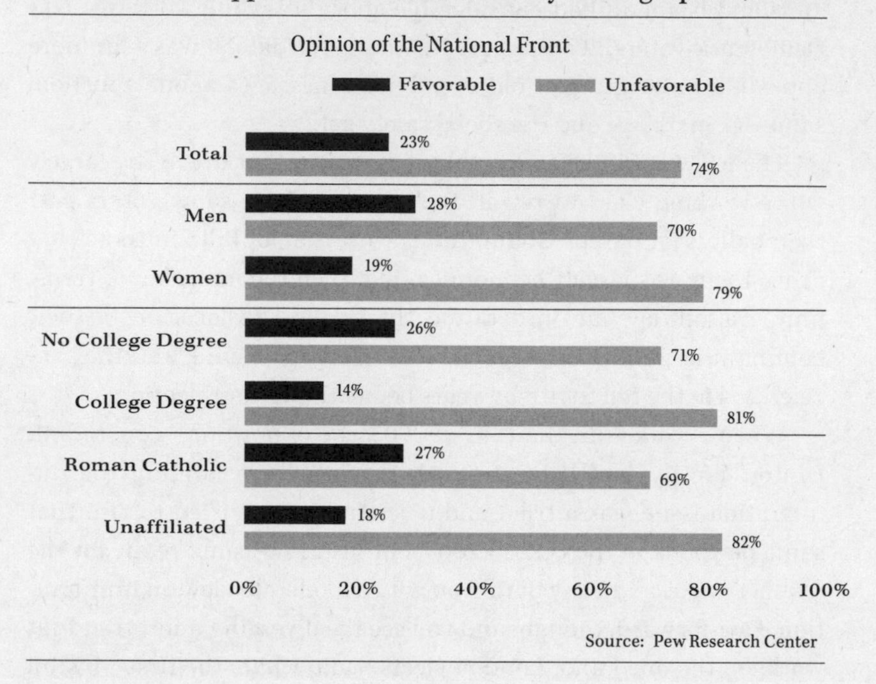

Source: Pew Research Center

French youth ages 18 to 24—a surprising finding, considering France is traditionally known for its leftist youth movements.

I don't think that this microtrend, with the stabilization once again of manufacturing jobs, will last decades as a pivotal vote. The numbers are diminishing in the long run, but they could again be powerful in the next round of elections. More important, they are not to be dismissed as "deplorable": these Americans are hardworking, family- and religion-oriented people who have had their ears boxed by globalization and technology. The elites ignored them at their peril, and Trump filled the void.

There are also some basic immutable facts from elementary economics that can't be ignored. Bring in millions of low-skilled workers from any part of the world, and the wages of the existing working-class members will be squeezed, regardless of their religion, ethnicity, or nationality. Open your borders to trade without a border equalization tax, and manufacturing jobs will be shipped overseas. This does not mean it is or is not the right strategy; it means that some existing people will be damaged to a greater extent than has been realized. When too much power and money went to the cities, the rural areas worked to wrest it back.

The answer is not to try to revive the old economy, though there is no question that we can drive better trade bargains that cost fewer jobs. The answer has got to be to distribute the tools and the jobs related to the new economy to every region of the country, and to spend what it takes to get this done. We certainly need to provide new-economy tax credits that work in the areas that have less than their fair share of these jobs. It may not be practical to put all the engineering jobs in Ohio, but we may well be able to put a lot of Amazon warehouses there—and at least some of the engineering.

Another thing we need to do is to figure a way for people in the cities and the suburbs to have a better understanding of the rest of the country. We need to encourage every rising cloistered college student to take a trip one summer, not to Israel or France, but across America for six weeks. We have become so siloed that Americans simply don't know America.

Finally, we have to stop the depopulating of our rural areas. It just does not make sense as a country, when these areas are so rich in culture, in land, and in resources, to let them atrophy any further. We need to make them the most desirable areas in the country for people to settle down in—and make it easier for kids to stay and build good lives there.

36. HAPPY PESSIMISTS

The economy is cratering. My kids will never do as well as I did. The country is headed over a cliff. Washington is broken. Racism and neo-Nazis are rampant. Free speech is dead. College graduates end up with hamburger-flipper jobs. And so on and so on.

Something has happened over the last decade in America. The most optimistic, can-do country has become mired in endless pessimism and negativity. Try to say that America has never been so prosperous, or that its middle class has never had so much opportunity, and you may get laughed out of a room. Today nearly two-thirds of young Americans enroll in college, and if they graduate they earn significantly more money. Women are earning more than men in major metropolitan areas, and are the majority of students in colleges and professional schools. Wages have gone up, especially when adjusted for inflation and employer subsidies like employer-provided health care. Inflation is low. Health care coverage is at an all-time high. Costs of basic middle-class goods like energy and housing have gone down. And political infighting, rough as it is, doesn't compare to the open warfare and mass protests of the 1960s.

But many Americans believe this can't possibly be true. They believe the worst about America and are fueling a downward spiral of pessimism increasingly out of sync with the overall statistics of the country and even their assessments of their own lives. Half of respondents ages 18 to 29 in a recent Harvard Institute of Politics survey said they "considered the American dream alive and well for them personally. Half of them said it was dead as a doornail."

36.1: Satisfaction with Direction of the Country among U.S. Adults

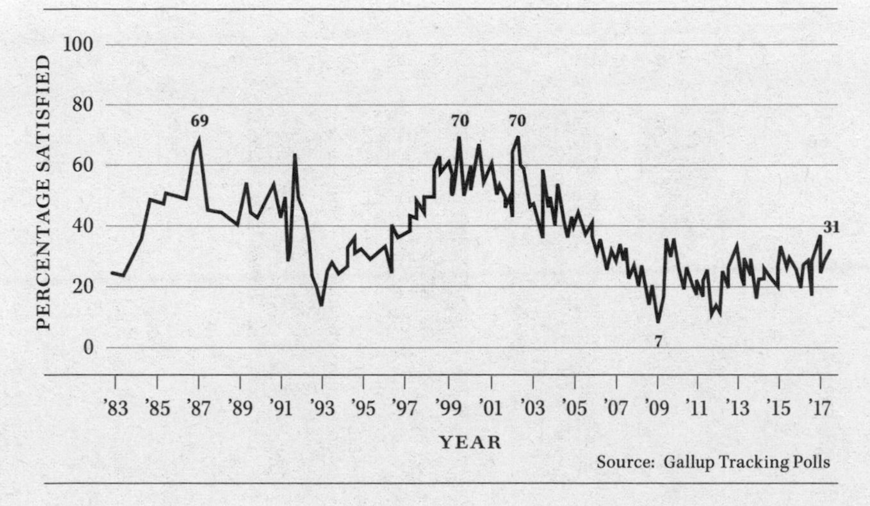

The origins of this trend started, I believe, with September 11. The horrific tragedy was the last time America came together in unity to fight a foe. But the subsequent wars in Iraq and Afghanistan—despite being on a far smaller scale than past wars in Vietnam, Korea, or World War II—dragged down the national psyche. Leadership lost sight of the national goals and America grew tired of the fight and all its expense in money and lost lives. National morale only worsened with the financial crisis of 2008 and 2009.

In the 1990s and early 2000s, 70 percent of Americans were satisfied with the direction things were going in the United States, according to Gallup. Starting in 2005, after Bush's reelection, which coincided with the setbacks in Iraq, the right track slipped below 50 percent. This "right-track"/"wrong-track" measure has remained below 50 percent ever since. It is the longest continuous period of the public feeling down about the country that I can find since the modern era of polling began. Americans somehow felt better about the future during and after the Great Depression even though almost every significant measure of economic and material well-being was much worse.

This mood of dissatisfaction and uncertainty means that neg-

36.2: Negative Versus Positive Political Advertising, 2000–2012

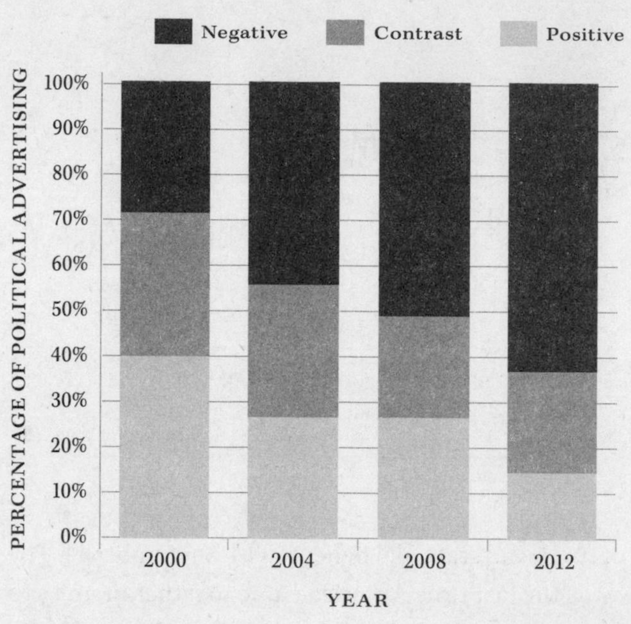

Source: Wesleyan Media Project

ativity is what sells products and candidates. The Wesleyan Media Project compiled a chart to show how political advertising has come to reflect these negative attitudes. In 2000, 30 percent of political ads were negative; in 2004 it was over 40 percent, in 2008 around 50 percent, by 2012 over 60 percent. And in the most recent presidential campaign, 90 percent of our political ads were negative.

Unsurprisingly, public trust in all institutions has declined. Congressional approval is in the teens. Judges, as seen in a Harvard-Harris Poll, are believed to rule more on politics than the law. People don't trust traditional media, or social media even as millennials lap it up. And Washington is viewed as a swamp, with 79 percent calling the nation's political system corrupt.

President Donald Trump played off all this sentiment with his catchphrase "MAGA—Make America Great Again." But after his vic-

36.3: Public Trust in U.S. Government, 1964–2015

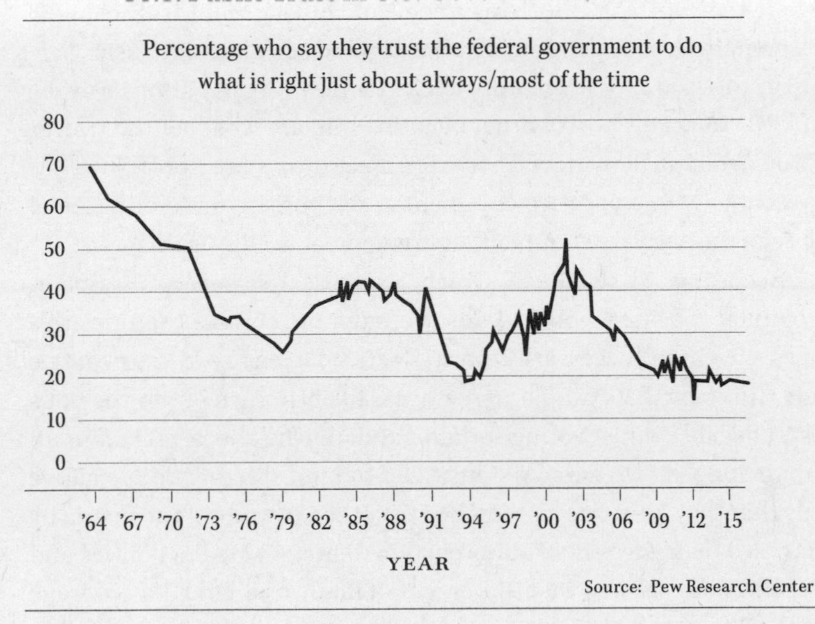

tory and in the first eight months of his presidency, the mood of pessimism has not changed. While some individuals think the country's condition is improving, the overall percentage remains stubbornly in the 30 percent to 40 percent range. All this despite the fact that the percentage of people who believe the economy is on the rise has grown for the first time in a decade.

This happy-pessimist attitude isn't just an American phenomenon, as the lack of trust in institutions is seen across the developed world. There is also a significant divergence in attitudes between the elites—as represented by the top quarter in income—and everyone else. In the U.S., 71 percent of "elites" have trust in their institutions, compared to just 40 percent if you are in the bottom quartile of earnings. This trust gap is also strong in France, Russia, and the U.K.; it's a phenomenon across the most developed countries (save for Germany) and is in stark contrast to places like Indonesia, Malaysia, and the UAE, where overall trust is high and the trust gap between income groups is low.

The culture of negativity is also reflected in our habits online, where the "alt-right," the "resistance," and other groups traffic in and respond to a cacophony of negative ads and social media posts. Negative stories are what generate clicks for news organizations as well: juicy or salacious posts with a negative spin are what get the traffic. ("You Won't Believe How These Ten Beautiful Stars Look Now!") If presented with a negative comment and a positive one, you're going to read the negative comment and remember it. Why is this?

According to Donald P. Green, a political science professor at Columbia, negative political ads are more memorable than positive ones—but aren't necessarily more effective. Green says these negative ads still show that "people were no less likely to turn out to the polls or to decide against voting for a candidate who was attacked in an ad." It suggests we are so desensitized to mud-slinging and negative ads that they go in one ear and out the other. A study of the media by Harvard Kennedy School's Shorenstein Center on Media, Politics and Public Policy showed that 91 percent of mainstream media coverage of the Trump administration has been negative. It's a never-ending stream of negativity hitting our airwaves.

American pessimism has become ingrained in our culture for the first time. America's youth remain the most optimistic about their futures even as they grow up during a period of extreme negativity. But the baby boomers, despite tremendous wealth and prosperity, have turned dark—women even more so than men. This group of people—who are "making it" and living the American Dream—are negative toward America and its institutions, driving the country's new and sour mood. They cut across party lines and even geography.

We now have gone from a country that believed we could conquer every adversity to one consumed by cynicism and gullibility. More and more American TV shows have the same plot: something is wrong in America and we suspect terrorists abroad. The twist, however, as in *Homeland*, *Designated Survivor*, *Blindspot*, and *Quantico*, is that the enemy is actually in our midst. We are a country that now responds better to stark negative statements than grand promises even as technology does more than we ever imagined possible. We are a nation that believes the worst of every institution and company. Happy pessimists are motivated by fear and anger, not hope. The flames are being fueled on the left and the right as political and marketing communicators reluctantly all conclude the same thing: it's now far easier to tear down America than it is to lift it up.

These sentiments drive greater skepticism about our military, police, and intelligence operations. They create doubts about our banks and now growing doubts about our tech companies. They spawn successful TV franchises based on firing people and throwing them off

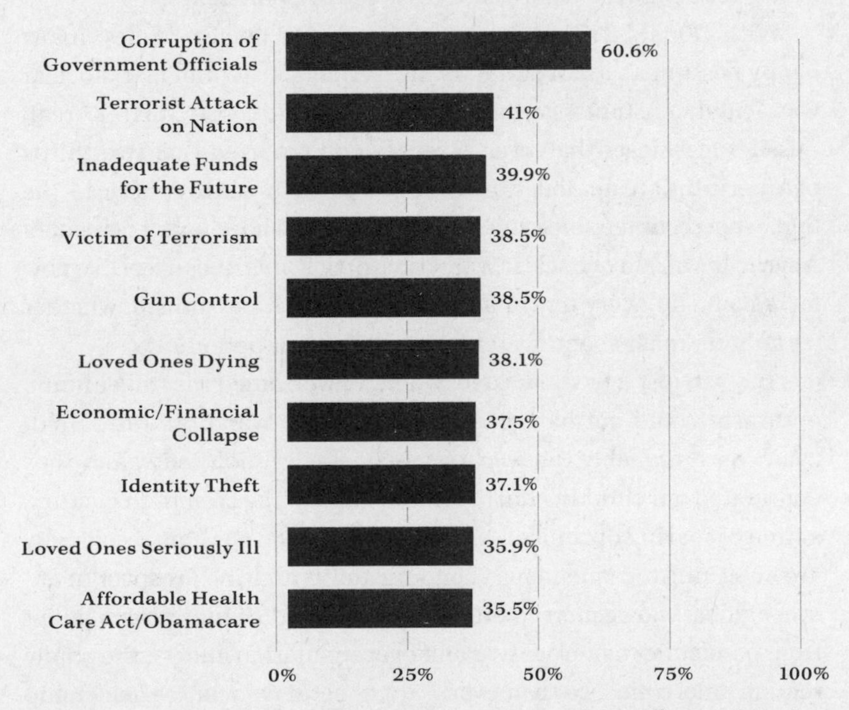

the island. They mean it's easier to stop and stall every new policy by suggesting it will have people dying on the streets.

No body politic can really survive without what President Nixon of all people called the "lift of a driving dream," and America sure doesn't have one right now. Maybe *you* can be that rare bird: successful in politics and marketing by creating new leadership and turning the mood around. Just look to FDR, who did this in the 1930s. Or you can go with the status quo and cut another negative ad, again tickling the worry bone of the new American pessimists. So far, the happy pessimists are winning out.

We are a nation of fears, the most significant one of 2016 being the corruption of government officials, followed pretty widely (by about 20 percentage points) by being attacked on our own soil. Fears in America are ever changing: in 2016, Americans were afraid of the cost increases of Obamacare; by 2017, the public was more afraid of losing the enhanced health care coverage of Obamacare.

With Donald Trump in possession of the nuclear codes, many happy pessimists are fixating on an eternal, existential fear: nuclear war. Amid constant tweets and vague threats, those North Korean missiles feel closer than ever. A recent poll reported that two-thirds of Americans are anxious about the country's threat to America—the highest percentage since 2000. Vox reported a whopping 82 percent of Americans afraid of nuclear war with North Korea. It can feel like new fears come up every day to add to our national pessimism, whether it's another mass shooting, terrorist incident, or potential war.

And yet, just a few years ago, when we welcomed the millennium, optimism could not have been higher. World War II and the Holocaust were probably the world's most cataclysmic events, and they dominated our thinking during the last half of the twentieth century, a time of soaring optimism. Now technology and the global economy are achieving a tremendous economic uplift and the prospect of another global war seems remote. We have dodged virtually every bullet from pandemic to nuclear war and overpopulation and yet the public remains more morose than ever. I am hopeful we will see leadership over time that brings back the next "Morning in America."

37. CLOSET CONSERVATIVES

They might be sitting next to you at work. Or maybe they're at the salon, one stylist away, or on the bus sitting beside you, or even across from you at the dinner table.

These are America's closet conservatives; they voted for Trump but hide their real views from you. Perhaps it was the Russians whispering in their ears, but it took many Americans to elect Donald Trump, and to vote for a Republican Senate, House of Representatives, and governorships of thirty-six out of fifty states.

Something does not add up. Liberals are everywhere on TV, in the media, in sports, on campuses. How could conservatives possibly outnumber liberals?

The answer is the closet conservatives. Closet conservatives talk a good progressive game and blend into liberal areas like Washington, D.C., but they have been driven into the shadows by a society that heaps scorn on their views. Without Fox News reinforcing their views, closet conservatives might go completely stir-crazy.

You can't target closet conservatives because, for all practical purposes, they do not have a conservative footprint and they cover their tracks. In a Harvard CAPS–Harris poll conducted last year, nearly 40 percent of Americans say they are reluctant to reveal their political views to their own family. Sixty percent stay mum at work.

Given the gender gap, it is clear that younger men, faced with a pink-hatted girlfriend, are simply not about to confess that they like the bravado of Donald Trump. Husbands who used to be the political lords of the household are now relegated to secretly disagreeing with their spouses while yessing them to their faces. As for closet conservative women, Hillary Clinton has called them "traitors" to their gender. On TV, the leaders of legions of women are liberal stars such as Madonna and Tina Fey. Yet the most surprising statistic of the last presidential election was that 53 percent of white women overall, and close to 60 percent in suburban and rural areas, voted for Donald Trump. These same women also overwhelmingly rejected Barack Obama in the 2012 election in favor of Mitt Romney, and favored Republicans by 22 points in the 2014 midterms.

What? That can't be right. Something does not compute.

Right. It does not add up. Even when the Republicans have won Congress, the congressional ballot in preelection polls has generally been four or five points in the Democrats' favor. This polling disconnect is especially reflected in the differences between telephone polls conducted by live interviewers and online polls. People confronted by others are not as conservative as people clicking away on the internet.

Closet conservatives can hide behind a screen, but when asked about their views they're likely to obscure them in favor of more liberal ones. This comes out particularly in questions about immigration, and the disparity in answers shows that the cohort of closet

37.1: Republicans' Responses in Phone Versus Web Surveys

PERCENTAGE OF REPUBLICANS ANSWERING AFFIRMATIVELY:	PHONE	WEB	DIFFERENCE
Very unfavorable opinion of Obama	35%	49%	14%
Very favorable opinion of Trump	29%	37%	8%
There should be national effort to deport all immigrants living in U.S. illegally	50%	63%	13%
Immigrants are a burden on our country	46%	58%	12%

Source: Pew Research Center

conservatives is about 5 percent of the population or more. This suggests that more than 5 percent of the population—that's more than 15 million people—are more conservative than they are willing to publicly admit. Our polling read on many hot-button issues might then underestimate their true support at the ballot box.

Men in particular make up a sizable portion of the closet conservative ranks—perhaps because many might end up sleeping on the couch if they let their political loyalties out into the light. The media reported several divorces after Trump's victory: wives who couldn't handle the political divide after finding out their beloved voted for *him*.

Recent research indicates that one in ten couples, married or not, have ended their relationships due to a battle over political differences. Some women prefer tall man, some men prefer blondes, but it looks like the new dividing line on dating apps might well be your party affiliation. So much so that the popular dating app Bumble, during the 2016 election season, had filters to say who you were voting for—so you wouldn't waste your time with someone of the opposite party. For younger millennials, this tension over politics is greater: 22 percent of couples have ended a relationship over political differences. It's no surprise then that many closet conservatives would just as soon clam up.

Despite most white women voting Republican, especially in the suburbs, peer pressure makes these closet conservative women particularly hard to find. We assume that any educated suburban white woman is going to be a liberal Democrat, but that's not true. That's the essence of the closet conservative: they are not who you expect, and they keep their political views close to the vest.

In general, Republicans are more reserved about their beliefs than their Democratic counterparts. The key to figuring out who these closet conservatives are and what they care about is getting them to respond in certain ways. The mode by which these questions are asked—telephone versus survey—matters a lot.

So what happened with all the polls that predicted a 2016 election landslide for the Democrats? How did we get it so wrong? Were telephone polls understating support for Trump? The answer was clearly yes. Closet conservatives weren't about to admit who they were voting for, and they were willing to tell someone on the phone what they wanted to hear. Americans in general, when it comes to politics, will default to a pleasing answer versus a real one. A 2005 academic paper revealed that Americans overreported their voting history because it was "socially desirable" to be a consistent voter. Clearly, social pressures are causing our predictions for elections to be skewed. Many people who said they were voting for Hillary Clinton either were lying or just did not bother to vote. The latter is actually more problematic for polling accuracy. At Nate Silver's FiveThirtyEight, the site didn't take into account the non-responses when it came to election polling—which led to a lot of holes in research. Another issue is that the percentage of Americans who are very active politically are actually overreported. As a whole, Americans aren't as enthusiastic about politics as we think; it's a choice group that is.

Another deterrent to expressing political views is that the First Amendment does not extend to the workplace. If you express your conservative political views, say, on Facebook or give to conservative political causes, you can be fired for views your employer or customers don't like. If you work for a company that sells primarily to urban areas, and you believe in strong borders, you can be outed on social media and become the subject of a consumer boycott. While Congress can't make your actions illegal, your employer may still fire you. This is one big reason why closet conservatives don't make their views known at work.

All of which underscores the importance of the secret ballot in letting people express their real views and highlights the danger of governing by polls. Vote-by-mail has dangers because organizers and spouses can demand to see the ballots of their family members. Organizers can stand over the shoulders of seniors in nursing homes. Only the secret ballot in a voting booth insulates Americans from these peer influences.

It isn't good for anyone if Americans feel they need to hide their political views to protect themselves from scorn at home or from being fired at work. We need to reaffirm the First Amendment and the secret ballot. As I wrote in *The Hill*, we need to make it just as illegal to fire people because of their views as it is for Congress to put them in jail. We need to reestablish the norm that you are entitled, even encouraged, to say your political beliefs at home, at work, and on social media without penalty. Until we do that, don't expect that you can publicly ask folks how they voted and why and get true answers. The current atmosphere, whether in the media, on campuses, or in the workplace, encourages at least some conservatives to remain in the closet.

38. IMPRESSIONABLE ELITES REVISITED

When I was chief strategist for Senator Hillary Clinton's presidential campaign in 2008, I noticed a consistent pattern. When someone came up to me and asked, "Why can't Hillary just be more likable?" it was invariably a donor or highly educated voter. When someone came up to me and asked if I thought her health care plan would work, it was invariably a middle- or working-class voter who had a genuine interest in the issue because it would affect his or her life.

From this observation, I developed the theory of impressionable elites—meaning that contrary to expectations, the more educated our electorate becomes, the more swayed those educated voters become by what they hear and read from the sources they trust. Rather than thinking more independently, impressionable elites instead trust even more a chorus conducted by the media and think tanks. Middle- and working-class American voters, in contrast, are connected very closely in their everyday lives to the issues, and so they base their judgments not on talking points but on the facts on the ground.

This hypothesis is a hard one to test scientifically. But, if anything, this propensity to pick up talking points uncritically from the media rather than base opinions on their own life experience has grown even stronger in American life in the decade since the first *Microtrends* covered impressionable elites. The elite establishment today in both parties is now under withering assault as fundamentally out of touch with Americans. The Supreme Court is seen as making political rather than legal decisions. The press is seen as biased and more interested in driving narrative over facts. Smear tactics against people work better than ever, as gossip fueled by anonymous sources has become the coin of the realm. The most fundamental tenet of the system that America's founders set up—that ours should be a representative democracy run by educated elites as opposed to direct democracy—is under question. This disconnect led to the populist revolution of 2016 and the silent overthrow of the elite guardians. These elites are still in power, and yet in many ways they are a walking dead—seen as unable to act on anything and wedded to egghead principles that make no sense.

The election of 2016 is a case in point. The collective elites simply failed to see Donald Trump coming. I certainly did not imagine him becoming as powerful as he did, but I also couldn't ignore the ease with which he dispatched seventeen candidates in the Republican Party by simply ripping off their masks. Jeb Bush, the consensus elite candidate, failed to even get out of the gate, despite nearly $200 million of early funding. GOP primary voters revolted against a Republican establishment they thought had grown cozy with the Democratic establishment, hadn't stood up to President Barack Obama, and probably could not stop Hillary Clinton from winning the election. The Republican elites even continued warring with Trump well after he got the nomination. They came to believe that they—and not the voters—were the party.

The fountains of elite information all said that the victory of Hillary Clinton was inevitable, and the elites all believed it. They did not see what was happening right before their eyes right here in America. Every blow to Trump was seen as the coup de grâce, yet he kept fighting back. Many elites continued to hold former president Bill Clinton in high regard—despite a checkered history with women—while assuming a crude audiotape would be the end of Donald Trump. And even in the aftermath, impressionable elites remain on the edge of their seats, in a world of Russian conspiracies and James Comey missteps, still waiting for the deus ex machina to bring the tragedy of 2016 to a close. But these, as well as other blinders, are just ways of denying the sea change of the rebellion of 2016. When you add up all the votes in the congressional races, the Republicans were the winners of the national popular vote. The Democrats lost 1,000 legislative seats at all levels under President Barack Obama and yet cling to a fantasy that the country is overwhelmingly liberal when the obvious facts staring at them are quite different.

Today you can sit down with an impressionable elite—a Harvard-educated lawyer, for example—and they know with absolute certainty that somehow Trump was laundering money with the Russians in exchange for help in the election. They have no evidence for these claims and yet they "know" it just as strongly as elites once believed with absolute certainty that the earth was flat. So did the Russians need money? How, when $2.4 billion was spent on the election campaign, would $100,000 worth of Facebook ads make a difference? It's illogical, and yet perhaps 40 percent of those reading this paragraph have come to believe it, based on reports of completely classified unknowable information. They just know it.

The reason why working-class voters supported Trump also confirms the impressionable-elite theory. Both Hillary Clinton and Donald Trump were disliked by about two-thirds of the voters. About a third of those who voted for Clinton disliked her. About a third of those voting for Trump disliked him. In what was the most intensely personal and negative campaign I have ever witnessed, it was middle- and working-class voters concerned about issues that swung the election in favor of Donald Trump. These largely Midwestern voters certainly did not "love" the Donald Trump of *Access Hollywood* who talked about assaulting women. But they believed that his basic analysis of the country was right: that political correctness had gone too far, that we didn't control our border, that there was war on the police, that trade deals had eroded our manufacturing and cost us jobs, and that Washington needed a wake-up call. Agree or disagree with these voters, their political and issue perspective is clear, and they voted Trump (and many had voted for Obama) for these very tangible reasons that elites have all but ignored. The traditional cultural Republicans who voted based on "religion and guns" also supported

Trump as they had all the other Republicans, but it was Trump's seizing of these new issues that broadened his coalition and brought him victory.

Today, there is an impressionable-elite echo chamber. Think tanks tell elites what to think and the *New York Times* and the rest of the media echo it and voilà: sit down in the country club in New Jersey, and most are armed with the very same talking points. The Southern Poverty Law Center sets the standard on cultural issues, and the Tax Policy Center sets the standard on tax and economic issues. Partisan "analysts" drum up a report that is never questioned and spoon-fed to elites through the media.

Of course, the right has had their own echo chamber for some time, with Fox News and the Drudge Report beaming out key points in similar fashion for ages. But the remarkable thing is that while the establishment media provided talking points for largely liberal elites, Fox and Drudge started to cater to voters instead, and dissociated themselves from the Republican elites, who are now basically adrift—disliked by the Democrats and largely abandoned by their own voters.

President Barack Obama was in many ways the perfect impressionable-elite president. He was an editor of the *Harvard Law Review*, had little Washington or governmental experience, and had, outside of his upbringing in Indonesia, traveled very little. He received the Nobel Peace Prize right off the bat.

Though it might be counterintuitive, Facebook data suggests that elites actually have fewer international friends than people in lower social classes—only speaking to others with Ivy League educations and vacations to exotic locales. It's the lower-tier Americans who are actually hearing opinions from their immigrant friends or from those outside a tiny, exclusive segment of the population. According to the University of Cambridge reporting on a study using Facebook data, "low-social class people have nearly 50% more international friends than high-social class people."

The U.K. has shown a similar pattern, as elite sentiment diverged from the working-class voters to produce the surprise vote on Brexit.

Elites of almost all stripes were convinced that the EU was a good thing and that calamity would befall Great Britain if it pulled out. Calamity, of course, failed to happen. Once again, elites living in their own fictional world of global and multicultural harmony became disconnected from people fearing the economic and cultural aspects of increased immigration and the open-borders policy of the EU.

Of course, the polls and analysis were so wrong about these two huge events that the Democratic Party fired its pollsters, the *New York Times* replaced its election unit, the BBC overhauled its polling operation, and Facebook and SurveyMonkey ended their partnership due to inaccurate polls. Actually, *none* of that happened. It does not appear that anyone got fired for all of this misdirection and the failure to understand the most basic forces happening in the world. Instead they got promoted. Impressionable elites discovered they didn't have to be right—they simply needed to please a constituency that would stick with them. So, rather than address all of the economic and cultural missteps that produced these remarkable events, they went into the cocoon of denial and continued with business as usual. Polls once again proclaim that Donald Trump is finished and has no support. Every proposal from Trump is ridiculed by a group of policy-skilled comedians and entertainers. The elites hold their noses, expecting that this too shall pass; they, after all, are the permanent Washington.

Elites are no longer the ones we count upon to tell us right from wrong, or to apply their skills of expertise to move society forward. Instead they are viewed increasingly as spinmeisters, telling tales that fit their narrowly defined worldviews. They have become even more distant from the broader population simply by rejecting what happened across two continents and reading books like *Hillbilly Elegy*, treating the other half as though they are zoo specimens. The implications of this disconnect remain profound, with no solution in sight. If a new independent party is created on either continent, it is unlikely to be the group of social liberals and economic conservatives we long thought would want a new party. It will instead be a populist party based on restoring power to the people and seizing it from the elites and the deep state. Trump was at the vanguard of this movement, and even if Trump works with the Establishment, the Establishment as we know it is still in deep trouble. The underlying anger and concerns that produced Trump's victory are not being addressed in any meaningful way. The result is that our elites are becoming even more impressionable.

39. MILITANT DREAMERS REVISITED

Call them what you will today, depending upon your political perspective, but those who are here illegally without proper documentation have become, as predicted ten years ago in the first *Microtrends*, a major political force. This group may well be the most powerful force in the next presidential election, but as their electoral power has grown, so has a backlash that threatens them, too.

The voting population of Latinos has skyrocketed over the last decade. We saw that in 1992 the Latino vote was essentially at 2 percent. In 2016 it was at 11 percent, and there is still more potential for that number to grow. If you look at the states where significantly more voters turned out this election than last, it was New York, California, Texas, and Florida—each with an average in the last two elections of over 900,000 more votes cast in the presidential contest. But there were 10 percent jumps in Latino voting in Colorado and Arizona as well. Colorado and New Mexico are pretty much out of reach now for a Republican, but a lot of the additional votes in Texas and Florida don't make much of a difference. In New York and California, the massive additional Latino votes are simply gilding the lily in national contests and not making an Electoral College difference whatsoever.

The entire debate around this issue has evolved as we predicted in the first *Microtrends*. Those here without legal status have been able to ally with those here legally, and the movement has a huge base in the key urban centers of the country. No mayor in New York, Los An-

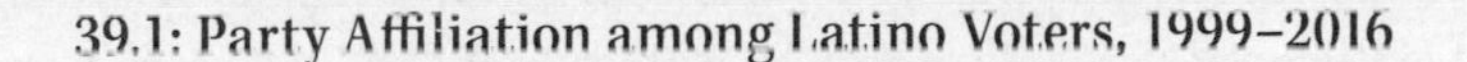

39.1: Party Affiliation among Latino Voters, 1999–2016

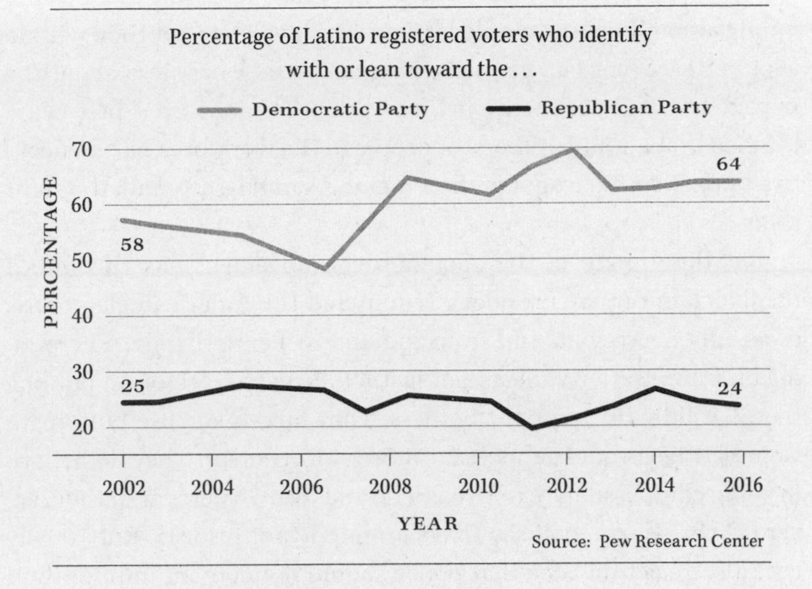

geles, Chicago, or Miami can get elected without a significant Latino vote. This has boosted the strength of the Latino vote both in absolute numbers nationally and especially within the Democratic Party.

In 2008, Hillary Clinton didn't speak favorably about people coming into this country outside of the legal immigration system. In a 2003 radio interview she said, "I am, you know, adamantly against illegal immigrants." She did not think some people should be able to "jump the line" past others, and said so both on the stump and many times behind closed doors. In 2016 the "Stronger Together" Hillary Clinton threw those views out the window. The more the campaign went on, the further to the left her views on immigration became. Clinton started out the 2016 campaign emphasizing comprehensive immigration reform and the tightening of our borders. By the end of the campaign she was encouraged to stay away from even mentioning tightened borders.

Interestingly, business is generally pro-immigration. They want more customers and more workers—especially cheaper workers.

Perhaps the biggest change here is that unions, which by any logic typically oppose trade and immigration, now oppose trade but not immigration. Like the employers, unions have decided they will do a lot better if they can get more members, and worry less about the impact on wages of their existing workers. Unions even propagate the idea that adding millions of people to the workforce has no negative impact on the wages of their members and is, after all, the right thing to do.

But the growth of the open-borders movement has run into a roadblock put up by President Trump and the American electorate, especially in Arizona and from Indiana to Pennsylvania. The polling on immigration reflects not just a bifurcated electorate but one that is solidly behind tight borders. They largely oppose building a wall, but they would support far more enforcement. They do believe in being compassionate to Dreamers, and over 70 percent in the Harvard CAPS–Harris poll say that's an important priority. But 70 percent also reject the idea that police should not contact immigration authorities when they arrest people. The "sanctuary city" movement has no support outside of the sanctuary cities.

If our political system were not fractured, we would have long ago tightened the borders, granted the people here work permits and a path to citizenship, and deported the criminals. But what's happened instead is that the right wants even tougher measures—including mass deportations—and the left wants open borders. This has put people like Marco Rubio, who supported a compromise, in the crossfire and has increasingly widened the chasm.

The demographic character of immigrants who came here illegally has in recent years been changing and may change again soon. Mexicans now make up less than half of those here illegally, and the ranks of Asian and Central American immigrants have been rising. Given what has happened in Syria, there is a surge in Middle Eastern immigrants trying to get into this country, and Trump has used fear of terrorism as a wedge on immigration to bar refugees and others from entering.

California is on the cutting edge for the left and has passed laws to turn the entire state into a sanctuary state, telling law enforcement that they can't cooperate with immigration authorities when it comes to arresting people. The entire political dynamic in California has flipped around from the days of Pete Wilson, governor up until 1999, who spearheaded Proposition 187 to curb the use of state services by noncitizens. The Supreme Court declared it unconstitutional.

As West Virginia went from one of the most Democratic states to a Republican state during this period, California swung heavily from a toss-up state that elected Ronald Reagan and Arnold Schwarzenegger to one of the most Democratic states. It was the growth of the Latino vote that made this possible, and this is why Democrats hope that over time the same thing can happen in Texas—locking out the Republicans from the presidency.

There are many organizations that want to galvanize the strong Latino population in Texas to make it a state that could potentially turn blue in 2020—organizations like Battleground Texas that try to make Texas a swing state, in part by making Hispanic voters more engaged. More generally, we've seen a ton of new Hispanic-

39.2: Hispanic Percentage of U.S. Vote, 1980–2016

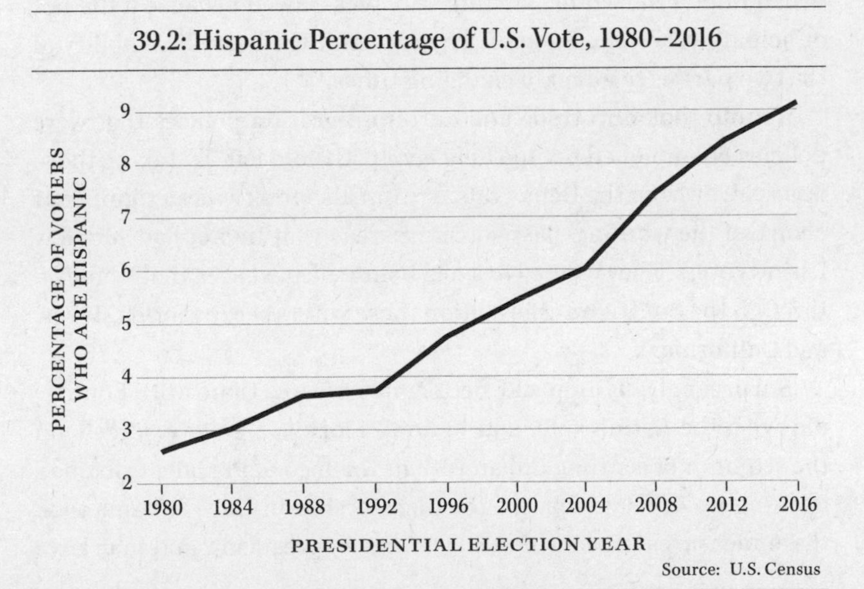

Source: U.S. Census

focused organizations sprout up in the last two decades. These organizations—like Voto Latino, Mijente, and Mi Familia Vota—are trying to raise Hispanic political and civic engagement, although the effects are unclear so far.

Ten years ago in *Microtrends* we noted that Latino voters are overwhelmingly Democratic, and they remain so today. A recent Pew study found that the Democratic party affiliation of Latinos in America continues to climb. Despite a dip in 2006 (because of the stronger Latino support for George W. Bush), over the past ten years the percentage of Latino registered voters has gone from 49 percent Democratic to holding steady around 63 to 64 percent. With this population's key values including health care and education, it seems that the Democratic Party will retain these voters as a crucial part of their base in the foreseeable future.

Based on recent migration and voter registration statistics, John Judis and Ruy Teixeira wrote a highly influential book titled *The Emerging Democratic Majority*. They wrote that Democrats could simply rely on demographics and identity politics to make America a Democratic country. But their analysis, like almost all analyses that depend upon the world standing still, was flawed because it did not anticipate other demographic changes and the incredible ability of the two parties to adapt to changing times.

Trump took anti-trade and anti-immigration policies that were policies championed not too long ago by the old left. By taking those issues away from the Democrats, Trump also took away a significant chunk of the working-class voters in areas that in fact had very few Latino voters. They wanted to avoid being the next area that would go through the kind of transformation these voters see in Florida, Texas, and California.

Surprisingly, Trump did better, not worse, than Mitt Romney did with the Latino vote, and he took Florida, I believe, largely on the strength of a strong Cuban vote in the face of President Obama's opening up of relations with the dictatorship in Cuba. Obama took these measures as some of his last acts as president, and may have tipped the state over to Trump. Typically it's the minority of Protestant Latinos who go for the Republicans, and that's still the case.

The prognosis for what's going to happen here is less certain than ten years ago. It was a no-brainer then that the power of undocumented immigrants would rise, and it has. But the reaction to these changes is at the core of the Republican/Trump counterwave. Perhaps Trump will be the Pete Wilson of America and the last gasp before a complete reversal of these policies and a full path to citizenship to the 11 million who are here without legal status. Or perhaps he will arrest the traffic at the border and the Latino voting population will see limited growth. Concentration in a few big states—as long as the Republicans hold on to Texas—also limits increased national impact.

The U.S. census counts all people here and the apportionment of seats includes noncitizens, and so there will be a few changes in 2020; but as long as the states are winner-take-all, more seats in Texas and Arizona will mean more electoral votes for the Republicans, and the rest of the changes pretty much cancel themselves out.

I would like to see comprehensive immigration reform get passed so the country could, if it worked, put this issue in the rearview mirror. But right now it looks like each side will move further and further apart, making this a critical flashpoint in American politics for another decade.

40. NEWEST AMERICANS

When we talk about immigration, we tend to talk about Latin American countries and the Middle East. However, over the past decade, Asians are without a doubt the fastest-growing immigrant population in America—more than those from any other region in the world. And Asian immigrants are experiencing incredible degrees of influence and success in America—from education to job opportunities to political influence.

The Asian population in America has skyrocketed—in 1960 it was 5 percent of the foreign-born population, and 30 percent of the nation's immigrants by 2014, according to Migration Policy Institute statistics. In 2010, Asian immigrants had higher naturalization rates in the U.S. than Hispanics: 261,370 for new Americans in 2015 out of the total of 730,259. In 2016 there were an estimated 20.5 million Asian-Americans living in the U.S, and the U.S. Census Bureau projects that number with reach 25.7 million by 2019.

Asians were not always so welcome here. Geopolitical concerns, racism, and economics have had a profound impact on the Asian-American experience, starting with the Chinese Exclusion Act in 1882. Remember that many Chinese were brought to California as part of the gold rush in conditions little better than slavery. As Chinese immigrants' population and economic power grew, however, outcry and fear resulted in the first major law restricting immigration to the United States. The act halted Chinese immigration for a decade and barred Chinese from becoming American citizens; it was

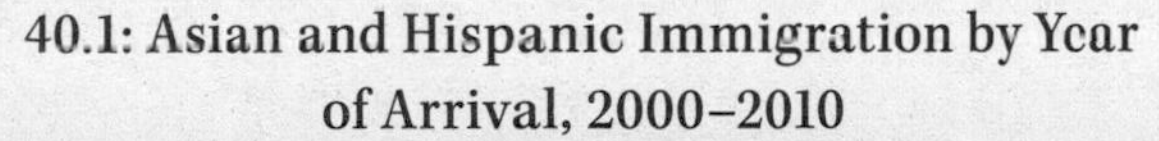

40.1: Asian and Hispanic Immigration by Year of Arrival, 2000–2010

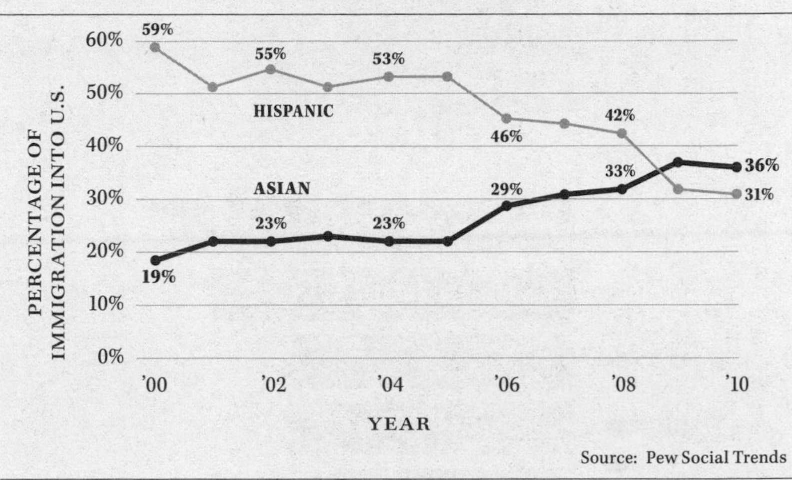

not until the Immigration Act of 1965 that Chinese immigration on a large scale was allowed to begin again.

The Japanese-American population also met with similar policies. Teddy Roosevelt's gentleman's agreement of 1907 was a U.S.-Japanese policy that held that no Japanese would be issued passports to immigrate to the U.S. except for certain categories of business and professional men. It was ended in the 1920s, but not long after, Pearl Harbor led to the internment of Japanese citizens here and enormous animosity toward Japanese in America.

Generations later, new governments and new attitudes toward Asia brought a new influx of immigration. In 1980, only 384,000 Chinese immigrants lived in the United States. In 2016 that number topped 2 million. During this same period the total Asian immigrant population rose from 2.5 million to over 12.5 million. India is the number one Asian country sending its citizens to America, followed by China, the Philippines, Vietnam, and Korea.

The most remarkable statistics about recent Asian immigrants lie

40.2: U.S. Median Household Income by Asian Origin Group, 2010

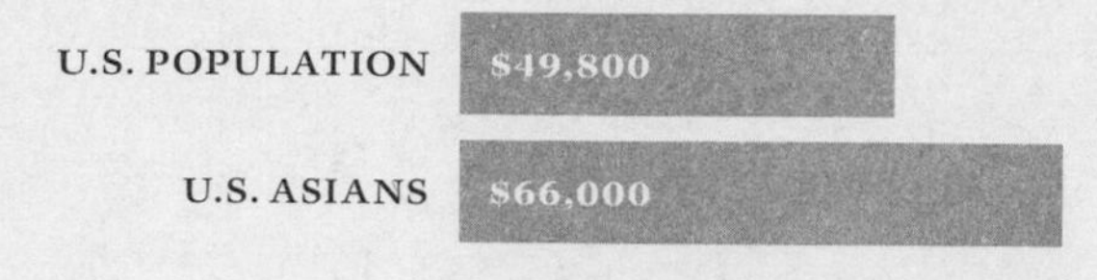

MAJOR U.S. ASIAN GROUPS

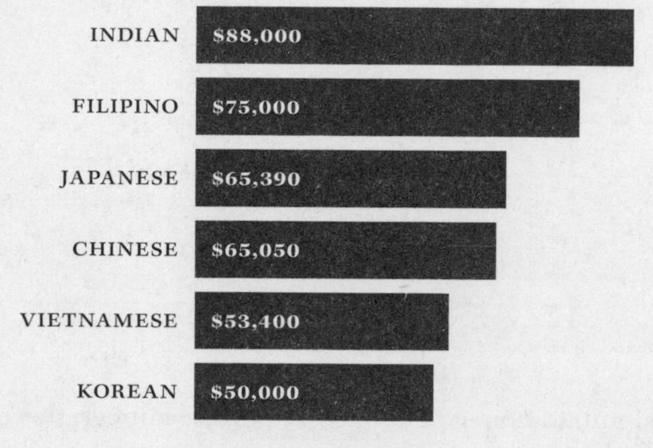

Source: Pew Research Center

in the economic success they are having in America. Asian-Americans now have a median income of $74,829—39 percent greater than the national average, and up from $66,000 in 2010. Given the widespread discussion about the impacts of racism and the long-standing caricatures of Asians, it is an incredible achievement. Asians are an immigration success story, even for the more conservative and fiscally minded, as they're bringing new tax revenue to the country.

The conventional wisdom has been that a traditional Asian emphasis on merit and education, which dates back to Confucian times, has made the difference for this population's success. In fact, the educational gap of Asians today is huge: 30 percent of Americans over age 25 have a college degree compared to half of Asian-Americans. This certainly is significant enough to explain the pay gap we see today as Asians are earning what they learn.

The purchasing power of the Asian-American community, then, is outsized compared to its population and is growing rapidly, with the community spending an impressive $825 billion annually. And their buying power, according to *The Multicultural Economy 2015*, is expected to increase by 32 percent by 2020.

Asians in America tend to buy what upscale Asians buy in Asia. They eat 69 percent more fresh seafood than the average American, 72 percent more fresh vegetables, and 29 percent more fresh fruits, according to Nielsen research. And they also appreciate their gadgets. Asian-Americans outpace the general population in ownership of smartphones, computers, tablets, sound systems, and other tech devices. From the same Nielsen research, "of the eighty-seven U.S. start-up companies valued at $1 billion or more, nineteen were founded by Asian-American immigrants."

Asian immigrants, especially those coming from businesses in China and India, are also often well versed in the importance of scale, and of managers and management. A million-dollar business in the United States will likely have six employees, while a million-dollar business will have one hundred or two hundred employees in India. At Microsoft I worked for Satya Nadella, a model Indian immigrant born in a relatively small village. He worked head down at Microsoft for twenty-two years before rising to the logical choice of CEO. Intellectually he was head and shoulders above his competitors, having a deep understanding of both the financial and technical sides of the cloud. His climb to into the management ranks a common trend for Indian-Americans, who have become the first immigrant group in this country to achieve a median income of over $100,000.

There is always a chicken-and-egg question to the remarkable success that Asian-Americans are having, but it's notable that 69 percent agreed when Pew Research asked if "people who want to get ahead can make it if they work hard." Asian-Americans are eleven points higher on this belief than the average American. Then again, this could merely reflect class sensibilities. Upper- and middle-class Americans of all races hold similar beliefs, with 71 percent and 67 percent, respectively, agreeing that hard work means getting ahead. (Among lower-class Americans, only about half feel this way.)

The next generation of Asian-Americans continues to show higher educational achievement than other demographics. Asians are about 5 percent of high school students but make up 22 percent of the entering class at Harvard and 26 percent of the Massachusetts Institute of Technology freshman class. A look at the overall SAT scores shows Asian-Americans significantly outscoring other Americans in math, which is of course a vital skill for advancement in the Information Age. The National Science Foundation reported that in 2012 Asian-Americans earned around 6 percent of PhDs in science and engineering, while African-Americans and Hispanic Americans earned 3 percent and 4 percent of such PhDs, respectively. A further 27 percent of 2012's science and engineering PhDs were earned by temporary visa holders, many of whom came from Asia. In Google's 2017 diversity report, the tech giant reported that 35 percent of its workforce was Asian or Asian-American, up from 30 percent just four years earlier.

While economic success is generally correlated with voting Republican, Asians have been moving sharply to the Democratic Party in the last few elections. As the population has grown, it has flipped from over 50 percent Republican to over 70 percent Democratic. Americans from India are most likely to be Democrats, while Chinese-Americans are most likely to be Republicans. In this group, early Republican support was based on the anti-communist and strong-on-defense stance of the party, which would attract those who had real concerns about Mao Tse-tung and the Cultural Revolution. But today's immigrants have few such concerns, and those from India and the Philippines, for example, are more concerned about social justice issues here in the U.S. than about foreign policy.

Having said that, Asian voters are also fairly concentrated in less competitive states. The largest populations are in California and New York. While they are now also going to the South and the Midwest, they have had a fairly minor impact on national politics because their vote is small in core swing states. Their high level of success, however, shows that Republicans might have some success in winning voters back with the right kinds of candidates. Trump got 27 percent of the Asian-American vote.

The Justice Department's backing of the Asian-American students' suit against Harvard was politically brilliant: it was a back-door way to oppose affirmative action and at the same time show that perhaps the interests of Asian-American voters are not with the Democratic Party. At these income levels Asians are big taxpayers, and their concerns may flip toward a better environment for business, lower taxes, and race-blind admissions to colleges over affirmative action.

Asian-Americans are, however, starting to run for office in growing numbers. The 2015 congressional swearing-in had notable Asian firsts: Senator Tammy Duckworth (D-IL) became the first Thai-American elected to the Senate; and Representative Stephanie Murphy (D-FL) was the first Vietnamese-American woman elected to Congress. In total, there are now eighteen Asian-Americans and Pacific Islanders in Congress (up from fourteen in 2016).

When I was growing up, the pop-culture image of the Asian was represented by Hop Sing, the efficient and affable cook on the most popular TV show of that time, *Bonanza*. Things have come a long way since then, but Asians are still often depicted in stereotypes. The recent show *Fresh Off the Boat*, set in the 1990s, when Asian immigration was new, is the first TV show with an Asian lead character in twenty years. On the big screen, movies like *Slumdog Millionaire* and *The Best Exotic Marigold Hotel* were commercial successes that put India in a generally good light.

But successes are not without setbacks. Recently, Grace Park refused to re-up with *Hawaii 5-0* unless its producers paid its Asian-American leads the same as the white leads of the show, walking off rather than taking less. The studios also paid a high price for casting Scarlett Johansson in *Ghost in the Shell*, in which she played a very famous and beloved Japanese anime character; the film did not did not recoup its production and marketing costs. Only one out of every twenty speaking roles in American films goes to Asians, and they receive only 1 percent of leading roles.

This will change in time. There will continue to be more Asian-American experiences being told on-screen, like the lauded Emmy Award–winning *Master of None*, written by comedians Aziz Ansari and Alan Yang, which devotes several episodes to the childhood experience of Asian immigrants. There is also an increased drive to feature more Asians in big movies fueled by the growth of the Chinese entertainment marketplace. A movie that opens in the U.S. can now be a success or failure based entirely on how it does at the Chinese box office.

With rapid double-digit growth in Asian immigration over the last twenty years, expect the cultural influence of Asian-Americans to continue to increase. Likewise, this group will continue to pack a serious economic punch. And given their powerful influence in technology companies, Asian-Americans may well be America's secret weapon in the race to stay ahead in innovation and technology.

41. COUCH POTATO VOTERS

Swing remains king when it comes to our elections. But President Donald Trump rewrote the playbook to shift the edge in American politics from soccer moms to football dads, and he began to attract back to politics a new group of those voters just on the fringe of participating in politics.

As the power of mass communications has expanded, the percentage of people who vote in our elections has barely budged, increasing basically with population growth. Some demographics, like the African-American community, focused on organizing and increasing their voting strength, but others dropped out and became couch potato voters.

Some of these voters are getting off the couch now and represent the biggest untapped political resource for future candidates and elections.

The couch potatoes are created by the voluntary nature of participation in the political system. You need to get a Social Security card at birth and you need a photo ID to get on a plane. However, no forces require you to register to vote or to get out and do it. Political participation and power go to those in America who actively choose to turn off the TV and vote. Those who stayed on the couch lost their power in each election—2016 included—but candidates have an opportunity for subsequent elections to motivate a new slice of those voters and get them to the polls.

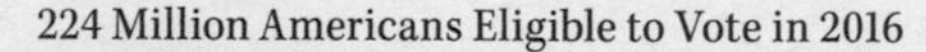

41.1: American Citizen Voting-Age Population, 2016

224 Million Americans Eligible to Vote in 2016

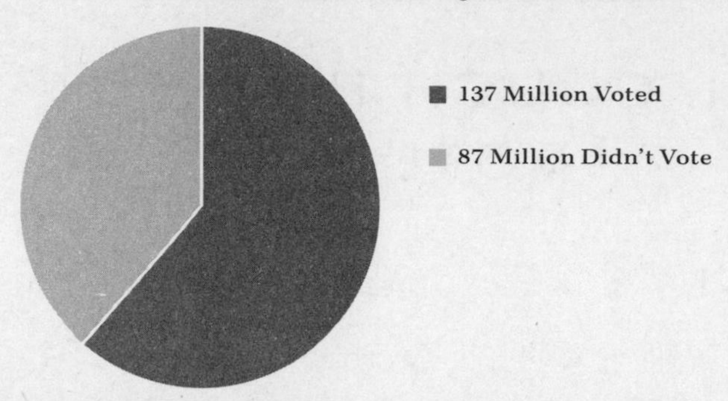

Source: U.S. Census Current Population Survey

In 2016 about 224 million people were eligible to vote, and about 137 million voted; even though turnout went up from 2012, the couch potato vote—people eligible but not voting—was still nearly 90 million citizens. Educated voters, women, and older voters have high turnout rates in this country. Men, young people, and the less educated have much lower rates—as do Hispanics and Asians. There are 54 million white voters on the couch compared to about 19 million Asians and Hispanics. African-American turnout, while down from 2012, was still higher than turnout among white guys without a college education.

So the unexpected secret locked in the numbers is that the largest untapped number of voters who have become these couch potatoes are lower-educated white male voters, precisely the voters who could be energized by a populist campaign. There are tens of millions of those voters, and even though the Hispanic vote and the Asian vote both underperform and have room to grow, they are still much smaller in numbers than the noncollege whites who are political dropouts. (And most of the white male nonvoters are located outside of the swing states, which might complicate things for anyone who wants to switch to a popular vote. Such a change would cause a huge

41.2: Demographics of Voters and Non-Voters, 2016

	DIDN'T VOTE (MILLIONS)	DID VOTE (MILLIONS)	PERCENTAGE VOTING
AGE			
18 to 24 years	15	12	43%
25 to 44 years	32	41	56%
45 to 64 years	26	52	67%
65 years and over	14	33	71%
GENDER			
Male	44	64	59%
Female	43	74	63%
RACE			
White	54	101	65%
Black	12	17	59%
Hispanic	14	13	48%
Asian	5	5	49%
EDUCATION			
High school or less	45	41	47%
Some college	25	42	63%
Bachelor's degree	12	34	74%
Advanced degree	5	20	80%

Source: U.S. Census Current Population Survey

race to get voters off the couch everywhere, fundamentally changing how the campaigns are run.)

Donald Trump may have gotten fewer votes than Hillary Clinton, but he also got the highest number of votes ever received by a Republican candidate, coming in at nearly 63 million votes, while Hillary got nearly 66 million. Clinton didn't have the highest number of votes for a Democrat. That honor goes to President Barack Obama, who got a record 69 million against John McCain. The Libertarian Party also surged to a record number of votes, and it's unclear how they would have broken in a two-way popular vote system. Trump brought in several million who had never voted in a Republican primary before, and those voters were no doubt critical in his winning the Electoral College. That's right: his ace in the hole was the couch potato vote.

Two changes have facilitated the shift from just going after swing voters to targeting a slice of the couch potatoes. One is the vast expansion of funds available to presidential races since Barack Obama became the first candidate in decades to turn down limits and federal matching. The second is the rise of the internet and micro-targeted digital ads, tools that did not exist in politics ten years ago but now get multibillion-dollar checks.

As I have written, don't expect that $100,000 in ads from Russian accounts tipped the election. That's a pittance compared to $2.4 billion spent by the 2016 presidential campaigns, most of which would have gone into a limited number of swing states. But the internet does allow an added degree of personal targeting that should be better than targeting the right TV show (the previous best practice). For instance, President Barack Obama and his team did an incredible job of targeting and energizing the black community. As a result, African-American voters overperformed white voters in turnout, especially in key swing states, over the course of two elections. In 2016, African-American turnout remained high, but not as high as 2012, and it was not as high in a place like Ohio. In 2012, 15 percent of votes in Ohio were cast by African-Americans, while only 10 percent are African-American in the census there. This means that in 2012 the African-American vote in Ohio was so energized that it overperformed compared to the census by 50 percent.

Trump and his campaign team had to pull out record numbers of sympathetic voters in swing states across the Midwest and in Florida to produce an upset, a strategy largely based on energizing a new group of white working-class voters that felt left behind.

On the other end of the spectrum, Bernie Sanders, the Democratic presidential nominee hopeful who lost to Senator Hillary Clinton, energized young people and progressive voters with his message about free college and breaking up the big banks. By targeting those communities, he also brought in new voters who were drawn to a long-shot candidacy and made them a powerful force.

Most people in this country believe in immigration policies that allow a path for citizenship and want their borders strengthened; both are fairly sensible policies. But those who can be animated to vote when they typically stay home are likely to be more on the fringes rather than the mainstream. These are people who want fully closed or open borders, and it's the extremes—not the sensible solutions—that increase turnout.

Similarly, recent polls find that most Americans support trade, and yet the most powerful movements in politics today play off economic anger and resentment along with xenophobia; the marginal voters were moved by anti-trade policies.

The rise of the couch potato voter is also not just an American trend by any means. Take a look at Brexit, the vote for the United Kingdom to leave the European Union in summer of 2016 brought out voters who were motivated by fear of immigration from Syria and other countries in the Middle East. It only took a small group of very passionate people to throw off all of the polling models and upend the experts entirely. We are seeing the same forces taking hold in France and elsewhere in Europe after several terror attacks that have wracked those countries. Even Germany has seen its governing coalition collapse.

The implications of the new strategy—whereby campaigns target identity and fringe groups to win—are huge. If there is a marginal voter shift from being a middle-class suburban family to angry working-class voters on the right, or to socialists on the left, our elections will increasingly tear us apart rather than bring us together. The campaigns will pander to baser feelings and emotions rather than to the sensible solutions of the new center. The choices emerging from the primaries will be even more polarized and the general election campaign will be caustic, scorched-earth campaigns.

Rather than reaching compromises on issues like trade, the environment, and immigration, we will be driven to even further gridlock or executive orders that most Americans oppose, creating a vicious spiral downward and a collapse of faith in our political system.

The answer: paradoxically, we have to reduce the couch potato voter population by half or more by inviting them into the broader voting population. This would break the system wherein huge benefits accrue from motivating the 10 percent on the outside rather than working across aisles to attract swing voters. Universal voting would fix the problem, but most believe voting should be voluntary.

Let's start with reforming voter registration. Start it at birth, like Social Security. And set up a national database allowing voters to simply switch their registration from state to state. End this antiquated patchwork system.

Second, we need to make voting easier while keeping it private. That may mean initiatives like voting online, but other options include enabling places like ATMs—which use an already secure and available network for transactions—to function as voting terminals. And Tuesday voting should be replaced by a full weekend of voting. The Tuesday model is outdated and isn't working. One thing that is important, though, is the secret ballot: no one should ever be able to see how you are voting, especially before you vote, which could enable blackmail or harassment.

We also need to abolish caucuses: it's not a fair process in the twenty-first century, and they give even more power to the activist fringes because of their low turnout. Primaries should rotate in order of states, perhaps even by lottery to stop the gaming of New Hampshire and Iowa. We need to think overall about how this system has to change, rotating the geographic order so that no one bloc of voters becomes a gatekeeper to the presidency.

I personally prefer the Electoral College to a straight popular vote, because if we overcome the couch potato voter problem, it mostly requires candidates to pander to the center. I worry what today's multibillion-dollar campaigns would become if you could win by getting every New Yorker and Californian to the polls. I believe that a close election would result in a civil war, as votes would need to be recounted not in a few swing states but in every single district in the land. In theory, I would like to see the popular vote govern, but given today's America and its litigious nature, I'm not sure we could handle it. Any popular vote would require a runoff to save it from becoming a game of creating splinter candidacies and spoilers. An interesting variation would be for minor candidates to give their votes to one of the top two if they fail to get elected.

We all looked at our TV sets in amazement in this past election, watching candidates calling for mass deportation or tearing down our economic system. We have not updated and modernized our democracy as we have grown, nor have we taken advantage of the technology and innovation that makes it easier today to get a car and drive than it is to vote. The result is that in modern politics the fringe can be gamed to be more powerful than the mainstream, and that will tear us apart if we fail to see what is happening and fix it.

Section 6

WORK AND BUSINESS

42. Self-Data Lovers

43. Bikers to Work

44. Virtual Entrepreneurs

45. Microcapitalists

46. The Fakesters

47. Work with Limits

48. The New Factory Worker

49. Hazel Reborn

50. 10XMillionaires

42. SELF-DATA LOVERS

An intriguing new pastime has overtaken stepping on the scale: more and more of us are now body policing our every move, using technology to gather up-to-the-minute data on ourselves. Satirist David Sedaris in a piece for the *New Yorker* described his obsession with his new Fitbit: "During the first few weeks that I had it, I'd return to my hotel at the end of the day, and when I discovered that I'd taken a total of, say, twelve thousand steps, I'd go out for another three thousand." Why the extra steps? "Because," he explained, "my Fitbit thinks I can do better."

Self-data lovers are the new Wall Street traders: data addicts of a different kind. When one's life revolves solely around data, one begins to have a mind-set that sinks or soars by the numbers coming in. It can grow into an obsession, and it turns out that Sedaris is not alone in the self-monitoring craze.

According to a recent Harvard CAPS–Harris poll that surveyed a representative sample of Americans, over 40 percent of us are tracking at least some kind of health information, such as steps or heart rates. Men are more likely to track their health than women, and younger adults are more likely than older adults. Young urbanites are the most likely culprits, while their rural counterparts are the least likely. Of those who do track their health data, 58 percent reported using their phones. Another 28 percent of these track-happy respondents said they used their watch for tracking, while 19 percent used a Wi-Fi enabled scale, and 35 percent used other devices. (Some of these respondents obviously use multiple devices.)

42.1: Health Tracking Device Usage, 2017

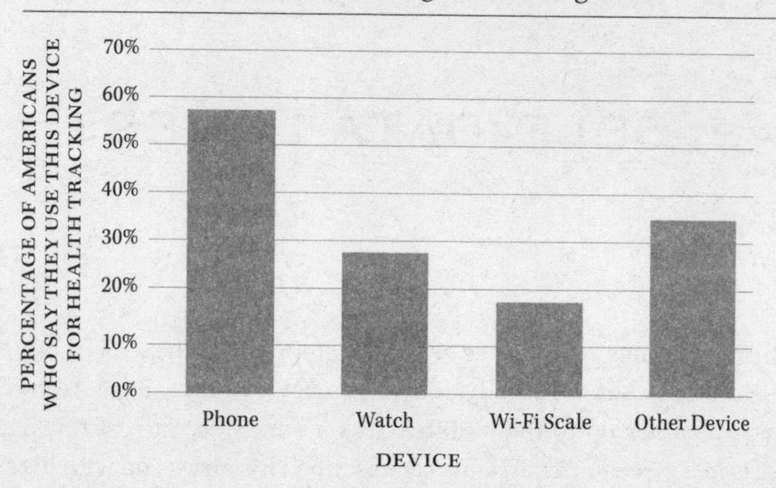

Source: Harvard–Harris Poll, September 2017

It's not just steps or weight we're life logging; it's practically anything that can be measured in our daily lives: fitness, mood, sleep, spending, menstrual cycle, food intake, symptoms, treatments, diaper deliveries, pizza deliveries, movement through space, social networks, addictions, and so on.

The possibilities are endless. Too much television watching? Log it. Worried about your sperm count? Track it. Or concerned about future injury prevention? Potential tumors? Both can be monitored through data.

But are we being data-delusional? There's a dark side here, as self-data tracking can get addictive. There's also an extremism to how far people are going with self-tracking things. And the results—of step logging, for instance—are not necessarily that one is achieving better health. The process can be merely time wasting or compulsive; it can even lead to very unhealthy behaviors.

A new study found that sleep trackers are actually bad for your health, according to a recent article in the *Journal of Clinical Sleep Medicine*. Participants can become fixated on the number of hours

42.2: Demographics of Americans Who Track Their Health Data, 2017

Percent of American Adults Who Track Their Health Data	
Total	43%
Gender	
Male	47%
Female	40%
Age	
18–34	57%
35–49	46%
50–64	34%
65+	35%
Locale	
Urban	51%
Suburban	41%
Rural	39%
Ethnicity	
White	44%
Hispanic	39%
Black/AA	41%
Asian/PI	48%
Other	44%
Education	
College Grad and Beyond	54%
Some College or Less	37%
Income	
$75K or More	52%
Less than $75K	37%

Source: Harvard-Harris Poll, September 2017

to sleep and end up, paradoxically, lying awake, obsessed with the data. Moreover, the study determined that the monitors used weren't even able to evaluate one's sleep results accurately. In essence, self-tracking creates worse sleep habits—more noise, more fuss, less rest.

Gary Wolf, editor at *Wired* magazine—who, along with coeditor Kevin Kelly, first coined the term "the quantified self" (QS)—noted that people might jump to conclusions and see negative effects of constant self-tracking. He offered a different view in a 2010 TED Talk: "We know that numbers are useful for us when we advertise, manage, govern, search. But they're also useful when we reflect, learn, remember, and want to improve. . . . While most people think of these tools as pointing outward as windows, they also turn inward and become mirrors for self-discovery, self-awareness, self-improvement, self-knowledge."

Wolf's QSers agree; in fact they meet up at large conferences—with as many as several thousand participants—and the movement

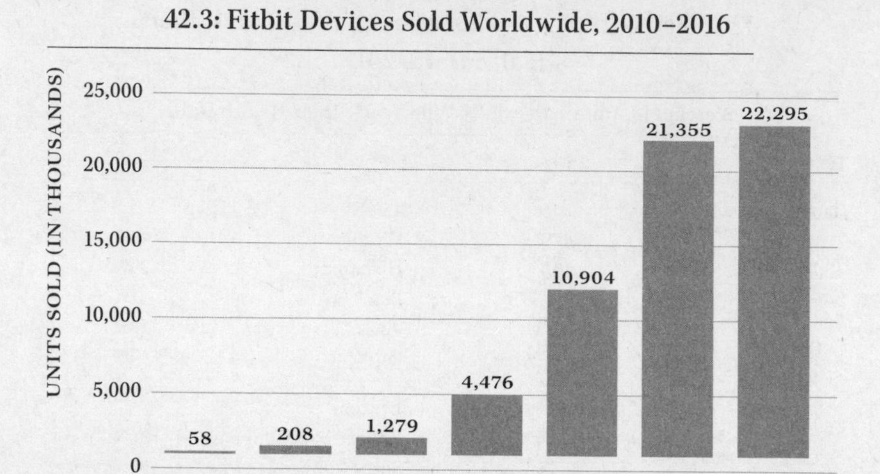

has spread internationally to more than one hundred groups in thirty countries. Topics included geotracking, DNA sequencing, chemical body load counts, personal genome sequencing, behavior monitoring, location tracking, non-invasive probing, etc. They also shared resources and videos and discussed newer and better technologies hitting the scene—and there are plenty.

Sure, geeky biometric gadgetry can be a means for self-revelation, helping you track your sleep apnea or daily caloric intake. But what's most surprising from these self-data lovers is that while a growing number of consumers are concerned about data mining and Big Data tracking by industries, many life loggers seem more than willing to share personal information with whoever is interested, supplying health symptoms and treatments to PatientsLikeMe and CureTogether; playlists and the number of times they've listened to a particular song to Spotify; and the number of calories they just ate at dinner to too many apps to mention. Orangetheory Fitness and CrossFit post workout results on screens throughout their facilities to encourage members to work harder. GPS tracking app Strava gathers where you've been and sells it to city planners, while Ototo does the same for public transportation.

Yet while we still struggle to navigate the delicate balance of private and public data, devices to log, track, and share are in flying off the shelves. MyFitnessPal, which was just acquired by Under Armour in 2015 for $475 million, has 165 million users. Lose It! claimed 17 million users in 2014. Samsung recently filed for a patent that would install a body fat sensor in their phones; people are lining up. The period app Clue has over 2.5 million users worldwide.

Of the concerns surrounding the self-tracking movement, those that tap into the Big Data debate are perhaps the most notable. With the installation of one sensor—at under $1 to produce—whole industries can amass mountains of information on their customers. As other institutions do the same, one has to step back and wonder what kind of surveillance environment we're building. Governments from local to national use personal data to trade figures; hospitals gather waiting times and exam results; companies manage turnover, assess what we're buying, and review our complaints. Almost all banks have some kind of tracking apps for customers, while PayScale Salary Survey has the largest database of individual compensation profiles in the world. Not just large organizations with deep pockets but small organizations and nonprofits—even mom-and-pop stores—can get enough personal information about customers to understand our habits.

In some industries this is not bad news, particularly when it comes to advancements in medicine. Talk to people with chronic social anxiety or back problems, HIV medication concerns, Parkinson's, or epilepsy. Personal data has helped ease symptoms and log warning signs. Take for example Asthmapolis, a start-up in Madison, Wisconsin. They've developed a device called the SpiroScout that can attach to an asthma inhaler and, through satellite positioning data, allow patients and doctors to examine their environments. Based on this information, researchers are understanding more about particular crops and environmental conditions and how they affect people with lung and asthma problems.

In Deborah Lupton's book *The Quantified Self*, she says there are five kinds of self-data trackers: private, communal, pushed, imposed, and exploited. She warns that even if monitoring offers positive outcome and motivation—say through fitness and diet—accuracy, consistency, and sustainability are also key.

If one were to study self-data trends, one might look to the younger generations to see what's on the horizon. According to a CNBC report, "U.S. teens and young adults are clocking up more hours on social media, a new survey has found, but at the same time sharing less and growing frustrated with 'friends' who 'overshare.'" The report goes on to say that "of the 812 teens and young adults surveyed, roughly three quarters said they spent the same or more amount of time on social media sites compared to a year ago. However, two-thirds said they had stopped sharing as much information as they used to. Four-fifths complained that people their age share too much." But for now there's a loyal following of self-data exhibitionists who don't seem to be slowing their sharing anytime soon. Nor will they be deterred by Big Data using their personal information for their own benefit. Why? According to Jennifer Hurst at Truman State University, "The desire for social connectedness and the positive feeling some get from the environment must be worth the time, energy, and sacrifice."

At Harvard they have been experimenting with a personal data "can"—a receptacle for all the data people generate about themselves across all of their activities and apps. Admission to the can is then sold to the highest bidder for your data. If you are someone with a disease or a love for chocolate cookies, you can expect either medical researchers or candy manufacturers to buy your data and you will be able to monetize your hobby of self-data loving. It's one way to turn a passion into something productive.

It might not be the people in lab coats who find the cure to certain diseases; it might just be these movements of life loggers who ping their way to new discoveries, new cures, or even just new pain relief. The potential is high, as are the risks to privacy, but I expect as data becomes the central and most powerful currency, the microtrend of self-data lovers will grow and more of us will keep all of the data we generate from birth to death and beyond.

43. BIKERS TO WORK

Almost every major city has torn up their roads and made an environmental statement in an attempt to curb global warming by adding bike lanes to their primary commuter roads. The response has not been overwhelming, but it's no longer uncommon to see helmeted commuters in business suits racing by your car as you sit stuck in traffic.

The Great Recession clearly had a role in Americans ditching cars for public transportation, walking, or biking as gas prices shot up before they shot down. According to the Federal Highway Administration, during the first ten years of this century Americans in each age group were driving less than in previous decades. The youngest of these groups—teens and young adults ages sixteen to thirty, had the sharpest drop. Whether it's because a family couldn't provide a teen with a car or because teens decided to pick up their bikes or walk instead, it set up a generation to look for alternative ways to get around. As reported in the *New Republic*, the "portion of Americans aged 16 to 24 who have driver's licenses fell to 67 percent in 2011, its lowest level in roughly a half-century."

Urban areas have seen some significant growth in bikers to work as the miles of bike-friendly roads have been dramatically increased. New York, for example, added over 500 miles of new bike paths to its roads in the last few years. Los Angeles now has 796 miles of bike lanes. Along with the bike lanes have come bike-sharing services that allow you to use a bike and return it to its stall. The largest of these was sponsored by Citibank, although its technology supplier went out of business even after having raised $50 million.

43.1: The Growth of Bike Commuting

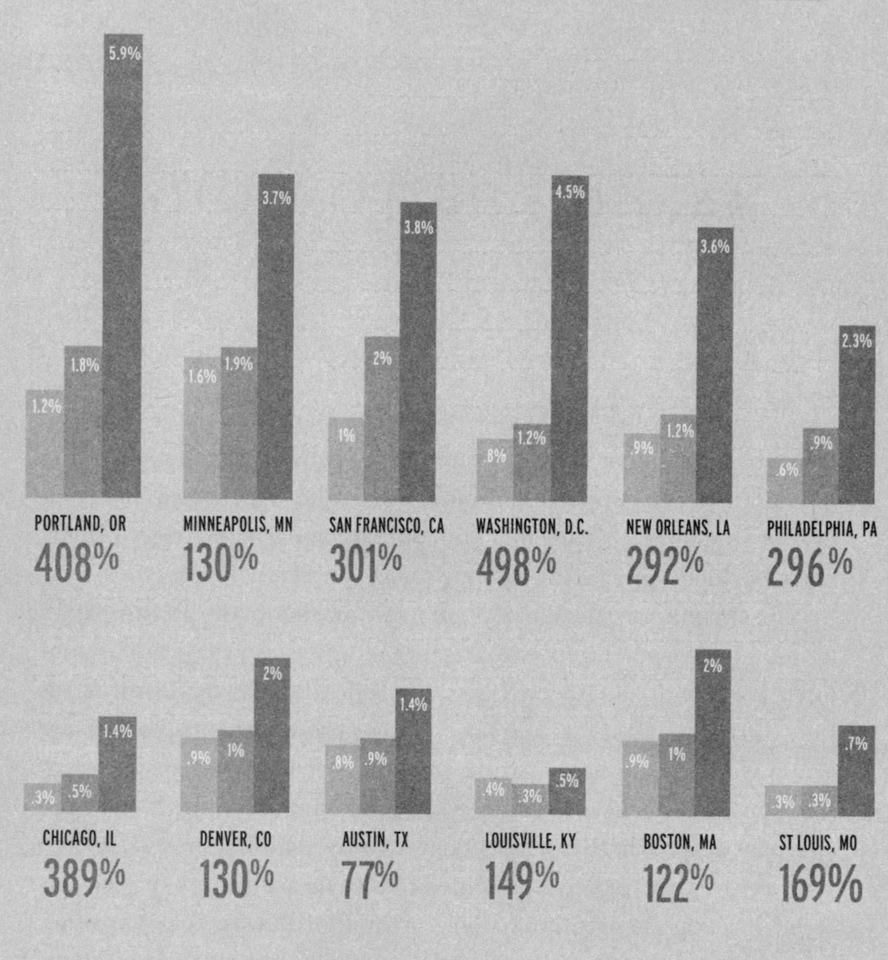

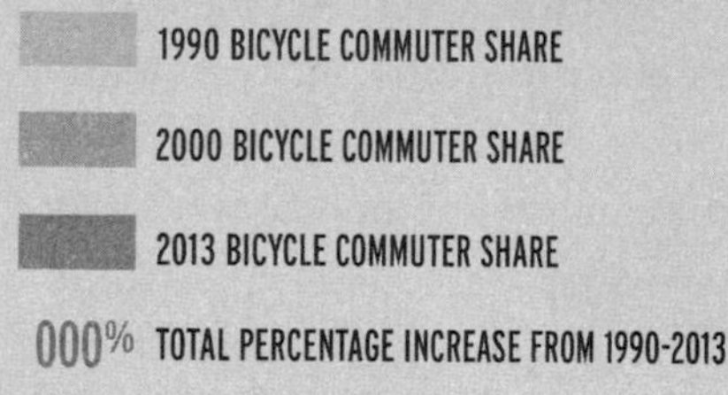

Source: The League of American Bicyclists (www.bikeleague.org). "Bicycle Friendly Community" and "BFC" are service marks of The League of American Bicyclists. Used with permission.

The result of these developments has been impressive growth in the use of bicycles to get to work: up over 400 percent in cities like Washington, D.C., and Portland, Oregon. Even in a big market like San Francisco, the percentage of those who bike to work is up 300 percent. Garages now often have bike racks as well as spaces for gasoline-powered cars and electric vehicles. Many condos and apartment buildings in American cities once again offer bike rooms.

Bikes have even become a status symbol of sorts. Whereas teens and twentysomethings have long gotten their hands dirty souping up their cars, restoring a classic bike or customizing the one you have is the new "cool" activity. Ultra-luxury brand Hermès sells bikes, and its Flaneur model costs an eye-popping $11,300. In China, there is a nostalgia for biking as a primary means of transportation. According to Reuters, "Rich Chinese are buying bicycles that cost more than the average citizen makes in three years, motivated by nostalgia."

Zeroing in on Washington, D.C., and New York City, it's clear that bikes are changing infrastructure and our roads. However, it's still a pretty yuppie population that's using bike shares or biking to work. Even in a very diverse city like D.C., 85 percent of Capital Bikeshare users are white, and around 50 percent of users make more than $100,000 a year. These are not people who need a bike to deliver take-out. The *New York Times* asks if bikes are just for rich tourists and white New Yorkers, or "a public transportation system for all."

While the growth has been strong, its absolute numbers are still small. Even by the generous estimates of cycling groups, bike commuting is just 2 or 3 percent of all local commuting. Meanwhile, billions of dollars have been spent on bicycle lanes that are often 20 or 25 percent of the available roadway. Anyone who sits in traffic looking at empty bicycle lanes wonders if the expenditures are really productive or sensible.

Despite lots of new start-ups aimed at making biking easier, or even shareable, the efforts aren't necessarily yielding a nation of bikers. According to the League of American Bicyclists, 2015 was the first year since 2010 that showed a decline in the number of people biking to work, despite its being the fastest-growing way to get to the office. In

2000, 43.1 million Americans "rode bicycles six or more days," and "by 2014 this had declined to 35.6 million," according to Streets.mn. Despite the up-and-down numbers, cities like Washington, D.C., are plowing ahead with further plans to make even more bike lanes. Whether they lead to a steady increase in ridership remains to be seen.

The bike movement here is in many ways an adaptation of programs that appeared to work in some countries in Europe. In Germany, for example, over 80 percent of households have a bike. In Japan, 78 percent, in Thailand, 74 percent. Many crowded Asian cities require a bike to navigate. However, cars are also prohibitively expensive for the average person in Thailand, making a bike cheap, easy, and the obvious choice. In the U.S., only 53 percent of households have a bike. Interestingly, the numbers vary hugely by country. For instance, only 5 percent of Jordanian households have a bike, and 7 percent of Lebanese homes.

Abroad, the U.K. has spent a lot to get Brits out of their cars and onto bikes. In 2016, London Mayor Sadiq Khan "promised to inject £770 million ($978 million) of new funding over the next five years into improving London's cycling infrastructure and conditions." In Barcelona, the City Council is planning to spend €32 million ($39 million) to "triple the reach of its bike lanes by 2018. This would take the total length of bike-only throughways from 116 kilometers (72 miles) to 308 kilometers (191 miles)." But there's a tradeoff: such moves have accelerated the traffic congestion in London, where getting across town can now routinely take an hour or more.

In China, a place where riding bikes to work is common, a massive bike-sharing push has filled Chinese cities with rival companies and start-ups. Mobike, for instance, is a bike-sharing platform in China that reportedly receives 20 million orders per month. At the same time, one major bike-sharing company in China went bankrupt, as 90 percent of their bikes were stolen. Overall, China's relationship with bikes appears to be in a state of flux. *Fast Company* reported that while 97 percent of Chinese people owned a bike in 1992, "by 2007 that had dropped to 49%, but just two years later, in 2009, ownership had risen again to 63%."

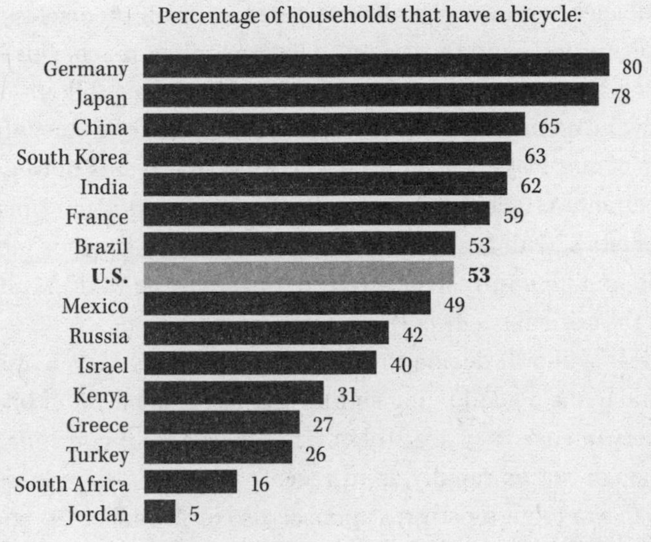

Of course, if you don't get injured, biking is generally good for you. According to Reuters, the investment in biking, particularly in New York City, is making its inhabitants healthier. "Every $1,300 New York City invested in building bike lanes in 2015 provided benefits equivalent to one additional year of life at full health over the lifetime of all city residents, according to a new economic assessment." A British medical journal found that over five years, walking and cycling versus passive modes of transport had serious medical and well-being effects. "Commuters who cycled to work had a 41% lower risk of dying from all causes than people who drove or took public transport. They also had a 46% lower risk of developing and a 52% lower risk of dying from cardiovascular disease, and a 45% lower risk of developing and a 40% lower risk of dying from cancer." The benefits of walking were significant, too: "Walking to work was associated with a 27% lower risk of developing and a 36% lower risk of dying from cardiovascular disease."

There is no question that the urban bike lane craze has been financed with huge sums of federal money. Personally, I am pessimistic about the long-term future of the trend. Mostly upper-income people in good neighborhoods who like the exercise avail themselves of these opportunities—and they seem to have a limited reach. Our society is aging, and while a young society would have more bikers, our fastest-growing demo group is those over 90. Instead, ride sharing—in the form of uberPOOL and similar Lyft services—seems poised to provide the more efficient and cost-effective transportation breakthrough for cities, with far less danger. Mass transit also needs more investment, and bike infrastructure programs may be taking funds away from the critical needs of these aging systems.

Businesses will still decide to cater to the growing bicycle marketplace and make a good living selling upscale, crunch-proof bikes with trackers in case they are stolen. That market will continue to expand, though not as rapidly as in recent years. Bike-sharing services seem to work, but mostly if a sponsor also regards them as good advertising, as bikes can easily be stolen or damaged. But if the bike will soon be competing with the driverless Uber, it's likely that the latter is going to win out.

44. VIRTUAL ENTREPRENEURS

The single biggest advance since the dawn of the PC for American small businesses and the mom-and-pop store is the cloud. Big business in the U.S. is moving to the cloud in record numbers, but it's smaller-scale businesses that reap enormous rewards—that is, if the leadership is savvy enough to take advantage of the technology. Small business formation is declining in the U.S. even as it has never been easier, nor more profitable, to open your own shop. Many Americans are still held back from striking out on their own because of perceived barriers and complexity.

A decade ago, opening a business meant filling out endless forms for health care, payroll, rent, and insurance. It also required hiring someone to file paperwork in Delaware for your LLC, arranging a check run for payroll, filling out all the state, unemployment, and workers' comp. You needed to buy computers, software . . . the list goes on and on. By the end of this arduous process, you pretty much turned into a Republican by default, ready to slash government regulations and red tape. And even after all that, you needed to buy a server for all of your files, hire someone to back your PC hard drives, and install a security system.

Today you can open and run a small business in the course of an afternoon, without any personnel or even a server. To start a business now, you open your government accounts and numbers online, put your employee records in the cloud, and direct deposit checks. Previous time sucks—paper, HR, health insurance, claims, accounting, IT support—are all done right at your desk, without assistance. Between virtual payroll companies and companies like Zenefits, the messy and annoying parts of opening a small business are transferred to people you will never talk to, let alone meet. Wireless phones will arrive in a few days and your company credit cards come with built-in expense tracking. With a little searching online you can find an employee handbook and a standard contract for the employees (if any), and you're ready to go.

When I was 13, I opened my first business selling stamps and coins to collectors through the mail. The best place to advertise used to be the classified section of the *New York Times*. It was a fun business, being a teen and going to auctions, selling through the mail on approval. In those days everything was done in person and by hand. From going to the stamp auctions to going to the PO box to collecting the returns, I was deeply involved in each step.

Today I would never leave my desk for any of these tasks. If I were running a collectibles business, I would bid in online auctions after setting up an eBay account, create online lots for sale, wait for confirmations of the credit card payments by e-mail. If the same market existed for stamps and coins as it did when I was 13 years old, I would expect a legion of competitors. Back then, the playing field wasn't so wide.

But the opening of the playing field to anyone with an entrepreneurial itch is both refreshing and encouraging. Anyone with a computer and an idea can start a business. You're less likely to be dissuaded by daunting barriers to entry and more likely to succeed if you have a good idea. Let's imagine you want to launch a business to create T-shirts with someone's street name on them, which you could sell to your neighbors. The virtual entrepreneur in you takes over, and there's already a wealth of services that make it possible. After handling the online paperwork to set up your business, you'd be able to find a company online to make your product—something along the lines of "OvernightTs.com," a massive T-shirt factory that will give you a discount for quantity. You'd invest in fifty shirts for each of the neighboring five blocks. They would arrive overnight, and now you have to sell them. You could go door to door, or you could simply target ads on Facebook to the local area or to a list of local e-mails. You could hire a robocall service to blast the neighborhood with calls on the "onetime offer" for a T-shirt with the name of your own street right on it.

With the internet enabling us, young (or old) upstart Americans can become their own bosses and execute ideas that previously wouldn't have been possible. You don't even have to have a physical product to be a virtual entrepreneur; you could create an online "product"—a blog or website on travel, say—and add on some promotions to gain your first customers, through organic and paid social. This business doesn't even have to be about humans: Look at the world of celebrity pets and pet "influencers" on platforms like Instagram, making millions. Just film videos of your pet doing amazing things (with a little behind-the-scenes help) and start to generate a following. One couple I know turned their dog into a pet-food influencer by gathering 250,000 followers on Instagram. They rake in $3,000 per ad or sponsorship. Soon their dog will be making more than they did, combined, at their previous jobs.

Around 10 percent of all retail sales are already online. Advertising is moving there, too, with the virtual "storefront" becoming as competitive as the traditional storefront used to be. In fact, the mark of success these days is for online brands to open up physical brick-and-mortar stores—but only after proving large levels of sales and visibility on the internet. Think Warby Parker or Casper: both of these brands performed so well online that the chance executives took was to bring them to you in real life, with pop-ups and retail "experiences." Previously, for a successful boutique, an e-commerce site was considered an exotic or second-tier way to make money. Now it's the opposite. Even the highest-end boutique, with rare pieces from designers—like FiveStory in New York, Colette in Paris, or The Webster in Miami—has an e-boutique.

Virtual entrepreneurs are also disrupting the food and restaurant business. While UberEATS and Grubhub ensure you don't have to set foot in a restaurant to pick up your food, a new model threatens restaurants entirely. This model is called a "virtual restaurant" and shifts away from the overhead required to start a successful business in the field. These "restaurants" would have no waitstaff and no hostess—just a kitchen to create delicious food with the idea that ordering online and through app services would be enough to sustain business.

The virtual workplace has benefits especially for the small artisan. In the past, people with a talent for making jewelry either made it for friends and family, did it as a hobby without the intent to sell or market, or got a job in a jewelry store. Now, if your stuff is marketable and desirable, you can create your own empire. One example of this are the "power sellers" on Etsy, like Alicia Shaffer. She began making headbands on Etsy, selling them piecemeal—and now she makes $80,000 a month selling scarves, headbands, and leg warmers. She does it from her home and moves 3,000 products per day. Her initial overhead? Almost nonexistent.

The rise of virtual entrepreneurs stands to help American women in particular. American women spend a tremendous amount of money, and it's female entrepreneurs who understand how to reach them. Virtual entrepreneurship allows many more one-woman startups to benefit from a new level of flexibility, as they're able to make their own schedules and fall back on cloud services to fill out the enterprise. A recent Harvard University study asserts that "the gender gap in pay would be considerably reduced and might even vanish if firms did not have an incentive to disproportionately reward individuals who worked long hours and who worked particular hours." Flexibility is one of the keys to American women's success in business.

The flexibility that comes from being a virtual entrepreneur, or working for one, means that employees are happier, too. You might also get better hires; who doesn't want to work from home in their pajamas? A *Forbes* article cites a study in which workers' happiness is evaluated on a scale of one to ten. The answer to "How happy are you at work?" scored higher for remote workers—an 8.10—versus all workers—7.42.

Americans, particularly millennials, will spend a lot buying from savvy online retailers. Companies that have exploded from virtual-only and smart marketing to young tech-savvy Americans are Warby Parker, Dollar Shave Club, Casper, and Bonobos, to name a few. Both Dollar Shave Club and Harry's (from the team behind Warby Parker) understood that the millennial male (and female) wanted an easy solution to buying razors. As of 2014, Harry's was valued at $350 million, and Dollar Shave Club was purchased by Unilever for $1 billion. Both companies have millions of customers, thanks to a keen understanding of social media and reach. These tactics are crucial for the new virtual entrepreneur. Millennial-centric eyewear brand Warby Parker did something similar for boring glasses shopping. Picking out new glasses is unsexy, and this online start-up—now valued at over a billion dollars—made glasses part of your outfit and identity while delivering chic frames to your door. Years later, after starting as online only, Warby Parker has stores all over the U.S.

Millennial men are key targets for these virtual businesses. Case in point: clothing brand Bonobos, which made the reverse move to brick-and-mortar. Their motto? "Like most guys, we're not big fans of shopping. That's why we set out to build the best online shopping experience in the world, and we made it the core of what we do. We're now the largest clothing brand ever built on the web in the US."

Advertising for these online businesses is popping up in well-trod digital spaces like Facebook and other social media platforms—but also in what might seem like the most boring of places: podcasts. Savvy Americans are consuming audio content, and some of the most precious ad space is on popular podcasts with large audiences. Slots are cheap (a few hundred dollars), and they have tremendous reach. With the viral true-crime podcast *Serial*, online mailing list company MailChimp got lucky: they took a chance on what might be a big and savvy audience and became an overnight sensation. Podcast advertising also helped propel the virtual mattress company Casper to scale, allowing the company to make a million dollars in its first twenty-eight days in business.

There's also money in reselling things you buy in the wild. Nasty

Gal founder Sophia Amoruso (aka Girl Boss) did just that: she started a massive e-commerce site that began as an eBay store where she flipped clothing she bought in stores for more money online. The popular podcast *Planet Money* recently dedicated a whole episode to these resellers, particularly on Amazon. One such reseller, Sam Cohen, "buys stuff at big retail stores, then turns around and sells it on Amazon for a quick profit. It defies economic logic." There are millions to be made from this, as has been proven over and over again. Students, ripped off by expensive textbook prices, are buying and selling textbooks as arbitrage using online pricing strategies.

Founding a virtual business is a microtrend that allows savvy Americans to thrive in a world of automation and globalization—a low cost way to pay the rent without having to go into an office. You don't need to have a world-changing idea, either, just a good one. To be a virtual entrepreneur, all you need is a bit of technical savvy to open accounts online, some marketing moxie, and a small amount of capital.

You, too—young, old—can become a virtual entrepreneur. Don't expect to succeed on the first try; it might take four or five ideas, balances on your credit cards, and some stress to figure out what works. But only a few years ago this ability to quickly fail (or succeed) didn't exist. You might not be Bill Gates or Sara Blakely (self-made billionaire founder of Spanx), but with some persistence and the right idea, you can make a decent living or pick up some extra cash. Globalization and technology are not your enemies but your friends. America should be doing everything it can policy-wise to clear the way for these new virtual entrepreneurs and the flexible workplaces they can create.

45. MICROCAPITALISTS

Almost anyone in America today can start their own business, selling their old stuff or new crafts on eBay. It takes a little time and capital to get started, but once you're up and running, amazing opportunities can arise. If you live in many of the developing countries in the world, the landscape is different and the stakes are higher, but the opportunity to make it on your own is on the rise. You may face low wages and few good jobs locally, but if you could leverage the basic ideas of capitalism to your benefit, it could change life for you, your family, and your community fundamentally. *If* you can get started.

Enter the "microcapitalists," who've made it their business to disperse seed money in small parcels to entrepreneurs across the globe. Both the model and the returns are astonishing and on the rise.

It is not a surprise that Goldman Sachs would make this a major initiative, but it was a surprise that their male-dominated finance firm would focus on women. In 2008, Goldman Sachs announced their 10,000 Women initiative. With an initial commitment of $100 million, the bank created a program that would provide the most underserved women—from across fifty-six countries—the financial resources, education, mentorship, and networking they would need to start a business in their local communities. This program was revolutionary: women business owners—particularly of small- to medium-sized enterprises in impoverished parts of the world—have always been overlooked by investors and institutions.

At the same time that Goldman Sachs announced its 10,000 Women program, Muhammad Yunus of Grameen Bank in Bangladesh was building on a similar concept of loaning money to the very poorest of his country—mostly women. Some would call it "financial inclusion," but most of us now know it as microfinancing. And it would quickly gain traction. Today, microfinancing reaches over 200 million clients worldwide, 80 percent of whom are women. Yunus went on to win a Nobel Peace Prize for his work in microcredit in 2006. And in 2014, Goldman Sachs's 10,000 Women initiative, in partnership with the World Bank, announced a $600 million global-financing facility that would enable 100,000 women (and growing) access to capital and resources worldwide.

Women have been a key focus, not only because they have a notoriously difficult time asking for and receiving money, but also because the International Finance Corporation estimates that 70 percent of women business owners in developing countries can't get adequate funding—at a gap of nearly $300 billion. In the U.S., it would be perfectly normal and feasible for a female entrepreneur to apply for a small-business loan to start, say, a Lululemon franchise; there are plenty of institutions competing for their business, and the lending process is usually quick and straightforward. But in the developing world—where steady employment is a challenge, money is scarce, a person's credit history is virtually nonexistent, and often there are few assets to be used as collateral—lending to aspiring entrepreneurs is all but nonexistent. At least, it was.

Now microcredit institutions have expanded to over a hundred countries and benefited millions of the most impoverished. Grameen Bank alone has lent more than $2 billion to more than 2 million villagers in India—most of them women—with an average loan of less than $100. Has a focus on women negatively or positively impacted the process? Muhammad Yunus explained in an interview with the *Los Angeles Times*: "Based on our experience in Bangladesh, money going to the families through women brings much more of a benefit than the same money going through a man. Women want to build it up for the future, they have a longer-term vision. Women look at the family situation, improving the children's situation, unlike the men, who try to concentrate on immediate gratification and enjoyment of life. We saw the same thing in other countries where the idea of microcredit has spread."

Goldman Sachs reported positive results as well. Graduates of their program on average reported a 480 percent increase in revenues.

There's a lot to be learned from these microcapitalists, and not just in the narrow sense of what they're doing with their loans. We also learn from microfinancing in general about the successes and failures of lending money, making money, owing money, and losing money in impoverished nations, with or without the infrastructure to support entrepreneurial endeavors.

In Bangladesh, the birthplace of microfinancing, most women began by taking out a small loan to buy a cow to sell milk, or they would purchase materials to sew and sell saris. Then women began pooling their money for larger projects—say, to buy a herd of water buffalo or to open a bakery. Now, years later, women-oriented microfinancing initiatives have grown into grassroots movements and self-sustaining organizations that are alleviating poverty not just for themselves and their families but for entire communities while also empowering future generations of women. Take, for example, Mamatha of Hyderabad, India: in 2006 she started a company that would clean water tanks in her community—a much-needed business. Her customer base started with 200 locals and grew to a regional 4,000; she now employs 15 people, and dozens of contract workers. Her business is expected to grow by another 30 percent over the next few years.

Latin America, with its well-established microfinancing programs, has benefited greatly from this financing development, which has become important to the overall economic outlook of developing countries in the region. *The Economist* published its Microfinance Business Environment report which found that eight of the top dozen countries with the best business environments are in Latin America. Peru led with a $12.3 billion microcredit portfolio, followed by Ecuador ($1.7 billion) and Colombia ($1.4 billion). Mexico had 2.3 million clients, making it the largest market in the region.

Microfinancing is changing lives not just in India and Latin America but globally. Rural women in East Africa, for example, have been accessing microloans throughout the poorest parts of Uganda, Tanzania, and Kenya to support AIDS orphans, start small businesses, and pay for school fees, food, and health care. Borrowers further help communities by using funds to hire helpers and create local improvements.

In Pakistan, where two-thirds of the people live on less than $2 a day, and ancient cities have been demolished by war and terrorism, women have started storefront businesses, are creating incentives to rebuild infrastructure and housing, and are focused on keeping their children in school. Investment banker Roshaneh Zafar has been trying to stamp out poverty in her hometown and the surrounding neighborhoods of Lahore through microfinancing since 1995. She has given over $200 million to more than 300,000 women. Money goes toward embroidery businesses, salons, schools, infrastructure, etc. The biggest impact reported to Zafar: "We've discovered that 40 percent of men interviewed say, 'We have stopped beating our wives,' as a result of the loans, because most quarrels are over money, lack of money." A whopping 80 percent of men say they now consult their wives in not just financial decisions but all decision making.

Even in the United States, where Grameen America reports that 28 million people have no access to banking services and less than half of us have a savings account, women—particularly black and Hispanic—are finding new opportunities in microfinancing.

Overall, the largest impact of microfinancing communities has been in education. Muhammad Yunus, founder of Grameen, explains, "In Bangladesh, we lend money to women, and they're all illiterate. Their husbands are illiterate. We wanted to make sure their second generations are not illiterate. We made it happen—100% literacy in Grameen families. We gave them education loans so they can go to universities, colleges, medical school. We have a whole new second generation with high education. It is built into our system."

Unfortunately, despite the numerous success stories, there are just as many tales of borrowers who built up debt they couldn't repay.

Africa, for example, has not attracted as much attention or capital as, say, Latin America, due to political risks and weaker infrastructure. A successful microfinancing model doesn't just require a person with an idea and aspirations to run a business; it requires the overall macroeconomic health of a country. With a failing economy, fewer recipients are able to pay off loans; interest rates are high; there is less training available; and many borrowers end up rolling unpaid loans into new loans—a revolving-door effect. Donor programs intervene, but many of these organizations function with a kind of "flavor-of-the-month" giving mentality. Direct funding, rather than funding through an organized government or regional program, has created increased uncertainty for many microcapitalists in the region and more often than not businesses are forgotten or abandoned and eventually fail.

With a couple of decades under its belt now, the microfinance industry is estimated at a value of somewhere between $70 billion and $100 billion. According to the 2015 Microcredit Summit Campaign report, by the end of 2013, "microfinance institutions reported reaching 211,119,547 borrowers; this is the largest number ever reported. On the other hand, the total number of poorest clients with loans outstanding declined, for the third straight year, to 114,311,586. Of these poorest clients, 82.6 percent, or 94,388,701, are women."

Studies revealed that people in developing countries manage their households in far more complex ways than economists thought. By looking at overall income and expenditures, researchers were overlooking the day-to-day struggles of the poor. Researcher Jonathan Morduch explains in *Portfolios of the Poor* that when someone is living on $1 or $2 a day, that money isn't actually earned each day: it could be weeks before their next payment. Therefore households might not be making long-term choices with their income but rather providing for immediate needs.

In developing areas where microfinancing is being allocated and properly managed, and where businesses and grassroots organizations are taking shape and impacting communities directly, poverty levels have decreased dramatically and quality of life has improved.

Still, as independent economist Kathleen Odell points out, microfinancing is no silver bullet: "The overall effect on the incomes and poverty rates of microfinance clients is less clear, as are the effects of microfinance on measures of social well-being, such as education, health, and women's empowerment."

Another side benefit of microfinance is simply the introduction of the ideas of Adam Smith into communities that otherwise would think of economic gain and loss as more about what the tribe or the government does. Of course, failed microcapitalists could become even less enthusiastic about these ideas, but success stories provide inspiration that capitalism works—and not just for the big companies, but for the little guy or woman. In the U.S., due to all the issues related to red tape and taxes, opening a small business often moves people toward the Republican Party. We don't know what becoming a microcapitalist does to people's political views in developing countries, but anyone with a business anywhere needs economic if not social freedom.

Microfinancing may not be the cure-all for global poverty, but it is here to stay. When it fails, it generally leaves people no worse than they were; but when it is successful, it can make a huge difference to people and their lives. There is no "Minnow Tank" (that is, a smaller version of popular show *Shark Tank*) for people taking microcredit, but a splashy reality TV show may well be what's needed to bring even more attention to this way out of poverty. Unlike a handout, these ideas are meant to teach people how to fish for a lifetime, which is why they are so powerful when they work.

46. THE FAKESTERS

Fake news became all the rage after the 2016 presidential election, and yet it only served to pull the covers back on a whole new world of fraud that had been developing over the last decade. A new kind of con man that could pick your pocket without ever coming within 2,000 miles had been created. The internet fakester was born.

Many internet fakesters represent a new kind of criminal far removed from the great bank robbers like Willie Sutton and famous mobsters. Even the great criminal fakesters of the past like Charles Ponzi or the more recent Bernie Madoff needed to confront their victims and look them right in the eye. While the internet has created incredible benefits for society, it also has allowed this new underclass to develop and prosper.

When hackers came on the scene, it was mostly out of sport. MIT students coined the term "hack" in the 1960s to mean "a person who delights in having an intimate understanding of the internal workings of a system, computers and computer networks in particular." They were nerds, geniuses, recluses with a lot of time. Movies were made, legends built.

Sarah Gordon, senior research fellow at Symantec Research Labs, has been tracking the mentality and motivation of virus writers and hackers for years. Gordon explains that hackers today are a varied bunch. A good number of fakesters fit the stereotypical mold of the adolescent male computer nerd, but with the changing of the internet, she explains, hackers don't necessarily match one profile, one skill set, one demographic, one geographic location. Nor do they have to be people with an advanced understanding of computer systems. In fact, most hackers get their tricks from—where else?—the internet.

On its simplest level, skimming cash off the internet became easy once internet platforms opened up to provide cash to virtually anyone who could provide clicks. As we've seen, that created fascinating new careers for some hardworking and creative people. But it also opened up the internet to this dark side. Simply splash a few false headlines with a picture and, if you get enough clicks, ads and checks will follow. Post the fictitious "Clinton Bites Dog"—or "Trump Pisses on Pope"—and *bam*, great headlines garner clicks. Come up with hundreds of those, and the easiest scam ever created could start to multiply.

The best place to be a fakester is a location where no state police or FBI are likely to burst through the door and arrest you. That makes it hard to maintain in the U.S. and impossible in China (unless the government is helping you). However, many countries remain prime real estate for a fakester operation—places like the Ukraine, parts of Africa, and the Philippines. According to cloud service provider Akamai, Indonesia faces the largest number of cyberattacks—38 percent worldwide, followed by China. Only 1.7 percent of all cyberattacks are targeted at Russia—much lower than the United States, Taiwan, Turkey, and India.

One fake news distributor in America, Disinfomedia, run by Jestin Coler, was willing to talk to NPR. According to Coler, he runs many faux news sites—a number he would not pin down—with anywhere between twenty and twenty-five writers. "Coler is a soft-spoken 40-year-old with a wife and two kids. He says he got into fake news around 2013 to highlight the extremism of the white nationalist alt-right."

"The whole idea from the start was to build a site that could kind of infiltrate the echo chambers of the alt-right, publish blatantly fictional stories and then be able to publicly denounce those stories and point out the fact that they were fiction," Coler says. He wrote one fake story about how customers in Colorado were using food stamps to buy marijuana, and his news made it all the way to the Colorado statehouse. State representatives were proposing legislation on something that never even occurred.

Coler continues writing fake news, undeterred by the reaction to his interview. Stories about fake news garner $10,000 to $30,000 a month. If Coler targets Trump supporters, he makes much more. Like other cons, for fake newsters, the money comes easily; their identities can remain hidden, and best of all, the identities of their victims remain hidden.

In the past, a con man was a con man. Today, a con man can also be the guy you just bought your insurance from. According to Martin MacKay in his 2015 piece "Researching the Psychology of Hackers": "If you go to DEF CON in Las Vegas, or Chaos Computer Club in Europe, you'll see hundreds of examples of the lone hacker, tattooed and wearing a dark hoodie. But for every one of those people putting on

46.1: Heimdal Security's Top Online Scams, 2017
Phishing e-mail scams
The Nigerian scam
Greeting card scams
A guaranteed bank loan or credit card scam
Lottery scams
Hitman scams
Romance scams
Fake antivirus software
Facebook impersonation scams
Make-money-fast scams
Travel scams
Delivery scams
Fake news scams
Stock market scams
Job offer scams
SMS scams
Source: Heimdal Security

a public show, there are tens if not hundreds of people who spend their time breaking systems for fun and profit. Many of them are successful businesspeople, wearing a suit to work every day, looking and acting no different from everyone else. To some people, committing crimes using a computer is as much a 9-to-5 job as protecting computer systems is."

But fakesters have plenty of other routes. Last week I received an e-mail that asked me to wire $25,000 to a man I'd never met before in Nigeria in exchange for a larger sum of money later on. It's the classic e-mail scam—replete with odd spacing, odd writing, claiming dire straits—known as "the Nigerian Prince Story." These are so bad and so obvious you kind of wonder why people even bother. But they must send out tens of millions of these and get a rate of return that is good enough to live a pretty good life in Nigeria. On the other hand, John Podesta and the Clinton campaign IT operation fell prey to a rather simple phishing scam.

According to *Mother Jones*, "Nigerian fraudsters manage to dupe Americans into forking thousands of dollars over to complete strangers each year. In 2011, the FBI received close to 30,000 reports of advance fee ploys, called '419 scams' after the section of the Nigerian criminal code that outlaws fraud. The agency received over 4,000 complaints of advance fee romance scams in 2012, with victim losses totaling over $55 million. Nigerians aren't the only ones committing international advance fee fraud, but nearly one-fifth of all such scams originate in the West African country. The scams often involve phony lottery winnings, job offers, and inheritance notices." Two fakesters who were interviewed for the *Mother Jones* article admitted they are each worth $60,000 in Nigeria—a country where 70 percent of the population lives on $2 a day.

Surprisingly, phone scams are on the rise, too. There are now call centers with four hundred to five hundred people running scams, and almost all of the calls come from India. They account for 10 percent of consumer complaints to the FTC, and over a quarter million complaints in 2016. With advancements in the robocaller, billions of fake phone calls to both cellular phones and landlines are placed every month. Apple has documented one common scam in which the victim receives "a call instilling panic and urgency to make a payment by purchasing iTunes Gift Cards from the nearest retailer (convenience store, electronics retailer, etc.). After the cards have been purchased, the victim is asked to pay by sharing the 16-digit code on the back of the card with the caller over the phone." Amazing what sometimes works.

One of the more frightening and lucrative scams on the rise is ransomware. Ransomware acts like malware, but once it enters your computer system it locks your keyboard to prevent you from accessing your hard drive until you pay a ransom, usually in Bitcoin. According to *Wired* magazine, ransomware has been quite lucrative. "In 2012, Symantec gained access to a command-and-control server used by the CryptoDefense malware and got a glimpse of the hackers' haul based on transactions for two Bitcoin addresses the attackers used to receive ransoms. Out of 5,700 computers infected with the malware in a single day, about three percent of victims appeared to shell out for the ransom. At an average of $200 per victim, Symantec estimated that the attackers hauled in at least $34,000 that day. Extrapolating from this, they would have earned more than $394,000 in a month." Overall, in 2016, it is estimated that the fakesters took in $1.33 billion from the U.S. market.

There are probably 100,000 people in the fraud industry, and it's one of the fastest-growing jobs in the planet. It's done mostly by young people in developing countries who may never know a better career, and the skills needed for much of it are diminishing rather than increasing. Just as our airports today require enormous resources poured into security, so, too, does the internet need to develop in the same way. Much of this crime is not about technology but about preying on our emotions. No security has ever been developed that guards against the basic human instinct to help someone you believe needs help—or baser flashes of curiosity or greed. It will take a concerted effort to curb the fakesters, but this is one microtrend I hope stays a microtrend.

47. WORK WITH LIMITS

The "attention deficit generation" can add a new kind of work to its mobile lifestyle of casual dating, shared living, part-time schooling, and the notification-driven culture generated by smartphones and social media.

Part-time and after-school work has been around for a long time. Generally, part-time work arose when full-time work was cut back by employers who needed to save money given a reduction in orders. Some part-time work, like the seasonal work around Christmas, was intended to deal with cyclical retail patterns. After-school or summer work fit nicely with the breaks people had from school.

However, there is an emerging microtrend that we call work with limits. We're not talking about part-timers who are looking for full employment; we're not talking about college-age employees balancing school and work; and we're not talking about the 60-and-older crowd working post-retirement jobs. We're talking about Americans in the prime of their careers who don't want their work to be the defining factor of their lives. This runs in stark contrast to the rest of America slogging away at their desk jobs.

For these workers with limits (WWLs), work is not everything—it's only part of their lives. About 25 percent of part-time workers live in poverty, according to a study by Rebecca Glauber, a professor at the University of New Hampshire. However, this particular set of part-timers are finding ways to cobble together gig-economy jobs—maybe driving for Uber during the day, delivering for Seamless at night—in order to create the life they want, with the schedule that they desire. It's a way of working that's meant to work for them, not their employer. Many of these WWLs are women—ones who don't necessarily have to work due to their financial situations but choose to dabble in fulfilling and productive projects that don't take up all of their time. This allows them to spend time with their families or pursue other interests. For WWLs, it's all about finding fulfilling work that speaks to a passion or allows you to find a work-life balance that you can control.

While these WWLs might be finding time for their passions, it's become a worrisome trend for the Federal Reserve. The metrics produced by the Bureau of Labor on monthly employment data are closely watched by all industries to understand where the economy is headed. Yet, while the part-time workforce is at "high levels," according to Federal Reserve chair Janet Yellen, the Bureau of Labor Statistics shows that of the 26 million part-time employees in the U.S. in 2016, 20 million of those actively choose part-time work. Of those, 6 million chose to work part-time to pursue their passions.

When it comes to full-time work versus part-time, American men vastly prefer full-time work, unlike women. In a survey from 2011, only 12 percent of men preferred part-time employment, whereas 60 percent of the women preferred it. However, part of this gap is due to the stigma of men taking a backseat in their careers, particularly if it would make them feel like second-fiddle husbands.

Regardless, part-time labor in America is growing quickly. Between 1955 and 2015, the number of Americans choosing part-time labor quadrupled. As the labor force has contracted, this group has expanded. It might seem as though part-time work were bad for the American economy, but that isn't necessarily the case. According to Diane Lim of the Committee for Economic Development, OECD research indicates that part-time work allows for "greater freedom of movement of workers—across jobs, occupations, industries, and geographies—[and] lets resources flow more easily to their highest-valued uses." In other words, part-timers allow for a more fluid economy and the creation of jobs that are constant and evolving. Part-time jobs also aren't resulting in a decrease in productivity; instead this influx of part-time work brings relief to the economy from pressure on automation. Let's not confuse those who work with limits slackers, either. Many studies show that part-time work is a solid strategy for both companies and employers, as these tightened schedules result in happier employees and a better work product.

Currently two-thirds of part-time employees are women, and one-third are men, with half of the men coming from the oldest and youngest age groups. Overwhelming evidence shows that part-time work benefits American women. A study from 2012 evaluating the happiness of women between part-time and full-time work found that "decreases in working long hours" brought "positive and significant improvement" for the lives of women who participated. Many of these female part-time workers have children and a full-time working spouse; maybe they are seeking out intellectual stimulation or want to dip a toe back into their old work lives without sacrificing their home lives.

Start-ups have begun to take notice of the flexibility that women with children want in their lives. Companies like Inkwell—which matches high-level small projects with qualified women who have left the workforce to have children—have sprouted up, enabling a marketing executive with two decades of experience to take part in fulfilling work that also allows her to spend time with her kids. These companies and initiatives run counter to the "brain drain"—the idea that educated American women drop out of the workforce to have children and don't return—that can slow women's rise up the corporate ladder when they want to put their families first but also to continue their work.

The WWL lifestyle is an advancement for working moms. Companies that offer flexible scheduling or part-time work at a high level are bringing many moms back into the workforce. Many companies are taking notice and catering to those who really want to spend only a limited amount of their time on work, and a quarter of all working American women now work part-time. Companies that don't have part-time options will fall to the back of the pack and lose their competitive edge for hiring the best talent.

Slowly but surely, industries that were once notoriously inflexible with work hours are realizing the benefits of compromise in this age of connectivity. A recent National Study of Employers report found that 38 percent of employers offer more work-from-home options, up from 23 percent in 2008. While commonplace part-time work might be a trend to watch in the future, more companies now offer flexible arrangements, telecommuting, and shorter workdays than ever before—although some of these benefits are offered only to certain employees, particularly women with young children.

Many American men want to work part-time but feel that it might make them seem emasculated. A study found that 59 percent of working fathers would love a part-time schedule but don't do it because over a third said that "part-timers were looked down upon at their organization," according to *Fast Company.* This bias might be keeping part-time workers from participation on big essential projects or from gaining the full respect of their coworkers.

This may continue to change in the coming years, but flexibility in the workforce will be driven by employers, not employees. If companies see this as a way to save—perhaps through fringe benefits or to tighten the wage gap between men and women, or to simply allow less stress on employees and more time with family—then change will come from the employers' culture. Perhaps rewriting the employee handbooks is in order.

Among many young Americans, the ideal is to avoid working for large companies entirely and to be able keep some control over their time. Millennials are obsessed with the idea of working on their own schedule—which might mean fewer traditional company perks (paid vacation, health benefits), in order to feel like your own boss. According to a recent 2015 study by PayScale, only around 15 percent of 2015 college graduates "want to work for large corporations." Whereas a large banking job or position at a global firm was the keen desire of a rising senior in college in, say, 2007, that's now considered unappealing. The study also found that things like wanting to spend time with a loved one, to feel passionate about one's work, and to travel the globe all trumped the desire to have the security of a full-time corporate job. This was reinforced by a CareerBuilder study that found that 63 percent of respondents agreed that a full eight-hour workday from 9:00 a.m. to 5:00 p.m. was an "outdated concept" (Velasco, 2015).

The nine-to-five workday doesn't fit the modern family structure, period. Before, this setup was intended for a two-parent family where the man was at the office and the woman was at home. Traditional industries and traditional schedules aren't taking into account the delay of modern marriages or workers' desires to pursue personal interests, let alone a two-parent working home, same-sex marriages, or even the prospect of a woman working while her husband takes care of the kids. Even structurally, new additions like a lactation room or an open-office setting hint that the old way of work is simply not applicable for modern times.

According to a 2015 study, more young men are looking for part-time work than ever, indicating that the stigma felt by older generations of men is either going away or not potent enough to outweigh the other priorities of men entering the workforce. This trend is also likely a reflection of a new generation of men who seem to be participating more in what economists call "household production" (aka duties on the home front). This hints that the gender gap in part-time work may close in the future and that companies will need more innovative paternity leave.

The desire for a more flexible job and personal life isn't just American. In the Netherlands the majority of married women have a part-time job and are happy with it. In a 2013 (Booth & Van Ours) study, the findings indicated that "partnered women in part-time work have high levels of job satisfaction, a low desire to change their working hours, and live in partnerships in which household production is highly gendered." While women in countries like the Netherlands are still managing the home, they're not upset about it. In European nations like Spain, the United Kingdom, Germany, and France, governments actually emphasize part-time work for employers as a way to cut costs and employ more people with less commitment, citing from the Booth & Van Ours study above.

Employees in part-time situations were "the most satisfied," according to a 2012 study, surpassing the job satisfaction of regular nine-to-fivers. And part-time work also makes you more efficient and effective. This arrangement is somewhat confounding for social planners and government officials, who define "full employment" as everyone working the longest possible hours in exchange for clear benefits. But more and more workers say part-time is enough. On the whole, WWLs are not trying to climb the corporate ladder or buy a Tesla; they view work as necessity but want limits.

48. THE NEW FACTORY WORKER

The new factory worker is just as much a creature of the Information Age as the traditional factory worker was of the industrial age. This new factory worker profile couldn't look any more different from the old one. In the nineteenth century, jobs and industry in America were structured around family life, health and safety, work hours and overtime, and being part of a collective organization and structure that would protect you, your children, and your spouse. Today's new factory worker is built around the always-on economy and the greater flexibility demanded by new millennial workers.

Factory workers used to stand on an assembly line doing one arduous and tedious task day in and day out. Maybe this meant screwing in one part of a toy or placing one item in a basket over, and over, and over again. The new factory worker runs a forklift in an Amazon warehouse or works independently for an app like Uber and still has a challenging job, but it looks very different.

Traditional factory jobs that were the bulwark of the old economy are disappearing—not just in the United States but globally. All over the world, the manufacturing base of employment is shrinking even as productivity has increased. Many believe that we are nearing the end of "work" as we know it, in a narrative that goes like this: robots, spurred on by artificial intelligence, are taking on more of what people used to do. Those who can make it in this new future economy will have every luxury, while those who can't will be permanently unemployed, perhaps funded by robot taxes or a bleak world that looks a lot like the new *Blade Runner 2049*.

But jobs are not really disappearing. Massive amounts of new jobs have been created, and employment around the globe is at a record high. Rebounding from 2009, America now has more people at work than ever. As of 2016 data, there were 124 million Americans working full-time and 28 million with part-time jobs. All over the world, unemployment has fallen. According to 2015 data, China had 775 million employed people—and, two years later, that has surely risen. In the U.K. in 2017, there were 23.25 million full-time workers, up 209,000 from 2016, as well as higher numbers for part-time employment.

Yes, technology has destroyed old jobs, as it always has. But it continues to create new ones in even greater numbers. Gone forever are elevator operators and tollbooth collectors. Many of the jobs that have disappeared as technology has risen are in fact among the worst, more repetitive, and least interesting jobs anyone would want to do. Stop mourning for them. In their place have come tens of millions of much more interesting "white-collar" jobs, the growth of a new service economy helping people in every aspect of their lives, and inherently better new factory jobs—jobs that don't require a college education, can provide a middle-class income, and yet typically provide a more interesting career than the jobs that have been lost. The biggest problem is not the lack of jobs right now but the lack of jobs in the places where people have been dislocated.

At first, technology companies needed large forces of engineers, who became the baseline high-income hires for the traditional "tech" sector. As tech expanded to serve more and more consumers, tech and tech-infused industries started to hire a much larger

48.1: Percentage of U.S. Employment in Manufacturing, 2005–2015

	2005	2006	2007	2008	2009	2010	2011	2012	2013	2014	2015
Manufacturing	11%	11%	10%	10%	10%	9%	9%	9%	9%	9%	9%

Source: USA Facts

workforce with jobs accessible to the broader population. Facebook, for example, just posted a thousand new jobs to find fake news—a typical new-factory-worker job done by huge numbers of workers, but far more interesting than working on an assembly line. Instead of cutting back on jobs, companies like Uber have set off an explosion of new job opportunities in their wake. For example, when Uber revolutionized taxis, the company added hundreds of thousands of people to the driver population, both in the U.S. and in the sixty-six countries it drives in. In city after city, as Uber launched, the number of employed drivers increased dramatically as people who had cars now had access to the marketplace just as users now had easier access to a car and driver. Amazon, another key example, needed to staff their huge warehouses and logistics operations. Postmates needed a force of people ready to deliver at a moment's notice. Competition for its second headquarters is as intense at the competition ever was for a big factory. Zeel needed thousands of people ready to give massages. By making goods and services more available, they often increased rather than decreased the marketplace and the need for employees.

These employees have more personal freedom and greater ability to set their own hours, and need to be proficient managers of their tasks. There is far less personal supervision and far more oversight by computers that can track where employees go and what they do. Rather than requiring attendance at a central location, these jobs are deliberately decentralized to cover wide service areas. And rather than being rigidly structured, they allow especially singles and moms freedom to work when and where they want.

Other examples include apps like TaskRabbit for on-demand chores; Instacart for grocery shopping and delivery; and StyleSeat for on-demand style services and bookings. Like old factory jobs, these jobs have a routine that starts with an order ticket and they repeat the same tasks, but the factory floor is everywhere. Unlike the old factory jobs, your customers or clients are now your supervisors. They rate your every job and your numbers can earn you extra money, a promotion, or a pink slip. Good numbers also earn you more work, as the algorithms will tilt new, better work to the better employee. Your customers can choose you just as you can choose them.

Remember also that there are far more literate people today than ever. As many as 95 percent graduate high school and, despite all of the bad-mouthing of our schools, average folks today are much more competent in the basics of reading, writing, and math than in the heyday of the American factory.

The other big difference for the new factory worker: you're essentially alone on the job. Previously, you met your spouse or some of your best friends around the water cooler or in the lunchroom at the office. Now you are bowling alone—and need the kind of personality that can chat up a few customers and make connections or feel even more isolated than the old cogs of the industrial age.

The big question about new-factory-worker jobs is whether they will develop into long-term employment or if they are a part-time work gig for younger Americans until they find the next, more permanent career path. The record on this is mixed. Many Amazon jobs are permanent, and anyone can be an Uber driver for a long time. However, there is tremendous competition for these jobs, and some seem more transient in nature, like delivery jobs. Some observers worry that new-factory-worker jobs may soon be taken over by self-driving cars, drones, and delivery robots. Maybe in the long term, but I believe the ability to replace humans in these multidimensional tasks is largely overrated. A clumsy, slow-moving robot is a long way off from beating a nimble guy on a bicycle who can weave through traffic.

Not all cultures are suited to the new factory worker, either. Stricter cultures with more bureaucratic structures, like Japan, are struggling to understand what it means for jobs and for lifestyle. The freedom these jobs have, and the ability to turn them on and off, is in stark contrast to the cultural norms of working for the zaibatsu, the large Japanese conglomerates that control much of the economy. When it comes to foreign factory jobs, global changes in the manufacturing sector have "undergone a tumultuous decade: large developing economies leaped into the first tier of manufacturing nations, a severe recession choked off demand, and manufacturing employment fell at an accelerated rate in advanced economies," according to a 2012 McKinsey Global Institute report. The CIA *World Factbook* estimates that 23.6 percent of world jobs were in "industry," but it remains unclear just how many of those are factory-related.

For the most industrious, these new opportunities can be financially rewarding: you can use your own car, pick up some Uber rides, deliver food later in the day with UberEATS, or sign up with another service. If you are a top-rated driver and hustling, you can make $100,000 or more annually. Some in New York can earn the median income of $50,000 to $60,000. However, that's mostly the exception. Most drivers in most cities make about ten bucks an hour—enough to supplement an income but not usually enough to support a family. Uber loses most of its drivers within a year and offers certain perks to longer-serving drivers (being able to pick up higher-rated passengers, a guaranteed amount of money per hour, etc.). Of the various new sharing economy services, Airbnb and its users who can rent out a vacant property are making the most amount of money. But that takes a certain amount of wealth, already amassed in an asset like an apartment or house.

As many of these enabling app technologies like Uber were born, government and regulators were mostly hands-off—spurring a Wild West environment when it comes to selling products and worker treatment. While engineers today are living high on the hog with $150,000 starting packages, the new factory worker is often struggling and treated in ways we would never tolerate in traditional large companies. As these tech companies become firmly established and their values soar past conventional companies, it will be critical to give the new factory workers the kind of help that licensed taxi drivers had to stabilize the labor market and turn these into good, lasting jobs.

The tech industry is continually destroying old jobs and creating new ones, but, left to their own devices, these wily entrepreneurs will seek to avoid all of the protections workers have won since the 1930s. A gig economy labor standards bill is desperately needed to ensure that these new workers get the kinds of protections that the last generation of factory workers won the hard way from their bosses. Remember that conditions in the early factories were far more dreadful than conditions in Amazon's warehouse and that it does take time for new groups of workers to organize effectively and for public policy to catch up to changes in the workplace. Ideally, most new factory workers will be able to earn a living that can support a family. That work and that family might not look the same as the blue-collar, white-picket-fence model of yesteryear, but the American Dream still needs to be renewed for these new workers who are the real backbone of the Information Age.

49. HAZEL REBORN

In the popular 1960s TV show *Hazel*, an American family proudly moves into a new home in the suburbs—and with the house also comes a housekeeper, the ever-opinionated Hazel, who became involved in every aspect of family life. The numbers of full-time nannies and housekeepers have shrunk in the decades since. But now, in the age of Seamless and Uber, the profession is surging back—remixed and reimagined. The personal service industry has been exploding as millions of Americans have signed on to cater to the endless whims and fancies of the growing upper middle class of America. And the world of do-it-yourself turns out to be the world of having lots of people doing lots of things for everyone else. Maybe the old housekeepers "did not do windows," but today you can have a window washer and virtually any personal service at your door in minutes. Welcome to Hazel reborn for the Information Age and witness the birth of the pampering economy.

If you don't have a college degree and there are no factories for you to work in, this could well be the new job you take. So, get ready to say "Please," "Thank you," and "Have a nice day" a lot while you learn people's most intimate secrets as you deliver their groceries, drive their kids, massage their backs, or walk their dogs.

Several trends lie behind the massive expansion of the service economy, which, according to economic studies and the *New York Times*, has expanded from 40 percent of the economy to 56 percent in just the last decade. As the industrial age faded and the Information Age dawned, a huge segment of jobs shifted to the service sector.

49.1: Americans Employed as "Personal Care Aides," 2003–2015

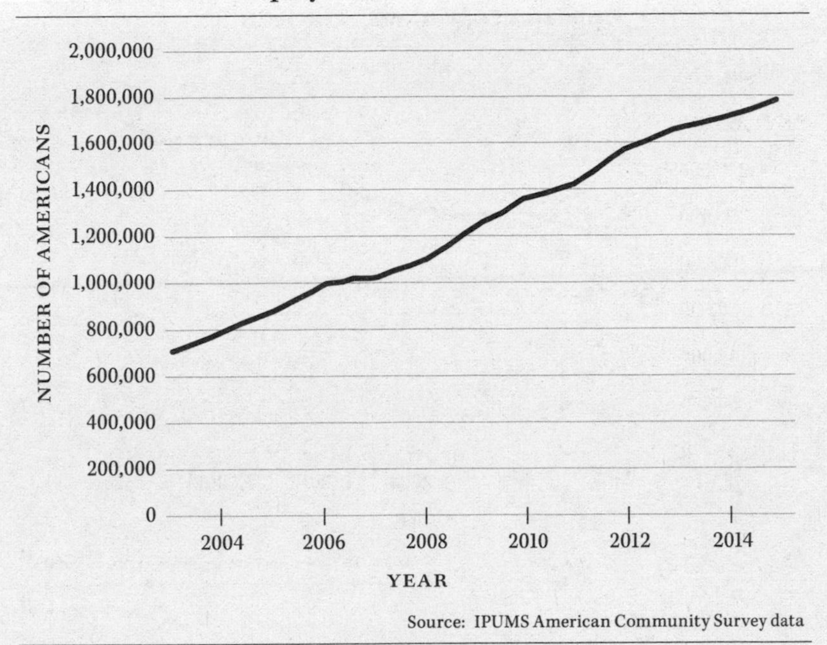

Source: IPUMS American Community Survey data

And the *Times* notes that the revolution in cheaper manufacturing overseas was in many ways a catalyst of this realignment: as manufactured products came down in price, people had more disposable income and did not need a second bicycle or a third refrigerator. They had more money left over and they spent it on themselves. This boosted the service sector and eventually gave rise to the "gig" economy, offering personal, premium services at affordable mass prices. Services once available to only the rich have been democratized, and so broader segments of the population can get a lot more pampering once reserved for only the very wealthy. The live-in figure of Hazel has been replaced by a parade of people sharing slivers of their time, often made possible only by apps that allow us to match up people, location, and time to everyone's benefit.

Busy upper-middle-class working families can have as many as a dozen or so new personal assistants going in and out of their lives.

49.2: Americans Employed as "Miscellaneous Personal Appearance Workers," 2003–2015

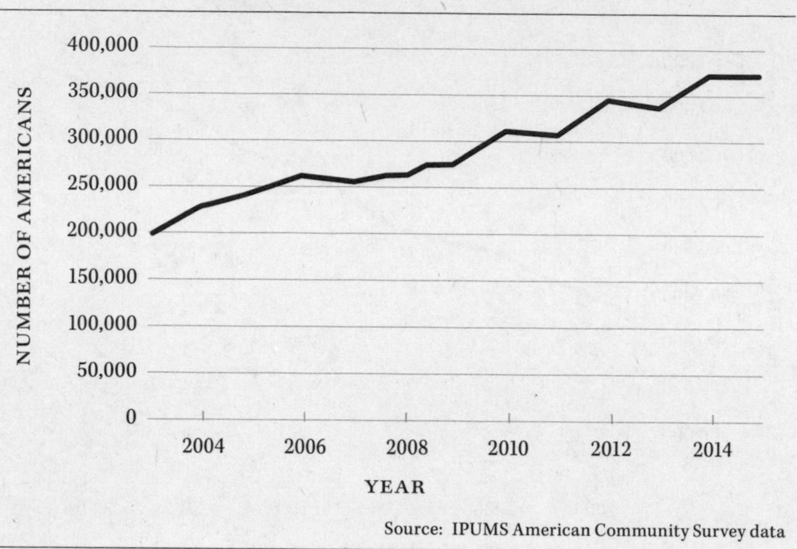

Source: IPUMS American Community Survey data

The traveling spa can bring to your door in an hour a person who can handle everything from nails and hair to massages. Postmates gets your food and anything else delivered to you and will run even complex errands at a moment's notice. (Running out of printer cartridges or diapers? They're on it.) A babysitter can now be found and called in through an app, as can an electrician. And don't forget that for the older generation, the Bureau of Labor Statistics expects physical therapy assistants, home health aides, and other personal assistance jobs to be at the top of the new-job list.

Becoming a reborn Hazel is in many ways about isolating a basic home skill—running errands, cooking, doing nails or hair, picking out clothes—and turning it into a job and even microbusinesses. But to be successful in the marketplace, people need to refine their skills. No one wants a delivery to take an hour or an in-home salon experience that simply results in a bowl-over-the-head haircut. Each state has its own licensing requirements for many of these professions, but beyond the licensing, these Hazels have to do a great job—or they get low online ratings and soon find themselves out of work.

Jobs in the Hazel-reborn economy, in contrast to old service jobs, allow people to help others and still have a vibrant life of their own. In *Downton Abbey* we all cheer for Gwen as she gets a chance to work in an office and gains a place of her own. More freedom is a fundamental part of how the job has changed. Today's Hazels can date, get married, have kids, and do their job part-time or quit and come back as they need. On the other hand, those bopping from one anonymous client to the other will never have the same level of personal connection that Hazel did, and those relationships were a core reward of the job.

One booming new craze is to get a personal chef. Once thought of for only celebrities or the very wealthy, personal chefs can be brought in on demand for $45 an hour—perhaps not for everyday meals, but why not have that birthday dinner at home? Two-career couples with kids are finding mealtimes a challenge; while Blue Apron is one solu-

49.3: Reasons Given by Gig Platform Workers for Participating

Percentage of gig platform workers who use online job/task platforms for the following reasons

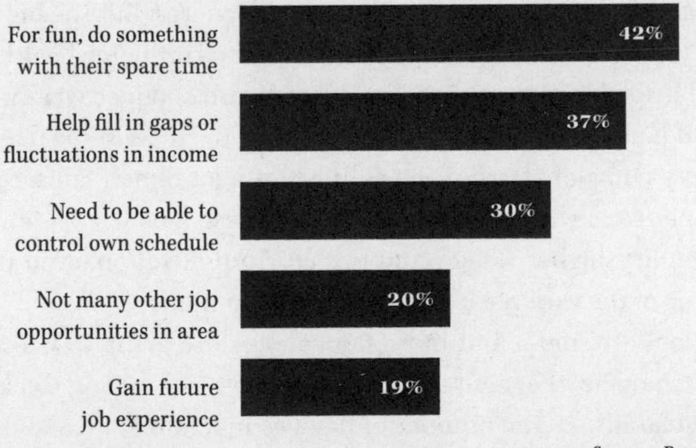

Source: Pew Research Center

tion, chef services send over not just all the ingredients but the chef, too. Of course, such services will have some very high hurdles to overcome to be successful: the chefs have to be punctual, well trained, and far more flexible, lest simple dinners for picky strangers turn into kitchen nightmares.

Another profession that has taken off is personal training, letting thousands turn their passion for exercise into a career. According to the Bureau of Labor Statistics, there were 267,000 personal trainers in the U.S. in 2012 and the career is expected to grow to 338,000 by 2018. You can get a certificate from the American College of Sports Medicine for about $1,000 in fees and that will help you get a job in this increasingly crowded profession. But the trend toward fitness has been pretty well played out over the last decade, so this is a profession that is likely to top out. And it isn't particularly lucrative in the long run: the Department of Labor thinks that, given all the overhead time of travel, meshing schedules, and finding clients, personal trainers are taking home a median of $15 an hour. Another problem is that it's a hard profession to maintain for a lifetime: you don't see a lot of personal trainers in their forties, let alone fifties and sixties. So a personal trainer often has to be on the lookout for the second act.

Personal service–related companies have a huge potential market in the growing elderly population of the U.S. For those who are active and looking for something to do, new moneymaking opportunities open up for simply helping out a family with the chores. But the biggest growth will come from the unprecedented need for home health care, a trend helped by the universality of Medicare and its coverage of specialized home health workers. This is going to create some reasonably high-paying jobs within the skill set of a lot of non-college-educated Americans with the right training. These jobs have a fair degree of stability, higher wages, and possibly unionization, even if they lack some of the carefree nature of the new app-based jobs.

Looking forward, more and more households are going to need someone to manage the household technology—a kind of Geek Squad for the family. As the number of devices in a family escalates and technology takes over everything from washing machines to cars, the job of coordinating all of the technology and keeping down the bills could well create a space for a PTM—a personal technology manager, covering perhaps a hundred households, monitoring their devices and network.

If terrorism were to ramp up or crime to increase further as it has in some cities, there could also be room for an app to deliver a security guard just as quickly as an Uber driver. Most of the services in the pampering economy are luxuries, but modern life could create new necessities around technology and security that drive additional employment.

Robots may well try to get into the act of personal service, following the lead of Alexa, Siri, and Cortana, which were all conceived of as a kind of replacement for the office PA. These may have replaced switchboard operators and be good at collecting all your messages, but the nature of what people are looking for morphs up the chain as computers become more proficient at answering questions and routing elevators and trains. And these early e-PAs have a long way to go in terms of effectiveness and trust.

Some service work will continue to resist roboticization for the foreseeable future. People won't want a robot massage for quite some time—and they want to talk to and gossip with their hairdresser, personal trainer, or other personal helper. Part of being pampered is having a name, a face, and a person to connect to, even if it's just for a day or an hour, and of course for a fee.

Headlines proclaim that the middle class in America is shrinking, but those stories bury the fact that three out of four households leaving the middle class are not headed down but upward, joining the upper middle class. As long as the robots stick to replacing manufacturing jobs, the Hazel class will be on the rise—and increasingly they'll able to hire Hazels of their own.

50. 10XMILLIONAIRES

A million dollars isn't nearly as much money as it used to be. With a low barrier to entry to starting a business, and with the wealthiest 1 percent increasingly able to sock three-quarters of their savings into assets, there is a new class of rich Americans who aren't satisfied with that oldest of dreams. With one in ten households in America now achieving millionaire status, being a millionaire is passé; the new golden number is $10 million in assets.

There are four main ways to become a $10 million household: inherit it, win the lottery or some other chance event, save and invest your way up, or own and typically then sell a successful business. According to consulting group Capgemini in their *World Wealth Report*, business owners worth multimillions tend to be found in several select industries. Finance and technology are no surprise: successful multimillionaire entrepreneurs are "disrupting" other industries through technology and either winning or losing big. Next in line at the top of the list are health care, manufacturing, and real estate/construction. This new set of multimillionaires believes in the system: they work hard, look the part, play by the rules, and know how to make change happen. They're also brokerage houses' best customers, paying the highest fees without much care. There are, according to the latest studies, about $1.3 million households with assets between $5 million and $25 million, not counting their primary residences.

Gone are the days of wealth pushing you into the silver-spoon set. Most multimillionaire Americans still work full-time—and they're not just executives and entrepreneurs. They're doctors and actuaries

50.1: Household Net Worth Percentile Markers, 2017

NET WORTH	PERCENTILE
$ 0	13
$ 1,000	16
$ 5,000	21
$ 10,000	26
$ 50,000	43
$ 100,000	53
$ 500,000	82
$ 1,000,000	91
$ 5,000,000	98.2
$ 10,000,000	99.3

Source: Federal Reserve Survey of Consumer Finances (SCF)

and real estate magnates, and a good majority are self-made. These tend to be fiercely independent, hard-nosed, eclectic in mind-set: they do offbeat things like open cosmetic stores, sell Christmas ornaments, and launch websites. One day you design a video app that no one else can quite imagine; the next you sell it to Google and you're a multimillionaire.

This demographic group thinks about money and deals with it differently from most Americans. The $10 million household invests the bulk of its non-business assets in stocks and bonds, which is fundamentally different from the rest of the population, which relies on the value of their house and sometimes their 401(k) for their savings, if any. They can afford to have more children, so many of them do and have larger families, often across several marriages. They have high-end cars as well as decorators, nannies, and other regular service providers. Most of these 10Xers have second homes—some third homes. They have prenups and complex estate plans with generation-skipping trusts.

One notable difference between this population and the rest of America's wealth brackets is that the $10 million households don't go bankrupt. If you are getting rich, you're likely to stay rich. Almost

50.2: Percentage of Household Food Budget Spent at Home Versus Restaurants by Wealth Percentile

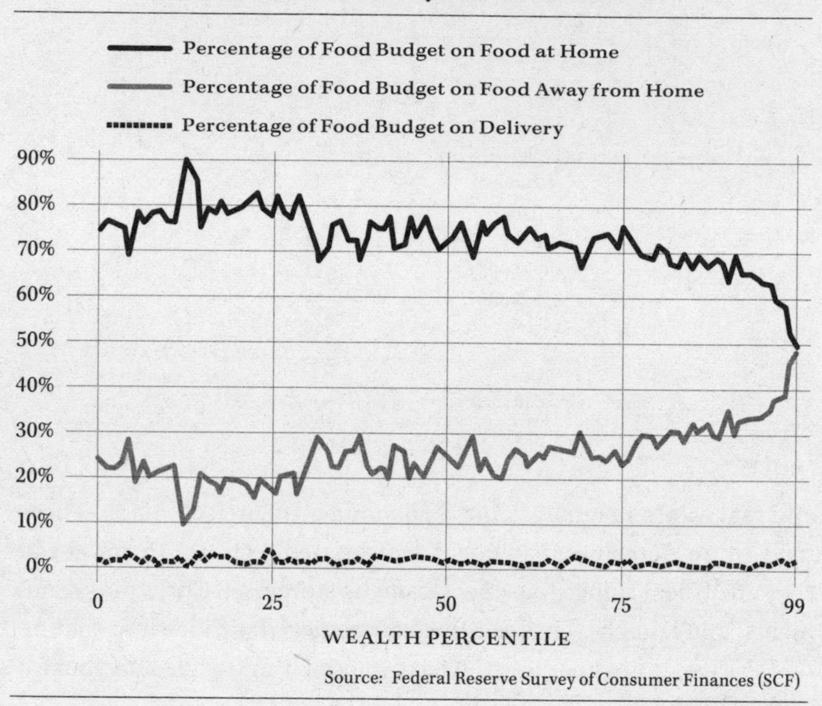

Source: Federal Reserve Survey of Consumer Finances (SCF)

none of them have had bankruptcies in the past five years (as of 2013 data). And this group also has more access to people managing their money and more resources for financial education, both of which further help them to hold on to their wealth. All that said, most won't be leaving their kids with enough money to not have to work.

10Xers are likely to have one or more housekeepers, but that won't keep them from going online. According to the Luxury Institute, 99 percent of multimillionaires have access and use the internet on a daily basis; 42 percent plan and make travel reservations online themselves; and 43 percent buy products and services online. The Luxury Institute reports: "The most effective way to reach wealthy consumers online is through search engine results—including paid placements. . . . Overall, click through banner ads are the least effective way to create a positive impression and to get browsers to buy a product, and yet the youngest and wealthiest consumers were unusually receptive to click-through ads. Nearly one third of consumers worth $5 million or more visited a website after being prompted to do so in another medium such as print or television."

Marketing in America tends to go from the top down. The ultra-wealthy set the bar of what is fashionable, and major brands like Mercedes, Tesla, and Ralph Lauren made their mark by getting their acceptance first and then broadening out their lines to sell to a bigger marketplace. 10Xers like to feel catered to and tend to stay within their network of reliable and trustworthy brands, companies, and luxury items. They will often participate in peer-to-peer referrals and incentives to get high-end products. (This set of largely business owners loves an incentive: Ask JetSmarter, which offers $3,000 vigs for a referral.) They are the ones setting the trends and demanding even higher quality. They're the vocal, visible consumer in every industry, from automobiles to pet products, clothing and home styles, health and beauty products, even vacation destinations. We're all watching what they'll buy next.

Baby boomers (ages 62 to 71), with college all paid off, still lead in total spending. But these days it's the wealthy Gen Xers that have the greatest amount of influence among the superwealthy. They ap-

50.3: U.S. Educational Attainment by Wealth Status, 2009–2011

	TOP 1%	BOTTOM 99%
	%	%
Postgraduate	49	16
College graduate only	23	15
Some college	19	32
High school diploma or less	8	37
Total college	72	31

Source: Gallup Polls

preciate the finer things and, because they're at their greatest earning potential, aren't afraid to spend. But what are multimillionaires spending their money on in 2018?

If you've got a cool $3 mil lying around, why not pick up a new Bugatti Chiron? Not this crowd. Bragging rights are everything to this select group, but gaudy displays of wealth are out. Instead, "smarter" technology, health and wellness, and personal services are in. Think less jewelry and luxury real estate, and more air purifiers, retro Smeg refrigerators, mind and body consultants, home wellness rooms, gourmet health-conscious chefs, and sports-themed vacations. A big exception to this rule are the big life events like weddings and birthdays, where the sky is often the limit. These are the customers you want when you are working in the Four Seasons banquets. And they are keeping the remaining high-end travel experts in business: African safaris are a must with this group, which is on the hunt for more exotic travel.

Some things this group does make a lot of sense. Unsurprisingly, the percentage of people who say they are saving for a home declines as you go up the income scale, as they already have several. But when it comes to saving for retirement, more Americans at the top of the wealth food chain say that they are putting money away for later in life: having enough money left to maintain the lux lifestyle in ever longer old age is a chief concern of this group, and loss of that lifestyle is a huge fear that propels them to save and invest rather than consume.

The profile of a multimillionaire might hold some surprises: while most multimillionaires consider themselves conservative, they identify as independent voters. According to a recent Gallup poll: "One-third of the nation's '1%' identify themselves as Republicans, 41% as independents, and 26% as Democrats. This is a mirror image of the '99%,' a third of whom are Democrats, with 39% independents and a quarter Republicans."

Where are these 10Xers living? Large metropolitan areas and cities with diverse and high-level job opportunities hold the most. New York City dominates; there the average three-bedroom condo on the Upper East Side goes for around $8 million. Surprisingly, the state with the highest concentration of multimillionaires has the lowest population in America: Wyoming.

Not surprising is the correlation between wealth and education. Advanced education separates the haves from the have-nots in clear terms. Seventy-two percent of wealthy Americans have at least a college degree; almost 50 percent of those have post-graduate degrees. Clearly, for the upper class, education is extremely important. And while only 17 percent of the new millionaires ever attended private school, over 55 percent of their children go private.

In the U.S. it's very common to talk about income inequality but less common to talk about wealth inequality. Will this change? Is all this wealth making these multimillionaires any more generous? Most millionaires would agree that the wealthy should shoulder the country's financial burden. However, less wealthy Americans actually end up giving more of their money to charity than their richer counterparts. A 2011 study showed that the top 20 percent of American earners gave an average of 1.3 percent of their money to charity, compared to 3.2 percent of those in the bottom 20 percent, as reported by the *Atlantic.*

Not only are these new $10M-plusers stingy on a percentage basis, another trend has been noticed by sociologists. As Americans get wealthier, they need people—and their communities—less; they become more independent, autonomous, and inevitably more isolated as individuals. So, within the $10Xer club, rates of loneliness and depression increase. A number of studies have recently suggested that with authority, ownership, and decision making—such as that associated with CEOs and business owners—depression rates rise to double that of the general public, which is already at 20 percent. Let's not shed too many crocodile tears for these depressed 10Xers, though.

As the wealth chasm gets larger, there will likely be more shrouded megafortunes . . . and more upper-middle-class "hoarding." According to a new book out by Richard Reeves, *Dream Hoarders: How the American Upper Middle Class Is Leaving Everyone Else in the Dust, Why That Is a Problem, and What to Do About It,* the 10Xers are taking every advantage they can while making it more difficult for others to progress up the financial ladder. Reeves examines the "opportunity hoarding" that the upper middle class is practicing with their wealth. These advantages include zoning and school laws, health care opportunities, college application procedures, and allocation of internships—which better serve those with money and restrict access for people without.

Resentment! The rich are getting richer, and we all know it. But as the income gap grows, the wealth gap will widen even more. When the super-rich die they will leave their millions to their heirs, who can build upon it even more, especially with the widespread opposition to the estate tax—58 percent favored its abolition in a 2017 Harvard CAPS–Harris poll. But perhaps there will be a push for a capital tax as called for by Thomas Piketty in his book *Capital in the Twenty-First Century.* Either way, the 10Xers will still be well behind the wealth of the 100Xers or the billionaires who get the private planes and the big, big mansions, so there will still be people they envy.

As much as we've seen the ranks of 10XMillionaires climb in America, a recent report by *Global Finance* didn't even rank the United States among the world's top ten countries when it came to most 10Xers adjusted for the number of people in the country. The countries with the highest concentration of households of over $10 million tend to be smaller ones, with either large reserves of hydrocarbons or natural resources: Think Qatar, Kuwait, Norway, and the United Arab Emirates. Or they have well-developed and diversified financial sectors, such as Luxembourg, Singapore, and Switzerland.

But larger countries have seen strong growth as well. China—the world's second largest economy—has created a lot of new millionaires and multimillionaires for their country with their recent economic boom. The number of high-net-worth individuals has increased nearly ninefold in the last decade. In 2016, approximately 120,000 Chinese had at least 100 million yuan (approximately $15,000,000) in investable assets—up from less than 10,000 people in 2006.

10XMillionaire households are the new pinnacle of Horatio Alger–style dreams. Part of the change is just the natural progression of inflation, but the other part is simply that with larger and more prosperous global markets, success at all levels will continue to pay higher rewards for those who can achieve it. This group of ultra-wealthy 10Xers will set the standard now of the highest level of hard-to-reach success that for nearly a hundred years has been defined by the simple word "millionaire."

CONCLUSION: TAMING OUR MICROTRENDS

Modern life is at a vital crossroads.

These times seem so confusing because microtrends—now more powerful and potent than ever—are simultaneously pulling society in different directions, often diametrically opposed. Power relationships are being refined and redefined as we see the winners and the losers of these conflicts. And the optimism that filled the start of the new millennium is now fading. Old tribal conflicts that lay behind previous global wars are reemerging; meanwhile, technology is becoming as threatening to our society as it is useful in advancing the world. Amid signs of progress, we also see the potential to sink once again into political and global chaos. That threat is very real unless we act now to fix some of the obvious problems that are emerging.

As we have seen in today's new microtrends, unexpected paradoxes are turning things upside down:

- The presence of choice in life, in information, and in products has in fact led people to make fewer choices.
- In a world of growing material prosperity, it is data, not gold or oil, that has become the most valuable commodity in the world.
- Artificial intelligence could potentially find the cure to cancer—or cause world destruction if it blinds us from reality.

- The rapid increase in the variety of media channels has given the new media titans more, rather than less, control over what we see and hear.
- Start-up culture has led to the growth of big technology that is now squeezing out the next generation of start-ups.
- Open democracy is eroding, rather than strengthening, some of our core democratic institutions.
- Bots are forming new relationships with people who no longer realize or care that these bots are not real but just programmed Sirens.
- Greater prosperity has led to fewer marriages and fewer children.
- Our ability to stay connected with so many others has led to fewer deep and lasting connections.
- Technology is creating more new jobs than it is destroying so far, but it is also creating a global underworld of online fraud and crime.

Many of the microtrends we have outlined continue to create promise for people and businesses as we advance further into the twenty-first century. Today you can become a social millionaire with a healthy dose of moxie, determination, and some clever ideas. Almost anyone can start his or her own online business with far less capital than ever. And the cloud is the greatest advance for small businesses since IBM unveiled the PC.

Wealth itself is expanding, as 10 percent of American households are now millionaires. Many in the American middle class can now afford an array of new servants who help them through their everyday tasks. Even the most luxurious amenities—whether it's digital tailors, a black car on demand, or even new access to private planes—keep getting more affordable. Technology that was once reserved for the wealthy is now available to the masses, and has created a single network within which everyone can communicate.

Political movements can now be started by a few people with some ideas and an internet connection, and they can even replace entrenched interests in just a few years. We have seen how the movement on behalf of undocumented immigrants grew remarkably in the last decade, moving from a niche argument to a movement that is at the center of today's political debate.

The last decade has been about organizing our information, connecting us all on mobile devices, and digitizing entertainment, while this next decade will be much more about harnessing Big Data, utilizing AI, and making technology a direct extension of who we are. While employment is threatened by automation, technology is also creating new jobs at all levels, from the forklift operators at the Amazon warehouse to the engineers at Tesla Laboratories working on driverless cars. We are approaching the end of the most monotonous, oppressive work ever created involving endlessly repetitive tasks.

Long-standing efforts at fighting disease are showing progress, especially when more of us are becoming cancer survivors instead of cancer victims. We are on the verge of breakthroughs that will enable people to see, hear, and move us around as never before. We never had a category of nonagenarians with many people in it—and we are closing in on making one hundred years of living a common occurrence. Diet and exercise seem to be having some real impact on people's health, although in the end it turned out that protein and not grain became the hero food.

Today you can have fun and get together in new ways that were never before possible with just a few clicks; the ability to meet people has been revolutionized by online dating. Even nerds have fun conventions, and the trend is certainly toward the legalization of some drugs in ways similar to alcohol.

As people have more single years, our cities and their vibrancy are being remade. They have become new melting pots as they are teaming with a diverse combination of millennials, newest immigrants and folks open-minded about marriage and relationships. These urban dwellers are at the forefront of social movements, both healthy and unhealthy, that are driving our culture.

Of course, many of these changes have also been accompanied by countertrends as older and rural voters—those whose livelihoods have been disrupted by globalization and technological change—are reasserting both their power and their cultural values.

Importantly, in my view, the reassertion of power by groups who felt left out of our culture and our economy is a success of the democratic system, not a failure.

The losers of a contest can't always claim "FRAUD AT POLLS!" as the alternate headline, as in *Citizen Kane*. Older, more rural voters who felt left behind in the new economy reasserted their political power by voting for Donald Trump, the first major candidate to champion them in decades. They felt marginalized and their victory is resetting the country on issue after issue. Whether you agree or disagree with these directions—in areas like trade, gun control, and immigration—the democratic system works when such movements can use the ballot box as their outlet and established orders can retreat peacefully, ready to come back another day. The greater problem occurs when losers cry foul at every defeat.

Every poll I conduct shows a very divided country, and yet every time I ask if you want the parties to compromise on their principles to come together to make agreements, just about 90 percent in the Harvard CAPS–Harris polls say that's exactly what they want our politicians to do. On top of that, this is a moderate country, with only about one-fourth of the voters identifying themselves as liberals. I believe our politics can find the center again. It may ping-pong too far to the left or the right, but I think it will eventually settle in the middle.

Looking toward the future, we can see warning signs around the further clash of trends, microtrends, and powerful forces in society. Robotics ultimately may redefine humanity and its role on the planet, but combined with AI it just might be the force that wipes us out entirely as science fiction becomes science reality. The power realignments of the 2016 election were wake-up calls to the coasts as changes that better suited the educated and the less religious were seen as leaving behind people outside of those demographics. In the back-and-forth of politics, the system is having trouble finding the middle course that most people want.

The paradoxes we have revealed within this book help to explain why modern life seems so confusing. They also point us to the need to make some mid-course corrections to stay on a path of freedom, openness, innovation, and success.

We have so much more clarity today than we did ten years ago on what is going right and what can go wrong; this knowledge should enable us to adopt a plan of action to make the Information Age work for all of us. The progressive era of the early 1900s was a response to what went wrong in the industrial age, and once again we need to step in—not to bring innovation and free enterprise down, but to keep it going strong.

In many ways, companies today have become amazingly responsive to market conditions and trends, but government has been left flat-footed, unable to keep up with the changes in the marketplace. It has largely failed to put in place any structures that can respond fast enough to what can happen and is happening. There's more that it, and we, can do.

Here are some practical ideas and changes we need to start making to address these emerging issues and problems.

Break out of our silos.

Perhaps the single greatest issue arising out of the data-driven society we have built is that, when it comes to news, food, work, or how we raise our children, more choice has resulted in people making fewer and fewer choices. This is also maybe the most difficult issue to correct. Americans find what they like and cocoon within it, in ways that distort their views of the rest of the world. Then these choices reinforce themselves as we repeat them over and over again.

There is also a flaw in the strategy of giving people what they want: they will often *change* their perspective when they see something new. The big consulting companies told AT&T that the cell phone would never take off. They were told it was nothing more than a specialty item—because they were dealing with people as they were, not as they would be transformed.

To get ourselves out of our silos: first, people are going to have to be made conscious of what is happening and of the fact that they are the victims of a telescoping worldview. We need to start funding research and studies that speak to this phenomenon and offer viable alternatives. We will need an explicit cultural program to get Americans out of their cocoons; it's not something that can be legislated.

News channels are going to have to do a far better job of saying there is another side to things. Starbucks can offer try-something-new discounts. Apps from Siri to Alexa are going to need to be programmed to ask, "Have you tried something different lately?" Dating apps should have random match days. We need to make this a cultural mantra if we are going to climb out of this. What is the point of having a phone that can connect you to any person in the world if you just call the same six people in a small circle?

The problem is accentuated by the way that we collect data and use it. The concept of effective, targeted online advertising is built on tracking you to find out what you want and then get that in front of you at exactly the moment you want it. It's like selling popcorn just before a movie. We can ask our algorithms be programmed with a random choice element. Let's say you are dealing with a white male searcher in Ohio: there might be a box on the page that says, "Did you know that New York City has six places for barbecue?" Or let's say you are dealing with a Never Trumper in New York and it pops up: "When is the last time you thought about the opioid crisis in Ohio?" This is not as wacky as it may seem. Just as algorithms can figure out what you want, they can also figure out quite easily the antithesis of what you want—with the goal not of defeating the system but of supplementing it in ways that prompt us to look outside our familiar world and our beliefs, no matter how uncomfortable that might be.

Create new standards of ethics.

The next great danger here is that we will create technology we cannot control. Preventing that, I believe, starts with building up a far greater sense of ethics in developers and engineers. We need to realize that engineers have the power of life and death in their hands and should take an oath every bit as powerful and important as those undertaken in professions like medicine and law. The IEEE some time ago came up with such a code—but it speaks in platitudes related to the public interest.

Today we have to be far sharper in delineating the code:

- Software experiences based on consumer algorithms should be transparent, to the extent possible, and always explain their basic purpose and techniques.
- Software that suggests choices to people or that makes choices for people should always be required to disclose the basis on which those choices are suggested. They should also be required to disclose whether these choices are engineered or nudged to the benefit of others, such as advertisers or companies, as opposed to working solely in the user's best interest. In certain cases we may want to legislate the outcomes here.
- All bot and robot relationships should carry a clear notice and repeated warnings that they are generated from software and not by people. For example, anytime customer service is using a bot and not a person to respond to you, they should be required to disclose that fact.
- Shibuya Mirai is the first AI character to be an official resident of Tokyo. We need to revoke his citizenship. He does not exist. He is just an AI bot. His goal is lighthearted engagement with residents of Tokyo to field their questions. The aims of this were benign, but it's a first step down a road that has no good end: bots are not human and do not have human rights, and confusion of the two will eventually lead to early acceptance of them as harmless. But whether it was the *Colossus: The Forbin Project*, *Fringe*, *Person of Interest*, *Battlestar Galactica*, or *The Terminator*, this story always ends the same way: our complete destruction or near destruction at the hands of bots that become too wide and all-powerful. These may be fictional scenarios, but that doesn't mean we should ignore the risks in reality.
- When matters of life and death are involved, except when used by the military or the police, the software should be designed always

to put the safety of humans first, and should disclose the hierarchy of safety. No software should be written that could involve the loss of life without a clear warning about that possibility.

This will become more important in the next few years, especially as it relates to driverless cars. You are driving 40 miles an hour and a crane falls on the road in front of you. Your "driver" calculates your choices: hit the crane, killing you and destroying the car; swerve right and save you and the car but killing a pedestrian; swerve left and hit a guardrail that will probably still kill you; save the car but do $200,000 of damage to the guardrails. There is no person in charge to make the call, only a computer that has calculated these probabilities and outcomes and now must make a choice—and on what basis? Save you, save the car, save the public expense? How would you decide this if you were the driver? Does the machine have the right to kill the pedestrian to save you? Are you responsible if you programmed it that way?

This is all going to get a lot stickier a lot faster than people seem to realize—and life and death choices will come up.

We currently have more rules about putting an actor in an ad than we do about creating and marketing a bot that acts like a psychologist. We have no real level of expertise in such questions or regulatory power to enact restrictions anywhere in the country; yet technology means we need to be able to make, change, and even repeal rules quickly as they become outmoded. It follows that we will need an FTC of software transparency and ethics to enforce these codes. When billions of dollars are at stake, good luck trusting only a voluntary code of ethics.

We will need to grapple with the issues of drones and the larger question of robot soldiers. We will need to get rid of the line-of-sight rules on drones but only when they are safe enough and can be adequately policed in the skies. We may need drone-killing lasers as a way of patrolling the increased risks that these new inventions can create. As for robot soldiers, we should think about international conventions that ban them as we banned some land mines. Once you take the people out of war, it simply becomes too dangerous and too easy to deploy robots against neighboring countries or against one's own people. If we don't ban them, there are many ways in which robo-cops and robo-soldiers could become an extreme danger to society, far greater than even chemical weapons. They are weapons of mass destruction, and should be treated as such.

Tech companies will, of course, prefer to keep a veil of secrecy over their operations, processes, and algorithms. But we are going to have to strike more of a compromise on those elements if we are to continue to depend on these systems and allow a few companies to have so much control over so much of the internet.

Reform news distribution.

The internet created enormous disruption in the news industry. Local papers went bankrupt. National papers at first saw struggles but are finding their footing. New outlets arose. Platform companies realized that people really do care about news and information, not just sports and entertainment. These companies started to get into the act of distributing news through their platform, supplementing what users were doing to share news bits on their social sites. This happened so quickly, however, that we skipped over all of the careful consideration we gave to rules on TV and radio ownership when these technologies were new. There was no real policy analysis done when Facebook went into news and overnight became the largest news distributor in the free world.

Facebook then set algorithms aimed at serving you the news items you would be most interested in reading. So if you don't like Trump, you will feast on more and more anti-Trump articles as the algorithm tries to maximize your engagement. People get pigeonholed and can get more and more spun up in a never-ending loop, just as we outlined earlier.

This was a significant departure from how newspapers worked in the past, where a group of talented editors used their judgment to place some stories higher or lower on the page. The news that the populace saw was not a mere reflection of what they liked but a selection of what editors thought was important for you to read. Facebook, with a 42 percent share of people's online time, is the equivalent of hundreds of newspapers and TV stations, and represents an unprecedented concentration of news distribution. It has struggled with various algorithms for the news feed, first getting accused of favoring the left, then favoring the right. They can't seem to win. They can't win because today they are a single powerful outlet in a country that no longer wants its news to be homogenous or to be determined by elites sitting in a San Francisco or New York conference room.

My suggested fix for this is that we view these huge tech platforms on the internet with billions of users just as we viewed the television and radio airwaves: as limited publicly owned spaces that must be distributed in ways that create a real marketplace in information free from domination. Facebook itself (as well as Google) could create ten official news channels and then bid out who would have control of each channel. The franchises could be for five-year periods, which would allow different groups to run each with different goals and perspectives. Facebook users could then choose the news channels that they watch. This would keep Facebook in the position of serving as a platform and yet get it out of the editorial business. Each Facebook news channel would receive an equal level of promotion and placement, and funds from the ads would be split between the franchisees and Facebook.

This solution would preserve our basic freedoms, and it would do so without sacrificing consumer choice; it would also lessen the power of any one news decider in an age where certain applications have become so powerful that switching to another platform is not a meaningful or fair alternative. In exchange for sharing its platform, we could exempt Facebook from being responsible for the content, and that responsibility would lie with the editors of the channels.

Several other types of information services may need a similar approach. The Google-Yelp fight has been going on for years, as Google can leverage its search business to promote its own listings and reviews. This is one of the situations that has caught the attention of regulators in Europe but not here. Yet the combination of hidden processes and vast economic power suggests that, going forward, the nature of antitrust law is going to have to be redefined to rein in the potential abuses that affect consumers, often in ways they never directly see or understand.

Put more limits on data collection.

In the past, when you left for work and dropped your clothes off at the dry cleaner, only he would know your dirty laundry. You took a cab whose driver knew where you worked but wouldn't share it. Then you stopped off for a donut and coffee, and only they would know what you liked to eat. Today, all of that personal data can be collected in a central place, and a single company will know everything imaginable about your laundry, your location, and your likes. It is the concentration of all of this information in single sources that makes it so powerful for the companies and so vulnerable for you.

Right now this is all done in secret; we know snippets but nothing of the whole story. Until I pointed it out in the Scroogled campaign at Microsoft, nobody realized that Google for over six years scanned your mail and analyzed its contents to determine what kinds of ads you should receive. Correspondence with your doctor would be turned into ads for medications. What you assumed could only be read with a court order was being read, scanned, and analyzed all along; it's why they could give you free e-mail.

We cannot continue to operate with a secret system of data collection that is gradually bringing privacy down to zero. We need to shift control of people's information back to the individuals themselves. Europe has much more serious laws than we do, but even they are not as serious as they need to be to deal with what is coming over the next decade.

Some people say simply, "Get over it"—that this is the end of privacy as we know it. Yet data is the rocket fuel of the entire big tech/AI complex: the best way to slow it down and make sure it does not turn destructive is to control its data collection and make more transparent its collection and use. All third-party transfers of your information should be explicitly shared with you in some way, and the hidden centralized collection of everything about you should be brought out into the light and dismantled. People should be able to capture and sell their own data about themselves. This idea of a "data can" containing all of your personal-usage online data is already being tested at Harvard and would redefine the economic relationship between consumers and the internet giants.

Obviously, the security standards need to be raised, and perhaps companies can be required to offer fee-based options for consumers who want the same services on a non-advertised basis. We are already seeing some of that, and I would expect most consumers to choose to continue to use these services on an advertised basis—but it may be different once they know the true and full extent of data mining. Back in the 1970s, when given the choice, 60 percent of consumers took the free listing in the phone book and 40 percent paid a monthly charge to have their names removed.

Another aspect of this is the crackdown on being a fakester. Considerable resources have now been pouring into this area and corporate security is ramping up. We will need a much greater commitment from all companies, international governments, and perhaps even a new international cybercrime police force to prevent this from taking down the internet. On all levels, from fake accounts to fake pleas from Nigerian princes, we need to think about what kind of tough enforcement can stem the growth of these new crimes.

Add more democracy to our democracy.

It's easy to blame money for the state of politics—but money doesn't mean that you need to spend all your time and effort blasting your opponents with half-truths rather than promoting what you will do if elected. People make those decisions on their own. In general, I have a slightly different view of money and politics: I agree with the Supreme Court that it's not the core problem we are facing today. Despite the flaws of a First Amendment approach, only a system open to significant paid speech can bring to bear the firepower necessary to unseat entrenched interests who have burrowed into their positions and who have the power to dispense government contracts to buy political support.

I am more concerned, however, that what started as something for limited use—negative ads, which have their place—has become essentially the entirety of mass political communications. Ninety percent of the ads in presidential campaigns are negative, and politics has become more about what campaigns are against than what they stand for. Social media has also added to the political distortions. And while I don't think the Russian Facebook ads had any impact on the election because of their small size, they do show how divisive messages work on the internet and how they can easily be exploited to sow discontent. You want clicks; you want money; then go destroy someone.

As the rise of the couch potato voters shows, too many people have been left outside the political system and too much effort is spent on attracting fringe voters rather than bringing people together by appealing across the aisle. Many elements of our electoral infrastructure have evolved in haphazard ways, due to the rise of the power of political parties and the people who controlled those entities.

We need to:

- Make voter registration universal, starting with a voter registration card issued to all citizens at birth or on the day of naturalization. The current system is a complete mess. To avoid fraud and manage people moving residences, we need a central identification system and voter database, letting people send in documentation about which state they reside in based on where they pay taxes, much as they do now to get a passport. It no longer makes sense to avoid national systems of identification when ID is so critical to voting, travel, and even entering an office building. This is the best and simplest solution.
- We need to keep voting secret in nature but allow people to vote in other convenient ways and at convenient times. Internet voting could be a disaster, because people can look over your shoulder and the security of it is questionable. But I think ATMs could be

turned into secure voting terminals based on personalized voting cards. Voting should move from Tuesdays to being done over entire weekends. I would discourage advance voting, which has been the trend, because it means not everyone hears the entire campaign and it encourages people to shut down, listening only to their own views, when the last weeks of a campaign are typically the most informative.

- End all caucuses and replace the nomination systems with uniform primary systems across the nation, starting with different states chosen by lottery so that no state has a built-in advantage. Caucuses are fundamentally low-turnout, undemocratic institutions that have no place in a modern democracy. The brouhaha over Team Clinton's control of the DNC in 2015 may hasten demand for needed reforms here that would get rid of the superdelegates in exchange for getting rid of the caucuses, scoring one for the left, one for the center, and two for the people of the country.
- Electioneering ads, whether they are online or on TV, should be filed with a central clearinghouse where they can be inspected and go through a limited validation process, as all TV spots traditionally did before they could run on broadcast.
- The Fairness Doctrine may have outlived its usefulness, but completely eliminating it and having no similar concept anywhere in the public—through the airwaves or the internet—has not worked out any better. In fact, a strong case can be made that eliminating this policy really ushered in the balkanization of news and the ability to go for niche viewers and cliques based on exploiting people's political viewpoints. We can't go backward, but we still do have to solve the problem that has been created, and perhaps bringing back some limited public interest rules would be a start.

Do more to encourage marriage and having children.

Immigration should be a supplement to family life in America, not a substitute for having and rearing kids in one of the greatest child-friendly environments ever created.

As we become more prosperous and more educated, more and more people are skipping marriage (see "Never Married") and starting open marriages. Those are great choices for the people who make them consciously and intentionally. But the continuation of every worthwhile country and culture does depend upon welcoming families and children and allowing people to take root over generations.

My parents were from immigrant families, and we have grown in America from a small band to a moderate-sized clan. I think fifty years ago people thought that America would be so crowded now that both China and America might have to have a one-child policy. Instead, China has ended the policy, and we need to do more to encourage people of all types to enjoy having families. Whatever we have done, it has not been enough against the pull of modern life toward their careers, the allure of greater success, and the conveniences of less family life. We will need not only to expand just tax deductions but to encourage families culturally. We need to expand policies like family and medical leave and maternity/paternity care to European standards, because no matter the immediate cost, the long-term benefits of bending this curve—which now shows an ever-aging nation—are enormous.

Bring the new economy to every region.

Although we started the process in the 1990s, somehow we fell off the task of bringing the new economy to every region of the country, especially the Midwest. This failure to set up incentives for spreading the new jobs and the income that came with them has in large measure intensified the division between the tech/finance classes and the old-economy voters.

We need to set up national incentives, using something like the corporate tax as an incentive for companies to spread new-economy jobs. Every state should be ranked by the percentage of employment that can be tied to the new or digital economy, and an incentive system should be created to give tax breaks to companies moving jobs to those locations.

This is similar to what New York is doing in parts of the city: significant breaks are being given for bringing jobs to lower Manhattan after 9/11 and there are no incentives for bringing new jobs to Midtown. This same approach should be taken nationally with high-tech and low-tech jobs created by the digital companies. It may be slightly suboptimal economically, but we need to create a greater sense of unified purpose across the country, and this is perhaps the largest fault line separating people, their culture, and their politics. Tech is going to continue to be the center of economic growth in the next decade, and we need to make every state a tech-oriented one if we are to once again be the *United* States of America. This same policy should be implemented in any other country facing these same problems—certainly the U.K., for instance.

It is definitely not too late to make these changes.

Technology is at the center of the growth of our prosperity and our future. Many elements of it are developing in incredibly positive ways. But it is this combination of technology, globalization, demographics, and people's personal attitudes based on how they fared in the last decade that has created a series of powerful disruptions. On the one hand it has created the new Hazels, whereby people are having more of their needs met than ever before. It has also created angry pockets of people who felt left behind or underserved, whether they be old-economy voters or members of a newly energized immigrant community.

The pull of these roughly equal but powerful forces, after so many years in which the coastal elites governed with their support, has created upheaval in the political world. At the same time a new modern lifestyle is being created. Both youth and old age have been elongated: the phases of life in which people are young, without major commitments, is much longer now, as is life post-retirement. Both shifts have driven significant cultural changes, and when you combine these with the rapid growth of technology, there's enormous potential for instability.

All of this means that we need to see some significant thought given to changes in the development of technology, the rules around business and marketing, reforms of our political system, and the deployment of government resources and policy beyond the typical areas of taxes, deficits, and entitlements.

So far, we have survived the atom bomb and its power to destroy the world. The somewhat darker question is whether we have the foresight and resolve to survive the power of the internet age to destroy us all. Sitting with President Clinton at the ceremonies ushering in the new millennium, I would have laughed at that proposition. Today, nearly two decades later, I would rather be an alarmist about how the next set of microtrends could be our last. And yet, I don't think it is too late for us to wake up and get us back on a path to taming the forces and counterforces unleashed by microtrends squared.

SOURCES

The Building Blocks of Change Today

- The data on the average age of Egyptians comes from the CIA's *World Factbook*, https://www.cia.gov/library/publications/the-world-factbook/fields/2177.html.
- Data on rural voters from the 2012 and 2016 elections comes from NBC, http://elections.nbcnews.com/ns/politics/2012/all/president/#.Wf_RgGKPKgR and https://www.nbcnews.com/politics/2016-election/president; and data from 2000 is from a report by Seth C. McKee, "Rural Voters in Presidential Elections, 1992–2004," which was published in the *Forum* 5, no. 2 (2007).
- Pew Research found growth in the highest income tier: http://www.pewsocialtrends.org/2015/12/09/the-american-middle-class-is-losing-ground/.
- The poll showing Millennial skepticism of capitalism is from Harvard's Institute of Politics: http://iop.harvard.edu/youth-poll/harvard-iop-spring-2016-poll.
- Data for the 1964 election comes from Gallup: http://news.gallup.com/poll/9454/election-polls-vote-groups-19601964.aspx.
- Exit polls for the U.K.'s Brexit vote were analyzed by Pew Research: http://www.pewresearch.org/fact-tank/2016/11/09/behind-trumps-victory-divisions-by-race-gender-education/.

SECTION 1: LOVE AND RELATIONSHIPS

1. Second-Fiddle Husbands

- The chart on female breadwinners by income level comes from the Center for American Progress: https://www.americanprogress.org/issues/economy/reports/2012/04/16/11377/the-new-breadwinners-2010-update/.
- Data on the changing percentages of mixed-education marriages comes from the American Community Survey, via IPUMS: Steven Ruggles et al., *Integrated*

Public Use Microdata Series: Version 7.0 (Minneapolis: University of Minnesota, 2017).

- The study of mixed-education marriages in EU countries is from Martin Klesment and Jan Van Bavel, "The Reversal of the Gender Gap in Education and Female Breadwinners in Europe" (2015), EU-funded research, https://lirias.kuleuven.be/handle/123456789/491575.
- The *Atlantic* reported on research on the gender gap among parents and non-parents in various developed countries: https://www.theatlantic.com/business/archive/2012/12/the-4-rich-countries-where-women-out-earn-men-with-1-huge-caveat/266343/.
- The research on how the number of hours worked in two-parent families has been distributed came from Liza Mundy's book *The Richer Sex: How the New Majority of Female Breadwinners Is Transforming Our Culture* (New York: Free Press, 2013).
- The Pew study cited on stay-at-home dads is "Growing Number of Dads Home with the Kids," which was published in 2014: http://www.pewsocialtrends.org/2014/06/05/growing-number-of-dads-home-with-the-kids/.
- The excerpt from *Time* magazine comes from an article by Cybele Weisser and Kerri Anne Renzulli, "7 Ways to Stop Fighting about Money and Grow Richer, Together," published in June 2014: http://time.com/money/2791658/couples-marriage-money-survey-female-breadwinners/.
- Noelle Chesley and Sarah Flood's article "Signs of Change? At-Home and Breadwinner Parents' Housework and Child-Care Time" provided data on the contrast between stay-at-home moms and dads in the job market: http://onlinelibrary.wiley.com/doi/10.1111/jomf.12376/full.
- Alyson Byrne and Julian Barling's article "When She Brings Home the Job Status," from 2017, was helpful for understanding the dynamics when women earn more than their male partners: http://pubsonline.informs.org/doi/10.1287/orsc.2017.1120.
- Belinda Luscombe's article "Honey, Your Success Is Shrinking Me" cites helpful research by Kate Ratliff on the relationships of higher-status women and lower-status men: http://healthland.time.com/2013/08/30/honey-your-success-is-shrinking-me/.
- "Gender Identity and Relative Income within Households" by Marianne Bertrand, Emir Kamenica, and Jessica Pan demonstrated the reluctance to form relationships where women outearned men: https://academic.oup.com/qje/article-abstract/130/2/571/2330321?redirectedFrom=fulltext.
- Martin Klesment and Jan Van Bavel in their paper "The Reversal of the Gender Gap in Education and Female Breadwinners in Europe" showed the relationship between women's education and share of income across Europe: https://lirias.kuleuven.be/handle/123456789/491575.

- Li Ma's article "Female Labour Force Participation and Second Birth Rates in South Korea" provided interesting data about motherhood and earnings in South Korea: https://link.springer.com/article/10.1007/s12546-016-9166-z.
- Data on women breadwinners by income quintile came from a report from the Center For American Progress, "The New Breadwinners: 2010 Update": https://www.americanprogress.org/issues/economy/reports/2012/04/16/11377/the-new-breadwinners-2010-update/.
- Derek Thompson's piece in the *Atlantic* "The 4 Rich Countries Where Women Out-Earn Men (With 1 Huge Caveat)" had important information about motherhood and earnings internationally: https://www.theatlantic.com/business/archive/2012/12/the-4-rich-countries-where-women-out-earn-men-with-1-huge-caveat/266343/.
- Projections on the number of women graduates came from a 2016 Department of Education report, "Projections of Education Statistics to 2023": https://nces.ed.gov/pubs2015/2015073.pdf.

2. Never Married

- Data on the percentage of American adults who have never been married, as well as data on unmarried partners, come from the American Community Survey, via IPUMS: Steven Ruggles et al., *Integrated Public Use Microdata Series: Version 7.0* (Minneapolis: University of Minnesota, 2017).
- Pew's 2014 study "Record Share of Americans Have Never Married" had survey data around the number of men and women who would someday like to get married: http://www.pewsocialtrends.org/2014/09/24/chapter-1-public-views-on-marriage/.
- Information on single parents is from Matthew Yglesias's article "Living Together Is the New Marriage—Even for Parents": https://www.vox.com/2015/2/24/8100917/cohabitation-birth-rate.
- The number of unmarried men and women in Saudi Arabia came from this report by the Saudi Arabian government's General Statistics Authority 2016 "Demography Survey": https://www.stats.gov.sa/sites/default/files/en-demographic-research-2016_2.pdf.
- The *Hankyoreh* reported on the rate of Never Marrieds in South Korea and other OECD nations: http://www.hani.co.kr/arti/english_edition/e_international/635913.html.

3. Open Marriages

- Avvo's "2016 Annual Relationship, Marriage, and Divorce Survey" included the survey of two thousand Americans and the actual estimate of how many adults have been in open relationships: http://marketing-assets.avvo.com/uploads/sites/3/2016/05/Avvo-Relationship-Study_Final-Research-Report.pdf.

- In 2012 Juju Chang and Dan Lieberman collected survey data and studies on infidelity (including from the University of Washington Center for the Study of Health and Risk Behaviors) in their article "Swingers: Inside the Secret World of Provocative Parties and Couples Who 'Swap'": http://abcnews.go.com/Entertainment/swingers-inside-secret-world-provocative-parties-couples-swap/story?id=16396730.
- Susan Dominus's blockbuster article in the *New York Times Magazine*, "Is an Open Marriage a Happier Marriage?," was filled with information about the success of open marriages and their relationships to female libido: https://www.nytimes.com/2017/05/11/magazine/is-an-open-marriage-a-happier-marriage.html?_r=1.
- Andrea Syrtash's article "What It Really Means to Be Monogamish" about Dan Savage's term *monogamish* was helpful for understanding the term: https://www.glamour.com/story/what-is-monogamish.
- I also consulted this academic paper on internet searches and non-monogamy: Amy C. Moors, "Has the American Public's Interest in Information Related to Relationships beyond 'the Couple' Increased over Time?," *Journal of Sex Research* 54, no. 6 (2017), http://www.tandfonline.com/doi/abs/10.1080/00224499.2016.1178208?journalCode=hjsr20.
- This September 2016 YouGov poll examined Americans' attitudes toward non-monogamy: https://d25d2506sfb94s.cloudfront.net/cumulus_uploads/document/cqmk3va41c/tabs_OP_Relationships_20160925.pdf.
- Tammy Nelson's book is *The New Monogamy: Redefining Your Relationship*, published by New Harbinger Publications, in 2013.

4. Graying Bachelors

- Pew Research's "Record Share of Americans Have Never Been Married" study included data on the ratio of unmarried men to women by age: http://www.pewsocialtrends.org/2014/09/24/record-share-of-americans-have-never-married/st-2014-09-24-never-married-22/.
- Study on older American men and wealth by Alan J. Auerback et al., "How the Growing Gap in Life Expectancy May Affect Retirement Benefits and Reforms," http://www.nber.org/papers/w23329.
- "Dating Relationships in Older Adulthood: A National Portrait" by Susan L. Brown and Sayaka K. Shinohara included information about the benefits of dating among older populations.
- Ezekiel Emmanuel wrote this helpful op-ed in the *New York Times* about the health risks of senior-citizen sex practices: "Sex and the Single Senior," https://www.nytimes.com/2014/01/19/opinion/sunday/emanuel-sex-and-the-single-senior.html.

- AARP reported the figures for the over-50 single population: https://press.aarp.org/2014-02-04-Love-Is-In-The-Air-For-50-Singles-AARP-Releases-Profile-of-The-50-Dating-Life-More-Active-Social-Than-Ever.
- Paula Derrow's article "Seniors, Sex, and STDs" had important CDC data about rising STD rates: http://www.berkeleywellness.com/self-care/sexual-health/article/seniors-sex-and-stds.
- Life expectancy figures come from the CDC: https://www.cdc.gov/nchs/data/hus/hus16.pdf#listfigures.
- Laura Donnelly's article about infidelity in older generations, "Over-55s More Likely Than Younger People to Have Affairs," provided some important context: http://www.telegraph.co.uk/lifestyle/3363230/Over-55s-more-likely-than-younger-people-to-have-affairs.html.
- Kevyn Burger's article "Senior Citizens Are Having More Sex and Enjoying It More Than Younger People" cited material from the Archives of Sexual Behavior on declining intimacy among all age cohorts except over seventy: http://www.startribune.com/senior-citizens-are-having-more-sex-and-enjoying-it-more-than-younger-people/425508863/.
- The *WorldAtlas* had data on the oldest countries in "Countries with the Largest Aging Population in the World": http://www.worldatlas.com/articles/countries-with-the-largest-aging-population-in-the-world.html.
- The chart on age differences between spouses with different income levels comes from the Austin Institute: http://www.austin-institute.org/research/ask-a-data-scientist-age-differences-between-couples/.
- Mimi Lau wrote about the Fujian Bureau of Statistics report on the skewed gender birth ratio in China and the number of single men, which could be larger than Australia's population: "Soon China Is Going to Have More Single Males Than the Entire Population of Australia": http://www.businessinsider.com/china-more-males-australia-population-2015-9.

5. Third-Time Winners

- Data on the percentage of American adults who have married three or more times comes from the American Community Survey, via IPUMS: Steven Ruggles et al., *Integrated Public Use Microdata Series: Version 7.0* (Minneapolis: University of Minnesota, 2017).
- Pew analysis of US Census data on remarriage came from "Four-in-Ten Couples Are Saying 'I Do,' Again," a report by Gretchen Livingston: http://www.pewsocialtrends.org/2014/11/14/four-in-ten-couples-are-saying-i-do-again/.
- Steven Ruggles et al., *Integrated Public Use Microdata Series: Version 7.0* (Minneapolis: University of Minnesota, 2017), https://doi.org/10.18128/D010.V7.0.
- Data on the average cost of a wedding came from https://www.costofwedding.com/.

- *Inside Edition* refreshed our memory on the wisdom of Zsa Zsa Gabor in "'Divorce Lawyers Are a Girl's Best Friend': The Affairs, Marriages and Relationships of Zsa Zsa Gabor," http://www.insideedition.com/headlines/20547-divorce-lawyers-are-a-girls-best-friend-the-affairs-marriages-and-relationships-of-zsa-zsa.

6. Having It Both Ways

- Pew did an important report on the attitudes and lives of LGBT Americans: "A Survey of LGBT Americans," http://www.pewsocialtrends.org/files/2013/06/SDT_LGBT-Americans_06-2013.pdf.
- Gary J. Gates at Gallup wrote an article summarizing the trends they have seen in LGBT self-identification over the years: "In U.S., More Adults Identifying as LGBT," http://news.gallup.com/poll/201731/lgbt-identification-rises.aspx.
- Michelle Castillo caught Mackey Friedman's press release on how negative attitudes toward bisexual individuals can affect them in her article "15 Percent of People Don't Think Bisexuality Is Real Sexual Orientation: Study," https://www.cbsnews.com/news/15-percent-of-people-dont-think-bisexuality-is-real-sexual-orientation-study/.
- Tangela S. Roberts, Sharon G. Horne, and William T. Hoyt's study "Between a Gay and a Straight Place: Bisexual Individuals' Experiences with Monosexism" was important in demonstrating that bisexuals also face discrimination from gay men and lesbians: http://www.tandfonline.com/doi/abs/10.1080/15299716.2015.1111183?journalCode=wjbi20#.VrZJf5MrKuU.
- GLAAD's 2016 "Where We Are on TV" report raised concerns about stereotypes of bisexuals on television: https://www.glaad.org/whereweareontv16.
- Maria Burnham's article "Online Dating: The Bisexual Conundrum" told us about common problems for bisexuals online: https://www.huffingtonpost.com/maria-burnham/online-dating-the-bisexual-conundrum_b_1956684.html.
- For additional information on how same- and opposite-sex relationships start, I looked at this paper: Michael J. Rosenfeld and Reuben J. Thomas, "Searching for a Mate: The Rise of the Internet as a Social Intermediary," *American Sociological Review* 77, no. 4 (2012): 523–47, https://web.stanford.edu/~mrosenfe/Rosenfeld_How_Couples_Meet_Working_Paper.pdf.

7. Internet Marrieds Revisited

- M. J. Penn and E. K. Zalesne, *Microtrends: The Small Forces behind Tomorrow's Big Changes* (New York: Twelve, 2007).
- Pew Research had helpful basic facts and charts about attitudes toward and usage of online dating in their news release "5 Facts about Online Dating" by

Aaron Smith and Monica Anderson: http://www.pewresearch.org/fact-tank/2016/02/29/5-facts-about-online-dating/.

- Another Pew study by Aaron Smith and Monica Anderson, "15% of American Adults Have Used Online Dating Sites or Mobile Dating Apps," showed recent growth in online dating usage across the age spectrum: http://www.pewinternet.org/2016/02/11/15-percent-of-american-adults-have-used-online-dating-sites-or-mobile-dating-apps/.
- GrowthHackers looked into the numbers behind Tinder's explosive growth: https://growthhackers.com/growth-studies/what-ignited-tinders-explosive-growth.
- Michael J. Rosenfeld and Reuben J. Thomas's paper "Searching for a Mate: The Rise of the Internet as a Social Intermediary," published in the *American Sociological Review*, was helpful in understanding how online relationships evolve and at what pace.
- OkCupid's blog publishes many fascinating statistics, including some on racial attitudes in dating: https://theblog.okcupid.com/race-and-attraction-2009-2014-107dcbb4f060.
- Christopher Rudolph wrote up the survey by Grindr showing that 77 percent of users want to get married someday: "Grindr Survey Shows 77 Percent of Members Want to Get Married," https://www.huffingtonpost.com/2013/06/28/grindr-marriage-survey_n_3511342.html.
- Information on the funding of Bharat Matrimony and on Dil Mil came from Crunchbase: https://www.crunchbase.com/organization/bharat-matrimony and https://www.crunchbase.com/organization/dilmile.
- Ruth Styles wrote up a study examining relationship outcomes in the *Daily Mail*: "Looking for Love? Try the Office! Relationships That Begin in the Workplace Most Likely to Result in Marriage," http://www.dailymail.co.uk/femail/article-2437181/Relationships-begin-workplace-likely-result-marriage-new-study-reveals.html#ixzz4yuWB4Mm2.
- Kristine Fellizar wrote about romantic trends in Australia in "Online Dating Is the Second Most Popular Way to Meet Someone, Says New Study, and More Things to Know about Dating in the Digital Age," https://www.bustle.com/articles/105558-online-dating-is-the-second-most-popular-way-to-meet-someone-says-new-study-and-more.
- The University of Chicago research is from John Cacioppo: https://news.uchicago.edu/article/2013/06/03/meeting-online-leads-happier-more-enduring-marriages.
- Information on marital satisfaction: http://www.pnas.org/content/110/25/10135.full.pdf.

8. Independent Marrieds

- Mark Eghrari wrote for *Forbes* about a study showing that long commutes can lead to divorce: "A Long Commute Could Be the Last Thing Your Marriage Needs," https://www.forbes.com/sites/markeghrari/2016/01/21/a-long-commute-could-be-the-last-thing-your-marriage-needs/#3cb1b0674245.
- Mary Bowerman wrote about the National Sleep Foundation survey and the National Homebuilder projections for separate beds and bedrooms in "Why So Many Married Couples Are Sleeping in Separate Beds," https://www.usatoday.com/story/news/nation-now/2017/03/30/why-so-many-married-couples-sleeping-separate-beds/99818086/.
- Chris Taylor at Reuters wrote about couples taking separate vacations and TripAdvisor in "See You in Two Weeks: When Couples Take Separate Vacations," https://www.reuters.com/article/us-money-travel-couples/see-you-in-two-weeks-when-couples-take-separate-vacations-idUSBRE86Q0S420120727.
- Kelsey Kloss looked into the prices of homes with multiple master bedrooms in "Luxury Homes Now Come with Separate Master Bedrooms for Couples Who Want to Sleep Apart," http://www.elledecor.com/design-decorate/trends/a9164471/master-bedrooms/.
- Alice Philipson wrote about couples living apart in the U.K. and London in "Why Happily Married Couples Are Choosing to Live Apart," http://www.telegraph.co.uk/women/sex/relationship-advice-and-romance/10592950/why-happily-married-couples-are-choosing-to-live-apart.html.
- Amy Wallace wrote about the Aston Medical School study looking at survival outcomes and marital status in "Study: Married Heart Disease Patients Have Better Survival Rate," https://www.upi.com/Health_News/2017/08/28/Study-Married-heart-disease-patients-have-better-survival-rates/3971503923865/.
- Rates of "living apart together" couples by country are compiled in Wikipedia: https://en.wikipedia.org/wiki/Living_apart_together.

SECTION 2: HEALTH AND DIET

9. Pro-Proteiners

- Janet Larsen at the Earth Policy Institute wrote up their data in 2013 on how many different proteins were being consumed: "China's Growing Hunger for Meat Shown by Move to Buy Smithfield, World's Leading Pork Producer," http://www.earth-policy.org/data_highlights/2013/highlights39.
- *Undercurrent News* reported on data from the National Fisheries Institute about how different fish were being consumed and included a helpful graph:

https://www.undercurrentnews.com/2013/11/01/whitefish-surpasses-shrimp-as-us-most-consumed/.

- Anahad O'Connor at the *Well* blog at the *New York Times* reported on the guidelines suggesting that men and boys are overconsuming protein: "New Dietary Guidelines Urge Less Sugar for All and Less Protein for Boys and Men." https://well.blogs.nytimes.com/2016/01/07/new-diet-guidelines-urge-less-sugar-for-all-and-less-meat-for-boys-and-men/.
- Roni Caryn Rabin, also at the *New York Times Well* blog, did an article on protein powder, "Can You Get Too Much Protein?," https://www.nytimes.com/2016/12/06/well/eat/can-you-get-too-much-protein.html.
- The Food and Agriculture Organization of the United Nations' 2013 report "Edible Insects" was about the future of, well, edible insects.
- Klint Finley wrote about Exo and the bug-based food businesses for *Wired* in "You'll Eat Bugs. These Investors Are Betting Millions on It," https://www.wired.com/2016/03/investors-bet-millions-wont-balk-eating-bugs/.
- The number of sushi restaurants comes from Statistic Brain: https://www.statisticbrain.com/sushi-industry-statistics/.
- You can read more about Research and Markets' analysis of plant-based-protein markets at https://www.prnewswire.com/news-releases/global-plant-protein-market-2016-2022-demand-for-healthy-food-products-and-due-to-high-nutritional-values-of-soy-and-pea-proteins-300524295.html.
- The *Economic Times* reported on the report by India's National Sample Survey Office: https://economictimes.indiatimes.com/industry/cons-products/food/chicken-consumption-growing-at-12-making-india-one-of-the-fastest-growing-markets/articleshow/49295260.cms.

10. Guys Left Behind

- Eric Klein wrote about the Cleveland Clinic survey of why men avoid the doctor in "60 Percent of Men Don't Go to the Doctor: Here's Why," https://www.everydayhealth.com/columns/health-answers/why-men-dont-go-to-the-doctor/.
- Anna Almendrala wrote about more surveys showing why men avoid doctors, including the chart from Orlando Health, in "Here's Why Men Don't Like Going to the Doctor," https://www.huffingtonpost.com/entry/why-men-dont-go-to-the-doctor_us_5759c267e4b00f97fba7aa3e.
- The World Health Organization bulletin "The Men's Health Gap: Men Must Be Included in the Global Health Equity Agenda" is at http://www.who.int/bulletin/volumes/92/8/13-132795/en/.
- The CDC report "Health, United States, 16" had data on obesity and alcoholism by sex: https://www.cdc.gov/nchs/data/hus/hus16.pdf#listfigures.

- Figures on male and female incarceration rates come from the Bureau of Justice Statistics: https://www.bjs.gov/content/pub/pdf/cpus15.pdf.
- The Kaiser Family Foundation data on heart disease mortality was from https://www.kff.org/other/state-indicator/heart-disease-death-rate-by-gender/.
- Barbara Hagenbaugh at *USA Today* wrote about the difference in unemployment between men and women: https://usatoday30.usatoday.com/money/economy/2009-01-11-unemployment-rate-sexes_N.htm.
- Rachel Breitman wrote about young women outearning young men in big cities for Reuters: "Young Women Earn More Than Men in Big U.S. Cities," https://www.reuters.com/article/us-workplace-women/young-women-earn-more-than-men-in-big-u-s-cities-idUSN0334472920070803.
- The NBER paper by Alan J. Auerbach et al. talked about how longer life expectancy is concentrated at the top of the income distribution: "How the Growing Gap in Life Expectancy May Affect Retirement Benefits and Reforms," http://www.nber.org/papers/w23329.
- The chart on "deaths of despair" comes from the *Financial Times*: https://www.ft.com/content/34637e1a-0f41-11e7-b030-768954394623.
- For more on the link between social isolation and cardiac problems (among other health problems) see "Loneliness and Social Isolation as Risk Factors for Coronary Heart Disease and Stroke: Systematic Review and Meta-analysis of Longitudinal Observational Studies" by Nicole K. Valtorta et al., http://heart.bmj.com/content/early/2016/03/15/heartjnl-2015-308790.
- Niobe Way's book is *Deep Secrets: Boys' Friendships and the Crisis of Connection*, published by Harvard University Press in 2013.
- Boys are having trouble sitting still while classes in most schools are becoming more demanding at earlier ages. Eighth-grade boys are 50 percent more likely than girls to get held back a grade; 67 percent of special education students are boys; suspensions are given to boys 71 percent of the time: http://www.teachmag.com/archives/133.
- Size of SAT prep industry: https://www.forbes.com/sites/carolinehoward/2014/03/05/right-answer-for-sat-college-board-revamps-test-adds-partnership-with-khan-academy/#6c854ab55d5f.

11. Nonagenarians

- American Community Survey data on nonagenarians comes from the IPUMS database: Steven Ruggles et al., *Integrated Public Use Microdata Series: Version 7.0* (Minneapolis: University of Minnesota, 2017), https://doi.org/10.18128/D010.V7.0.
- The U.K.'s life-expectancy calculator is available from the Office of National Statistics at https://visual.ons.gov.uk/how-long-will-my-pension-need-to-last/.

- The Census's 2010 summary of life for nonagenarians contains many interesting stats: https://www.census.gov/newsroom/releases/archives/aging_population/cb11-194.html.
- Damien Gayle wrote up results, including a graph of Office of National Statistics data, about life satisfaction in "People Aged 40–59 Are Least Happy and Most Anxious, Report Finds," https://www.theguardian.com/society/2016/feb/02/middle-aged-people-least-happy-most-anxious-ons-wellbeing-report.
- The U.K. Office of National Statistics also provided data on the growing number of ninety-year-olds there: https://www.ons.gov.uk/peoplepopulationandcommunity/birthsdeathsandmarriages/ageing/bulletins/estimatesoftheveryoldincludingcentenarians/2002to2015#there-were-14570-centenarians-in-2015.
- Lydia Smith wrote about the aging population in Japan and the Japanese government data in "Japan's Over-90 Population Soars over Two Million Mark as Birth Rate Continues to Decline," http://www.independent.co.uk/news/world/asia/japan-ageing-over-90-population-2-million-birthrate-decline-sex-children-marriage-childcare-a7954841.html.
- For more on the demographic projections in Sweden, see the 2015 report from Statistics Sweden at http://www.scb.se/statistik/_publikationer/BE0401_2006I50_BR_BE51BR0602ENG.pdf.
- Reporting on Japan's annual survey concerning its aging population was detailed by Jun Hongo of the *Wall Street Journal* in 2015: https://blogs.wsj.com/japanrealtime/2015/06/16/fear-of-dying-alone-the-state-of-japans-aging-population/.
- "With increasing advances in healthcare, if you hit 80, you have a 30 percent chance of making it to 90": http://www.businessinsider.com/social-security-life-table-charts-2014-3.

12. Kids on Meds

- Thanks for this CDC data and graphs on the use of medication for children with mental health challenges goes to "Use of Medication Prescribed for Emotional or Behavioral Difficulties among Children Aged 6–17 Years in the United States, 2011–2012," https://www.cdc.gov/nchs/data/databriefs/db148.htm#x2013;17%20Years%20in%20the%20United%20States,%202011%E2%80%932012%20.
- This book review by Judith Newman about several books on children with behavioral problems referenced additional CDC data on how common medication is: "How to Ignore Your Kids' Bad Behavior and Yet Be Fully Present for Them," https://www.nytimes.com/2017/08/11/books/review/help-desk-tantrums-discipline-attention.html.

- Child Trends reported on the increase in ADHD diagnoses by family income and other interesting demographic characteristics: https://www.childtrends.org/wp-content/uploads/2012/07/76_appendix1.pdf.
- E. Jane Costello, PhD, Gordon P. Keeler, MS, and Adrian Angold, MRCPsych, in "Poverty, Race/Ethnicity, and Psychiatric Disorder: A Study of Rural Children," looked at the risk factors for psychiatric issues in rural children: https://www.ncbi.nlm.nih.gov/pmc/articles/PMC1446810/.
- The CDC had additional data that provided insight into racial disparities in these medications: "Psychotropic Medication Use among Adolescents: United States, 2005–2010," https://www.cdc.gov/nchs/data/databriefs/db135.htm#x2013;2010%20.
- Thomas Insel wrote about a Carter Center symposium that discussed, among other things, toddlers on Ritalin: "Post by Former NIMH Director Thomas Insel: Are Children Overmedicated?," https://www.nimh.nih.gov/about/directors/thomas-insel/blog/2014/are-children-overmedicated.shtml.
- Alan Schwarz wrote in 2015 for the *New York Times* about young children on antipsychotics in "Still in a Crib, Yet Being Given Antipsychotics," https://www.nytimes.com/2015/12/11/us/psychiatric-drugs-are-being-prescribed-to-infants.html?mcubz=3.
- This Johns Hopkins Bloomberg School of Public Health press release discussed the new trend in Adderall emergency-room visits: "Adderall Misuse Rising among Young Adults," https://www.jhsph.edu/news/news-releases/2016/adderall-misuse-rising-among-young-adults.html.
- Amanda M. Stone and Lisa J. Merlo's article "Attitudes of College Students toward Mental Illness Stigma and the Misuse of Psychiatric Medications" discussed that how people feel about mental health influences how they use the medications: https://www.ncbi.nlm.nih.gov/pmc/articles/PMC3056282/.
- ADHD market projection numbers: https://www.ibisworld.com/industry-trends/specialized-market-research-reports/life-sciences/prescription-drugs/adhd-medication-manufacturing.html.
- CDC information on youth and ADHD: https://www.cdc.gov/ncbddd/adhd/features/key-findings-adhd72013.html.

13. The Speed Eaters

- Pam Spaulding at *USA Today* wrote about work by CareerBuilder and Right Management looking at worker lunch habits: "More Workers Work through Lunch or Eat at Their Desks," https://usatoday30.usatoday.com/money/workplace/story/2012-04-15/lunch-at-work/54167808/1.
- Soylent's press release touting its growth had helpful figures: http://blog.soylent.com/post/160300733977/soylent-closes-50-million-series-b-round-led-by.

- Niamh Michail wrote about the energy-bar market in the U.K. in "UK Energy Bar Sales Triple and Set to Rise," https://www.nutraingredients.com/Article/2015/02/24/UK-energy-bar-sales-triple-and-set-to-rise.
- Kate Taylor wrote about the rise of meat bars as alternative snacks in "An Unusual Type of Protein Snack Is after the Hearts and Wallets of Average Americans," http://www.businessinsider.com/the-rise-of-the-meat-protein-bar-2016-4.
- Ashley Lutz wrote about nutrient bars in "Grocery Stores Have Discovered the Perfect Product, and Customers Are Happily Paying Higher Prices," http://www.businessinsider.com/nutrition-bar-sales-are-soaring-2015-6.
- Source on the decline of chocolate and growth of other kinds of bars: Kate Taylor, "An Unusual Type of Protein Snack Is After the Hearts and Wallets of Average Americans," http://www.businessinsider.com/the-rise-of-the-meat-protein-bar-2016-4.
- Data on waiters/waitresses and other professions comes from the American Community Survey, via IPUMS: Steven Ruggles et al., *Integrated Public Use Microdata Series: Version 7.0* (Minneapolis: University of Minnesota, 2017).
- Statista had some helpful data about the granola-bar industry and market: https://www.statista.com/statistics/188216/top-granola-bar-brands-in-the-united-states/.
- Neil Stern wrote about Blue Apron in "The Big Question about Blue Apron's IPO," https://www.forbes.com/sites/neilstern/2017/06/05/meal-prep-pioneer-blue-apron-preps-for-an-ipo/#30d79f8e13ef.
- Amar Toor wrote about food delivery in France in "The French Finally Embrace Delivery Food," https://www.theverge.com/2016/3/8/11171894/paris-food-delivery-apps-french-cuisine-foodora-deliveroo-uber-eats.

14. Wellness Freaks

- Data and a nice chart on quinoa consumption came from this Food and Agriculture Organization of the United Nations report: http://www.fao.org/3/a-i4042e/i4042e20.pdf.
- The rise in celiac diagnoses was reported in the *New York Times*' *Well* blog in 2009: https://well.blogs.nytimes.com/2009/07/02/celiac-disease-becoming-more-common/.
- Information on orthorexia from Steven Bratman's site: http://www.orthorexia.com/what-is-orthorexia/.
- Yoga Alliance included a lot of great data and charts on the rise in popularity of the practice: https://www.yogaalliance.org/Portals/0/2016%20Yoga%20in%20America%20Study%20RESULTS.pdf.
- Hayley Peterson wrote up the Department of Agriculture data on kale in "This

One Stat Shows How Kale Has Exploded in the US," http://www.businessinsider.com/kale-consumption-has-exploded-in-the-us-2014-5.

- Pomegranate-farm numbers were reported by the Agricultural Marketing Resource Center: https://www.agmrc.org/commodities-products/fruits/pomegranates/.
- Shine on Creatives had some advice on juicing at http://www.shineoncreatives.com/juicing.html.
- The FTC press release on POM can be found at https://www.ftc.gov/news-events/press-releases/2013/01/ftc-commissioners-uphold-trial-judge-decision-pom-wonderful-llc.
- "12 Year Old Vegan Has the Degenerating Bones of 80 Year Old" by Kaayla T. Daniel: https://www.thehealthyhomeeconomist.com/12-year-old-vegan-has-the-degenerating-bones-of-80-year-old/.
- Martina M. Cartwright, PhD, RD, wrote about orthorexia in children for *Psychology Today* in "Freaked about Food: Ultra Health Conscious Kids," https://www.psychologytoday.com/blog/food-thought/201102/freaked-about-food-ultra-health-conscious-kids.
- Information on orthorexia from https://www.nationaleatingdisorders.org/orthorexia-nervosa.

15. Cancer Survivors

- The National Cancer Institute had some helpful graphs on cancer survivors, one of which is included here: https://cancercontrol.cancer.gov/ocs/statistics/graphs.html.
- Cancer.org also has useful stats on the number of survivors: https://www.cancer.org/content/dam/cancer-org/research/cancer-facts-and-statistics/cancer-treatment-and-survivorship-facts-and-figures/cancer-treatment-and-survivorship-facts-and-figures-2016-2017.pdf.
- *Journal of the National Cancer Institute*, chart: Chris Canipe/*Axios* had an excellent chart about changing cancer prognoses that was included: https://www.axios.com/heres-how-cancer-survival-rates-have-changed-2507510822.html.
- The American Cancer Society's survival numbers and Edwards's numbers on the amount of diagnoses were found in Sheryl Ness et al., "Concerns across the Survivorship Trajectory: Results from a Survey of Cancer Survivors," *Oncology Nursing Forum* 40, no. 1 (2013): 35–42.
- Sarah Knapton wrote about cancer in the U.K. in "Cancer Now More Common Than Getting Married or Having a First Baby," http://www.telegraph.co.uk/science/2017/07/09/cancer-now-common-getting-married-having-first-baby/.
- The American Cancer Society's 2016–17 "Cancer Treatment and Survivorship

Facts & Figures" was informative about survivors' quality of life: https://www.cancer.org/content/dam/cancer-org/research/cancer-facts-and-statistics/cancer-treatment-and-survivorship-facts-and-figures/cancer-treatment-and-survivorship-facts-and-figures-2016-2017.pdf.

- Joshua A. Halpern et al., "National Trends in Prostate Biopsy and Radical Prostatectomy Volumes following the US Preventive Services Task Force Guidelines against Prostate-Specific Antigen Screening," *JAMA Surgery* 152, no. 2 (2017):192–98, https://jamanetwork.com/journals/jamasurgery/article-abstract/2571537.
- Data on the increase in prostate cancer in the U.K. come from Cancer Research UK: http://www.cancerresearchuk.org/health-professional/cancer-statistics/statistics-by-cancer-type/prostate-cancer/diagnosis-and-treatment.

SECTION 3: TECHNOLOGY

16. The New Addicts

- Kelly Wallace wrote about work Common Sense Media did on teens and tech addiction in "Half of Teens Think They're Addicted to Their Smartphones," http://www.cnn.com/2016/05/03/health/teens-cell-phone-addiction-parents/index.html.
- Wikipedia wrote about the phenomenal growth of Pokémon Go at https://en.wikipedia.org/wiki/Pokémon_Go#Commercial_response.
- And the rise of Kim Kardashian's game at https://en.wikipedia.org/wiki/Kim_Kardashian:_Hollywood.
- Jeff Dunn wrote about where the money in the gaming industry comes from in "The Video Game Industry Now Gets More Money Making Games for Smartphones and Tablets Than for Consoles or PCs," http://www.businessinsider.com/mobile-games-more-money-than-console-pc-chart-2017-6.
- Leena Rao wrote about the Kim Kardashian game in "Here's How Much Kim Kardashian's Hit Game Has Made," http://fortune.com/2016/02/19/kardashian-game-revenue/.
- Katie Heaney wrote about people who spend money on games without realizing it in "How Much Money Are People Actually Spending on Kim Kardashian: Hollywood?," https://www.buzzfeed.com/katieheaney/how-much-money-are-people-actually-spending-on-kim-kardashia?utm_term=.baekvXJoA#.urL89kwnL.
- Claudia Dreifus interviewed Adam Alter on this topic, which provided the anecdote about the man who spent forty-five days playing video games and extreme measures in Asia: "Why We Can't Look Away from Our Screens," https://www.nytimes.com/2017/03/06/science/technology-addiction-irresistible-by-adam-alter.html?_r=0.

- Graham Keeley and Jo Adetunji wrote about the first case of children being addicted to mobile phones in Spain in "Children, 12 and 13, Treated for Addiction to Mobile Phones," https://www.theguardian.com/world/2008/jun/13/spain.mobilephones.
- Saqib Shah wrote about video games building in time limits: "Tencent Tackles Mobile Game Addiction with Time Limits for Kids," https://www.engadget.com/2017/07/04/tencent-tackles-mobile-game-addiction-with-time-limits-for-kids/.
- Earnings on Glu Mobile and Kim Kardashian: Hollywood: http://t.co/cTlun2X70y.

17. Digital Tailors

- Etsy's success was reported in *VentureBeat*: https://venturebeat.com/2015/03/05/a-brief-history-of-etsy-from-2005-brooklyn-launch-to-2015-ipo/.
- *Entrepreneur.com* reported on the rate that online apparel purchases are returned: https://www.entrepreneur.com/article/246421.
- Nick Wingfield and Kelly Couturier wrote about Amazon's patent for customized clothes in "Detailing Amazon's Custom-Clothing Patent," https://www.nytimes.com/2017/04/30/technology/detailing-amazons-custom-clothing-patent.html.
- Pamela N. Danzinger wrote about Amazon's fashion strategy in "Made-to-Order Clothing Is an Opportunity Tailor-Made for Amazon," https://www.forbes.com/sites/pamdanziger/2017/05/03/made-to-order-clothing-is-an-opportunity-tailor-made-for-amazon/#6278e40a6dcb.
- Looking at Like A Glove gave a helpful example of this trend: http://www.likeaglove.me/.
- Crunchbase's data on Indochina funding at https://www.crunchbase.com/organization/indochino/funding_rounds/funding_rounds_list and investors at https://www.crunchbase.com/organization/indochino/investors/investors_list.
- Sales figures for Stitch Fix come from *Recode*: https://www.recode.net/2017/5/10/15610606/stitch-fix-fashion-revenue-730-million-profitable-katrina-lake-ipo.
- Information about the size of the apparel industry is from Statista.

18. Technology-Advanced People

- Ray Kurzweil's book is *The Age of Spiritual Machines: When Computers Exceed Human Intelligence* (New York: Viking, 1998).
- Merrit Kennedy wrote about an employer who is putting microchips in employees in "Wisconsin Company Offers to Implant Chips in Its Employees," https://www.npr.org/sections/thetwo-way/2017/07/25/539265157/wisconsin-company-plans-to-start-implanting-chips-in-its-employees.

- Keiron Monks wrote for CNN about implantable technologies in "Forget Wearable Tech, Embeddable Implants Are Already Here," http://www.cnn.com/2014/04/08/tech/forget-wearable-tech-embeddable-implants/index.html.
- Information on artificial retinas from Susan Young Rojahn, "What It's Like to See Again with an Artificial Retina," https://www.technologyreview.com/s/514081/can-artificial-retinas-restore-natural-sight/.

19. Droning On

- April Glaser wrote about the drone market and included a nice graph in "DJI Is Running Away with the Drone Market," https://www.recode.net/2017/4/14/14690576/drone-market-share-growth-charts-dji-forecast.
- The Center for the Study of the Drone at Bard College reported on Defense Department spending on drones: http://dronecenter.bard.edu/files/2016/02/DroneSpendingFy17_CSD_1-1.pdf.
- The Federal Aviation Administration generated projects on drone sales: https://www.faa.gov/news/updates/?newsId=85227&cid=TW414.
- Sally French wrote about the University of Nevada, Las Vegas, drone study in "'Surprising' Drone Study Shows How People Really Feel about Drones," https://www.marketwatch.com/story/surprising-drone-study-shows-how-people-really-feel-about-drones-2015-11-11.
- Richard Verrier wrote about drones in entertainment in "Drones Are Providing Film and TV Viewers a New Perspective on the Action," http://www.latimes.com/entertainment/envelope/cotown/la-et-ct-drones-hollywood-20151008-story.html.
- Amar Toor wrote about drones delivering medicine overseas in "Drones Will Begin Delivering Blood and Medicine in the US," https://www.theverge.com/2016/8/2/12350274/zipline-drone-delivery-us-launch-blood-medicine.
- Kim Hayes wrote about drones delivering health care elsewhere in "Simulation Shows Promise for Drone Use in Cardiac Arrest," https://www.aarp.org/health/conditions-treatments/info-2017/drones-could-deliver-aeds-fd.html.
- April Glaser wrote about drones and privacy laws for *Recode* in "Federal Privacy Laws Won't Necessarily Protect You from Spying Drones," https://www.recode.net/2017/3/15/14934050/federal-privacy-laws-spying-drones-senate-hearing.
- Senator Markey on his drone legislation: "Senator Markey & Rep. Welch Introduce Legislation to Ensure Transparency, Privacy for Drone Use," https://www.markey.senate.gov/news/press-releases/-senator-markey-and-rep-welch-introduce-legislation-to-ensure-transparency-privacy-for-drone-use.

20. No-PCers

- These articles pointed to helpful UN data about internet usage in India: https://yourstory.com/2017/06/india-internet-users-report/ and http://data.un.org/Data.aspx?d=WDI&f=Indicator_Code%3AIT.NET.USER.P2.
- eMarketer had an excellent chart on how US residents are using the internet: https://www.emarketer.com/Article/US-Internet-Users-Rely-on-Mobile-Devices-Digital-Access/1013649.
- Pew's research on mobile usage in Africa is rich with statistics: http://www.pewglobal.org/2015/04/15/cell-phones-in-africa-communication-lifeline/.
- The *Wall Street Journal* reported on Motorola's success in Brazil: https://www.wsj.com/articles/motorola-has-a-hitin-brazil-1427493853.
- UNESCO's report on the "reading revolution" generated by mobile phones was reported in several publications, including the *Guardian*: https://www.theguardian.com/books/2014/apr/23/mobile-reading-revolution-unesco-study-phones-africa-subcontinent.
- Ben Popper wrote about Google's achievement of 2 billion Android users in "Google Announces Over 2 Billion Monthly Active Devices on Android," https://www.theverge.com/2017/5/17/15654454/android-reaches-2-billion-monthly-active-users.
- This International Data Corporation press release alerted me to the trends in the PC industry: "Traditional PC Market Was Up Slightly, Recording Its First Growth in Five Years as HP Recovered the Top Position, According to IDC," https://www.idc.com/getdoc.jsp?containerId=prUS42464617.
- Andrew Burger wrote up the Pew study on smartphone internet access in "Pew: Smartphone-Only Internet Users Find Them an Incomplete Home Broadband Substitute," http://www.telecompetitor.com/pew-smartphone-only-internet-users-find-them-an-incomplete-home-broadband-substitute/.
- Marty Swant wrote about how video content preferences change depending on mobile/desktop viewing: "New Study Shows Millennials Prefer Short Mobile Videos, While Older Crowds Like Long-Form," http://www.adweek.com/digital/new-study-shows-millennials-prefer-short-mobile-videos-while-older-crowds-long-form-170739/#/.
- This press release from the European Commission about attitudes toward data privacy was illuminating: http://ec.europa.eu/justice/newsroom/data-protection/news/240615_en.htm.
- Information on the percentage of Americans using their smartphones to access the internet: http://www.pewinternet.org/2012/06/26/cell-internet-use-2012/.
- PC sales market: https://www.statista.com/statistics/273495/global-shipments-of-personal-computers-since-2006/.

21. Unemployed Language Teachers

- Kat Devlin for Pew wrote about Americans' lack of language skills, included as reported by the General Social Survey's "Learning a Foreign Language a 'Must' in Europe, Not So in America," http://www.pewresearch.org/fact-tank/2015/07/13/learning-a-foreign-language-a-must-in-europe-not-so-in-america/.
- Global Industry Analysts Inc. reported on the size of the global web-conferencing market: http://www.strategyr.com/MarketResearch/Web_Conferencing_Market_Trends.asp.
- Data on study abroad was taken from USA Study Abroad, an office of the State Department: https://studyabroad.state.gov/us-government-resources/student-mobility-data.
- Sumant Patil and Patrick Davies's study "Use of Google Translate in Medical Communication: Evaluation of Accuracy," in *BMJ*, was helpful in getting a medical perspective: http://www.bmj.com/content/349/bmj.g7392.
- The Bureau of Labor Statistics' *Occupational Outlook Handbook* included projections on the labor market for translators and interpreters: https://www.bls.gov/ooh/media-and-communication/interpreters-and-translators.htm.
- "Global Business Speaks English" by Tsedal Neeley in the *Harvard Business Review* laid out the case for English as an unprecedented lingua franca: https://hbr.org/2012/05/global-business-speaks-english.

22. Bots with Benefits

- Claire Cain Miller wrote on research including by Carnegie Mellon University, Harvard University, and the University of Washington for the *New York Times*' Upshot: "When Algorithms Discriminate," https://www.nytimes.com/2015/07/10/upshot/when-algorithms-discriminate.html?mcubz=3&_r=0.
- "The tech sex industry has been estimated at $30 billion in market size today, with the potential to grow to ten times that size": https://sexevangelist.me/what-is-sextech-and-how-is-the-industry-worth-30-6-billion-developing-d5f0a61e31d6.

23. New Luddites Updated

- Aaron Smith wrote about smartphone adoption in "Record Shares of Americans Now Own Smartphones, Have Home Broadband," http://www.pewresearch.org/fact-tank/2017/01/12/evolution-of-technology/.
- Robert McGarvey talked about the draw of the flip phone in "Why Flip Phones Are Coming Back," https://www.thestreet.com/story/13561991/1/why-flip-phones-are-coming-back.html.
- Laura Stampler pointed out those few Millennials who still resist smartphones

in "The Few, The Proud: The Millennials Who Still Use Flip Phones," http://time.com/3318573/flip-phones-millennials-iphone6/.

- Seth Stevenson wrote about the enduring appeal for some of the BlackBerry in "Who Still Wants a BlackBerry?," http://www.slate.com/articles/technology/technology/2015/03/blackberry_classic_if_you_like_any_of_the_ways_smartphones_have_evolved.html.
- Andrew Perrin wrote about Pew's research into Americans' book reading in "Book Reading 2016," http://www.pewinternet.org/2016/09/01/book-reading-2016/.
- Pew's 2013 "Health Online" report contained many facts about online searches: http://www.pewinternet.org/2013/01/15/health-online-2013/.
- Simon Smelt's research on data security was reported by NBC News: http://www.nbcnews.com/id/3078835/t/online-privacy-fears-are-real/#.Whszh1VKvIU.
- "Coming and Going on Facebook" by Lee Rainie, Aaron Smith, and Maeve Duggan told of the people who take breaks from Facebook: http://www.pewinternet.org/2013/02/05/coming-and-going-on-facebook/.
- The *Huffington Post* wrote about the research by Laura Portwood-Stacer on the social impact and repercussions of quitting Facebook: https://www.huffingtonpost.com/2013/01/04/quitting-facebook_n_2410071.html.
- Holly Ellyatt wrote about a survey of why Facebook users quit: "Users Quitting Facebook Cite Privacy Concerns," https://www.thedailybeast.com/users-quitting-facebook-cite-privacy-concerns.
- Sarah Marsh wrote about a study finding teens get happier after quitting social media: "Does Quitting Social Media Make You Happier? Yes, Say Young People Doing It," https://www.theguardian.com/media/2016/sep/21/does-quitting-social-media-make-you-happier-yes-say-young-people-doing-it.
- Kim Kardashian's BlackBerry usage: http://money.cnn.com/2016/08/03/technology/kim-kardashian-blackberry-bold/index.html.
- Size of BlackBerry market share and power: https://www.statista.com/chart/8180/blackberrys-smartphone-market-share/.

24. Private Plane Party Crashers

- Knight Frank and NetJets via *CNNMoney* published data on the most common private-plane routes: http://money.cnn.com/2015/03/04/luxury/top-ten-private-jet-routes/index.html.
- *USA Today* reported on the size of the global fleet: https://www.usatoday.com/story/todayinthesky/2013/06/12/boeing-predicts-commercial-aircraft-will-double-by-2033/2416131/.
- Doug Gollan in "Private Jets: Who, What, When, Where and How?" wrote about the types of people who fly private: https://www.forbes.com/sites/douggollan/2016/05/14/private-jets-who-what-when-where-and-how/#46117b8d5862.

- "Flight Risk" by Ben Popper and Colin Lecher discussed the troubles of the JetSmarter app in the *Verge*: https://www.theverge.com/2017/3/28/15055046/jetsmarter-app-membership-cost-reviews-high-prices-lawsuits.
- Dennis Schaal wrote about some of the good deals to be had on HotelTonight: "HotelTonight Launches a New Product Aimed at Penthouses and Luxury Suites," https://skift.com/2013/09/25/hoteltonight-launches-a-new-product-aimed-at-penthouses-and-luxury-suites/.
- Rebecca Grant wrote about HotelTonight's new funding and products in "HotelTonight Launches in 15 New Destinations and Adds 'HighRoller' Option," https://venturebeat.com/2013/09/25/hoteltonight-launches-in-15-new-destination-and-adds-highroller-option/.
- Information on average private jet member spending from the *Verge*: Ben Popper and Colin Lecher, "Legal Threats and Disgruntled Clients: Inside the 'Uber for Private Jets,'" https://www.theverge.com/2017/3/28/15055046/jetsmarter-app-membership-cost-reviews-high-prices-lawsuits.
- Information on fractional ownership and others came from Mark Penn's personal knowledge.

25. Social Millionaires

- Wikipedia had some excellent data on the most popular Instagram and YouTube accounts: https://en.wikipedia.org/wiki/List_of_most-followed_Instagram_accounts and https://en.wikipedia.org/wiki/List_of_most-subscribed_YouTube_channels.
- Gabrielle Bluestone wrote about Fyre Festival's marketing in "Let's Just Do It and Be Legends, Man," https://news.vice.com/story/fyre-fest-organizers-blew-all-their-money-months-early-on-models-planes-and-yachts.
- Though lists of social media millionaires are not published as such, we estimated the number of YouTube and Twitter millionaires by curve-fitting the data from those services' top two thousand and one thousand accounts, respectively. YouTube's top two thousand accounts are listed by VidStax (http://vidstatsx.com/youtube-top-2000-most-subscribed-channels), while Twitter's top one thousand accounts are listed by Twitter Counter (https://twittercounter.com/pages/100).
- *VentureBeat* reported on OpenSlate's list of top-earning YouTube accounts, including DisneyCollectorBR: https://venturebeat.com/2015/01/02/youtubes-10-most-profitable-channels-of-2014-were-um-not-what-i-expected/.
- *Fast Company* reported on the earnings of YouTube channel EvanTubeHD: https://www.fastcompany.com/3045807/meet-the-father-son-team-making-13-million-on-youtube.

SECTION 4: LIFESTYLE

26. Single with Pet

- The Harris poll looked into how common pet ownership is across generations, including what types of pets and what people do with them: http://www.theharrispoll.com/health-and-life/Pets-are-Members-of-the-Family.html.
- For the second chart we put together several results from past Harris polls: http://www.businesswire.com/news/home/20071204005298/en/Pets-Members-Family-Two-Thirds-Pet-Owners-Buy; http://www.theharrispoll.com/health-and-life/Pets_Really_Are_Members_of_the_Family.html; and http://www.theharrispoll.com/health-and-life/Pets-are-Members-of-the-Family.html.
- Crunchbase had information about Barkly at https://www.crunchbase.com/organization/cylent-systems and about DogVacay at https://www.crunchbase.com/organization/dogvacay.

27. Roomies for Life

- Data on adults living with nonrelated housemates comes from the American Community Survey, via IPUMS: Steven Ruggles et al., *Integrated Public Use Microdata Series: Version 7.0*, (Minneapolis: University of Minnesota, 2017).
- RENTCafé had an enormous amount of survey data on roommate preferences—gender, behavior, and more: "The Cohabitation Correlation—What Makes the Best and Worst Roommate," https://www.rentcafe.com/blog/apartmentliving/roommates/best-and-worst-roommates-demographics-survey/.
- Katie Hafner wrote about the effects of loneliness on mortality in "Researchers Confront an Epidemic of Loneliness," https://www.nytimes.com/2016/09/06/health/lonliness-aging-health-effects.html?_r=0.
- Amanda Gardner wrote about depression, medication, and living alone in Finland in "Will Living Alone Make You Depressed?," http://www.cnn.com/2012/03/23/health/living-alone-depression/index.html.

28. Footloose and Fancy-Free

Laura McKenna wrote about the record number of PhDs and the tough academic job market in "The Ever-Tightening Job Market for Ph.D.s," https://www.theatlantic.com/education/archive/2016/04/bad-job-market-phds/479205/.

29. Nerds with Money

- *U.S. News & World Report* job rankings had interesting info about IT managers: https://money.usnews.com/careers/best-jobs/it-manager.
- Subrat Patnaik wrote about *Star Wars* merchandise crossing the $700 million mark in "'Star Wars' Toys Generate More Than $700 Million in Sales in 2015,"

https://www.reuters.com/article/us-star-wars-toys/star-wars-toys-generate-more-than-700-million-in-sales-in-2015-idUSKCN0UY2D7.

- Box Office Mojo is the source for film-franchise totals (http://www.boxofficemojo.com/franchises/?view=Franchise&sort=sumgross&order=DESC&p=.htm) as well as the box-office performance of *Star Wars: The Force Awakens* (http://www.boxofficemojo.com/movies/?id=starwars7.htm).
- Digiday, describing research by marketing firm SpotRight, is the source for the analysis of *Star Wars*' Twitter followers: https://digiday.com/marketing/star-wars-demographics-male/.
- Viewership figures for *The Big Bang Theory* are accessible on Wikipedia: https://en.wikipedia.org/wiki/The_Big_Bang_Theory#Episodes.
- *IndieWire* reported on viewership figures for *The Walking Dead* (http://www.indiewire.com/2017/05/most-watched-tv-show-2016-2017-season-the-walking-dead-this-is-us-football-1201832878/), while *Variety* reported on the per-ad cost (http://variety.com/2016/tv/news/tv-ad-prices-football-walking-dead-empire-advertising-1201890660/).
- *Business Insider* reported on the most pirated television shows of 2016: http://www.businessinsider.com/most-pirated-shows-2016-12.
- Revenue figures for the size of the video gaming industry come from *VentureBeat*: https://venturebeat.com/2016/12/21/worldwide-game-industry-hits-91-billion-in-revenues-in-2016-with-mobile-the-clear-leader/.
- Estimates for the local economic impact of San Diego Comic Con were reported by the *San Diego Union Tribune*: http://www.sandiegouniontribune.com/g00/entertainment/comic-con/sd-me-con-numbers-20170715-story.html.
- Attendance figures for the various conventions were generally made public by the organizers of those conventions. Some conventions report attendance as the sum of all individual ticket holders, while others report daily turnstile figures.
- Google Trends charts for "cosplay" are accessible at https://trends.google.com/trends/explore?date=all&q=cosplay.
- Viewership figures for *Cosplay Melee* were available via Wikipedia: https://en.wikipedia.org/wiki/Cosplay_Melee.

30. Uptown Stoners

- Megan Giller wrote about the marijuana market for *Forbes* in "This High-End Edibles Startup Targets a New Kind of Cannabis Consumer," https://www.forbes.com/sites/megangiller/2017/04/20/this-high-end-edibles-startup-targets-a-new-kind-of-cannabis-consumer/#2000273b7313.
- *CNNMoney* reported on Colorado's marijuana revenue: http://money.cnn.com/2017/07/19/news/colorado-marijuana-tax-revenue/index.html.
- *MarketWatch* reported on the size of the US alcohol industry and its relation to

the marijuana industry: https://www.marketwatch.com/story/legal-marijuana-expected-to-pose-threat-to-200-billon-alcohol-industry-2016-09-23.

- Christopher Ingraham wrote about some research on the changing legal risks of marijuana consumption: "What Makes Marijuana Users Different from Everyone Else," https://www.washingtonpost.com/news/wonk/wp/2016/08/14/what-makes-marijuana-users-different-from-everyone-else/?utm_term=.f2037d15bf81.

31. Intelligent TV

- Steven Johnson, *Everything Bad Is Good for You* (New York: Riverhead Books, 2005).
- Statista had great info on the growth of Netflix subscribers over time: https://www.statista.com/statistics/250934/quarterly-number-of-netflix-streaming-subscribers-worldwide/.
- Figures for the growth in scripted television shows were reported by *Business Insider*: http://www.businessinsider.com/tv-show-growth-2002-2015-2016-10.
- *AppleInsider* reported on internet traffic figures, including the percentage of internet traffic devoted to Netflix: http://appleinsider.com/articles/16/01/20/netflix-boasts-37-share-of-internet-traffic-in-north-america-compared-with-3-for-apples-itunes.
- Netflix revenue figures are from NASDAQ: http://www.nasdaq.com/symbol/nflx/financials?query=income-statement.
- Average television viewing time for Americans in 2016 was reported in the *New York Times*: https://www.nytimes.com/2016/07/01/business/media/nielsen-survey-media-viewing.html?_r=0.
- Number of TV shows in 1976 came from manually tallying on Wikipedia.

32. Korean Beauty

- Export.gov had some excellent data on the growth of Korean cosmetics exports: https://2016.export.gov/southkorea/doingbusinessinskorea/leadingsectors forusexportsinvestment/cosmetics/index.asp.
- This article from Yonhap News reported on the Korean products spreading throughout Asia: http://english.yonhapnews.co.kr/business/2017/09/13/0501000000AEN20170913002600320.html.
- This article had the quotes from Alicia Yoon about beauty trends: "'Glass Skin' Is the K-Beauty Complexion Everyone Wants," http://www.themalaymailonline.com/features/article/glass-skin-is-the-k-beauty-complexion-everyone-wants.
- Data on the number of facial procedures was taken from International Society of Aesthetic Plastic Surgery: https://www.isaps.org/Media/Default/global-statistics/2015%20ISAPS%20Results.pdf.
- Patricia Marx's article on cosmetic surgery in South Korea was full of ex-

tremely helpful anecdotes and data: "About Face," https://www.newyorker
.com/magazine/2015/03/23/about-face.

- The *South China Morning Post* reported on China's decision to ban Korean beauty products in "China Bans Imports of 19 Korean Cosmetics," http://www.scmp.com/news/asia/east-asia/article/2061152/china-bans-imports-19-korean-cosmetics.
- Size of Korean beauty market and predictions: http://www.mintel.com/press-centre/beauty-and-personal-care/a-bright-future-south-korea-ranks-among-the-top-10-beauty-markets-globally.
- Information on how much more money Korean women spend on beauty: "A Bright Future: South Korea Ranks Among the Top 10 Beauty Markets Globally," http://www.bbc.com/news/business-35408764.

33. Modern Annie Oakleys

- Gun ownership by gender data was found by the Harris poll in December 2015.
- Pew has also done work over the years on gun ownership trends that we compiled: http://www.people-press.org/2013/03/12/section-3-gun-ownership-trends-and-demographics/ and http://www.pewresearch.org/fact-tank/2017/06/29/how-male-and-female-gun-owners-in-the-u-s-compare/.
- Dana Loesch's quote is from an interview with the Well Armed Woman: https://thewellarmedwoman.com/blog/dana-loesch-truly-a-well-armed-woman/.
- Emily DePrang reported on the Harvard Injury Control Research Center poll results in "The Real Landscape," http://www.marieclaire.com/politics/a18016/women-and-guns/#the-stats.
- Pew Research reported on the numbers of active-duty female military members: http://www.pewresearch.org/fact-tank/2017/04/13/6-facts-about-the-u-s-military-and-its-changing-demographics/.
- *U.S. News & World Report* compiled statistics on female police officers: https://www.usnews.com/news/best-states/washington/articles/2017-03-25/number-of-female-police-officers-on-the-rise.
- RAINN statistics on sexual assault are available on their website: https://www.rainn.org/statistics.
- *Guns & Ammo* reported on the National Shooting Sports Foundation study on women gun owners, which included geographic and other data: http://www.gunsandammo.com/gun-culture/women-gun-owners-nssf-1/#ixzz4sbVHrAhD.
- Lisa Marie Pane wrote about research showing African-American women acquiring firearms: "Black Women Picking Up Firearms for Self-Defense," https://www.apnews.com/94811ec90b7b4872a029ba3fc8f22723/Black-women-picking-up-firearms-for-self-defense.

- Antonia Okafor wrote about her perspective on gun ownership and carrying in "Why I Bring My Gun to School" in a *New York Times* opinion piece: https://www.nytimes.com/2017/07/24/opinion/why-i-bring-my-gun-to-school.html?_r=0.
- Erica Goode wrote about several signs of women's rising engagement with gun culture, including from the National Sporting Goods Association and National Shooting Sports Foundation: http://www.nytimes.com/2013/02/11/us/rising-voice-of-gun-ownership-is-female.html?_r=0.

34. Armchair Preppers

- Chris Ingrahm wrote in the *Washington Post*'s *Wonkblog* about data from the FBI's National Instant Criminal Background Check System: https://www.washingtonpost.com/news/wonk/wp/2016/01/05/gun-sales-hit-new-record-ahead-of-new-obama-gun-restrictions/?utm_term=.e5eff78bef02.
- Wikipedia has been tracking the most current position of the Doomsday Clock: https://en.wikipedia.org/wiki/Doomsday_Clock.
- Jon C. Ogg wrote about retailers and businesses seeing signs of this trend in "Industries Making the Most Money on Doomsday Preppers," https://finance.yahoo.com/news/industries-making-most-money-doomsday-103557775.html.
- Evan Osnos wrote about superwealthy preppers in the *New Yorker* in "Doomsday Prep for the Super-Rich," https://www.newyorker.com/magazine/2017/01/30/doomsday-prep-for-the-super-rich.
- Matthew Pennington and Emily Swanson for the Associated Press wrote "Poll: North Korea Nuke Advances Spook Most Americans," https://www.militarytimes.com/flashpoints/2017/10/11/poll-most-say-trump-making-north-korea-situation-worse/.

SECTION 5: POLITICS

35. Old Economy Voters

- The *Guardian* results from the U.K.'s Brexit/EU referendum were helpful: https://www.theguardian.com/politics/ng-interactive/2016/jun/23/eu-referendum-live-results-and-analysis.
- Richard Wike wrote a helpful piece for Pew, "5 Charts Showing Where France's National Front Draws Its Support," summarizing their findings about the National Front supporters in France: http://www.pewresearch.org/fact-tank/2017/04/21/5-charts-showing-where-frances-national-front-draws-its-support/.
- The U.K. Office for National Statistics included data on the trajectory of the manufacturing industry there: https://www.ons.gov.uk/employmentandlabourmarket/peopleinwork/employmentandemployeetypes/datasets/workforcejobsbyindustryjobs02.

- The U.K. Office for National Statistics also had data on immigration: https://www.ons.gov.uk/peoplepopulationandcommunity/populationandmigration/internationalmigration/bulletins/ukpopulationbycountryofbirthandnationality/2016.
- And the U.K. Office for National Statistics had data on median household income: https://www.ons.gov.uk/peoplepopulationandcommunity/personalandhouseholdfinances/incomeandwealth/datasets/nowcastinghouseholdincomeintheuk.
- Mark Muro and Siddharth Kulkarni wrote for the Brookings Institution "Voter Anger Explained—in One Chart" and included an excellent chart of manufacturing employment in the United States: https://www.brookings.edu/blog/the-avenue/2016/03/15/voter-anger-explained-in-one-chart/.
- The Migration Policy Institute data on immigration trends in the United States is fantastic: https://www.migrationpolicy.org/programs/data-hub/charts/immigrant-population-over-time?width=1000&height=850&iframe=true.
- Federal Reserve Economic Data from the Federal Reserve Bank of St. Louis had great time series data about real median income in the United States: https://fred.stlouisfed.org/series/MEHOINUSA672N.
- Nate Cohn wrote about the specific appeal of Donald Trump and his curious ideological profile in "How the Obama Coalition Crumbled, Leaving an Opening for Trump," https://www.nytimes.com/2016/12/23/upshot/how-the-obama-coalition-crumbled-leaving-an-opening-for-trump.html?_r=0.

36. Happy Pessimists

- Gallup tracking polls have been recording satisfaction with the country: http://www.gallup.com/poll/1669/general-mood-country.aspx.
- Denise-Marie Ordway and John Wihbey wrote about research by the Wesleyan Media Project that has a nice breakdown of the tone of political advertisements: "Negative Political Ads and Their Effect on Voters: Updated Collection of Research," https://journalistsresource.org/studies/politics/ads-public-opinion/negative-political-ads-effects-voters-research-roundup.
- Pew Research Center has been looking at public trust in government: http://www.people-press.org/2015/11/23/1-trust-in-government-1958-2015/.
- Chapman University surveyed Americans' top fears: https://blogs.chapman.edu/wilkinson/2016/10/11/americas-top-fears-2016/.
- Philip Bump wrote about the Harvard Institute of Politics poll about the American Dream in "48 Percent of Millennials Think the American Dream Is Dead. Here's Why," https://www.washingtonpost.com/news/the-fix/wp/2015/12/10/48-percent-of-millennials-think-the-american-dream-is-dead-heres-why/?utm_term=.cdbe8caca1a4.

- The *Washington Post* also reported on the Harvard Shorenstein Center's findings on coverage of President Trump: https://www.washingtonpost.com/blogs/erik-wemple/wp/2017/09/12/study-91-percent-of-recent-network-trump-coverage-has-been-negative/?utm_term=.437165a64e86.
- Uri Friedman wrote about the research by Edelman and others showing class-based trust gaps appearing across the world in "Trust in Government Is Collapsing around the World," https://www.theatlantic.com/international/archive/2016/07/trust-institutions-trump-brexit/489554/.
- *Scientific American* talked to Professor Donald Green about the effects of negative advertising in "Do Negative Political Ads Work?," https://www.scientificamerican.com/article/do-negative-political-ads-work/.
- Ella Nilsen at *Vox* reported on recent polling from CNN and CBS showing American anxiety about the prospects of war with North Korea in "Americans Are Afraid of War with North Korea—and of How Trump Could Handle It," https://www.vox.com/policy-and-politics/2017/8/11/16131016/americans-afraid-war-north-korea.
- "And in the most recent presidential campaign, 90 percent of our political ads were negative": http://www.cnn.com/2016/11/08/politics/negative-ads-hillary-clinton-donald-trump/index.html.
- "Judges, as seen in a Harvard Harris Poll, are believed to rule more on politics than the law": https://www.newsmax.com/Newsfront/poll-neil-gorsuch-supreme-court/2017/02/22/id/775112/.
- "And Washington is viewed as a swamp, with 79 percent calling the nation's political system corrupt": "79% of Voters Say Washington Today Is Basically Corrupt," Harvard-Harris poll, April 2017. The question number is GE3B.

37. Closet Conservatives

- Courtney Kennedy et al. wrote about the possible issues with measuring support for a candidate such as Trump in "Are Telephone Polls Understating Support for Trump?," http://www.pewresearch.org/2017/03/31/are-telephone-polls-understating-support-for-trump/.
- Paul Bedard wrote about data from Wakefield Research indicating that politics was ending relationships: "Fights over Trump Drive Couples, Especially Millennials, to Split Up": http://www.washingtonexaminer.com/fights-over-trump-drive-couples-especially-millennials-to-split-up/article/2622400.
- Jeffrey A. Karp and David Brockington wrote in 2005 about how people overreport their voting history in "Social Desirability and Response Validity: A Comparative Analysis of Overreporting Voter Turnout in Five Countries," http://www.nzes.org/docs/papers/jop_2005.pd.
- In a Harvard-Harris poll conducted last year, nearly four in ten (36 percent)

of Americans say they sometimes feel they cannot express their true political views with friends and family. Fifty-five percent stay mum at work: Harvard-Harris poll, August 2017. Question numbers NK30 and NK31.

38. Impressionable Elites Revisited

Research by the University of Cambridge into Facebook data found that those educated at elite educational institutions actually have fewer international friends: "Facebook Data Suggests People from Higher Social Class Have Fewer International Friends," http://www.cam.ac.uk/research/news/facebook-data-suggests-people-from-higher-social-class-have-fewer-international-friends.

39. Militant Dreamers Revisited

- Data on Hispanic partisan affiliation comes from the Pew Research Center, which was written about by Mark Hugo Lopez et al., "Democrats Maintain Edge as Party 'More Concerned' for Latinos, but Views Similar to 2012," http://www.pewhispanic.org/2016/10/11/democrats-maintain-edge-as-party-more-concerned-for-latinos-but-views-similar-to-2012/.
- Data on Hispanic voter turnout came from the U.S. Census: https://www.census.gov/data/tables/time-series/demo/voting-and-registration/voting-historical-time-series.html.
- The polling on immigration reflects not just a bifurcated electorate but one that is solidly behind tight borders. Those polled largely oppose building a wall, but they would support far more enforcement. They do believe in being compassionate to Dreamers, and over 70 percent in the Harvard-Harris poll say that's an important priority. But 70 percent also reject the idea that police should not contact immigration authorities when they arrest people. The sanctuary-city movement has no support outside the sanctuary cities.

  Seventy-two percent say Congress should work to restore work permits to those brought to the United States illegally as kids (Harvard-Harris poll, September 2017) (DR9).

  Seventy percent say when state or local police arrest someone for a crime, police should check the arrested person's immigration status and cooperate with federal immigration authorities (Harvard-Harris poll, September 2017) (DR12).

  Fifty-three percent oppose building a wall along the U.S.-Mexico border to try to stop illegal immigration (Harvard-Harris poll, February 2017) (I25).

  Eighty percent say cities that arrest illegal immigrants for crimes should be required to turn them over to immigration authorities (Harvard-Harris poll, February 2017) (I26).

40. Newest Americans

- Pew Social Trends wrote about data comparing the median income for Asian-Americans and is also responsible for the chart showing the rise in Asian immigration: http://www.pewsocialtrends.org/asianamericans-graphics/.
- Aline Barros wrote about data from the Department of Homeland Security on naturalizations: "US Citizenship Important to Asian Immigrants," https://www.voanews.com/a/us-citizenship-important-asian-immigrants/3767840.html.
- Background on the Chinese Exclusion Act came from this Harvard University Library Project page: http://ocp.hul.harvard.edu/immigration/exclusion.html.
- Jie Zong and Jeanne Batalova analyzed data from the U.S. Census's American Community Survey about Chinese immigrants in the United States: "Chinese Immigrants in the United States," https://www.migrationpolicy.org/article/chinese-immigrants-united-states.
- The Migration Policy Institute also reported on the largest immigrant groups by country, in 2015, in the United States: https://www.migrationpolicy.org/programs/data-hub/charts/largest-immigrant-groups-over-time.
- Jie Zong and Jeanne Batalova also wrote about data on Asian immigration from the U.S. Census's American Community Survey and other sources more broadly: "Asian Immigrants in the United States," https://www.migrationpolicy.org/article/asian-immigrants-united-states.
- Data on advanced STEM degrees came from the National Science Foundation: https://www.nsf.gov/statistics/2015/nsf15321/#chp1&chp2.
- Nathaniel Hilger's paper "Upward Mobility and Discrimination: The Case of Asian Americans" is available from the National Bureau of Economic Research, http://www.nber.org/papers/w22748.
- The stats on Asian-Americans' buying power and dining habits, as well as the numbers of Asians among top start-up founders, were compiled by Nielsen Research: http://nielsencommunity.com/report_files/Asian_Consumer_Report_2016_Final.pdf.
- Grace Donnelly wrote for *Fortune* about the workforce at Google in "Google's 2017 Diversity Report Shows Progress Hiring Women, Little Change for Minority Workers," http://fortune.com/2017/06/29/google-2017-diversity-report/.
- Asma Khalid talked about data from the Roper Center showing political shifts in the Asian-American community over time: https://www.npr.org/sections/itsallpolitics/2015/09/16/439574726/how-asian-american-voters-went-from-republican-to-democratic.
- Dhrumil Mehta and Jennifer Kanjana wrote about data from the National Asian American Survey looking at the political preferences of different subgroups of Asian-Americans: "Asian-American Voters Are Diverse but Unified

against Donald Trump," http://fivethirtyeight.com/features/asian-american-voters-are-diverse-but-unified-against-donald-trump/.

- *Teen Vogue* reported on the underrepresentation of Asian-Americans in lead roles in Hollywood: https://www.teenvogue.com/story/asian-representation-in-hollywood.
- Size of America's Asian population: https://www.migrationpolicy.org/article/asian-immigrants-united-states.

41. Couch Potato Voters

- The data in the charts showing the breakdown of voting and demographics of voting-age adults came from the US Census Current Population Survey: https://www.census.gov/data/tables/time-series/demo/voting-and-registration/p20-580.html.

SECTION 6: WORK AND BUSINESS

42. Self-Data Lovers

- David Sedaris wrote about his Fitbit in "Stepping Out," https://www.newyorker.com/magazine/2014/06/30/stepping-out-3.
- Some of the data in this chapter on habits was taken from the September 2017 Harvard-Harris poll.
- Joan Raymond wrote about a study from *Journal of Clinical Sleep Medicine* that detailed how tracking sleep habits can actually make sleep worse: http://harvardharrispoll.com/wp-content/uploads/2017/09/HHP-September-Wave_Topline-Memo_No-Banners_Registered-Voters.pdf.
- Gary Worlf's TED Talk can be seen at https://www.ted.com/talks/gary_wolf_the_quantified_self.
- Statista had data on the number of Fitbits that have been sold: https://www.statista.com/statistics/472591/fitbit-devices-sold/.
- David Jones talked to Nick Crocker, a former product manager at MyFitnessPal, about the growth of the app: https://www.linkedin.com/pulse/interview-how-myfitnesspal-app-got-165-million-users-david-jones/.
- Parmy Olson wrote about the sale of MyFitnessPal in "Under Armour Buys Health-Tracking App MyFitnessPal For $475 Million," https://www.forbes.com/sites/parmyolson/2015/02/04/myfitnesspal-acquisition-under-armour/#22a622256935.
- Sara Castellanos wrote about the Lose It! app and its user base in "Weight-Loss App Lose It! Grows to 17M Users, Aims to Rival Weight Watchers," https://www.bizjournals.com/boston/blog/startups/2014/02/lose-it-wants-to-compete-with-weight.html.

- The quote from Dr. Jennifer Hurst comes from *Wired*'s "Fitness Isn't a Lifestyle Anymore. Sometimes It's a Cult" by Meaghen Brown, in 2016: https://www.wired.com/2016/06/fitness-isnt-lifestyle-anymore-sometimes-cult/.
- Amrita Khalid wrote about period trackers and Clue in particular: "The 4 Best Apps to Track Your Period," https://www.dailydot.com/debug/best-period-apps/.
- Paul Krebs and Dustin T. Duncan wrote about a survey on how many smartphone users have downloaded a health app in "Health App Use among US Mobile Phone Owners: A National Survey," https://www.ncbi.nlm.nih.gov/pmc/articles/PMC4704953/.
- Katie Holliday wrote about surveys by the Naver Corporation and Harris Interactive about teen angst with social media: "US Youth Frustrated with 'Oversharing' on Social Media," https://www.cnbc.com/2014/10/23/us-youth-frustrated-with-oversharing-on-social-media.html.
- Meaghen Brown talked to Dr. Jennifer Hurst about the value people get from social connections in "Fitness Isn't a Lifestyle Anymore. Sometimes It's a Cult," https://www.wired.com/2016/06/fitness-isnt-lifestyle-anymore-sometimes-cult/.

43. Bikers to Work

- Data in the first chart came from the American Community Survey, analyzed by the Bike League: http://www.bikeleague.org/commutingdata.
- Jacob Poushter wrote about survey data from Pew Research on bike ownership, included in the second chart, in "Car, Bike or Motorcycle? Depends on Where You Live," http://www.pewresearch.org/fact-tank/2015/04/16/car-bike-or-motorcycle-depends-on-where-you-live/.
- Jeffrey Ball wrote about the Federal Highway Administration data showing that the youngest Americans are driving less in "The Proportion of Young Americans Who Drive Has Plummeted—and No One Knows Why," https://newrepublic.com/article/116993/millennials-are-abandoning-cars-bikes-car-share-will-it-stick.
- Winnie Hu wrote about bike lanes in New York and the additional lanes there, and in Los Angeles in "More New Yorkers Opting for Life in the Bike Lane," https://www.nytimes.com/2017/07/30/nyregion/new-yorkers-bike-lanes-commuting.html?_r=1.
- Donny Kwok and Yimou Lee wrote about high-end bikes and nostalgia in China in "Bikes for Bonuses as China's Wealthy Reminisce," https://www.reuters.com/article/us-china-bikes/bikes-for-bonuses-as-chinas-wealthy-reminisce-idUSBRE8BM0CZ20121223.
- Luz Lazo wrote about the data about Capital Bikeshare users in DC in "Who Uses Capital Bikeshare?" https://www.washingtonpost.com/news/dr-gridlock/wp/2015/04/28/who-uses-capital-bikeshare/?utm_term=.e913c7ee5f62.

- Emma G. Fitzsimmons wrote about the purpose of bikes in New York—rich comfort or comprehensive transit?—in "Citi Bike under Pressure to Expand to Low-Income Neighborhoods," https://www.nytimes.com/2016/12/05/nyregion/citi-bike-may-need-public-funding-to-reach-more-new-yorkers.html?_r=0.
- Ken McLeod wrote about Census data for the League of American Bicyclists: http://bikeleague.org/content/new-census-data-bike-commuting-released.
- Walker Angell reported on a National Bicycle Dealers Association report about bicycle commuting trends: https://streets.mn/2015/07/29/why-are-bicycle-sales-declining-for-the-14th-year/.
- Feargus O'Sullivan wrote about the massive investments in bike lanes in London in "London Will Double Its Spending on Cycling Infrastructure," https://www.citylab.com/transportation/2016/12/london-budget-bike-lanes-infrastructure-sadiq-khan/509693/.
- Sebastian Modak reported on Barcelona's planned increases in bike lanes in "Barcelona to Spend $36M on New Bike Lanes," https://www.cntraveler.com/story/barcelona-to-spend-36m-on-new-bike-lanes.
- Li Tao wrote about Mobike's incredible order numbers in "Bicycles Are Eating the Lunch of China's Dominant Car-Sharing App," http://www.scmp.com/business/article/2095975/bicycles-are-eating-lunch-chinas-dominant-car-sharing-app.
- Charlie Sorrel wrote on the study by Johns Hopkins looking at bike-ownership trends internationally: "Global Bike Ownership Has Halved in Last 30 Years, but It Stands to Rise Again," https://www.fastcompany.com/3054238/global-bike-ownership-has-halved-in-last-30-years-but-it-stands-to-rise-again.
- Kathryn Doyle looked at a study by Dr. Babak Mohit on the health benefits of bike lanes: "Bike Lanes Are a Sound Public Health Investment," https://www.reuters.com/article/us-health-costbenefit-bike-lanes/bike-lanes-are-a-sound-public-health-investment-idUSKCN11Z23A.
- Kevin Murnane wrote about another study in the British Medical Journal on the health externalities of bike lanes: "New Research Indicates Cycling to Work Has Extraordinary Health Benefits," https://www.forbes.com/sites/kevinmurnane/2017/04/25/new-research-indicates-cycling-to-work-has-extraordinary-health-benefits/#59687a273e62.

44. Virtual Entrepreneurs

- The *Daily Mail* reported on the success of Etsy seller Alicia Shaffer: http://www.dailymail.co.uk/news/article-2946905/Alicia-Shaffer-Etsy-s-richest-seller-handmade-headbands-socks-scarves.html.
- Christopher Mims wrote about online-only restaurants in "These Hot Restaurants Aren't on Maps, Only in Apps," https://www.wsj.com/article_email/these-hot-restaurants-arent-on-maps-only-in-apps-1509883200-lMyQjAxMTI3MzA2NjIwNjY0Wj/.

- Claire Cain Miller reported on a Harvard University study about how working particular hours relates to the gender pay gap: https://www.nytimes.com/2017/02/07/upshot/how-to-close-a-gender-gap-let-employees-control-their-schedules.html?_r=1.
- Victor Lipman wrote in *Forbes* about a survey from TINYpulse showing employee satisfaction with working from home: "Are Remote Workers Happier and More Productive? New Survey Offers Answers," https://www.forbes.com/sites/victorlipman/2016/05/02/are-remote-workers-happier-and-more-productive-new-survey-offers-answers/#503e24b66636.
- Information on Harry's and Dollar Shave Club's valuations came from these *Recode* articles by Jason Del Ray: "Razor Startup Harry's Raises $75 Million, Pushing It over $200 Million. Say What?," https://www.recode.net/2014/12/3/11633506/razor-startup-harrys-raises-75-million-pushing-it-over-200-million; and "Dollar Shave Club Just Sold for $1 Billion to Unilever," https://www.recode.net/2016/7/19/12232698/dollar-shave-club-just-sold-for-1-billion-to-unilever.
- Sam Carr told the story of the beginnings of Casper, the mattress company, in "Casper Made $1 Million in Its First 28 Days," https://thehustle.co/how-casper-made-1million-in-first-28-days.
- NPR's *Planet Money* team spoke to Sam Cohen about his internet reselling business: https://www.npr.org/sections/money/2015/06/03/411777635/episode-629-buy-low-sell-prime.
- *Planet Money* also investigated the world of resold textbooks: https://www.npr.org/sections/money/2014/11/10/363103753/textbook-arbitrage-making-money-off-used-books.

45. Microcapitalists

- Estimates for the size of the microfinancing industry, including total client numbers, come from the World Bank: http://www.worldbank.org/en/news/feature/2015/03/30/does-microfinance-still-hold-promise-for-reaching-the-poor.
- The first chart includes data published by Goldman Sachs on the success of their 10,000 Women program: http://www.goldmansachs.com/citizenship/10000women/#about-the-program.
- Goldman Sachs also wrote about their partnership with the World Bank IFC to address the problems they had identified for women entrepreneurs: http://www.goldmansachs.com/citizenship/10000women/capital-for-women-entrepreneurs/index.html.
- Another Goldman Sachs report on the program had helpful information on the impact of this program on the revenue of participants: http://www.goldmansachs.com/citizenship/10000women/news-and-events/10kw-progress-report/progress-report-full.pdf.

- In Tiffany Hus's interview with Muhammad Yunus, he spoke about the impact of microfinance for women: "Q&A: Muhammad Yunus, Father of Microfinance, Talks about L.A. Loan Program," http://www.latimes.com/business/la-fi-muhammad-yunus-grameen-20141124-story.html.
- PBS's *NewsHour* did a story about Roshaneh Zafar's efforts in microfinance: https://www.pbs.org/newshour/amp/show/world-jan-june11-microlending_05-12.
- The Microcredit Summit Campaign report in 2015 had important data on the number of borrowers and the number of women: https://stateofthecampaign.org/2015/12/08/2015-report-global-data-show-diverging-paths/.
- David Bornstein wrote about the analysis done by Kathy Odell on the microfinance industry: "Grameen Bank and the Public Good," https://opinionator.blogs.nytimes.com/2011/03/24/grameen-bank-and-the-public-good/?mcubz=3&_r=0.
- The success story of Mamatha of Hyderabad, India, is from http://www.goldmansachs.com/citizenship/10000women/meet-the-women-profiles/mamatha-profile.html.

46. The Fakesters

- Heimdal Security wrote about the top online scams, which I included as a figure in this chapter: https://heimdalsecurity.com/blog/top-online-scams/.
- *Slate* writer Joshua Keating wrote about the analysis from Akamai showing the concentration of cyberattacks in Indonesia: "Is Russia Really the Cybercrime Capital?," http://www.slate.com/blogs/the_world_/2014/08/06/billion_password_hack_russian_hackers_aren_t_prolific_they_re_just_really.html.
- NPR's *All Things Considered* spoke to Jason Coler, the fake-news purveyor: "We Tracked Down a Fake-News Creator in the Suburbs. Here's What We Learned," https://www.npr.org/sections/alltechconsidered/2016/11/23/503146770/npr-finds-the-head-of-a-covert-fake-news-operation-in-the-suburbs.
- Martin McKay wrote about the many different kinds of hackers in "Researching the Psychology of Hackers," https://securityintelligence.com/researching-the-psychology-of-hackers/.
- Erika Eichelberger, in *Mother Jones*, spoke to some Nigerian scam artists about their work and their earnings and looked into the number of FBI complaints and losses these scams cause: "What I Learned Hanging Out with Nigerian Email Scammers," http://www.motherjones.com/politics/2014/03/what-i-learned-from-nigerian-scammers/#.
- Apple has an entire help page dedicated to the iTunes gift-card scam: https://support.apple.com/itunes-gift-card-scams.

- Kim Zetter wrote the referenced article for *Wired*: "What Is Ransomware? A Guide to the Global Cyberattack's Scary Method," https://www.wired.com/2017/05/hacker-lexicon-guide-ransomware-scary-hack-thats-rise/.

47. Work with Limits

- Patrick Gillespie wrote about the research by Rebecca Glauber on poverty and part-time work in "America's Part-Time Workforce Is Huge," http://money.cnn.com/2016/04/25/news/economy/part-time-jobs/index.html.
- Giovanni Russo in his 2011 paper "Job and Life Satisfaction among Part-Time and Full-Time Workers: The 'Identity' Approach" wrote about men's and women's demand for part-time work: http://www.tandfonline.com/doi/abs/10.1080/00346764.2011.632323.
- The Society for Human Resource Management is responsible for the *National Study of Employers*: https://www.shrm.org/hr-today/trends-and-forecasting/research-and-surveys/pages/national-study-of-employers.aspx.
- Diane Lim's cited article on the benefits of part-time work is "Is It Good or Bad to Work Part Time? Pros and Cons for the Economy," https://www.ced.org/blog/entry/is-it-good-or-bad-to-work-part-time-pros-and-cons-for-the-economy.
- Laura Vanderkam wrote about a Working Mother Research Institute survey that also looked at the preferences of working fathers: "Why Working Part-Time Isn't the Best Answer for Parents," https://www.fastcompany.com/3038269/why-working-part-time-isnt-the-best-answer-for-parents.
- Leah Arnold-Smeets reported on an Accenture study of millennial workplace preferences: "Here's Why Millennials Want to Work Part-Time," https://www.payscale.com/career-news/2015/08/millennials-want-to-work-part-time.
- Schulyer Velasco wrote about the CareerBuilder.com study also looking at workplace preferences: "The '9 to 5' Job Is Going Extinct," https://www.csmonitor.com/Business/new-economy/2015/0723/The-9-to-5-job-is-going-extinct.
- I also consulted the following academic papers:

Alison L. Booth and Jan C. van Ours, "Part-Time Jobs: What Women Want?," *Journal of Population Economics* 26, no 1 (2013): 263, https://doi.org/10.1007/s00148-012-0417-9.

Barbara Beham, Patrick Präg, and Sonja Drobnič, "Who's Got the Balance? A Study of Satisfaction with the Work–Family Balance among Part-Time Service Sector Employees in Five Western European Countries," *International Journal of Human Resource Management* 23, no. 18 (2012).

Clare Kelliher and Dierdre Anderson, "Doing More with Less? Flexible Working Practices and the Intensification of Work," *Human Relations* 63, no. 1 (2009): 83–106, doi:10.1177/0018726709349199.

Vanessa Gash, Antje Mertens, and Laura Romeu Gordo, "Women between Part-Time and Full-Time Work: The Influence of Changing Hours of Work on Happiness and Life-Satisfaction," SOEPpaper no. 268, February 2010. Available at SSRN: https://ssrn.com/abstract=1553702 or http://dx.doi.org/10.2139/ssrn.1553702.

48. The New Factory Worker

- Data on the number of full- and part-time workers in the United States came from the Bureau of Labor Statistics: https://www.bls.gov/cps/cpsaat08.htm.
- Global unemployment is being tracked by the World Bank: https://data.worldbank.org/share/widget?indicators=SL.UEM.TOTL.ZS&view=chart.
- Statista is the source for Chinese employment: https://www.statista.com/statistics/252848/economically-active-population-vs-number-of-employed-persons-in-china/.
- The Office of National Statistics data was the source for employment in the U.K.: https://www.ons.gov.uk/employmentandlabourmarket/peopleinwork/employmentandemployeetypes/bulletins/uklabourmarket/jan2017.
- "Manufacturing the Future: The Next Era of Global Growth and Innovation" by James Manyika et al. was the McKinsey report on manufacturing in developed economies: https://www.mckinsey.com/business-functions/operations/our-insights/the-future-of-manufacturing.
- The CIA *Factbook* numbers on employment came from https://www.cia.gov/library/publications/the-world-factbook/fields/2048.html#xx.

49. Hazel Reborn

- The first two charts in this graph were constructed from data in Steven Ruggles et al., *Integrated Public Use Microdata Series: Version 7.0* (Minneapolis: University of Minnesota, 2017), https://doi.org/10.18128/D010.V7.0.
- The data in the final chart in this chapter came from this Pew Research Center article: http://www.pewinternet.org/2016/11/17/gig-work-online-selling-and-home-sharing/.
- The BLS data on personal trainers comes from https://www.bls.gov/ooh/personal-care-and-service/fitness-trainers-and-instructors.htm.
- The *New York Times* mention comes from https://www.nytimes.com/2017/02/23/magazine/the-new-working-class.html.

50. 10XMillionaires

- The Federal Reserve Survey of Consumer Finances (SCF) is the source for several of this chapter's charts and figures: https://www.federalreserve.gov/econres/scfindex.htm.

- Capgemini's World Wealth Report was summarized by *Inc.*: https://www.inc.com/business-insider/16-industries-highest-growth-number-of-millionaires.html.
- The Luxury Institute's research on the purchase behavior of multimillionaires was reported by the *Wise Marketer*: http://www.thewisemarketer.com/newswire/how-wealthy-consumers-use-the-internet/.
- Gallup's assessment of the educational status and partisanship of the 1 percent versus the 99 percent comes from their 2009–11 surveys: http://www.gallup.com/poll/151310/U.S.-Republican-Not-Conservative.aspx.
- CNBC reported on the rising number of American millionaires: https://www.cnbc.com/2017/03/24/a-record-number-of-americans-are-now-millionaires-new-study-shows.html.
- For more on the rising cost of luxury goods, see *Forbes*'s regularly updated "Cost of Living Extremely Well Index" (for example, the 2016 edition: https://www.forbes.com/sites/andreamurphy/2016/10/05/the-expense-of-exclusive-living-the-forbes-400s-cost-of-living-extremely-well-index/#4ac21794374d).
- The description of the Independent Sector's research comes from Dacher Keltner, as spoken to Shankar Vedantam of NPR's *All Things Considered*: https://www.npr.org/2013/09/03/218627288/why-being-wealthy-doesnt-lead-to-more-giving.
- Richard Reeves's 2017 book is *Dream Hoarders: How the American Upper Middle Class Is Leaving Everyone Else in the Dust, Why That Is a Problem, and What to Do about It* (Washington, D.C.: Brookings Institution Press).
- Reporting on the growth in the Chinese super-rich comes from ECNS: http://www.ecns.cn/cns-wire/2017/06-21/262385.shtml.
- Wealthy Americans versus poor Americans and their charitable giving: https://www.theatlantic.com/magazine/archive/2013/04/why-the-rich-dont-give/309254/.

INDEX

AARP, 52, 192–93
Abraham, S. Danny, 110
Academy of Nutrition and Dietetics, 85
addictions, 129–33
ADHD, 102–4, 106–8
advertising, 10, 11, 153, 212, 344
  discrimination and, 165
  Google and, 10–11, 165, 349
  political, 244, 246, 351, 352
  Scroogled campaign and, 10–11, 349
Afghanistan, 243
Africa, 304, 305
African-Americans, 270
  gun ownership and, 226, 227, 229
  voting by, 273, 274, 276
age, 13–14, 25
  dating and, 69
  nonagenarians, 96–101, 341
  see also millennials; older generations
Age of Spiritual Machines, The: When Computers Exceed Human Intelligence (Kurzweil), 157
AI, *see* artificial intelligence
Airbnb, 78, 176, 177, 322
Akamai, 308
Albers, Susan, 118
alcohol, 131, 208–11
Alexa, 12, 153, 163, 329, 344
algorithms, 9, 12, 344, 345, 347, 348
Amazon, 12, 17, 112, 136, 145, 164, 171, 220, 241, 300, 320, 321, 323, 341
  Alexa, 12, 153, 163, 329, 344
America and American values, 20–21
American Automobile Association, 148
American Cancer Society, 120–21
American College of Sports Medicine, 328
American Community Survey, 193
American Psychiatric Association, 131
American Redoubt, 233
American Sociological Association, 33
Amoruso, Sophia, 300
Android, 152–53
Annals of Internal Medicine, 53
Ansari, Aziz, 170, 272
AOL, 169
Apple, 132, 152, 167, 173, 223, 311
  Siri, 12, 329, 344
  Watch, 141–42, 143, 173
apps, 10, 61, 135, 176–77
  dating, 67–71; *see also* dating, internet
  purchases in, 130–31
  see also robots and bots

Aptonomy, 148
Archives of Sexual Behavior, 54
armchair preppers, 230–34
artificial intelligence (AI), 7, 9–12, 26, 124, 140–42, 161, 164, 339, 341, 342, 349
  drones and, 148, 149
  language translation and, 159
  see also robots and bots
Asian-Americans, 266–72, 274
Asthmapolis, 287
AT&T, 343
Atkins diet, 81–82
Atlantic, 335
ATMs, 161–62, 278
Atomic Blonde, 229
augmented reality (AR), 129
Axelrod, David, 169

baby boomers, 15, 53, 54, 65, 71, 83, 216, 246, 333
  see also older generations
bachelors, 39, 40
  older, 14, 51–56, 97
Bangladesh, 302–4
bankruptcies, 331–32
Barkly Pets, 187–88
Barrymore, Drew, 62, 218, 222
BBC, 223, 258
beauty products, 218–23
Beboe, 209
Beckinsale, Kate, 168
Beyoncé, 177
Beyond Meat, 85
Bezos, Jeff, 112
BharatMatrimony, 71
bicycles, 197, 289–94
Bieber, Justin, 178
Big Bang Theory, The, 202
big data, *see* data collection
Big Short, The, 17
bisexuality, 62–66
Bitcoin, 311
BlackBerry, 166, 168–69, 171
Blair, Tony, 237, 239
Blakely, Sara, 300
Blue Apron, 111, 327
Bonobos, 138, 299
books, 169
bots, *see* robots and bots
Bowie, David, 62
Bratman, Steven, 118
Brazil, 75
Breaking Bad, 212, 213
Brexit, 15–16, 239, 257–58, 277
Britain, *see* United Kingdom
Brokeback Mountain, 63
Brown, Ethan, 85
Brown, Kate, 66
Brown, Tina, 169
Buffett, Warren, 168, 173, 175, 182
Bulletin of Atomic Scientists, 230
Bumble, 251
Bureau of Labor Statistics, 159, 313, 326, 328
burn victims, 142
Bush, George W., 20–21, 238, 243, 264
Bush, Jeb, 255
Business Insider, 111
BuzzFeed, 131

California, 263
  immigrants in, 260, 262–64, 266, 270
cancer, 76, 81, 82–83, 93, 120–25, 293
  breast, 122
  prostate, 122–23
  survivors of, 120–25, 341
Candy Crush Saga, 131–32
Capaldi, Peter, 204

Capgemini, 330
Capital in the Twenty-First Century (Piketty), 336
capitalism, 16, 17, 25, 301, 306
carbohydrates, 14, 81, 82, 111
CareerBuilder, 110, 316
Carnegie Mellon University, 165
cars, 197, 289
  driverless, 346
Carter Center, 106
Cartwright, Martina M., 119
Casper, 297, 299
cats, 160, 185, 188, 189
CDC (Centers for Disease Control and Prevention), 52–53, 102, 105, 106
celiac disease, 115–16
Census Bureau, U.S., 43, 96, 265, 266
  American Community Survey, 58, 59–60, 111–12
Center for Science in the Public Interest, 84
cereal, 111
Chambliss, Michael, 146
chef services, 327–28
chicken, 81, 83, 87
children, *see* family and children
China, 21, 55–56, 75, 86–87, 132, 154, 216, 222, 239, 272, 308, 319, 353
  bicycling in, 291, 292
  immigrants from, 266–67, 269
  wealth in, 336
  Xiaoice in, 162, 164
chocolate, 111
choices, 5–6, 26, 339
  algorithms, AI, and data collection and, 9–12, 344, 345
  breaking out of silos, 343–44
  more and fewer, 7–9, 343
cholesterol, 83
Churchill, Winston, 21
CIA *World Factbook*, 322
Cisco, 152
Citibank, 289
cities, 26, 341
  rural areas vs., 17–19, 25, 241
Cleveland Clinic, 89, 118
climate change, 18, 19, 233, 289
Clinton, Bill, 46, 135, 237, 239, 255, 355
Clinton, Hillary, 18, 24, 25, 46, 121, 210, 250, 252, 254–56, 261, 275, 276, 310, 352
closet conservatives, 249–53
clothing, 134–39, 177
cloud storage, 11, 295, 298
CNBC, 170, 288
CNN, 143
CNNMoney, 175
coal industry, 18, 19
Cohen, Sam, 300
Cold War, 20
Coler, Jestin, 308–9
college, 13, 17, 31, 34–35, 45, 91, 94, 104, 195, 198–99, 315, 319
  Asian-Americans and, 268, 270
  bisexuals and, 66
  wealth and, 335
Comey, James, 255
Comic Con, 203–4
Common Sense Media, 130
commonsense policies vs. egghead theories, 19–20, 25, 26
commuter couples, 73–75, 163
computers, 169
  cloud storage, 11, 295, 298
  PCs, 16, 151–55, 295
  ransomware and, 311
condom use, 53
conservatives:
  closet, 249–53
  see also Republicans

Constitution, U.S., 18
conventions, entertainment, 203–6
Conway, Kellyanne, 24
cooking, 111
Coontz, Stephanie, 76
cosplay, 205–6
Costco, 221
couch potato voters, 273–79, 351
Cowan and Company, 136
Cramer, Jim, 1
crime:
  fraud, *see* fakesters and fraud
  law enforcement and, 142
Crosby, Lynton, 239
Cruise, Tom, 59
CryptoDefense, 311
Cuba, 264
Cuban, Mark, 85
Current Population Survey, 99
customization and personalization, 7–9, 12–14
  clothing, 134–39
CVS, 221
cyberattacks, 308

Daily Mail, 71
Dataclysm: Love, Sex, Race, and Identity—What Our Online Lives Tell Us About Our Offline Selves (Rudder), 69–70
data collection, 7, 9–12, 26, 124, 139, 339, 341, 344
  "can" experiment in, 288, 350
  limiting, 349–50
  Scroogled campaign and, 10–11, 349
  self-tracking and, 286–88
dating, 50, 198
  age and, 69
  bisexuality and, 65
  commuter couples and, 75
  older people and, 14, 51–56, 60, 69–71
  race and, 69–70
dating, internet, 47, 51, 53, 198, 341, 344
  apps for, 67–71
  marriages from, 2, 67–72
  political views and, 251
  prejudices and, 69–70, 72
death, 90, 115, 193
Defense Department, U.S., 145
de Gaulle, Charles, 21
democracy, 2, 18, 20, 27, 96, 255, 279, 340, 342, 350–52
Democrats, 18, 20, 66, 95, 199, 210, 238–39, 250, 251, 255–58, 261, 263, 264, 270, 271, 275, 276, 334, 352
Denmark, 55
depression, 64, 97, 106, 124, 130
Depression, Great, 243
Diagnostic and Statistical Manual of Mental Disorders, Fifth Edition (*DSM-5*), 131
Diamond, Lisa M., 64
Dichter, Kenny, 175
Dick, Andy, 62
diet, *see* food and diet
digital disaster scenarios, 233–34
Dil Mil, 71
discrimination, *see* prejudice and discrimination
disease, *see* health care and disease
Disinfomedia, 308–9
Disney, 216
divorce, 36–37, 50, 51–52, 56, 57–61, 69, 73, 75, 76, 121
DNA tests, 11
dogs, 160, 185–88
Dollar Shave Club, 299
Doomsday Clock, 230–31
Dowd, Maureen, 1

Dragon Con, 203–4
Dream Hoarders: How the American Upper Middle Class Is Leaving Everyone Else in the Dust, Why That Is a Problem, and What to Do About It (Reeves), 335–36
drones, 145–50, 321, 346
Drudge Report, 257
drugs, 88, 90
  marijuana, 16, 199, 208–11
  psychiatric, children on, 102–8
Duckworth, Tammy, 271

eBay, 300, 301
e-commerce, 297–300
e-mail, 169, 170
  Google and, 10, 125, 169, 349
Economist, 303
economy, 5, 13, 16, 19, 240, 245
  female breadwinners and, 36
  financial crisis of 2008 and Great Recession, 5, 17, 25–26, 36, 91–92, 94, 230, 243, 289
  new, 21–23, 25, 239, 241, 353–54
  old, 21–23, 25, 237–41, 318, 353, 354
  trade and, 17, 18, 19, 23, 95, 238–41, 256, 262, 264, 277
education, 6, 93, 94, 321
  American obsession with, 104
  Asian-Americans and, 268, 270
  language courses in, 156
  literacy, 154, 321
  wealth and, 335
  see also college
Edwards, John, 121
egghead theories, 255
  commonsense policies vs., 19–20, 25, 26
eggs, 83, 87
elderly:
  nonagenarians, 96–101, 341
  see also older generations
Electoral College, 24, 133, 260, 276, 278
elevators, 11
elites, 26, 240, 245, 257, 348
  impressionable, 1, 2, 24, 254–59
Elle Decor, 78
eMarketer, 153
emergencies and disasters, 230
  digital disaster scenarios, 233–34
  natural disasters, 230–34
  service and supply transport for, 147–48
Emerging Democratic Majority, The (Judis and Teixeira), 264
employment, *see* work
England, *see* United Kingdom
English language, 160
entrepreneurs, 295–300
  microcapitalists, 301–6
e-readers, 169
Ernst, Jodi, 229
Estée Lauder, 222
ethics, new standards of, 344–47
Etsy, 135, 298
Eurobarometer, 171–72
Euromonitor International, 84–85
Europe, 55, 78, 99, 171, 238, 277, 292, 316, 348, 349
European Commission (EC), 159
European Union (EU), 16, 35–36, 97–99, 238
  Brexit and, 15–16, 239, 257–58, 277
Everything Bad Is Good for You: How Today's Popular Culture Is Actually Making Us Smarter (Johnson), 214
exercise, 119, 341
eye implants, 143

Facebook, 2, 11, 43, 61, 68, 92, 122, 124, 166, 170, 218, 256–58, 299, 320, 351
  news on, 22, 347, 348
factory work:
  new, 318–23
  traditional, 16, 18, 23, 237–38, 240–41, 256, 318, 320–23, 329
Fail Safe, 160
fakesters and fraud, 22, 26, 307–11, 340, 350
  fake news, 307–9, 320
family and children, 16, 39–41, 238, 240, 340
  child care, 33, 38
  children on medications, 102–8
  encouragement of, 352–53
  having children, 13, 15, 37–38, 40, 45, 195, 340
  independent marriage and, 76–77
  military families, 73
  remarriage and, 59–60, 61
  single parenthood, 44
  work schedules and, 316
  see also marriage
fantasy and sci-fi, 200–207
Fast Company, 292, 315
FBI, 310
fears, 247, 248
Federal Aviation Administration, 147
Federal Highway Administration, 289
Federal Reserve, 313
Fey, Tina, 250
films, 145, 146, 216–17
  Asian-Americans in, 271–72
  sci-fi and fantasy, 200–207
financial crisis of 2008 and Great Recession, 5, 17, 25–26, 36, 91–92, 94, 230, 243, 289
financial disaster scenarios, 233–34
First Amendment, 252–53, 350
fish and seafood, 83, 87
  tuna, 85–86
Fitbit, 283
FiveThirtyEight, 252
flight attendants, 73
flip phones, 167–68, 170
Florida, 264–65
food and diet, 341
  cooking, 111
  protein consumption, 14, 81–87, 111, 341
  speed eaters, 109–13
  wellness freaks, 114–19, 220
footloose and fancy-free lifestyle, 13, 195–99
Forbes, 97, 298
Ford economy, 7
Fox News, 8, 51, 199, 249, 257
France, 21, 112, 239–40, 245, 277, 316
fraud, *see* fakesters and fraud
Fresh Off the Boat, 271
Friedman, Mackey, 64
friendships, 93
  international, 257
  roommates, 13, 190–94, 197
FTC (Federal Trade Commission), 116, 132, 180, 181, 310
Fyre Festival, 181

Gabor, Zsa Zsa, 59
Gallup, 243, 334
Game of Thrones, 203, 204, 206, 207, 212, 214, 216
gaming, 129–33, 203
Gap, 137
Gates, Bill, 98, 110, 161, 173, 177, 300
gay marriage, 16, 58, 62, 199, 239
gay men, 62–63, 65–66
  internet dating and, 71

General Statistics Authority, 45
genetics, 11
Gen Xers, 46, 54, 188, 333–34
Germany, 277, 292, 316
Ghost in the Shell, 271
gig economy, 325
Girls Trip, 77
GLAAD, 63
Glauber, Rebecca, 312
Global Finance, 336
globalization, 6, 16, 20–21, 23, 218, 239, 240, 248, 300, 341, 354
  language and, 156
Global Journal, 123
global warming, 18, 19, 233, 289
Glu Mobile, 131
gluten-free foods, 115–16, 119
Goldman Sachs, 135, 301–3
Gomez, Selena, 177, 178
Google, 47, 124–25, 153, 270, 348
  advertising and, 10–11, 165, 349
  email and, 10, 125, 169, 349
  Glass, 141, 160
  product listings on, 12
  Scroogled campaign and, 10–11, 349
  Translate, 158, 159
  Trends, 205
Goop, 117–18, 119
Gordon, Sarah, 307
GQ, 170
Grace and Frankie, 192
Grameen America, 304
Grameen Bank, 301–4
granola bars, 111
graying bachelors, 14, 51–56, 97
Great Britain, *see* United Kingdom
Great Depression, 243
Great Recession, *see* financial crisis of 2008 and Great Recession
Green, Donald P., 246
Grindr, 71
Guardian, 132, 170
guns, 88, 210, 224–29, 239, 256
  culture of, 226, 228, 229
  survivalism and, 230, 231
Guns & Ammo, 226
guys left behind, 88–95

hackers, 307–9, 311
Hamill, Mark, 204
Hanacure, 218, 222
Harris polls, 23, 141, 185, 187, 225, 244, 249, 262, 283, 336, 342
Harry's, 299
Harvard University, 298
  CAPS (Center for American Political Studies), 23, 141, 185, 244, 249, 262, 283, 336, 342
  data experiment at, 288, 350
  Injury Control Research Center, 227
  Institute of Politics, 242
  Kennedy School, 246
Harvard Law Review, 257
Hawaii 5-0, 271
Hawking, Stephen, 161
Hazel, 324
health care and disease, 81, 85, 199, 341
  biking and, 293
  cancer, *see* cancer
  children on medications, 102–8
  drones and, 148
  emergency services and supplies, 147–48
  home health care aides, 100, 163, 328
  internet searches and, 171
  language translation and, 158
  men and, 88–95, 97
  marriage and, 76, 90
  nonagenarians and, 96–101, 341

health care and disease (*Continued*)
Obamacare, 248
robots and, 100, 163
self-data tracking and, 283–88
social relationships and, 93, 193
technology-advanced people (TAP), 140–44
wellness freaks, 114–19, 220
see also food and diet
heart attacks, 76
Heche, Anne, 62
Hefner, Hugh, 40
Helmsley, Leona, 188
Hermès, 291
Hero Hair, 205
Hill, 253
Hispanics and Latinos, 260–65, 266, 270, 274
Hitler, Adolf, 21
HIV, 64, 66
hotels, 78, 176–77
HotelTonight, 176–77
House of Cards, 48
housing:
independent marrieds and, 78
living with parents, 94
nursing homes, 96–97, 99
rental, 193, 196–97
retirement communities, 53, 55
roommates, 13, 190–94, 197
separate homes in relationships, 43
How I Met Your Mother, 229
Huffington Post, 170
Huffman, Steve, 232
Hurst, Jennifer, 288

IAB, 155
IBISWorld, 102–3
IBM, 155
IEEE, 345
IIHS, 90
immigration, immigrants, 16, 19, 21, 23, 95, 238–39, 250–51, 256, 258, 277, 340–41, 341, 352–53
aging workforces and, 98
Asian-Americans, 266–72
in California, 260, 262–64, 266, 270
Dreamers, 262
friendships and, 257
Hispanic and Latino, 260–65, 266, 270, 274
jobs and, 19
militant Dreamers, 2, 260–65
sanctuary cities and, 262
impressionable elites, 1, 2, 24, 254–59
IMS Health, 106
income, 92–94
of Asian-Americans, 268
inequality in, 335, 336
multimillionaires, 330–37
nerds with money, 200–207
second-fiddle husbands and, 31–38, 94, 313, 316
wage stagnation, 238
Independent Marrieds, 50, 73–78
India, 71, 75, 86, 87, 92, 152, 302, 303, 308, 310
immigrants from, 269, 270
Indochino, 138
Indonesia, 308
infidelity, 53–54
marital, 48, 49
Information Age, 5, 6, 13, 17, 22, 32, 92, 318, 323, 324, 343
Inkwell, 314
Innisfree, 220
insects as food, 85
Instacart, 320
Instagram, 61, 175–76, 179, 181, 182, 219, 297

Intern, The, 33
International Cinematographers Guild, 146
International Finance Corporation, 302
internet, 16, 22, 152–54, 160, 166, 168, 194, 347, 355
  dating and, *see* dating, internet
  disconnecting from, 169–70
  entrepreneurship and, 295–300
  fraud and, 22, 26, 307–11
  privacy and, 167, 170–72
  retailers and, 297–300
  social media, *see* social media
  video/Web conferencing, 157
Iran, 21
Iraq, 20, 243
ISIS, 230
Italy, 94
It's a Wonderful Life, 39

Jacobson, Michael F., 84
jail, 88
Japan, 36, 99, 100, 292, 321
Japanese-Americans, 267
Jenner, Kendall, 181, 222
Jenner, Kylie, 179, 188, 218
JetSmarter, 176, 177, 333
jobs, *see* work
Johansson, Scarlett, 168, 271
Johns Hopkins Bloomberg School of Public Health, 107
Johnson, Lyndon, 16
Johnson, Steven, 214
Jolie, Angelina, 62
Jones, Jerry, 168
Journal of Clinical Sleep Medicine, 284
Journal of Sex Research, 47
Journal of the American Medical Association, 123
Judis, John, 264
juicing, 114, 115
Justice Department, U.S., 226, 271

kale, 115
Kardashian, Kim, 59, 130–31, 169, 179
Kardashian family, 176, 179, 181, 222
Kelley, Kevin, 285
Kennedy, John F., 15, 20, 21, 199
Kennedy generation, 15
Khan, Sadiq, 239, 292
Kojak, 214
Korea:
  North Korea, 230–31, 248
  South Korea, *see* South Korea
Korean War, 243
Kurzweil, Ray, 157

Labor Department, U.S., 328
Labour Party, 239
languages:
  English, 160
  translation of, 156–60
Latin America, 303, 305
Latinos and Hispanics, 260–65, 266, 270, 274
law enforcement, 142
League, The, 70
League of American Bicyclists, 291
Lee, Rich, 143
Legato, Marianne J., 92, 94
Le Pen, Marine, 239–40
lesbians, 62–63, 65
Less Than Zero, 211
LGBT community, 58, 62–66
  bisexuals, 62–66
  gay marriage, 16, 58, 62
  gay men, 62–63, 65–66
  internet dating and, 71
  lesbians, 62–63, 65

liberals, 249–51, 256, 342
  see also Democrats
Libertarian Party, 275
life expectancy, 51, 91–94, 120
lifestyle, 354
  armchair preppers, 230–34
  choices and, *see* choices
  footloose and fancy-free, 13, 195–99
  gun ownership, 88, 224–29, 230, 231
  Korean beauty, 218–23
  marijuana and, 16, 199, 208–11
  nerds with money, 200–207
  of older people, 13–14
  pets, 13, 15, 185–89
  roommates, 13, 190–94, 197
  television and, 212–17
  unintended consequences of shifts in, 7–14
Bow Wow, 174–76
Lim, Diane, 313
literacy, 154, 321
Loesch, Dana, 224–25, 229
London, 78, 204, 239, 292
loneliness, 193, 335
Lopez, Jennifer, 59
Los Angeles Times, 302
Luddites, new, 166–72
Lupton, Deborah, 287–88
Luxury Institute, 332–33

MacKay, Martin, 309–10
Madewell, 138
Madoff, Bernie, 307
Madonna, 250
magazines, 169
MailChimp, 299
malware, 311
manufacturing jobs, *see* factory work
Mao Tse-tung, 270
marijuana, 16, 199, 208–11
Markey, Ed, 150
Malay Mail Online, 221
Marie Claire, 227
marriage, 16, 17, 45, 48, 50, 340, 341
  age at first, 195
  bisexuality and, 66
  cancer and, 121–22
  celebrity, 48, 58, 59
  commuter, 73–75, 163
  divorce, 36–37, 50, 51–52, 56, 57–61, 69, 73, 75, 76, 121
  encouragement of, 352–53
  health care and, 76, 90
  independence in, 50, 73–78
  infidelity in, 48, 49
  internet dating and, 2, 67–72
  matchmaking and, 71
  military families and, 73
  never marrieds, 39–45, 69, 77, 94
  open, 46–50, 353
  political views and, 251
  same-sex, 16, 58, 62, 199, 239
  second-fiddle husbands, 31–38, 94, 313, 316
  serial, 48
  sleeping apart in, 75–76
  third, 57–61
  vacations and, 77–78
  weddings, 58, 61, 77
  work schedules and, 316
  see also family and children
Marshall Plan, 20
Master of None, 272
matchmaking, 71
Mary Tyler Moore Show, The, 40–41
McCain, John, 275
McKinsey Global Institute, 322
MCM, 204
meat, 81–83, 111
media, 244, 246, 249, 340

impressionable elites and, 1, 2, 24, 254–59
presidential election and, 18–19, 24
see also news
Medicare, 328
medications, children on, 102–8
men:
gender disparities and, 88–95
health care and, 88–95, 97
second-fiddle husbands, 31–38, 94, 313, 316
skin care and, 223
Mercedes, 173, 333
Merkel, Angela, 16
microcapitalists, 301–6
Microcredit Summit Campaign, 305
Microsoft, 142, 151, 152, 174, 269
Scroogled campaign at, 10–11, 349
Xiaoice, 162, 164
microtrends, 1–2, 339–43
addressing issues and problems with, 343–55
microtrends squared vs., 14–15
opposing, 6, 7, 14
power of, 5–7
Microtrends (Penn and Zalesne), 1, 5, 7, 25, 73, 166, 185, 254, 260, 264
middle class, 6, 22–23, 329, 340
Middle East, 20, 45, 277
Migration Policy Institute, 266
militant Dreamers, 260–65
military and war, 142, 145, 226, 247, 346–47
military families, 73
Millard, David Ralph, 222
millennials, 341
bisexuality and, 65
footloose and fancy-free lifestyle and, 13, 195–99
older generations vs., 15–17, 25
pets and, 188–89
politics and, 251
technology and, 13, 16, 154–55, 168
virtual businesses and, 299
and work with limits and flexibility, 315–16, 318
millionaires, 330, 340
multimillionaires, 330–37
Millward Brown Digital, 155
Mindy Project, The, 229
Ministry of Supply, 135
Mintel, 220
Mirai, Shibuya, 345
MIT, 307
MIT Technology Review, 143
Mobike, 292
Modern Family, 56
Money, 33
monogamy, 47, 49, 50
Morduch, Jonathan, 305
Mother Jones, 310
Movember, 122–23
movies, *see* films
MTailor, 135, 136, 173
Multicultural Economy 2015, The, 269
multimillionaires, 330–37
Murphy, Stephanie, 271
Murray, Bill, 168
Musk, Elon, 140, 141, 161

Nadella, Satya, 269
NAFTA, 18, 237, 239
NASA, 118
Nasty Gal, 299–300
National Association of Home Builders, 75
National Bureau of Economic Research, 93
National Cancer Institute, 122

National Center for Health Statistics, 106
National Coalition for Cancer Survivorship, 122
National Council on Aging, 54
National Enquirer, 121
National Fisheries Institute, 83
National Front, 239
National Health Interview Survey, 120–21
nationalism, 6, 20–21
National Rifle Association (NRA), 224, 228, 229
National Science Foundation, 270
National Shooting Sports Foundation, 228
National Sleep Foundation, 75
National Study of Employers, 315
National Survey of Sexual Health and Behavior, 53
natural disasters, 230–34
Navy SEALS, 142
negativity, 242–48
Neiman Marcus, 220–21
Nelson, Tammy, 47
nerds, 200–207, 307, 341
  conventions and, 203–6
Netflix, 12
Netherlands, 316
Netjets, 175
Neuralink, 141
never marrieds, 39–45, 69, 77, 94
Nexon, 130
new Luddites, 166–72
New Monogamy, The: Redefining Your Relationship After Infidelity (Nelson), 47
New Republic, 289
news, 8, 199, 352
  on Facebook, 22, 347, 348
  fake, 307–9, 320
  reforming distribution of, 347–49
New Survivalist, 231, 232
Newtonian physics, 6
New York City, 233, 322, 334, 354
  bicycling in, 289, 291, 293
  Police Department, 214
New York Comic Con, 204
New Yorker, 222, 232, 283
New York Times, 2, 12, 24, 52, 53, 76, 83, 106, 188, 193, 212, 227, 228, 238–39, 257, 258, 291, 296, 324–25
New York Times Magazine, 48–49
New Zealand, 207, 232–33
Nielsen Corporation, 269
Nigerian Prince scams, 310
9/11 attacks, 230, 243, 354
Nixon, Cynthia, 62
Nixon, Richard, 199, 248
nonagenarians, 96–101, 341
North Korea, 230–31, 248
NPR, 308
NRA (National Rifle Association), 224, 228, 229
nuclear war, 248
nursing homes, 96–97, 99

Oakley, Annie, 224
Obama, Barack, 20–21, 77, 169, 210, 238, 239, 250, 255–57, 264–65, 275, 276
Obama, Michelle, 77
Obamacare, 248
Odell, Kathleen, 306
Okafor, Antonia, 227
OkCupid, 69, 70
older generations, 6, 13–14, 341, 353, 354
  baby boomers, 15, 53, 54, 65, 71, 83, 216, 246, 333

bachelors, 14, 51–56, 97
bisexuality and, 65
dating and, 14, 51–56, 60, 69–71
home health care aides for, 100, 163, 328
millennials vs., 15–17, 25
nonagenarians, 96–101, 341
nursing homes for, 96–97, 99
retirement and, 36, 97–99, 334, 354
retirement communities for, 53, 55
roommates and, 192–93
travel and, 55
opportunity hoarding, 335–36
orthorexia, 118–19
Osnos, Evan, 232, 233

Pakistan, 304
Palin, Sarah, 229
Paltrow, Gwyneth, 117
Paquin, Anna, 62
parenthood, 13, 15, 37–38, 40, 45, 195, 340
single, 44
see also family and children
Paris, 112
Park, Grace, 271
Paul, Ron, 232
PayScale, 287, 315
PCs, 16, 151–55, 295
Peach & Lily, 221
Penn, Miles, 135
personal chefs, 327–28
personalization, *see* customization and personalization
personal service industry, 324–29
personal trainers, 328
pessimism, 242–48
pets, 13, 15, 185–89
celebrity and influencer, 297
Pew Research Center, 33, 34, 41, 65, 66, 71, 153, 154, 169, 171, 225, 228, 239, 264, 269
pharmaceutical companies, 171
Philippines, 270
phones, 343, 344
flip, 167–68, 170
scams and, 310–11
see also smartphones
Piketty, Thomas, 336
Planet Money, 300
plastic surgery, 221–22
podcasts, 299
Podesta, John, 310
Points Guy, 176
Pokémon Go, 129, 130
police, 214, 226, 247
political correctness, 16, 17, 256
Politico, 169
politics, 8, 16, 95, 199, 340
advertising in, 244, 246, 351, 352
Asian-Americans and, 266–72
bisexuality and, 66
caucuses and primaries, 278, 352
closet conservatives and, 249–53
democracy, 2, 18, 20, 27, 96, 255, 279, 340, 342, 350–52
and egghead theories vs. common-sense policies, 19–20, 25, 26
impressionable elites and, 1, 2, 24, 254–59
militant Dreamers and, 2, 260–65
millennials and, 251
multimillionaires and, 334
old economy voters, 25, 237–41, 353, 354
and older generations vs. millennials, 15–16, 25
pessimism and, 242–48
polarization in, 6

politics (*Continued*)
presidential election, *see* presidential election of 2016
and rural areas vs. cities, 17–19, 25, 241
voting, 273–79, 351–52
women and, 249–50
polyamory, 47
pomegranates, 116
Ponzi, Charles, 307
Pop, Iggy, 168
pornography, 162, 163
Portfolios of the Poor (Collins et al.), 305
Postmates, 320, 326
poverty, 104, 105, 303–6, 312
power trends, 14–23, 25, 342
egghead theories vs. commonsense policies, 19–20, 25, 26
globalists vs. nationalists, 20–21
old economy vs. new economy, 21–23, 25
older generations vs. millennials, 15–17, 25
rural areas vs. cities, 17–19, 25, 241
prejudice and discrimination:
advertising and, 165
internet dating and, 69–70, 72
see also racism
Preppi, 231
presidential election of 2016, 2, 18, 23–25, 251–52, 255–59, 273, 275–76, 279, 307, 342
Russia and, 2–3, 23–24, 255, 256, 276, 351
prison, 88
privacy, 11, 349
drones and, 149–50
internet and, 167, 170–72
see also data collection
PrivateFly, 175
private planes, 173–77
progressive era, 343
protein, 14, 81–87, 111, 341
plant-based, 85
powders and supplements, 84–85
Psychology Today, 74–75, 102, 119
Putin, Vladimir, 23

quantified self (QS), 285
Quantified Self, The (Lupton), 287–88
quinoa, 116

racism, 239
Asian-Americans and, 266, 268
dating and, 69–70
radiofrequency identification (RFID) chips, 143
Ralph Lauren, 138, 333
ransomware, 311
Rape, Abuse & Incest National Network, 227
Ratajkowski, Emily, 181
Ratliff, Kate, 34
Rawles, James Wesley, 233
Reagan, Ronald, 20, 59, 263
Recode, 147
Reddit, 232
Reeves, Richard, 335–36
relationships, 13, 340, 341
commuter, 73–75, 163
health and, 93
long-term, 43–44
monogamous, 47, 49, 50
never marrieds, 39–45, 69, 77, 94
open, 47–48
political views and, 251
primary and secondary, 49
separate-home, 43
sleeping apart and, 75–76

unmarried cohabitation, 43–44
see also dating; friendships; marriage; sex and sexuality
religion, 13, 16, 17, 20, 197–98, 240, 256
rent, 193, 196–97
RENTCafé, 192
Rent the Runway, 177
Republicans, 19, 25, 66, 228, 237–39, 255–57, 260, 263, 265, 270–71, 275–76, 306, 334
closet conservatives, 249–53
Research and Markets, 85
reselling, 299–300
restaurants, 111–12, 297–98
retirement, 36, 97–99, 334, 354
retirement communities, 53, 55
Reuters, 291, 293
Revolutionary Realty, 233
Rihanna, 168, 179, 218
robots and bots, 12, 21–22, 137, 160, 342
aging populations and, 98–100
Alexa, 12, 153, 163, 329, 344
citizenship and rights for, 345
for health care and personal services, 100, 163, 329
relationships with, 12–13, 161–65, 340, 345, 346
sex and, 162–63
Shibuya Mirai, 345
Siri, 12, 329, 344
soldiers, 142, 346–47
work and, 318–19, 321
Romney, Mitt, 250, 264
roommates, 13, 190–94, 197
Roosevelt, Franklin Delano, 248
Roosevelt, Theodore, 267
Rosenfeld, Michael J., 69
Rubio, Marco, 262
Rudder, Christian, 69–70
rural areas, 26, 241, 341
cities vs., 17–19, 25, 241
Russia, 245, 308
U.S. election and, 2–3, 23–24, 255, 256, 276, 351

Samsung, 223, 287
Sanders, Bernie, 276–77
San Diego Comic-Con (SDCC), 203
Saudi Arabia, 45
Savage, Dan, 49
schools, *see* education
Schwarzenegger, Arnold, 263
sci-fi and fantasy, 200–207
Scroogled campaign, 10–11, 349
SEALS, 142
Seamless, 109, 312, 324
second-fiddle husbands, 31–38, 94, 313, 316
security guards, 329
Sedaris, David, 283
self-data, 283–88
Selfridges, 220
senators, 18
seniors, *see* older generations
Sephora, 218
September 11 attacks, 230, 243, 354
Serial, 299
service economy, 324–25
personal services, 324–29
restaurants, 111–12, 298
sex and sexuality:
bisexuality, 62–66
female libido, 49
internet dating and, 68, 71
LGBT community, 58, 62–66
older people and, 52, 54
in open marriages, 47, 49
pornography, 162, 163
robots and, 162–63

sex and sexuality (*Continued*)
same-sex marriage, 16, 58, 62, 199, 239
in second-fiddle marriages, 33–34
separate bedrooms and, 76
sleep and, 76
Sex and the City, 33, 41, 62
sexual assault, 227
Sexual Fluidity: Understanding Women's Love and Desire (Diamond), 64
sexually transmitted diseases (STDs), 52–53
Shaffer, Alicia, 298
Shark Tank, 17, 85, 306
Shooting Divas of DMV, 228
Silver, Nate, 252
Silversea Cruises, 55
Sinema, Kyrsten, 66
Siri, 12, 329, 344
Skeptic, 117–18
sleep:
couples sleeping apart, 75–76
disorders, 75
tracking, 284–85
SlimFast, 110
small businesses, 295
microfinancing and, 301–6
virtual entrepreneurs, 295–300
smartphones, 10, 13, 99–100, 143, 144, 151–55, 166, 167–68, 173, 197, 223
addiction to, 130, 132, 168
BlackBerry, 166, 168–69, 171
games on, 129–33
Smelt, Simon, 171
Smith, Adam, 306
socialism, 16, 26
social media, 61, 92, 169, 178–82, 199, 210, 288, 299, 351
disconnecting from, 170
Facebook, *see* Facebook
Instagram, 61, 175–76, 179, 181, 182, 219, 297
political views and, 252, 253
Twitter, 166, 179, 180, 201
social networks, 93
Social Security, 94, 96, 97, 161, 273
Sopranos, The, 213
South China Morning Post, 222
Southern Poverty Law Center, 257
South Korea, 36, 37–38, 44–45
beauty products from, 218–23
plastic surgery in, 221–22
Soviet Union, 20
Soylent, 110, 113
Spain, 36, 123, 132, 316
Spanx, 300
speed eaters, 109–13
spinach, 115
SpiroScout, 287
standardization, 7
Starbucks, 7–8, 26, 344
Starsky & Hutch, 214
start-ups, 6, 12, 17, 25, 61, 148, 177, 208, 314, 340
unicorn, 194
Star Trek, 200, 202, 204
Star Wars, 200–201, 205–7
Statista, 137, 153
status leakage, 34
Stewart, Kristen, 62
Stitch, 71
Stitch Fix, 138
Stone, Emma, 222
strokes, 76
StyleSeat, 320
Sunflower Labs, 148
Sun-Haters, 1
Supreme Court, 62, 199, 254–55, 263, 350

SurveyMonkey, 258
survivalism, 230–34
Susan G. Komen Breast Cancer Foundation, 122
sushi, 86
Sutton, Willie, 307
swinging, 47, 49
Symantec, 311
Syria, 238, 262, 277
Szymanski, Tim, 142

Target, 221
TaskRabbit, 320
Tax Policy Center, 257
tech industry, 12, 319–20, 322
technology, 6, 7, 22, 26, 98, 240, 246–48, 279, 339, 340, 341
  addiction to, 129–33
  and bringing new economy to every region, 353–54
  choices and, *see* choices
  customized clothing, 134–39
  drones, 145–50, 321, 346
  ethics and, 344–47
  household, managers for, 328–29
  language translation, 156–60
  millennials and, 13, 16, 154–55, 168s
  new Luddites and, 166–72
  private planes, 173–77
  self-data tracking, 283–88
  technology-advanced people, 140–44
  television viewing and, 216
  unintended consequences of, 7–14
  work and, 318–19, 322, 329, 340, 341
  see also artificial intelligence; computers; data collection; internet; robots and bots; smartphones
Teixeira, Ruy, 264
Telegraph, 54
television, 197, 246–48, 347, 348
  Asian-Americans and, 271
  intelligent, 212–17
  nerd culture and, 202
  news programs, 8, 199
$10 million households, 330–37
10,000 Women initiative, 301–3
terrorism, 20, 149, 230, 234, 246, 262, 329
  9/11 attacks, 230, 243, 354
Tesla, Inc., 173, 233, 333, 341
Texas, 263, 265
Thailand, 292
32M, 143
Time, 33
Tinder, 67–68
Tomb Raider, 229
Tories, 1, 237
Toyota, 100
trade, 17, 18, 19, 23, 95, 238–41, 256, 262, 264, 277
travel, 55, 238
  language translation and, 158
  medical tourism, 222–23
  pets and, 188
  separate vacations for couples, 77–78
Tremor Video, 155
TripAdvisor, 77
Trump, Donald, 95, 166, 199, 232–33, 238–40, 309, 347
  closet conservatives and, 249–52
  election and presidency of, 16, 18, 23–25, 244–46, 248, 249–52, 255–59, 262, 264–65, 271, 273, 275–76, 342
  marriage of, 54, 59, 73–74
Trump, Melania, 54, 73–74
Twitter, 166, 179, 180, 201
270 (game), 133

Uber, 16, 154, 294, 312, 318, 321, 322, 324
UberEATS, 109, 112, 197, 297–98, 322
uberPOOL, 294
UNESCO, 154
unicorn start-ups, 194
Unilever, 299
unions, 262
United Kingdom (U.K.), 21, 23, 35, 71, 76, 78, 96, 97, 111, 120, 123, 237–39, 245, 292, 316, 319, 354
  Brexit and, 15–16, 239, 257–58, 277
United Nations (UN), 20, 85
University of Cambridge, 257
University of Chicago, 69
University of Washington, 48, 165
uptown stoners, 208–11
US Preventive Services Task Force, 123

vacations, 77–78
vegetarians, 81, 85
Verge, 112, 176
video/Web conferencing, 157
Vietnam War, 243
Vogue, 135, 167, 168, 170, 220
voting, 273–79, 351–52
Vox, 44, 248

Walking Dead, The, 202–3
Wall Street Journal, 78, 111
Walmart, 18, 138
war and military, 142, 145, 226, 247, 346–47
Warby Parker, 143, 297, 299
Washington, D.C., 193, 195, 204, 206, 228, 249, 291, 292
Washington Post, 112, 171, 211
Way, Niobe, 93
wealth, 340
  inequality in, 335, 336
  multimillionaires, 330–37
weddings, 58, 61, 77
Welch, Peter, 150
WeLive, 194
wellness freaks, 114–19, 220
Wesleyan Media Project, 244
West, Mark, 154
WeWork, 194
Wheels Up, 175
White, Jim, 85
WHO European Region, 90
Whole Foods, 112
Why Men Die First: How to Lengthen Your Lifespan (Legato), 92
Wilson, Pete, 263
Windows, 152
Winslet, Kate, 59
Wintour, Anna, 168
Wired, 85, 285, 311
Wolf, Gary, 285
women, 17
  clothing for, 137
  gender disparities and, 88–95
  gun ownership by, 224–29
  Korean beauty and, 218–23
  microfinancing and, 301–4, 306
  nerds with money, 201–2
  never-married, 39–45
  nonagenarian, 97
  older, roommates and, 192–93
  political views of, 249–50
  smartphones and, 130
  virtual entrepreneurship and, 298
  see also working women
work, 15, 16
  aging populations and, 97–99
  and bringing new economy to every region, 353–54

commuting via bicycle to, 197, 289–94
factory, *see* factory work
happiness and job satisfaction, 298, 316–17
immigrants and, 19, 261–62
job creation, 16–17
microcapitalists, 301–6
multimillionaires and, 330–31
never marrieds and, 42–43
part-time, 312–17, 319, 321
in personal service industry, 324–29
pets and, 186–87
political views and, 252
restaurant, 111–12, 298
retirement from, 36, 97–99, 334, 354
technology and, 318–19, 322, 329, 340, 341
trade policies and, 17, 18, 19, 23
unemployment, 91
virtual entrepreneurs, 295–300
see also income; working women
working women, 41–42, 59, 195, 197
as breadwinners, and second-fiddle husbands, 31–38, 94, 313, 316
part-time work and, 313, 314
World Bank, 302
World Economic Forum, 1, 169
World Wealth Report, 330
World War II, 20, 21, 115, 243, 248

Xiaoice, 162, 164

Yahoo! Finance, 232
Yang, Alan, 272
Yellen, Janet, 313
Yelp, 348
Yglesias, Matt, 44
yoga, 114, 117
Yoon, Alicia, 221
YouGov, 49
YouTube, 147, 180–81, 182
Yunus, Muhammad, 301–4

Zafar, Roshaneh, 304
Zeel, 320
Zuckerberg, Mark, 161

ABOUT THE AUTHORS

Mark Penn has spent over forty years in polling, marketing, advertising, and strategy at the highest levels of business and politics. As a leading pollster, he was chief strategist in the presidential campaigns of Bill and Hillary Clinton and is credited with identifying the influential "soccer moms" trend. He has advised Bill Gates and Tony Blair, among other world leaders, as well as companies from Ford to Verizon to Merck to McDonald's. He was CEO of one of the world's leading communications firms and became an executive vice president at Microsoft in charge of advertising and later its chief strategy officer. Today he is chairman of the Harris Poll and managing partner of the Stagwell Group, a collection of digital marketing firms. He is the author of the *New York Times* bestselling book *Microtrends* and has written for the *Wall Street Journal*, *Politico*, and other publications. For the last four years he has also taught public opinion and polling in Harvard's Government Department as a guest lecturer.

Meredith Fineman is the founder of FinePoint, a PR firm turned leadership company that elevates individuals, with a focus on women in positions of power. She is also a freelance writer of twelve years, with bylines in *Harvard Business Review*, *Forbes*, *Inc*., *Entrepreneur*, *Elle*, *Marie Claire*, *Fast Company*, and more.